We Build a Navy

By
HOLLOWAY H. FROST
Lieutenant Commander
U. S. Navy

1940
U. S. NAVAL INSTITUTE
ANNAPOLIS, MD.

Composed, Printed and Bound by
The Collegiate Press
George Banta Publishing Company
Menasha, Wisconsin

ENGLAND

FRANCE

Harwich
London
Southampton
Dover
Spithead
Plymouth
Severn R.
Scilly Is.

Ostend
Dunkirk
Calais
Paris
Havre
St.Malo
Brest
23 March to
10 April
14 August
L'Orient
Quiberon Bay
13 Febr. to 22 March
Nantes–2 Dec.
to 12 February.
Mouth of Loire–
30 Nov.to 1 Dec.
Rochefort
Bordeaux

5 May
8 May

"Bon Homme Richard"
Groix
"Ranger"

14th. Takes
Brigantine

23d."Takes "Fortune"
Loves 2 boats and
24 men

25th. "Cerf" leaves

24th.

26th.

21st–Takes "Mayflower"

19th "Monsieur"
leaves

18th–Takes "Verwagting"

Ballinskelligs Bay
Bantry Bay
Cork
Cape Clear

CRUISES OF THE
"RANGER" AND
"BON HOMME RICHARD"
1778 –1779

We Build a Navy

From an engraving by Sartain, after the original painting by Thomas Birch

THE NIGHT BATTLE BETWEEN THE U. S. S. *Constitution*
AND H. M. SHIPS *Cyane* AND *Levant*

On the left is the corvette *Cyane*; in the center the frigate *Constitution*, and on the right of the sloop *Levant*. The
Constitution captured both vessels.

This Volume
is Dedicated to
MY FATHER

ACKNOWLEDGMENT

The author acknowledges with thanks the assistance he has received from Captain W. R. Van Auken, U. S. Navy, Bureau of Navigation; Captain D. W. Knox, U. S. Navy (Retired), Lieutenant Commander Richard Wainwright, Jr., U. S. Navy (Retired), and Mrs. Constance Lathrop, of the Navy Department Library; Lieutenant (J.G.) Elliott B. Strauss, U. S. Navy, U.S.S. *Toucey;* Lieutenant Commander A. H. Rooks, U. S. Navy, and the Officers and Board of Control of the U. S. Naval Institute.

PREFACE

THIS volume is a story, not a history. It recounts those chapters of our early naval annals which I conceive to be the most interesting, the most dramatic, and the most instructive.

I have made an earnest endeavor to insure the accuracy and completeness of the facts by basing them upon official correspondence, other contemporary documents, and the writings of our most reputable historians. The archives of the Navy Department have been of great value. A list of the publications chiefly consulted is contained in the bibliography.

The facts presented have been supplemented by frequent extracts from the journals of sailors, letters and diaries of officers, and newspaper stories, in order to diffuse around the reader the quaint atmosphere of the times. I have tried to present the stirring events of those long-past days in a realistic manner.

But the underlying purpose has been to make their story instructive as well. Thus may the past serve the present and the future. To that end much care has been devoted to analysis of the facts and exposition of the lessons they teach. Among these are: the vital necessity for a navy; the paramount importance of its morale, reputation, and prestige; the value of an offensive attitude in naval warfare; the traits of character essential to naval commanders; the means of coördinating naval strategy with diplomatic measures and military operations; and the advantages of a vigorous national policy. All this sounds rather formidable—but it has been administered in small doses and in a manner which I hope the reader will not find overheavy.

It has long been a habit for our naval historians to claim perfection for the American naval commanders of that early period. This attitude doubtless was forced upon them by the gross slanders of the British historian, William James. Roosevelt was the first to venture upon a more critical treatment of the subject. Admiral Mahan went further and there is much well-taken criticism in his excellent history of the War of 1812. I have gone much further than either of these eminent historians and along entirely independent lines.

If one writes for purposes of propaganda it is natural that he should manipulate the facts and color their discussion. But if one writes to deduce lessons for future use his facts must be exact and their discussion straightforward, frank, and impartial. "Ships are but boards," said Shakespeare, "sailors but men." I have tried to write of our sailors as men—not as demigods. "To conduct great matters," Plutarch wrote, centuries ago, "and never commit a fault is above the force of human nature." If our best commanders occasionally made mistakes, it proves only how difficult it is to avoid them. There is no reason to conceal such mistakes on the one hand, nor to consider that they ruined reputations on the other.

A blanket approval of all the events of our early history does not distinguish between the excellent, the good, and the mediocre. It lowers our standard of measuring ability. It often furnishes a precedent, unconscious perhaps, upon which future commanders may base their decisions—with unfortunate results. It gives us an idea of our own invincibility—which, though perhaps stimulating in small doses, may prove fatal in large. Certainly our record of these years is splendid enough to stand squarely upon its own merits, without being bolstered up, as an Englishman

TABLE OF CONTENTS

ILLUSTRATIONS

MAPS

PART I
We Harry the British Coasts, 1777-1779

CHAPTER I

AMERICA TAKES TO THE SEA

ON NOVEMBER 2, 1777, a little ship sailed out past the forts of Portsmouth, New Hampshire. From her peak fluttered the new flag of a young confederation. She was called the *Ranger,* and carried to France the news of the great victory at Saratoga, counted by one military authority as among the fifteen decisive battles of the world. In her sailed as captain probably the most remarkable man of the generation—Paul Jones! Off now on his Great Adventure, his boundless ambition for distinction and his loyal eagerness to serve his adopted country were to make him the sensation of the world—to his friends a patriotic hero; to his enemies a bloodthirsty pirate. What must have been his dreams as the gray, rock-bound coast faded into the misty horizon over his taffrail? Why sailed he upon this perilous mission—one little ship against the overpowering weight of British naval strength? And what could he hope to accomplish?

From earliest history the tremendous importance and effect of sea power have been recognized. Crete, Phoenicia, Athens, Rome, the Norse sea kings, the Arab rovers, Genoa and Venice, Portugal and Spain, and the Netherlands have in turn grown powerful and wealthy through its influence. Sir Walter Raleigh, languishing in prison, reviewed its history. In about 1600 he gave his dictum: "Whoever commands the sea commands the trade; whoever commands the trade of the world commands the riches of the world and consequently the world itself."

[3]

English statesmen heeded this advice; saw that their future lay upon the sea. Navy, merchant shipping, commerce, and colonies were the four great elements of their sea power. The Royal Navy soon became the primary element of British sea power; it was vital to security while commerce was vital only to prosperity; it was due to their overwhelming naval strength that Britons ruled the waves for three centuries. Even the merchant marine was maintained primarily as a support to the navy in war—its fostering of commerce was a distinctly secondary purpose. "Our ancestors," wrote Reeves in 1792, "considered the defense of this island as the first law in the national policy. Judging that the dominion of the land could not be preserved without possessing that of the sea, they made every effort to procure to the nation a maritime power of its own. They wished that the merchants should own as many ships, and employ as many mariners as possible. To induce, and sometimes to force, them to this application of their capital, restrictions and prohibitions were devised. The interests of commerce were often sacrificed to this object."

From the very date of their founding, the American Colonies took to the sea. They became one of the chief cogs in the great commercial machine of the British Empire. Their people were seafaring by nature and tradition; their precarious hold upon the Atlantic coast line depended upon shipping from the home country and between the Colonies themselves. Their forests provided in profusion the finest timber for planking, beams, and spars, as well as tar, pitch, and turpentine in unlimited quantities. As early as 1639 shipwrights in New England were exempt from compulsory military service, so essential was the shipbuilding industry then considered.

So rapidly did the sea power of the Colonies grow that

England began to look upon it with suspicion. As early as 1668 Sir Joshua Child expressed the prevailing idea: "Of all the American plantations, His Majesty has none so apt for the building of ships as New England; nor none comparably so qualified for the breeding of seamen, not only by reason of the natural industry of the people, but principally by reason of their cod and mackerel fisheries, and in my opinion there is nothing more prejudicial and in prospect more dangerous to any mother country than the increase of shipping in her colonies, plantations, or provinces."

In 1698 a colonial governor wrote: "I believe I may venture to say that there are more good vessels belonging to the town of Boston than to all Scotland and Ireland unless one should reckon small craft, such as herring boats." In 1700 Boston had 194 seagoing vessels—New York 124. During the year 1772 the tonnage of shipping built by the Colonies amounted to the enormous total of 26,544, over 400 vessels being completed during the year. In 1775 Massachusetts had one seagoing vessel for each one hundred inhabitants.

During the colonial period the frequent wars with the French and Indians had given our people considerable military experience. Hunting and constant fighting along the frontier had developed excellence in marksmanship. Their militia regiments had taken part in many a campaign —and Wolfe must have been in his worst humor when he called our troops "the dirtiest, most contemptible, cowardly dogs you can conceive." Therefore when hostilities commenced our people were fairly well fitted to meet the British and Hessians on land, particularly in their own methods of Indian warfare.

On the other hand, we had no naval force of any kind to pit against the greatest sea power in the world. While quite a few of our men had been pressed into the Royal navy at various times, scarcely a single American had served as a commissioned officer. It is true that we had many ships and seamen suited for privateering, and in this form of warfare we did remarkably well. By the end of 1778 we took about one thousand merchant vessels in this way—a staggering blow to British trade. As early as 1775 we attempted to organize a Continental navy, but only six of the thirteen cruisers then laid down ever reached the sea. Our commerce, of course, was swept from the seas, a great part being captured.

During 1776 and 1777 the efforts of our newly organized Navy were devoted mostly to cruising along our coasts for British transports and storeships. Its career was a very checkered one—the skill and courage of some captains. being balanced by the inefficiency and bad conduct of others. Notable cruises were made by John Barry in the *Lexington;* Nicholas Biddle in the *Andrea Doria* and in the *Randolph,* which ship he fought to the finish against a ship of the line; Elisha Hinman in the *Cabot;* Abraham Whipple in the *Columbus;* Isaiah Robinson in the *Andrea Doria;* John Manley in the *Lee;* Seth Harding in the *Defense;* Daniel Waters in the *Lee;* and James Mugford in the *Franklin.*

But even in those early years of the war the name of Paul Jones stood out above all others. In the tiny 12-gun brig *Providence* he took fifteen prizes and had many miraculous escapes from hostile frigates. In the 24-gun ship *Alfred* he took seven prizes, one of which was loaded with 10,000 uniforms for Burgoyne's army. Imagine what a godsend they were for our shivering soldiers. These successes made him a marked man. Robert Morris was his friend and planned a cruise for him in the West Indies.

Now Morris had real strategical insight, gained probably through correspondence with Paul Jones. On February 1, 1777, he wrote a letter to the captain about this cruise which never materialized; it shows a remarkable knowledge of naval warfare. "As I have said before," he wrote to Jones, "destroying their settlements, spreading alarms, showing and keeping up a spirit of enterprise that will oblige them to defend their extensive possessions at all points, is of infinitely more consequence to the United States of America than all the plunder that can be taken." It was only five years later that the maxims which Sun Tzu wrote on the art of war five centuries before Christ were first translated into an European language. "Appear at points which the enemy must hasten to defend," the old Chinese general had written, "march swiftly to places where you are not expected." There is an illustration of the unchanging principles of warfare. "It has long been clear to me," Morris continued, "that our infant fleet cannot protect our coasts; and the only effectual relief it can afford us is to attack the enemy's defenseless places and thereby oblige them to station more of their ships in their own countries, or to keep them employed in following ours, and either way we are relieved so far as they do it." Thus admirably did a Continental statesman stress the principle that, being too weak for defense, it was necessary to attack!

CHAPTER II

WICKES AND CONYNGHAM

ROBERT MORRIS was soon to receive a practical confirmation of these principles. It came about in rather an unusual manner. France and Spain, humbled to the earth by the great Chatham in the Seven Years' War, had long been working for a *revanche*.

In close political alliance they had been building up their navies and waiting for an opportunity to regain their lost prestige and colonies. The underlying idea of French strategy for centuries had been to take advantage of the disaffection of the Scotch and Irish toward the British government. As late even as the World War we see Great Britain's enemies endeavoring to capitalize the hatred of the Irish toward their British rulers. Thus we may imagine the delight with which the French politicians saw the bickerings in the American Colonies break into open fighting. Our struggle for independence also deeply interested the higher levels of French society, already stirred by the novel political ideas recently aired by Voltaire, Rousseau, Turgot, and Montesquieu.

Minister of Foreign Affairs Vergennes had been watchfully waiting for his chance to intervene, but had to be sure that we were in earnest and could put up a good fight. Even before the Declaration of Independence he had turned over to a French agent a million francs with which to buy us arms and ammunition and had induced Spain to place to our credit a similar amount. To take advantage of this welcome assistance Congress sent Silas Deane over to Paris in the summer of 1776. Later it was decided that this was the place for our greatest diplomat, venerable Benjamin Franklin. When he heard that Congress had selected him for this station he was already seventy years old and worn out by a busy life. "I am old and good for nothing," he replied, "but as the storekeepers say of their remnants of cloth, I am but a fag end—you may have me for what you please."

Captain Lambert Wickes, who commanded the little 16-gun brig *Reprisal,* was assigned the important duty of carrying Franklin to France. Certainly no captain in our Navy ever assumed a heavier responsibility, for the independence of our country well-nigh depended upon the fortune of his cruise. In October, 1776, Wickes set sail and in December landed his passenger in France. In Paris Franklin was greeted with enthusiasm by all ranks of society—became literally the man of the hour. He quickly gained the confidence of the ministry and induced the King to grant us a subsidy of two million *livres* a year and a million more in exchange for American tobacco. Arms and military equipment were bought in France with the money thus obtained and sent to the Colonies in three vessels. The French also agreed to permit American privateers to fit out and be equipped in their ports.

While the political developments in Europe were becoming so favorable, activities of another sort were providing an interesting subject for breakfast-table conversation. Lambert Wickes was of an adventurous disposition. He had taken two prizes while carrying Franklin to Europe. He had doubtless heard how Captain John Lee, of the Newburyport privateer *Hawke,* only a few months before had come into Bilbao, Spain, with the news that he had taken five British prizes—and had shown some prisoners to prove it. And also of how Captain Isaac Soams with the Cape Ann privateer *Union* only last November had made five captures twenty-five leagues west of Lisbon. Why should not he also with his fast little cruiser strike a blow at the enemy in his home waters? Provide the American commissioners with some much-needed cash by selling his prizes in French ports? And incidentally embroil the French with our great enemy? So, early in 1777, Wickes sailed out into blustery Biscay and commenced the first cruise of an American man-of-war in British waters—gallantly blazing the trail for Gustavus Conyngham and Paul Jones.

Five prizes soon fell to the little *Reprisal*. One of them was the packet from Falmouth to Lisbon and she put up quite a fight. "She is mounted with sixteen guns," so Wickes reported, "and had near fifty men on board. She engaged near an hour before she struck. I had one man killed. My First Lieutenant had his left arm shot off above the elbow and the Lieutenant of Marines had a musquet ball lodged in his wrist." In the middle of February the *Reprisal* came back to Lorient with her five captures after what her captain termed modestly "a tolerable successful cruise." Wickes had shown the way. Others did not delay to follow.

In March the privateer *Resolution* appeared in the Bristol Channel and delivered to two fishing vessels the crew of a British merchantman she had just taken. This was the fifth prize she had taken and sent to port. About the same time the *Rover* and *Montgomery* boldly came into Galway to buy provisions and water. "During the short time the Captains were ashore they behaved with the greatest politeness," according to the letter of an inhabitant. "The crews that came on shore with them were dressed in blue uniforms with cockades and made a genteel appearance, but were all armed with pistols." They informed the townspeople that they had taken and sent home four prizes. Their conduct does not sound very piratical.

During the early spring Wickes had been preparing for a new cruise, this time into sight of the British coasts. He was reënforced in April by the 14-gun brig *Lexington,* Captain Henry Johnson, which had made a swift voyage from Baltimore; and later by the 10-gun cutter *Dolphin,* Lieutenant Samuel Nicholson, which arrived upon the scene in a most mysterious manner. In February this same Nicholson, by Franklin's order, had been sent out to buy a likely ship. Finding none in Boulogne or Calais, he had crossed to England, where, if caught, he would soon have made the acquaintance of a firing squad. Indeed, we have recorded a cryptic note he wrote from London in which he admits that his business is "of such a nature as won't bare putting to paper." He had found the ship he wanted in Dover and on February 17 had calmly sailed her over to Calais. There he renamed her the *Dolphin,* commissioned her as an American cruiser and assumed the command— and well he deserved it. Very few naval vessels, we warrant, have thus been bought in the country whose coasts they were to harry.

While Commodore Wickes was preparing this mighty armada for a summer campaign, another picturesque Irish-American adventurer was creating enough sensations to cover the front pages of the European journals. The sedate readers of the Continent must have looked on with smiling faces as these wild, scarcely civilized Americans plucked John Bull's beard in such unceremonious fashion! These Britons had been wont to "singe the beard" of other kings—but now conditions were very much reversed.

Captain Gustavus Conyngham was the fellow to whom we refer. He had a fine new commission, but no ship. However, our commissioners were a handy lot—perhaps they could find him one, Wickes having eased their financial difficulties by selling seven prizes. William Hodge, one of the agents, bought a lugger in Dunkirk, which was thought suitable for the business at hand. But now difficulties multiplied. Wickes' foray had stirred up so much commotion that French neutrality had to be reckoned with. However, by dint of intrigue and subterfuge the lugger at last was slipped out of Dunkirk with Conyngham aboard on May Day, 1777—a day later made memorable by Dewey's victory at Manila. Another vessel was at hand with ten guns and the needful ammunition. It was an easy matter for the guns to be moved over and mounted, for Conyngham to read his commission to his miscellaneous crew, to christen his ship the *Surprise,* and to start off on a foray. Nearly a century later the British repaid us with interest for this trick when they allowed Captain Semmes to launch the *Alabama* upon our shipping in like manner; and that interest was not limited by any legal rates.

Conyngham was a fast worker. Within a few days he took the ship *Joseph.* Then he headed into the North Sea and brought to the mail packet *Prince of Orange.* With this rich capture the *Surprise* appeared suddenly in Dunkirk. Now there was hell to pay. The British were infuriated. They sent over some ultimatums, and two men-of-war to bring back the *Surprise,* her prizes, and Conyngham. The captain, accordingly, was thrown head-first into prison, and William Hodge found that he had been awarded free board and lodging in the Bastille. Such rewards did our early captains receive for their successful cruises.

With all this fuss being stirred up in Dunkirk over the capture of two paltry ships, it behooved Commodore Wickes, who was out for a limit bag of twenty, to hurry his preparations. And so he did. His operation order was issued on May 23; it appointed a rendezvous at the Orkney Islands in case separation was necessary when chased by a vessel of superior force; it warned the other captains to "be very attentive to your signals"; and gave detailed instructions as to the manning and handling of prizes. As prizes were not then being welcomed into French and Spanish ports, a novel expedient was to be resorted to: all prisoners were to be taken out and when entering port "the prize master must not report or enter her as prize, but as an American vessel from a port that will be most likely to gain credit according to the cargo she may have on board." We wonder whether this idea really worked—history does not tell.

On May 28 the squadron sailed from St. Nazaire. When out only two days the *Foudroyant,* 86, gave chase, getting close enough to ease off a few shot at the *Lexington.* Reassembling his ships, Wickes headed northwest and ran up the western coast of Ireland. Not until June 19 did he reach his cruising ground to the northward of Ireland, but then he soon took two brigs and two sloops. The next week he swept up the Irish Sea in real Van Tromp fashion, taking two ships, seven brigs, and five other vessels. Of these eighteen prizes, eight were sent into port, seven were sunk, and three were used to send away the prisoners. In one alone 110 seamen, in addition to women and children, came into Whitehaven. Thus honorably did our captains observe the laws of war.

On June 27 a large man-of-war chased the squadron off Ushant. The *Reprisal* was close to capture, for the en-

emy, as Wickes says, "was almost within musket shot and
we escaped by heaving our guns overboard and lightening
the ship. They pay very little regard to the laws of neutrality, as they chased me and fired as long as they dared
stand in, for fear of running ashore." That last is rather
naïve, should we not say, on the part of a captain who had
been making French territory his base of operations. All
the squadron escaped, a result which caused British agent
Lupton to write home: "These three fellows have three of
the fastest sailing vessell in the employ of the Colonies and
it's impossiable to take them unless it blows hard." Lupton's
information seems much more accurate than his manner
of putting it upon paper.

What a cruise Wickes had made with his little squadron!
Hats off to him and his comrades for a daring exploit, well
planned and perfectly executed—worthy even of that great
captain who was soon to follow him in the *Ranger* and *Richard*. Silas Deane wrote back to Robert Morris an account
of this campaign. "It effectually alarmed England," he said,
"prevented the great fair at Chester, occasioned insurance
to rise and even deterred the English merchants from shipping goods in English bottoms, at any rate, so that in a few
weeks, forty sail of French ships were loading in the
Thames on freight; an instance never before known." Yes,
indeed, here is some reprisal, perfectly legitimate and honorable, for those burnings along the American coasts which
have been thought such an effective means of bringing
home to the rebels the errors of their ways.

Meanwhile the British had other worries. That fellow
Conyngham whom we saw thrown into jail had broken
loose again. Now the French, in view of the insistent
protests of the British ambassador, had to make some pretense of neutrality. But they never had any intention of

giving up Conyngham and his ships. They could not have been displeased at seeing those forty sail of French ships loading in the Thames. They did not allow Conyngham's prizes to be sold in Dunkirk, but made no objection to buying them out on the high seas just outside the three-mile limit, under which conditions their merchants could drive a shrewder bargain. Conyngham himself was released. And his friends even had a new ship ready for him to commence his forays, our old friend Hodge, undeterred by his vacation in the Bastille, again playing a leading rôle in these intrigues. A crew of 106 officers and men was recruited; according to British information it was "composed of all the most desperate fellows which could be procured in so blessed a port as Dunkirk," 66 being Frenchmen. A battery of fourteen 6-pounders was got together.

Suddenly on July 16, Conyngham commissioned his ship as the *Revenge* and put to sea to "burn, sink and destroy the enemy." Her cruise came near ending before it began, for the next day her captain said that he was "attacked, fired on, chased by several British frigates, sloops-of-war and cutters." The *Revenge* showed her heels to the blockading squadron, sailed northward through the North Sea, passed to the north of Scotland and down into that fine hunting ground—the Irish Sea. During this cruise Conyngham took prize after prize; unfortunately we do not know the number. Being in need of a refit, he sailed boldly into an English port and had his repairs made. Then he took on provisions and water in Ireland and was off again, this time into the Atlantic. Many prizes were made. At length he came into Ferrol for another refit. For the rest of the year he used Ferrol and Corunna as his bases and sent prizes into the Spanish ports. Then he sailed home to the United States. Silas Deane, in the letter above mentioned, said: "In a word Conyngham by his first and second bold expeditions is become the terror of all the eastern coast of England and Scotland and is more dreaded than Thurot was in the late war." This opinion was confirmed by British statements. "It is true," said the *Annual Register*, "that the coasts of Great Britain and Ireland were insulted by the American privateers in a manner which our hardiest enemies had never ventured in our most arduous contentions with foreigners."

But now luck turned against our little cruisers. The *Lexington* was forced out when unready for sea and was taken by a British man-of-war. Her crew, among whom was Richard Dale, were brutally treated and starved on insufficient rations. The *Reprisal*, with gallant Wickes on board, foundered on the Newfoundland Banks. Conyngham, captaining a privateer, fell into the hands of the enemy and was treated with such deliberate cruelty that Congress brought the matter officially to the attention of the British government. Thus did our great enemy attempt to discourage attacks on his trade, with what lack of success we shall soon see. For a greater captain than Wickes or Conyngham was on the way—Paul Jones.

CHAPTER III

PAUL JONES: TRIPLE-THREAT MAN

THE *RANGER'S* captain carried a letter from the Marine Committee of Congress to the American commissioner in Paris. "Our design in sending him," wrote the committee, "is (with the approbation of Congress) that you may purchase one of those fine frigates that Mr. Deane writes us you can get, and invest him with the command thereof as soon as possible. We hope that you may not delay this business one moment, but purchase, in such port or place in Europe as it can be done with the most convenience and despatch, a fine, fast sailing frigate or larger ship." Little did the committee know what an arduous task they were thus lightly imposing on poor Dr. Franklin.

The *Ranger* made a good run past the Azores and thence headed up for the French coast. As she neared the Continent many vessels were sighted and brought to, but only two were found to fly the enemy colors. A group of eleven sail was next sighted and Jones bore down upon them with alacrity, only to find that one of them was the liner *Invincible,* 74 guns. The *Ranger* was maneuvered about the convoy for two whole days, but Jones finally had to report that notwithstanding all his efforts it was impossible to cut any of them out. On he sailed for France.

On November 30, the *Ranger* dropped anchor off the mouth of the Loire. Two days later she stood up the river to Nantes. From there on the fourth our captain reported by letter to the commissioners. "I am here," he wrote in characteristic style, "and ready to receive, and pay cheerful and prompt obedience to, your orders. It is my

[17]

first and favorite wish to be employed in active and enterprising service where there is a prospect of rendering acceptable service to America."

Then, taking his lead from Robert Morris, Jones stated
succinctly the principle which was to underlie all his operations in British waters. "Were strict survey observed on
our part," he continued to the commissioners, "the enemy
have many important places in such defenseless situations,
that they might effectually be surprised and attacked with
no very considerable force. We cannot fight their navy,
as their numbers and force is so superior to ours; therefore it seems to be our natural province to surprise their
defenseless places and thereby divide their attention and
draw it off from our coasts."

Never was an underlying principle of warfare more
clearly and correctly stated. Twenty-four centuries ago in
far China, Sun Tzu used almost the same words. "Numerical weakness," he wrote, "comes from having to prepare against possible attacks; numerical strength from com-
pelling our adversary to make preparations against us."
The World War furnished confirmation of this old idea.
About one hundred German submarines occupied the attention of some 3,500 British vessels, not to mention other
hundreds of the allied and associated powers. They compelled a tremendous proportion of the industry of Great
Britain and the United States to be diverted from the
manufacture of munitions and equipment for the army to
the building of naval and merchant vessels. While as a
decisive weapon the submarine failed, as a diversion it was
successful to the highest degree.

In present-day football we know the advantages of a
varied attack. The team is most successful which mixes
end runs, line plunges, forward passes, and trick plays in

such a manner that the opposing team can never guess what to expect next. We speak of the advantage of having a *triple-threat man,* who may run, pass, or kick without disclosing his intention until the last instant. Paul Jones was the original *triple-threat* man: he might cruise against merchant vessels, attack men-of-war, or seize a seaport; and no one could guess where he might appear or what he might do next. He reduced the British seacoast and countryside to a state of terror which seems scarcely credible today. Mothers quieted their babes with his dreaded name. The epithet of "pirate," which was hurled so continuously at German submarine commanders in 1918, already has fallen into disuse, but after 150 years our captain still remains in British minds as "the pirate Paul Jones, a rebel subject and criminal of state." As late as 1890 Mr. Rudyard Kipling wrote a genial ballad referring "to one of the exploits of the notorious Paul Jones, an American pirate." He stated that this was founded on fact. If one wishes to appreciate the love and friendliness of the British for Paul Jones let him read this ballad. It is called "The Rhyme of the Three Captains."

While Robert Morris had considered the cruise of Paul Jones primarily as a military diversion, our captain soon saw that he could make the political results of his cruises even more damaging to his enemies than the losses he could inflict upon their navy and the paralyzing pressure he could exert against their trade. Just as the entry of the *Goeben* and *Breslau* into Constantinople led to Turkey's espousing the cause of the Central Powers, so did Paul Jones, working hand in glove with sagacious Franklin, have a vital influence in bringing France and Holland heartily to our assistance. He just missed embroiling Russia and the Baltic powers with Great Britain. It was this combination of effects, added to a brilliant and remarkable personality, which transformed a poor boy of doubtful parentage into the idol of the European populace and the lion of its artistocratic society.

While the *Ranger* was receiving a refit at Nantes, Paul Jones rode up to Paris to report in person to our commissioners. At the head of this important body was the wise and patient Benjamin Franklin. His tactful, and at the same time aggressive, statesmanship probably did as much to win our independence as Washington's resourceful and resolute generalship. The second commissioner was Silas Deane, an able and patriotic man, who, in the words of Alexander the Great, was to do well and have much evil said of him. The third was that evil genius of American policy in Europe, Arthur Lee. Influenced by two secretaries in English pay, he was already the open enemy of Franklin and Deane and obstructed every plan. He soon became an implacable foe of Captain Paul Jones.

Such was the scene upon which fortune projected our impetuous sea captain. His disappointments were not long in beginning. And already Franklin was beginning to find that naval management was "a most complicated and embarrassing part of our affairs." Jones had been in Paris only a few days when he learned that there would be no "fine, fast sailing frigate" for him to command. So he hurried back and resumed command of the *Ranger,* well contented with even such a poor instrument to carry through his long-cherished plans.

It was on January 16 that Franklin and Deane signed the orders for the *Ranger's* cruise. Arthur Lee with characteristic ill temper refused to affix his signature. "As it is not in our power," wrote the commissioners, "to procure you such a ship as you expected, we advise you, after equipping the *Ranger* in the best manner for the cruise you propose, that you proceed with her in the manner you shall judge best, for distressing the enemies of the United States, by sea or otherwise, consistent with the laws of war and the terms of your commission."

Fortunate indeed the captain who may proceed upon a cruise with orders such as these. The shrewd commissioners had judged Paul Jones's character to perfection. They had given him the free hand so necessary for one of his fertile resource and bold initiative—and the stimulus which would set on fire a man with his aggressive and high-spirited temperament. Here was a perfect coördination of policy and strategy—perfect teamwork between statesman and warrior. May our captains ever have Franklins to sign their orders. And we like also that reference to the "laws of war," while Americans were being treated on land and sea like rebels, outlaws, and pirates. This observance of the laws of war, written and unwritten, has been one of the traditions in which our naval officers have taken most pride. Hard fighters, but fair and honorable, have our naval commanders ever been. And many have been even more than that—chivalrous as any Bayard or Sidney!

CHAPTER IV

THE BEGINNING OF THE
RANGER'S CRUISE

ON FEBRUARY 12 the *Ranger* sailed out of the Loire
and anchored off Quiberon Bay. There, not many
years before, on a wild, stormy day, English Hawke had bid
his pilot forget the rocks and shoals and put him alongside
the French commander in chief. Perhaps Paul Jones
thought that night, as his ship rolled lazily in the swell, of
that bright page in naval history—thought of eager, impulsive Hawke, a fighter after his own heart. But, if so, other
plans were revolving in his fertile brain. For now he was
not planning a naval campaign, but a shrewd diplomatic
move. Another French fleet now rode at anchor in the
bay, and over it flew the flag of Admiral La Motte Picquet.
Jones had designs upon it: in fact, he was determined here
to make his first essay in diplomacy by arranging in advance for an exchange of gun salutes between his little sloop
and the mighty three-decker which flew the admiral's flag.

The next day the *Ranger* stood into the bay. As she
neared the French fleet the white ensign of France fluttered
out at her fore truck and a salute of thirteen guns broke
the silence. How eagerly must the American captain have
watched the great three-decker? And what must have
been his satisfaction when the first black smoke puff appeared against her side? For this return salute of nine
guns was the first which the Stars and Stripes had ever received from a foreign man-of-war! This was the first result of the famous treaty of commerce and alliance which

From an engraving made in 1781 by J. M. Moreau LeJeune

PAUL JONES

From a painting by Edward Moran.   Copyright 1898

FIRST RECOGNITION OF THE AMERICAN FLAG BY A FOREIGN GOVERNMENT

(In the harbor of Quiberon, France, February 13, 1778)

Salute to the U. S. Ship *Ranger* in command of Paul Jones.

Franklin had concluded eight days before with the ministry of His Most Christian Majesty, Louis XVI.

As may well be imagined, Jones lost no time in reporting his diplomatic triumph to the commissioners. In the same letter he again indicated his plan of campaign for the *Ranger:* "I have in contemplation several enterprises of importance; where an enemy thinks a design against him improbable, he can always be surprised and attacked to advantage. It is true I must run great risk; no gallant action was ever accomplished without danger; 'although I cannot insure success, I will endeavor to deserve it.'" Fortunate the navy whose tradition is founded by such captains. The Royal Navy had its Drake; we had his equal in Paul Jones. Here is a subject for believers in reincarnation to consider!

On March 23 the *Ranger* entered Brest. Admiral Count D'Orvilliers, the French commander in chief, again formally recognized our flag, returning with eleven guns our salute. Paul Jones now had his ambition for social distinction gratified. The French officers entertained him repeatedly. There is a yarn that at the mess table of D'Orvilliers himself he astonished his hosts by a remarkably intimate knowledge of naval history and his shrewd comments on the strategy of French admirals in former wars.

For a time now the blustery spring gales subdued even the restless activity of Paul Jones. It was not until April 10 that the *Ranger* turned her bows seaward and hove her anchor out of the mud. Out she sailed along the track of the *Reprisal, Surprise,* and *Revenge.* While the *Ranger* was larger than any of these vessels and had been built as a man-of-war, our Yankee shipbuilders had not enhanced their reputation in her construction. Perhaps then, as now, there was a technique in the design of naval vessels which people accustomed to the construction of merchant vessels did not know. Already the *Ranger* had proved herself a dull sailer and speed was a prime essential for the daring forays which Jones had in mind. Also, her guns were very short for the weight of shell they threw.

Unfortunately, these material defects were overshadowed by a far greater handicap—the poor quality of the officers and crew. All the officers were New Englanders and, as such, had little regard for a captain from the South, which was regarded almost as a foreign country. Excepting the captain, none of the officers had seen previous naval service. The first lieutenant, Simpson, had come out in the *Ranger* with the understanding that Jones would get his "fast sailing frigate," while he fleeted up to command of the *Ranger*. Now he was disgruntled at having to remain in a subordinate position. Not only did he and the other officers lack the loyalty we know in the Navy today, but they actually did their worst to undermine the influence of the captain over the crew and to provoke open disobedience. Most of these men had been privateersmen; their object was to take rich prizes without danger to themselves, not to engage in desperate attacks on seaports or to fight men-of-war. Thus they looked with misgivings upon the wild schemes of their captain which began to be bruited about the decks; and, in truth, the prospect of spending the rest of the war, if not their lives, in British dungeons with Conyngham and Dale was hardly a pleasant one. It must be admitted that a campaign of "frightfulness" has its effects upon many persons in the opposing forces—it was lucky that we had a "captain of captains."

Even before sailing from Portsmouth these conditions aboard ship had been apparent to the captain. He had advanced from his own funds several thousand dollars to give the men their first installments of pay. He had neglected

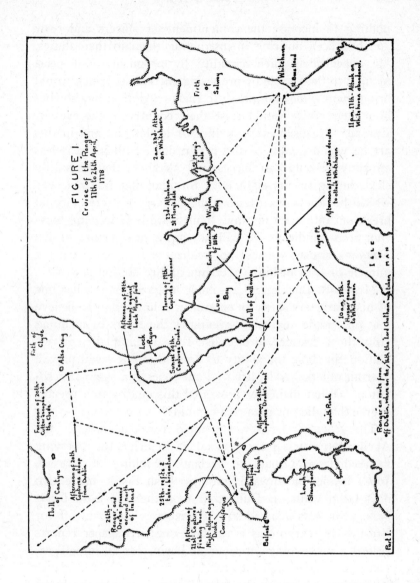

FIGURE I.
Cruise of the "Ranger"
11th to 26th April,
1778

Firth of Clyde

Mull of Cantyre

Ailsa Craig

Forenoon of 20th Cutter "escapes into the Clyde.

Afternoon of 20th Captures sloop from Dublin.

24th— Ranger and Drake passed around north of Ireland.

Afternoon of 14th Attempt against Loch Ryan fails

Loch Ryan

Sunset 24th— Captures Drake.

Morning of 19th— Captures schooner

Luce Bay

Afternoon of 21st. Captures fishing boat.

Night attempt against Drake

Carrickfergus

25th— refit & take a brigantine.

Afternoon 24th Captures Drake's boat.

Belfast Lough

Belfast

Lough Strangford

South Rock

Firth of Solway

Whitehaven

St Bees Head

2am 23rd— Attack on Whitehaven

St Mary's Isle

23rd— Attack St Mary's Isle

Wigton Bay

Early Morning of 18th

Mull of Galloway

Ayre Pt.

Isle of MAN

10a.m. 19th— Hussar escapes to Whitehaven.

Afternoon of 17th— Jones decides to attack Whitehaven.

11 p.m. 17th— Attack on Whitehaven abandoned.

"Ranger's route from off Dublin, where on the / 17th the Lord Chatham is taken

Pa.1.

nothing to increase the contentment of officers and crew
and had been untiring in instructing them in their duties.
He appealed to their cupidity by promising rich prize
money; to their pride by proposing enterprises which would
bring them fame and glory; to their patriotism by showing
how their cruise would raise their country in the eyes of
Europe. He used every artifice of leadership, and in this
art he was a genius of the first order. Still his ceaseless
efforts were only half successful. We hear that he hardly
slept during twenty-eight days for fear that the treachery
which he knew was fermenting among his crew would
break out into open mutiny. Unless we bear in mind these
enormous handicaps we will not get a true picture of the
Ranger's cruise; we will not realize so completely what a
miracle of seamanship, leadership, and resolution it was.

Mr. F. R. Buckley, in a notable magazine story, has one
of his characters speak an epigram: "I have come to believe
that one single quality differentiates the rulers of mankind
from those destined to be ruled. I mean the quality of resolution; in short the ability to insist that one's will prevail
over all others." The life of Paul Jones is a story of resolution. What man ever possessed this quality to a greater
degree than did our great sea captain?

The *Ranger's* head was pointed for Cape Clear. On
April 14 the first prize was taken—a brigantine carrying
flaxseed from Ostend to Ireland. Sinking this vessel,
Jones headed northward into the Irish Sea. There two
days later, while off Dublin, he took the ship *Lord Chatham*. She was manned with a prize crew and sent off for
Brest. Her cargo was a valuable one; newspaper reports
record a misfortune for General Irwin, for all his effects,
valued at £5,000, fell into rebel hands.

On the seventeenth the Isle of Man was passed. From

this islet in early centuries young Olaf Tryggeveson had been wont to launch many a viking foray against the Cumberland coast. Now this new sea rover—like sea kings of old—set his course for Whitehaven to try his long-meditated attack. About here he had sailed as a boy; as a young man he had put to sea in many a Whitehaven ship; he was familiar with every detail of the harbor and the locality; and he meant to strike terror into the enemy by an attack without precedent for boldness. France and England were hovering between war and peace—Spain trying to mediate. Perhaps some sensational stunt would break the *impasse* and, by demonstrating how easy it was to harry the English coasts, throw the great Continental powers into the war. Certainly it was worth while to try. Our captain would deserve success, even if he did not win it.

By ten o'clock in the evening the *Ranger* was off the port and the attacking party was ready to row off in two boats. But no sooner had they started than the wind came up strong from the seaward. The attack had to be called off, and in a hurry, for it was only by a fine display of seamanship that Jones was able to hoist in his boats and work the ship off a dangerous lee shore.

Early in the morning of the eighteenth the *Ranger* was in Luce Bay; thence she set sail for Ayre Point; when it bore east, distant six miles, a revenue wherry was sighted. Like the Coast Guard vessels of today, it was the duty of this little craft to search suspicious craft. Her captain, however, seems to have been extra suspicious of the *Ranger,* for he kept off at a distance. It would never do to let such a craft get away; so Jones gave chase. When he found that the wherry was outsailing him, he had to open with his guns. Imagine his mortification when she got clear, "in spite of a severe cannonade." Next day the

Hussar, Captain Gurley, ran into Whitehaven with a wild story, and shot holes through her sails to prove it. The dull sailing of his ship had lost to the American captain the only advantage he had thus far enjoyed—surprise!

On the morning of the nineteenth the ship was off the Mull of Galloway and here a small coasting schooner, loaded with barley, was made prize. Hearing from her that a fleet of merchant ships lay in Loch Ryan, Jones pointed the *Ranger* in that direction. But when he arrived at the entrance of the loch a heavy squall and unfavorable winds kept him from getting at his prey and this scheme had to be abandoned. Even the elements were against him.

On the twentieth the luck is no better. A cutter is chased as far as Ailsa Craig, but gets clean away. Here will be spread another report of the Yankee pirate; soon now will the royal frigates be gathering, like great hounds on the track of a lone wolf. Paul Jones must hurry now, if he is to carry through any of the daring plans he has had in mind. In the afternoon a little sloop from Dublin is run down and taken; the crew murmur; are beginning to speak out openly against the captain; where, they ask, are those rich prizes, about which so much has been promised? Where—though we care little for them—are those brilliant exploits about which there has been so much boasting? Where indeed?

On the twenty-first the captain receives some cheering information. While off the entrance to Belfast Lough the crew of a fishing vessel points out a brig anchored off Carrickfergus. That, Captain, is the *Drake* sloop-of-war; twenty guns she mounts, and her crew is none too good. Here at last is your chance, Captain; show this mutinous crew what an American ship of war can do. Jones is not so sure of his people; he wants to get on his side every advantage there is to be had. So he decides upon a characteristic plan. "I determined," he reported to the commissioners, "to attack her in the night. My plan was to overlay her cable, and fall upon her bow, so as to have all her decks open, and exposed to our musketry, &c.; at the same time it was my intention to have secured the enemy by grapplings, so that, had they cut their cables, they would not thereby have obtained an advantage." This plan reminds us of that famous surprise attack which Captain Müller of the *Emden* made with such complete success upon the unsuspecting Russian cruiser *Zhemchug* and the French torpedo boats in Penang Harbor. But will Jones, with his poorly trained and disciplined crew, have equal success? We fear not. The plan is good—but the quartermaster is drunk!

This is how it happened. The *Ranger,* all set for action, stood down into the lough. The night was pitch black; the breeze was fresh; the ship rolled heavily in the quartering sea. Jones conned her down into the proper position; gave the word to anchor. Nothing happened, for, as we have intimated, the quartermaster had been trying to work up some Dutch courage. By the time the captain could run forward and have the anchor let go it was too late. Instead of bringing up across the *Drake's* bow, the *Ranger* lay one hundred yards on her quarter. Now the plan would not work. The people on the *Drake,* mildly surprised to find that another ship was so close upon them, began to shout over inquiries, to which sooner or later response would be necessary. Jones cut his cable in such a manner as to make the people on the other ship believe that it had parted by accident. Then he made sail and stood out. Now the gale came on with blinding snow and it needed all our captain's seamanship to weather the lighthouse on the southern side of the lough. Another failure!

CHAPTER V

THE DESCENT ON WHITEHAVEN

O N THE twenty-second the weather moderated. Let's make another try on Whitehaven. In this tidal harbor lay 250 great ships. As they rested in the mud at low tide they were protected from the weather by two stone piers called the North Wall and the Old Quay. At either end of the latter were forts which mounted, together, some thirty heavy cannon. The harbor was divided by a third stone pier, called the Bulwark, into the northern and southern basins. In the former were about one hundred vessels and in the latter one hundred and fifty. There was such a range of tide that when the attack was made, at low tide, all these ships were high and dry out of the water.

The breeze was very light; it was eleven at night before the ship could reach her appointed station two miles off Old Quay. When Jones proposed his plan to the crew they were anything but happy. Here was no chance for prize money. On the contrary, a visit to an English prison seemed very probable. And if Conyngham had been nearly starved to death after taking a few prizes on the high seas, what would happen to the people who set on fire 250 ships in an English port? A night attack always has its terrors, even to the best disciplined men, and these fellows of the *Ranger* were waiting for a good excuse to mutiny. "Now a soldier's spirit," wrote Sun Tzu, "is keenest in the morning; by noonday it has begun to flag; and in the evening his mind is bent only on returning to camp." Under such conditions, it seems remarkable that the captain was able to obtain thirty-one volunteers. It can be explained only by

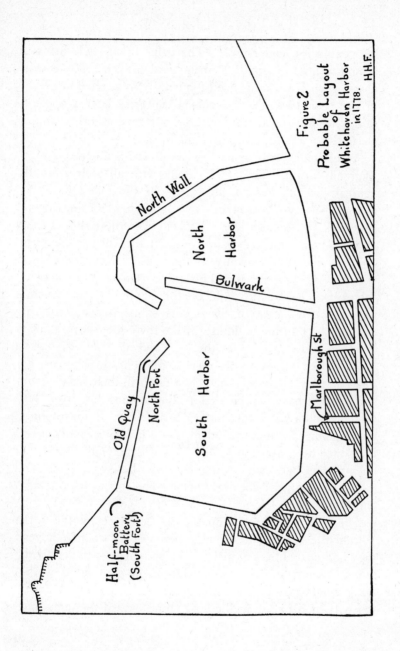

Half-moon
Battery
(South Fort)

Old Quay

North Fort

South Harbor

North Wall

North
Harbor

Bulwark

Marlborough St

Figure 2
Probable Layout
of
Whitehaven Harbor
in 1778.   H.H.F.

his genius for leadership. "The value of a whole army—
a mighty host of a million men—is dependent on one man
alone: such is the influence of spirit." So wrote Tsao Kuei
in the year 10 A.D. Seventeen centuries later Napoleon
said, "In war men are nothing; one man is everything."
Perhaps he was thinking of Paul Jones.

At midnight two boats rowed off from the *Ranger* on
their adventure. They had to pull with all their strength
against the full ebb of the tide. As the Old Quay was
neared the city clocks struck two. Dawn was commencing
to streak the eastern sky. Under cover of darkness they
at least had some concealment from the enemy; had not
quite realized the enormity of their task. Now the chance
of surprise was reduced and little time remained to complete
their work before it would be full daylight. In the cold
grey dawn a forest of masts was silhouetted against the
eastern sky and the buildings of the town loomed up darkly
in magnified masses. As the men looked from the objective of their attack to the two small boats which were to
make it, they might well have lost heart in their task. Paul
Jones must have sensed this feeling among his crew, but
this was no reason for him to turn back. It meant only
that he must be more confident, more inflexible, more resolute, that he must impose his iron will not only upon the
enemy, but upon his own men also. Let's go, Rangers;
we'll pull in toward the Old Quay! The fort at its outward
end must first be taken.

The first boat grated up on the beach below the fort.
Would the sentinel hear? Or perhaps, as we had hopes,
they had posted no sentinels. The second boat under Lieutenant Wallingford kept off a bit—willing to see how the
other would fare before committing itself too deeply. Leaving part of his crew in the boat, Jones scaled the quay and

the ramparts of the fort. The guard was asleep and easily overpowered. Even though an American ship was known to be in the vicinity, it had never occurred to these stolid Englishmen that their territory, held inviolate against many a great armada of Spanish, Dutch, and French ships of the line, would be invaded by thirty-one men from a rebel sloop. As a precaution to cover their retirement, the cannon in the fort were spiked.

While the captain and a few men were thus engaged, the men left in the boat had been plotting to shove off and return to their ship. The officers of the other boat seem to have been actuated by the same treachery. Lieutenant Meyer, a Swedish volunteer, later stated his belief that "they delayed a long time before landing from the other boat to second Jones in his plan, according to his directions. Jones called to them several times. Finally, however, when they saw their commander on the ramparts, and heard his summons to come and share the glory with him, they decided to join him."

The captain now sent Wallingford off in his boat to set fire to the ships in the northern basin. Directing his own crew to prepare to fire the vessels in the southern basin, Jones took one man with him and walked down to storm the fort at the other end of the quay. Here also there were no men on watch and the guns were duly spiked. While he was thus engaged, Wallingford was making a bluff at carrying out his orders. Probably he deliberately let his lights burn out for fear of the consequences of being taken prisoner under such circumstances. Then, according to the Cumberland *Chronicle* of April 23, 1778, he "landed ten men at Old Quay slip, when they proceeded to Nick Allisons, a public house on the Old Quay; they made very free with the liquor, etc., and would not permit any of the family to stir out." Well, Wallingford, this is a fine manner in which to execute your captain's orders!

Thus, when Paul Jones returned from the inner fort, he found a situation which must have been anything but pleasant. "I naturally expected," he reported to the commissioners, "to see the fire of the ships on the north side, as well as to find my own party with everything in readiness to set fire to the shipping in the south. Instead of this I found the boat under the direction of Mr. Hill and Mr. Wallingford returned, and the party in some confusion, their light having burnt out at the instant when it became necessary. By the strangest fatality my own party were in the same condition, the candles being all burnt out. The day came on apace; yet I would by no means retreat while any hopes of success remained."

A house in the outskirts of the town was entered and fresh lights there obtained. With these Jones boarded a large new ship, the *Thompson,* which lay in the midst of the vessels packed like sardines in the southern basin. Here he broke open a barrel of tar and started a roaring fire. Soon smoke was pouring from the hatches and flames licking along the decks. But just as it seemed that Jones had at last accomplished his purpose a most unforeseen incident occurred. One of the *Ranger's* people, David Freeman, slipped off and began to rouse the startled townspeople. "This much has been proved," reads a dispatch to the *Morning Post and Daily Advertiser* of April 28, "that a little after three o'clock he rapped at several doors in Marlborough Street (adjoining one of the piers) and informed them that fire had been set to one of the ships in the harbour, matches laid in several others; the whole world would soon be in a blaze, and the town also destroyed."

The consequences of Freeman's disaffection were soon

apparent. Let Captain Jones describe them. "The inhabitants began to appear in thousands; and individuals ran hastily toward us. I stood between them and the ship on fire, with a pistol in my hand, and ordered them to retire, which they did with precipitation. The flames had already caught the rigging, and began to ascend the mainmast; the sun was a full hour's march above the horizon, and sleep no longer ruled the world; it was time to retire. . . . After my people had embarked, I stood upon the pier for a considerable time, yet no persons advanced. I saw all the eminences around the town covered with amazed inhabitants." There was an example of "three-o'clock-in-the-morning" courage for a young naval service.

As the boat left the quay the people rushed down for the forts. After a long time they succeeded in firing off two cannon, whose shot fell short. They had better luck in putting out the fire. "Immediately after the alarm was effectually given," says an old newspaper account, "the fire engines were brought to the quay, and by the vigorous exertions of people of all ranks, the fire on board the *Thompson* was speedily extinguished, without damaging any of the vessel; thus were the malicious attempts of these daring incendiaries frustrated."

Thus after all his efforts the material results of Jones's daring attack were exactly nil. But the moral results were tremendous—Jones could truly report that what he had done was "sufficient to show that not all their boasted navy can protect their coasts; and that the scenes of distress which they have occasioned in America may be soon brought home to their own door."

A London newspaper of the time depicts the alarm caused by the wholly unexpected attack. "A gentleman who arrived in town on Saturday from Whitehaven in Cumber-

land says that the inhabitants of that place and at Work-
ington are very much alarmed at, and in daily expectation of
being plundered by the American privateers; three have been
cruising off that coast, one of which sent their boat towards
land, and it was beat back by the people on shore, who keep
guard every night, and the inhabitants mount in rotation.
There are the greatest preparations making, everyone fitting
up and repairing their old rusty guns and swords, making
balls, etc., resolved to give them a warm reception if they
should make any attempt."

Many years later an English writer, supposed to be Dis-
raeli, gave a vivid picture of the moral effects of Paul Jones's
daring expedition. "The descent at Whitehaven produced
consternation all over the kingdom. Expresses were immediately despatched to all the capital seaports; all strangers in
Whitehaven were immediately ordered to be arrested; similar
directions were forwarded throughout the country. Lookout
vessels were appointed at every port; continual meetings were
held down the coast; companies were raised by subscriptions;
and all forts and guns were immediately put into condition.
Rumor increased the terror for which there was but good
reason. The daily journals teemed hourly with circumstan-
tial accounts of strange 74's seen in the Channel, of expeditions which were never planned, and destruction which never
occurred! In one night Paul Jones was in all parts of England, and his dreadful name was sufficient for surveys of
fortifications, and subscriptions to build them."

Surely this little enterprise, which had such slight material results and such enormous moral ones, offers a dramatic proof of the great advantages to be derived from attacking the enemy in his own waters. It matters not how
powerful the attacking force may be nor how slight its
success. The populace will magnify a single vessel into a

squadron; and the mere fact that an attack has been made will induce them to fear others, much more effective. Many of us remember the alarm which spread along the coast when the *U-151* in May, 1918, commenced sinking her twenty-seven victims in our waters, and the press had prepared our people for such losses for over a year. Imagine the alarm which Paul Jones occasioned by entering a great seaport and nearly destroying 250 ships in a single night! No wonder that his name became dreadful to his enemies—and is still! No wonder that Englishmen never refer to his ships, his officers, or his crews, but always to Paul Jones. It was war to the death: the Royal Navy versus Paul Jones!

While the alarm was spreading along the coasts as fast as horses could gallop, Jones was heading for St. Mary's Isle with another wild scheme in his head. He had long had in mind a plan which he believed would induce the British to treat their American naval prisoners with some degree of humanity: the seizure of certain distinguished Englishmen and their retention as hostages. So now he planned to capture Lord Selkirk in his ancestral home. Rowing ashore in a single boat, Jones found that fortune again was against him—the lord was absent. He would then have returned at once had not his subordinate officers demanded that the silver plate be plundered. Much against his judgment and wishes, Paul Jones felt constrained to accede to this demand. In order to clear his name, he later bought the silver, valued at £650 sterling, from his own people, and returned it at his own expense to Lord Selkirk; the value of this action as a *beau geste* was much reduced, however, by the bombastic and highly affected style of certain letters to Lord Selkirk which he made public at the time. Though the captain had again failed to gain his objective, this second raid within twelve hours intensified the moral effects of the

Whitehaven attack.   And, had he known it, the good fortune which he had courted with such persistence was now
about to give Paul Jones her favor.   Yes, a better day was
at hand.

CHAPTER VI

THE CAPTURE OF H. M. S. *DRAKE*

EARLY on the twenty-fourth the *Ranger* arrived a second time off Belfast Lough. It would not be long now before British squadrons would be converging on her from north and south, blocking the exits from the Irish Sea. Whatever was to be done must be done quickly and Jones was determined to gain an outstanding success. His own prestige, as well as that of the United States Navy and the United States itself, was at stake. France and Spain were on the verge of war with Great Britain. Perhaps, if Paul Jones could show them what allies Americans could make, they would enter the war with their great fleets of ships of the line and give our weak armies the assistance of that sea power which Franklin and Washington knew was essential to our success. But an equally powerful incentive for Paul Jones was a passion for personal distinction, which could best be gratified by bringing into a French port a British man-of-war of equal strength, as visible evidence of his prowess as a captain and a fighter. Only when commanders are actuated both by patriotism and a passion for personal distinction do they reach the height of their profession and give their country the best service of which they are capable.

Thus Paul Jones was resolved to offer battle to the *Drake*. When he announced his intention to the crew they broke out into open mutiny. "I ran every chance," he said later, "of being killed or thrown overboard." Perhaps it was this time when, as related by Lieutenant Meyer, he had to point his pistol at the head of the master. At any rate, we know that it required all his genius for leadership to

[39]

impress his will upon his followers. The *Drake* fortunately eased the situation by coming out to fight; now our fellows would have to fight for their captain in self-defense. Once they saw that escape was impossible they fought well—as well as any captain could wish; and would continue to do so as long as those dark piercing eyes could watch them. Englishmen, you have one chance to win, only one. Better aim your shot, not at the *Ranger,* but at Paul Jones! Doubtless such was the command of the British captain, but the aim of his gunners and musketeers was poor!

Let's see why. The *Drake* had already been informed of the Whitehaven attack. Hasty preparations had been made for battle—as if hasty preparations ever were of any use, unless inspired by genius. A number of men volunteered for service; they would surely be of little use. Many more were gathered in by press gangs; they surely would be of less. Thus did her crew come to total 175—an impressive figure. A hogshead of rum was sent on board to celebrate the victory; or more probably to deaden the sensibilities of ill-trained men as they went into action for the first time; rather a doubtful expedient if the dose be too large. British accounts of the action, written after the event, said that the captain was sick; that the first lieutenant was an officer on leave from another ship who had just come on board the *Drake* as she was getting up anchor; and that there was no boatswain. Some scandal was bruited about that the gunner had been short in his accounts and that his powder charges lacked the proper amount of explosive. Now this was scarcely the way in which to send out a ship to fight Paul Jones; shows that his enemies thus far had given him scant credit as a fighter. They would be better able to estimate his abilities in that line before the day was over.

Now, if the *Drake* was hardly worthy of her illustrious name, conditions on the *Ranger* were no better. Officers and crew were mutinous. While moderately good seamen, they had received little training as man-of-war's men. Their total strength fell considerably short of that of the *Drake*. They certainly were little pleased at the prospect of fighting a regular cruiser of a navy which for centuries had imposed the *Pax Britannica* upon seafaring peoples. The *Drake* had on her side the well-established tradition of victory; even her name reminded her crew of a great and famous sea captain who had founded that tradition. The *Ranger's* men were reënforced by no tradition—for our young service had become accustomed to defeat as much as victory. They were aided, however, by the presence of a great leader, a man who, beginning with this fight, was to establish American naval tradition and make himself the Drake of our service. However these men of the *Ranger's* crew may have disliked and hated him, they must have been aroused by Paul Jones in battle—a picture which, dimmed by the passage of one and a half centuries, still inspires us.

Men fight, not ships. So we have told you about the men who were to fight and have not entered into an elaborate description of the ships—for what do such details matter when a Paul Jones is engaged. However, to satisfy those interested, it may be well to state that the *Ranger* mounted eighteen 6-pounders, whose length was much below the normal and thus reduced their power. There is dispute as to the size of the twenty guns which the *Drake* carried. The newspapers called them 6's; the proceedings of the court-martial said that they were 4's. It matters little. The British admitted that the two ships were a good match, for when did British captains concern themselves over a few pounds of gun metal? Not until 1812 surely!

Paul Jones had kept the *Ranger's* gun ports closed so she might be taken for a merchant vessel. While the *Drake* was beating out slowly against the tide her captain very foolishly sent a boat to board the suspicious stranger; he thus depleted his crew by a few good men. When the capture of this craft was seen from the shore, alarm clouds of smoke, just like those which drifted skyward when the Invincible Armada appeared off Plymouth, rose in lines along both sides of the narrow channel. Spectators thronged out to the cliffs to watch the battle. Little did they know that the captain of that sloop which waited for the fight was to become probably the most feared and hated foe of their great empire since the Spanish war galleons had appeared off their coasts!

Jones led the *Drake* well out into the middle of the channel and then deliberately shortened sail to allow her to come within range. The ships were on parallel courses— the *Ranger* directly ahead of the *Drake*. Then, answering the enemy's hail in a somewhat theatrical manner, Jones ordered the helm put up. He began the fight with a raking broadside into the *Drake's* bows. Not much maneuvering would there be with Paul Jones in the fight. He was always for downright fighting, believed in getting to point-blank range and keeping there. "The action," so he reported to the commissioners, "was warm, close, and obstinate." Sounds like an account of one of Jack Dempsey's fistic triumphs, does it not?

The *Ranger's* people, once fighting for their lives, did well. Even hostile historians—and there are many of them —admit that the Yankee ship was well handled and skillfully fought. Not so much could be said for the poor *Drake*. "The shipmaster being wounded," says a letter from Belfast, "and the rigging shot away, the *Drake* was unmanageable, so that the privateer raked her as she pleased." Her captain was killed by a musket shot through the head; the first lieutenant fell mortally wounded; some of the newly pressed men refused to fight. Then the rest, one hour and four minutes after the first shot, called out for quarter. She had lost in killed and wounded forty-two, against eight for the *Ranger;* her sails and rigging were cut to pieces, and as Jones said, "her masts and yards all wounded; and her hull very much galled." The injuries received by the *Ranger* were comparatively slight.

An English critic in a London paper, while crediting the *Ranger* with 9-pounders instead of the 6's she actually carried, said: "In our engagements with the French and Spaniards such a superiority would have been laughed at; but the case is widely different when we engage with our own countrymen; men who have the same spirit and bravery with ourselves."

Mrs. de Koven, who has written an excellent biography of Paul Jones, pays him a well-deserved tribute for his conduct in this famous action. "The personal element in Jones's conduct in this celebrated battle was therefore solely responsible for the victory. His ship, according to Professor Laughton's admission, was well handled and well fought, and this result was accomplished by the extraordinary character of its commander, who, at the moment of action, could inspire an inexperienced and rebellious crew with something of his own skill and enthusiasm. Nothing short of his unequalled pertinacity, his own inflexible determination and superb self-confidence, could have succeeded under such conditions."

A less resolute commander would have sunk his badly battered prize and hastily gone his way before greatly superior enemy forces could arrive upon the scene. But

Jones knew that the main object of his cruise was to create in France an impression favorable to America. He could do this only by showing visible proof of his victory, in other words, by bringing his prize into a French port for all to see. So all that night and the next day Jones remained in plain sight of both coasts, calmly and methodically refitting his prize for the homeward cruise. While so doing he was able to capture a large brigantine which had sailed out of Whitehaven. The command of the *Drake* was given to Lieutenant Simpson, first lieutenant of the *Ranger*. Though the conduct of this officer had been continually insubordinate during the cruise, Jones hoped that this kindness might change Simpson's attitude and create a spirit of harmony for the remaining days. While our captain could enforce discipline with an iron hand, he exhausted all his arts of persuasion and kindness before using such methods. In this case, unfortunately, he underestimated the strength of Simpson's bitter and vindictive spirit.

When the *Drake's* injuries at last had been repaired, the *Ranger* took her in tow and stood out through the North Channel. They were in the very nick of time, for only two hours later H. M. S. *Thetis,* a powerful frigate, arrived from Glasgow. The two little ships sailed about Ireland without incident of note; by May 5 they were again off the entrance to the English Channel. Here Jones intended, before entering port, to strike a heavy blow at the shipping which passed through this great artery of British trade. Giving Simpson his instructions, Jones cast the *Drake* loose. Many chances to take prizes were offered, but were lost due to Simpson's disobedience of orders. Finally he had to be relieved from command and placed under arrest. Course was set for Brest and there both ships arrived safely on May 8. Two hundred prisoners lay in their holds.

Jones dearly loved to make a *beau geste* and here was his opportunity. "I have the honor," he wrote to the commissioners, "to acquaint you that I arrived here last night and brought in with me the British ship of war *Drake,* of 20 guns, with the English colors inverted under the American stars." These sentences have a thrill for us even today. What must have been the effect as they passed from mouth to mouth through Parisian society as France hung upon the verge of war with her traditional enemy? The dream of Paul Jones had at last come true—he had defeated an enemy man-of-war of equal strength within sight of her own coast and brought her back to port as a prize.

Seldom in history has an enterprise on such a small scale created such immense effects. In twenty-eight days Paul Jones with his little sloop had spread terror along the English coasts. He had captured numerous prizes, made two descents upon the English coasts, and taken a British cruiser—all this by an exhibition of perseverence, resolution and will power which has seldom, if ever, been equalled. Insurance rates between England and Ireland had risen from $1\frac{1}{4}$ to 5 per cent. American prestige in France had been doubled by his exploits; this undoubtedly contributed toward the decision of the French ministry to enter the war openly on the side of the American Colonies.

Overnight Paul Jones became the hero of France, the idol of her society. His engaging personality heightened the effect of his adventurous cruises. He became the Lindbergh of the day.

CHAPTER VII

FRANCE BECOMES AN ALLY

MUCH as life amidst the high society of Paris pleased Paul Jones, he did not succumb to its enchantments. He was not the man to rest upon his oars after such minor successes as he had won. He used them and the social honors which had resulted from them merely as stepping stones to higher opportunities. But first he had to square away the difficult situation which had resulted from bringing the *Drake* into a technically neutral port. He had no food to feed his own crew and the prisoners, nor money to buy it with. Then there was the important question of exchanging these prisoners for Americans in English jails, whose relief had been one of the objects of the *Ranger's* cruise.

Once these questions were attended to with as much success as was possible under such difficult conditions, Jones set about to look for other opportunities to command an expedition into English waters. At first many came his way. Before officially entering the war the French wished to use the American flag to cover secret enterprises against English trade. With the American flag there should be an American commander, and what better one than Paul Jones could be found? If in the little *Ranger* he could terrorize the English coasts, what could he not accomplish with a large, well-disciplined, and carefully prepared squadron? The minister of marine requested Franklin to lend him the services of Captain Jones for such expeditions, and time after time there were brilliant prospects for a fine command. But each time there was some misfortune, some reason for abandoning the enterprise. Disappointment followed disappointment. At length, in July, France declared war, mobilized her fleets, and sent them to sea for a Channel campaign. Now French captains unemployed were clamoring for ships of any description; there was no hope for an American. On July 27 D'Orvilliers with thirty of the line met Keppel with an equal number and there was fought an indecisive action famous only for the recriminations among the British commanders and the charges and counter-charges which stirred public opinion in England in a fashion similar to the later Jellico-Beatty controversy. During the same month D'Estaing, who had sailed from Toulon on April 15 with twelve of the line, was commencing his American campaign in the approaches to New York.

The entry of France into the war seemed to have ended the opportunities for Paul Jones to get a command. Doubtless he would have been glad to have taken out the *Ranger* again, but she sailed for home. Despite every disappointment Paul Jones never gave up—never stopped trying. While in France, moving heaven and earth to get a ship, he might just as appropriately have made his famous saying, "I have not yet begun to fight," as on the decks of the *Bon Homme Richard*. That is the lesson for every naval officer—and every man too—from the career of Paul Jones.

At length, early in December, a friend sent in word that an old East India ship, the *Duras,* was on sale at Lorient. On his own initiative the captain hurried down to inspect her. "I am taking a step out of rule," he wrote, "but I see no remedy unless I wish to be trifled with until I die of grief." Ardent young Wolfe or restlessly impatient Nelson might have penned these very words. In neither heart burned a greater passion for distinction and fame!

And Paul Jones was equally eager to test whether "the paths of glory lead but to the grave."

The *Duras* was twelve years old, had been long out of service, was in very poor repair; even her timbers were rotten. But Jones believed that she could be made ready for sea, so he obtained an option for ten days. Where the money to purchase her was to come from he had no idea, but he wrote on to Paris to try his luck. Only vague replies were received, and the option had nearly run out. Chancing to read Franklin's "Maxims of Poor Richard," he saw the line: "If you would have your business done, go yourself; if not, send." This epigram impressed him as a Delphic oracle would have an ancient Greek. He went to Paris. There he nearly died of joy when the minister of marine promised him the ship; and Jones could hardly believe his ears when that worthy added that he might have a fine 64, three or four frigates, and five hundred soldiers of an Irish regiment.

But, unfortunately, there was a catch in this French generosity: no French seamen could be recruited to man the ships. Doubtless the minister had been unable to recruit the crews for these vessels and was willing for Jones to try his hand at sowing dragon's teeth and see if armed men would spring up. Our captain suspected that it would be impossible to provide his men by the expedient which Greek legends tell us once proved so successful; so he had to refuse all the vessels except the *Duras*. On February 4, 1779, this ship was formally delivered to him. With full permission of the French government the old Indiaman was named, in honor of Benjamin Franklin, the *Bon Homme Richard*.

Count Garnier, a very able man and well disposed toward America, was placed in charge of all arrangements for the projected cruise. Ray de Chaumont, not nearly so able

or well disposed, was ordered to supervise the procurement
of supplies and equipment. The financing of the enterprise
is still somewhat of a mystery. Chaumont was not to draw
guns and stores from royal magazines, but it seems that at
first he was allowed government funds to purchase them
from other sources. Jones had two main tasks to accomplish: to recruit a crew and to get some guns. Leaving
several officers to get the men, he started off on a grand
tour to beg, borrow, or steal some guns—or even to buy
them, if reduced to that extremity. On April 9, while thus
engaged, he received orders to come posthaste to Paris.
There he heard that Lafayette, who had just returned from
America in the frigate *Alliance* to induce his government
to send troops to Washington's assistance, had proposed
that he accompany the expedition with a large force of
troops.

Paul Jones was delighted at this turn of affairs. Passion-
ately as he loved distinction and fame, he was so sincerely
desirous of doing anything which would serve his country's
interests that he welcomed a plan which would have made
another the "headliner," while he was reduced to a position
of secondary importance. After arranging his plans with
this celebrated soldier and Count Garnier, the captain rode
back to Lorient to push the work on his ship. On April
27, Franklin wrote him that the *Alliance* would accompany
him. Our great statesman added words of advice which
should be quoted in the orders of every admiral and general
commencing a combined expedition: "The Marquis de la
Fayette will be with you soon. It has been observed that
joint expeditions of land and sea forces often miscarry
through jealousies and misunderstandings between officers
of the different corps. This must happen where there are
little minds, actuated more by personal views of profit or

honor to themselves, than by the warm and sincere desire
of good to their country. Knowing you both, as I do, and
your just ways of thinking on these occasions, I am confident that nothing of the kind can happen between you, and
that it is unnecessary for me to recommend to either of
you, that condescension, good will and harmony, which contribute so much to success in such undertakings." Ah,
what kindly tactfulness, what leadership, what knowledge
of human nature, and what an unerring insight into Paul
Jones's character do those beautifully worded sentences
disclose! Who can know, but Paul Jones himself, what
such support and encouragement meant to him amid his
unending difficulties of every imaginable kind? Certainly
we must award to Franklin a large share of Paul Jones's
successes and fame. Our captain was eternally grateful to
his considerate superior and kindly friend.

Paul Jones, delighted beyond words at Franklin's letter,
made haste to reply. "The letter I had the honor to receive from you today," he wrote, "together with your liberal and noble-minded instructions, would make a coward
brave. You have called up every sentiment of public virtue
in my breast, and it shall be my pride and my ambition, in
the strict pursuit of your instructions, to deserve success."

What a masterpiece of leadership our statesman had
achieved—and what a noble reply had our captain made!
Where can historians point a more perfect relationship between statesman and sailor?

Well it was that Franklin had played his part so ably
and that Paul Jones had a resolution steeled to bear every
misfortune, for now they came thick and fast. Chaumont,
who was rapidly becoming the evil genius of the undertaking, disclosed the secret of Lafayette's rôle and the King
ordered that the marquis should not sail. Then the govern-

ment seems to have withdrawn its financial support and told Count Garnier that his duties as its organizer were at an end. Chaumont invested his own capital in the enterprise and assumed entire responsibility for its preparation. Naturally, he was not in the business for his health, but was anxious for some dividends from his speculation. Thus, much to the disgust of Paul Jones, the combined military and naval expedition which he had been planning began to take on many of the aspects of a large-scale privateering venture.

Nor were these all the captain's troubles. He had ordered some cannon, but they did not arrive. He had to get his guns where he could; and many of them came from ordnance condemned by the French Navy as unfit for use; experience proved many even more dangerous to his own men than the enemy. On the main deck, which extended for the entire length of the ship, he mounted a collection of fourteen 12-pounders and an equal number of 9's, a very weak battery for a ship as large as the *Richard*. To make up for this deficiency on the main deck he cut some ports through the hull close above the water line and ran through them six old condemned 18-pounders. These guns could be used only in glassy water and events were to demonstrate that they had better been left on the scrap heap from which they had been dragged. Eight little 9's on the forecastle and quarter-deck brought the total to forty-two guns. So much for the battery.

If the *Richard's* guns were poor and her sides rotten, her crew was equally so. As a nucleus there were thirty Americans who had been exchanged from British prisons. The remainder were French peasants and British seamen residing in the jails of Brest and St. Malo. It would be easier to escape from the Yankee frigate than from the

French jails.   Jones himself had to admit that it was "as bad a crew as ever embarked in any vessel."   What other captain would have sailed in such a ship?

To give the devil his due, Chaumont showed considerable energy in fitting out the squadron.   He bought the *Pallas* and put in her thirty-two 12-pounders, a battery far better than Jones had been able to collect for his own ship.   He purchased the *Vengeance* and gave her twelve little 3-pounders.   These two ships he manned with French sailors, specially enlisted for the cruise.   Their captains were given American commissions, but these were only scraps of paper; their primary obligations were to Chaumont, who had selected them for their positions.   The *Cerf* also was added to the squadron; she was a regular 18-gun cutter of the French Navy, whose captain had received an American commission for the duration of the cruise.   The fine new 36-gun frigate *Alliance* completed the detachment.   In view of the friendship for France which her name implied it had been deemed appropriate to appoint a Frenchman as her captain.   The one most available proved to be Pierre Landais; he had been dismissed from the French Navy and was a scoundrel of the lowest order; also he was subject to fits of insanity.   Congress unfortunately had not thought it necessary to investigate his references.

At length this ill-assorted collection of vessels was ready for sea; not really ready, but able to get up anchor and sail about after a fashion.   On June 14, Chaumont presented the commodore—for so custom allowed him to now be called—with an extraordinary document.   Jones could scarcely believe his eyes when he read the fateful sentences.

"You shall not require from the said vessels," so the paper ran, after having enumerated the ships which composed the detachment, "any service but such as will be conformable with the orders which these officers shall have, and that in no case shall you require any changes to be made in the formation of their crews, which, as well the vessels as their armaments, shall be entirely at the dispositions of the commandants of the said vessels, who shall be answerable to those who have armed them." Here was something different from the noble orders of Franklin—here were instructions which reduced Paul Jones to the status of a mere figurehead, except in so far as his own ship was concerned. The situation was aggravated by Landais, who already had begun to demonstrate his insanity. Two of the best American officers on his ship deserted. This incident, coupled with the knowledge that there were many Englishmen among his crew, created grave misgivings. The original crew had been formed largely of seamen from the British cruiser *Somerset,* wrecked on the New England coast. Doubtless many of these fellows still remained.

CHAPTER VIII

PAUL JONES TRIES OUT HIS SQUADRON

WHILE our squadron had been making its final preparations a naval campaign on a grand scale had opened. On June 3, D'Orvilliers had slipped out of Brest with twenty-six of the line past the British Channel Fleet of forty. A short cruise found him in Spanish waters and on June 16 that country declared war against Great Britain. Her fleets prepared to join D'Orvilliers for a great campaign into the English Channel, which was to culminate in the seizure of the Isle of Wight by a French army. While this junction of the French and Spanish fleets was slowly being effected the Bay of Biscay was a veritable no-man's land, where cruisers scouted interminably for hostile fleets.

It was into this active sector that our heterogeneous squadron was projected. On June 18, Jones thought that perhaps it might be able to get up anchor and make sail, so he gave the word to proceed. His ships accordingly left their anchorage near Groix and started down the coast toward Bordeaux as escort for some merchant vessels, as did our naval forces so frequently in the recent war. Disasters could have been expected and doubtless were. These expectations were not disappointed. During the night of the twentieth Captain Landais, ignoring the commodore's signal, crashed his ship full into the *Richard*. His own mizzenmast snapped off and came cracking down in a splintering tangle of wreckage. The *Richard* lost her jib boom. After temporary repairs the voyage was continued and Bordeaux safely made.

[54]

Leaving the convoy there, Jones put to sea for a cruise against British men-of-war in the bay. His British sailors mutinied, but found that their captain was an old hand at handling such situations. He put the ringleaders in irons and the remainder said that they would turn over a new leaf. On the twenty-second three enemy sail were made out, but the *Richard* sailed so dully that they all got away. Without waiting for orders, the *Cerf* went after some enemy ships and got so much shot up that she headed home for repairs. On the twenty-sixth a fog came on and the *Alliance* and *Pallas* were lost. On the twenty-eighth the proceedings were varied by one of the gales for which Biscay is famous; in it the *Vengeance* vanished. So quickly had the squadron gone to pieces!

Perhaps Jones was pleased to be rid of such deadwood, for he was more determined than ever to meet the enemy. On the thirtieth, at seven-thirty in the evening, two large vessels, believed to be hostile frigates, were sighted. At last it seemed as though another opportunity had come for Paul Jones to perform a memorable feat. Under the conditions, who would have welcomed it? Certainly very few, but Paul Jones was one of those few. With a mutinous crew, a dull-sailing ship, a condemned battery, and the odds two to one against him, he eagerly welcomed the issue. "Captain Jones," thus quaintly runs the *Richard's* log, "gentleman-like, called all his officers, and consulted them whether they were willing to see them [i.e., attack the enemy]. They all said 'Yes.' Made sail after them; but they, being better sailors than we, got from us."

Now this is a little incident, almost forgotten by history. It had not the slightest material effect. But we suspect that its moral results were tremendous. The crew saw their captain for the fighter he was, and long they remembered the

confidence he had shown in their fidelity and ability. For
the captain it was another proof of his uncanny powers
of leadership; he had learned that he could make Englishmen fight against their own flag and that rude French peasants were willing to do their part even under such strange
conditions. He dashed off an order to his men which thrilled
like a Napoleonic bulletin. "It is with singular satisfaction," he wrote, without taking time even to spell correctly,
"that the Captain returns his thanks to the officers and men
for the noble ardour and marshall spirit which they manifested last night when in chase of two ships of war, which
appeared to be enemies, whom we expected every moment
to engage."

A few days later the *Richard* came into Lorient and
received orders for the long-planned foray about the British Isles. Many repairs were necessary before this could
be commenced and, in one respect at least, this delay was
helpful. It allowed another chance to improve the quality
of the crew. By this time a number of American prisoners
had been exchanged for the English seamen taken with the
Drake, and quite a few of them were willing and eager to
take another crack at the enemy who had treated them so
brutally. Another stroke of good fortune was the appearance of Richard Dale. He had been in Dartmoor since the
capture of the *Lexington* and only recently had made his
escape, boldly walking out through the gates in the uniform
of a British soldier. He accepted with alacrity an appointment as first lieutenant—and proved a splendid one. Lieutenant Samuel Nicholson, formerly of the *Dolphin,* also
joined. Another welcome reënforcement was a company
of French marines: 5 officers and 132 men. As finally constituted, the crew, exclusive of marines, consisted of men of
the following nationalities: 79 Americans, 61 Englishmen,

33 Portuguese, 18 Irishmen, 7 Swedes, 5 Scotchmen, 3 Norwegians, 1 Italian, 1 Swiss, 1 Frenchman, and 34 of unknown nationalities. These, with the marines, made up a total of 380 souls. Certainly no ship ever sailed on such a desperate undertaking with such a crew. Paul Jones would need every artifice of leadership at his command.

Just before sailing, Chaumont presented another paper to the commodore. This was the famous concordat. No inkling of it had reached his ears until the commissary placed it in his hands and showed him the signatures of all the captains. He said that Jones would have to sign under pain of dismissal from his command, and, since he was high in the favor of the Admiralty, could certainly have carried out his threat. The commodore saw at a glance the well-nigh fatal effects of the paper, but could do nothing but sign. He had set his heart upon this cruise, and was resolved to succeed regardless of the obstacles which were piling up along his path. The concordat stated that, as Chaumont had "furnished the expenses of the said squadron," all prizes were to be turned over to him for adjustment of prize money and its payment to the ships concerned—apparently after extracting his own share. Thus Chaumont was established as the real director of the expedition, and the commodore's prestige and authority were much reduced; in fact, except as to the *Richard,* his authority was practically nil. Chaumont further undermined his position by giving all captains copies of the secret orders for the cruise, so that each could place upon them his own interpretation. After the cruise was over the commodore reported these activities of Chaumont to the King. "According to my opinion," he wrote, "it was hardly possible for the commissary to render a worse service to his country." We leave it to the reader to decide whether this was an overstatement of the case.

For the time, however, Jones took these maneuvers of Chaumont to restrict his authority in good part. To counteract their effect he set about to win over the captains by tact, kindness, and generosity to a voluntary acquiescence in his leadership or at least to a *modus vivendi* by which they could coöperate loyally to make the enterprise a success. He doubtless hoped, also, that when the moment of danger arrived, his outstanding ability and superb confidence would induce the others to rely upon his directions and follow his lead. Thus had Xenophon, a simple volunteer, been thrust into command of the Ten Thousand Greeks. But, we fear, this comparison is a poor one, for they based their decisions upon reason, and strove for a common aim. Not so the captains of our squadron!

While thus endeavoring to match his leadership against the wiles of Chaumont, the commodore kept writing in cheerful vein to Franklin. "This little squadron," he wrote, the day before sailing, "appears to be unanimous, and, if that good understanding continues, we are able to perform essential service. I look forward with pleasing expectations and ardent desire to merit your friendship and that of America." Thus did Paul Jones, brave morally as well as physically, express complete satisfaction with a force he knew was rotten to the core, and assume full responsibility for a success which any other man would have known was impossible. Virgil, in describing a rowing race between two of Aeneas' galleys, told the secret of success. "They are able," he said of the winning boat, "because they think they are able." That, too, was the reason Paul Jones was soon to win for himself a place among the immortals.

CHAPTER IX

THE CAPTAIN OF CAPTAINS

O N AUGUST 14 the signal was hoisted to get under way, and the squadron put to sea. As then constituted, it had the following vessels:

Bon Homme Richard	Captain Paul Jones	42 guns
Pallas	Captain de Cottineau	32 guns
Alliance	Captain Pierre Landais	36 guns
Cerf	Captain de Varage	18 guns
Vengeance	Captain Ricot	12 guns

Monsieur and *Granville*—privateers.

The commodore had chosen a most favorable moment for his cruise. On July 22 the Spanish squadrons had joined D'Orvilliers and a week later the combined fleet had sailed for the Channel—sixty-six ships of the line and fourteen frigates. By August 14, when our squadron was leaving Groix, this immense armada was just entering the Channel, where the British were able to bring together only forty sail of the line to meet them. Unfortunately, D'Orvilliers' ships were poorly prepared for sea; food and water already were running short by the time he came in touch with the enemy. It proved difficult to coördinate the ships of two nationalities, and there were the usual jealousies and evidences of ill-feeling between the commanders—to be illustrated to perfection in the cruise we are about to describe. Also the orders were changed at the last minute and Falmouth instead of the Isle of Wight was indicated as the landing place of the French army. For these and other reasons the results of D'Orvilliers' gigantic campaign were practically nil; one ship of the line was the only important prize. But naturally it gave Paul Jones great indirect assistance in that it held the British squadrons in close concentration until September 20, when the French and Spanish returned to their ports. In fact, for over a month it gave him a chance to sail around the British coasts almost unopposed. Thus, though poor D'Orvilliers had to leave the service in undeserved disgrace, Paul Jones always spoke of him with high regard and sincere gratitude.

The American squadron sailed southwest into the Bay of Biscay. After several days it changed course to the northwest toward Cape Clear. On the eighteenth the first prize was taken. She was the Dutch vessel *Verwagting,* carrying a large cargo of brandy and wines. On board was a prize crew appointed by a British cruiser to take her into port. It was the privateer *Monsieur* which brought her to. According to the concordat, privateers accompanying the expedition were not to be allowed a share in the prize money; so the *Monsieur* made haste to plunder the prize. The commodore called a halt as soon as the *Richard* came up, manned the prize from his own crew, and sent her into port for Chaumont. The privateer went off in a huff.

On the twenty-first the squadron was still about one hundred miles south of Cape Clear when another vessel was sighted. She was found to be the brigantine *Mayflower,* with salt provisions and butter, bound from Limerick for London. She was manned and sent for a French port.

During this first week Paul Jones had been working with might and main to weld his crew into a disciplined and thoroughly trained fighting organization. He contemplated descents on the hostile coasts and battles with regular frigates, but before he could attempt such ventures he must know that his crew would support him to the finish. So he set about to win their loyalty. One of his officers tells us how he did it: "I sailed in my time with many captains; but with only one Paul Jones. He was the captain of captains. Any other commander I sailed with had some kind of method or fixed rule which he exerted to all under him alike. It suited some, and others not; but it was the same rule all the time and to everybody. Not so Paul Jones. He knew every officer and man in his crew as one friend knows another. Those big black eyes of his would look right through a new man at first sight, and, maybe, see something behind him! At any rate, he knew every man and dealt with each according to his notion. I have seen him teaching the French language to his midshipmen and the next hour showing an apprentice how to 'knot a Turk's head' or make a neat coil-down of a painter. He was in everybody's watch, and everybody's mess all the time. In fact, I may say that any ship Paul Jones commanded was full of him himself all the time."

It was well that the commodore had devoted such energy to building up the *esprit* of his crew. For now there began a series of accidents which would have dulled the fighting edge of nearly any body of men. On the twenty-third Cape Clear was seen. Away on the northwestern horizon were the sails of a brigantine. The sea was calm; sails flapped against masts. The commodore sent out his boats; after a long pull they drew up alongside the stranger; found her to be called the *Fortune,* bound from Newfoundland for Bristol. Had Ulysses made the prize he would have thought the name a good omen, and perhaps Paul Jones did also. If so, the next few hours convinced him that ancient methods of predicting the future were not always so correct as Plutarch would have us believe.

As evening came on the boats were still far away. The current was carrying the *Richard* near some outlying rocks. The captain's barge was lowered and sent ahead to tow the ship out of danger. In the excitement no one thought to hand pick her crew. In fact, seven British sailors had slid down into the barge with unwonted agility. "Soon after sunset," the commodore reported, "the villain who towed the ship cut the tow rope and decamped with my barge. Sundry shot were fired to bring them to without effect." What a sorry spectacle for the rest of the crew and the other ships to watch. What a humiliation for the commodore. Here, if ever, was a time to curse, and we'll lay odds that Paul Jones did so from the heart. Now the other boats returned. The master, Mr. Cutting Lunt, conceived an idea of giving the deserters a run for their money. So he placed twelve good American sailors and four French marines in a boat and rowed away, without even telling the commodore. A dense fog came down and pitchy darkness followed. Lunt and his people soon found that they were lost. Signal guns boomed from the *Richard,* but Lunt did not return.

Next morning the fog lifted. The *Alliance* was close to the flagship, so Landais came over to pay his respects. The commodore tells us how he did it. "He behaved toward me with great disrespect, affirming in the most indelicate manner and language, that I had lost my boats and people through my imprudence in sending boats to take a prize." Now Paul Jones was as hot and impulsive by nature as any man who ever lived, and his natural inclination would have been to put Landais in irons and appoint his first lieutenant to the command of the *Alliance;* perhaps it is unfortunate that he did not use such decisive measures at the first sign of insubordination. But the commodore, with all his passion for personal distinction, was resolved to use every means of maintaining the spirit of kindly coöperation among his captains which he felt was so essential for a successful cruise. So here he repressed his feelings in a truly remarkable manner and listened quietly to Landais' insane harangue. First he tried to explain to his colleague the true facts of the case. Then seeing that this had no effect, he called in the French marine officers. They endeavored to reason with Landais, still to no effect. He answered with volleys of abuse. Finally, he declared that he had no intention of obeying any orders of the commodore. Chaumont's leaven had begun to work.

After Landais had gone back to his ship, the commodore called over Captain Cottineau of the *Pallas*. He advised that the *Cerf* be sent in to look for the boats. Then he sent for Varage of the *Cerf* and had Cottineau suggest the plan to him. Thus he gained the "free consent and approbation" of the cutter's captain to the plan. Accordingly the *Cerf* stood off toward Cape Clear. All that afternoon the squadron waited for her to return and all the next day. No sign of her was seen, nor was she ever seen again by the squadron. Apparently her captain had been influenced by motives of his own in agreeing so readily to Cottineau's scheme.

During the evening of the twenty-sixth a southwest gale swept the Irish coast. Jones decided that it was time to leave his unlucky cruising ground and proceed northward. He signalled the course and when the weather thickened the *Richard* "carried a toplight and fired a gun every quarter of an hour." Seas carried away the *Pallas'* rudder and she parted. The *Granville* took a prize and made haste to get off with it. Landais deliberately sailed off. Only the little *Vengeance* followed the flag. She was the only craft in sight when day broke. Imagine the commodore's feelings as he scanned the horizon. Was this the way all his ardent hopes were to be dissipated? Was it thus that he was to do service to his country and win fame for himself? Steady, Commodore! No weakness! Perhaps, if you try and try and try—keep trying always—the fates, who are now testing and steeling you with their buffets, may relent a bit and give you your chance at last! Now the watchword must be *"Durchhalten,"* as a famed Prussian *feld-marschall* used to say a few years ago. Yes, stick it out! Who knows what the morrow will bring—or the next month?

The morrow brought nothing of cheer. In fact, had he known it, Paul Jones's only asset, surprise, had been taken from him. For at one o'clock in the morning of the twenty-fourth the seven deserters had landed at Ballinskellix. They had news to tell, and they told it; made a good story of it too. On the twenty-seventh an assistant of the lord lieutenant of Ireland issued far and wide a startling proclamation: "The people imagine that Jones's intentions are to scour the coast, and burn some principal towns, having a quantity of combustibles shipped on board the vessels in France. I am directed forthwith to make this intelligence known in the most extensive manner, that all persons, particularly those resident on the coast, may be on their guard to repel any hostile attack."

If such was official intelligence, imagine what the rumors were which sped from mouth to mouth, from village to village, from town to town. Jones was reported to have landed in person *with seven men;* what man ever had such a compliment paid to him? In Cork an attack was considered "inevitable" and two companies, each of sixty men, were formed in haste to resist it. A French fleet was reported sailing up the Shannon and two regiments went off by forced marches to resist its landing. A letter from

Cork, dated September 11, shows the extent of the terror and alarm created by the terrible name of Paul Jones. It was then sixteen days since he had left the Irish coast and actually he was far away in the North Sea. "Not a day passed," runs this remarkable epistle, "but we are receiving accounts of the depredations committed by Paul Jones and his squadron on our coast. A report is current this day that he is with his whole fleet in Bantry Bay, and had with him five prizes." Is it not amusing to compare the actual story of our squadron's cruise with the fantastic tales which the enemy spread about it? What better proof could one wish of the enormous moral effects to be gained by attacking the enemy in his own waters? That is the lesson Paul Jones spent his life in teaching! It is all very well to be prepared for defense, but let's remember that to attack is the best defense—in boxing, in football, and in war!

CHAPTER X

HARRYING THE BRITISH COASTS

IN COMPANY with the *Vengeance* the commodore sailed up the Irish coast. Far on the starboard hand was Bloody Foreland, where in Armada days many a great galleon had foundered, many a brave Spaniard had met his death at the hands of the savage Celts. On the thirty-first were made out the Flannie Islands, outposts of the Hebrides. There it was on the island of Skye that, in the days of Ossian, beautiful Bragela, daughter of car-borne Sorglan, had waited four long years for her warrior chief, Cuchullin. Alas, Bragela, never will your eyes see his sails! For mighty Cuchullin has fallen! Four mossy stones at Lego mark his grave! The songs of the bards tell his fame. Now after many centuries another fighter—a man of the same race—comes in his place. The sails of his ship gradually take form through the mists. His course is set toward fame. Of him, too, will the bards sing—as long as history lasts!

Early on September 1 a sail was sighted and the *Richard* made chase. While so doing the *Alliance* appeared again with a prize—the *Betsey,* bound from Liverpool for Jamaica. At noon Jones brought to his chase and found her the privateer *Union,* "bound from London for Quebec, with a cargo of naval stores on account of government, adapted for the service of British armed vessels on the lakes." Again Landais commenced his bickering, demanding to man the prize. The commodore acted with marvelous generosity; in hopes of inducing a more reasonable spirit, he gave the ship to the *Alliance!* What cared he for prize money if he could get Landais to play the game straight and work for the common cause. What self-repression such conduct required only Paul Jones could know—but we can guess. Here was patriotism worthy of Plutarch's Roman heroes!

But again the commodore's tactful conduct failed to have the desired effect. In the afternoon he ordered Landais to chase another sail, only to have the *Alliance* sail away in the opposite direction. On the second the *Pallas* rejoined. On the third the *Vengeance* took an Irish brigantine. The *Betsey* and *Union* this day drifted in dangerously close to the rugged shores of the Shetlands. So Jones sent the *Vengeance* to order them to sail south of Fair Island, which was the second appointed rendezvous. The rest of the squadron sailed for this station. On the fourth the *Vengeance* did not rejoin, so the *Alliance* was sent to bring up the prizes. Next day Landais came up with two little craft he had recently taken, but there was no sign of the *Union* or *Betsey*. Ricot then appeared and told the commodore that in consequence of orders given by Landais these two vessels had sailed off, he knew not where. "I am at this moment," the commodore wrote in his report after the cruise, "ignorant what orders these men received from Captain Landais, nor know I by what authority he ventured to give his orders to prizes in my presence and without my knowledge or approbation." In consequence of leaks the Irish brigantine had to be destroyed.

Still the commodore, in spite of rebuff after rebuff, resolved to make another trial to bring his captains into agreement or to establish at least a *modus vivendi*. To see if personal contact could accomplish anything he invited all the captains to come on board the flagship "to discuss further plans of operations." Landais refused.

On the seventh, just as D'Orvilliers' campaign was ap-

proaching its climax, a pilot boat near the Shetlands gave
the commodore information which induced him to proceed
toward Flamborough Head, the third and last of the appointed rendezvous. No sooner had he issued the orders
when the turbulent North Sea was lashed by a gale. The
Alliance, as per routine, went off on her own and it took
until the thirteenth for the rest of the squadron to assemble
off the Firth of Forth, famous as the base of the battle
cruiser fleet during the World War.

On the fourteenth many vessels were sighted; two carrying coal out of the firth were captured. The commodore
now saw a chance to carry out a characteristically daring
plan. Before him lay the prosperous town of Leith, the
seaport of Edinburgh. "They lay there," he said, "in a
perfect state of indolence and security, which would have
proved their ruin." What was to prevent him from going
ashore and levying a contribution of £200,000 sterling—
one million dollars—upon the city?

It was only a score of years before that eager young
Wolfe had taken part in the ill-starred Rochefort expedition. After having witnessed its failure he gave his opinion
in memorable sentences: "Experience shows me that, in an
affair depending upon vigour and despatch, the generals
should settle their plan of operations, so that no time may
be lost in idle debate and consultations when the sword
should be drawn; that pushing on smartly is the road to
success, and more particularly so in an affair of this sort;
that nothing is to be reckoned an obstacle to your undertaking which is not found really so on trial; that in war
something must be allowed to chance and fortune, seeing
that it is in its nature hazardous, and an option of difficulties; that the greatness of an object should come under consideration, opposed to the impediments that lie in the way;

that the honor of one's country is to have some weight."

We quote these sentiments of Wolfe because they coincided so exactly with those of Paul Jones. If they had then been published, we can imagine Jones reading them off to his French captains, just as on a later famous occasion Perry read to his captains some telling paragraphs of Nelson's memorandum before Trafalgar. Incidentally these were still worthy of casual perusal as late as May 31, 1916. As a further digression, we invite attention to the idea expressed by a recent British historian that it was very lucky indeed for these United States that gallant, dynamic Wolfe fell before the French musketry on the Plains of Abraham. Dying Montcalm saw his grenadiers shoot down the only general who could have upheld the British arms in the American Revolution.

The commodore called over the other captains and used all his powers of persuasion to get them to accept his plan. What a disappointment for him to see the hours slipping past and his chance slipping away. We blame him not for the note of irony which crept into his report. "So much time," he wrote, "was unavoidably spent in pointed remarks and sage deliberations that night that the wind became contrary in the morning." Nevertheless, he seems at length to have won his point, for the squadron started to beat up into the firth, spreading consternation along the coast.

As day broke on the seventeenth the ships were within gunshot of Leith—all was ready for the landing. Fortune again changed—as did the wind. "A very severe gale of wind came on," the commodore wrote, "and being directly contrary, obliged us to bear away, after having in vain endeavored for some time to withstand its violance." The townsfolk might call this gale the "Divine Wind," as the old Japanese did the gale which destroyed the mighty Mongol Armada. The alarm now was given; it was too late to attack.

During the gale one of the prizes sank. On the nineteenth three more were taken. The *Pallas* and *Vengeance* headed southward for Flamborough Head. The *Richard* had to make repairs aloft, so she followed at a slower speed. Two more prizes were taken and destroyed. The coast was in a reign of terror. Here is a letter from Newcastle to the London *Evening Post:* "The little squadron commanded by Paul Jones, after leaving the Firth of Forth, directed its course along the coast southward, and excited no small fears in the inhabitants along the shore as they passed. About five on Sunday afternoon they appeared off Tynemouth, and after parading a little in the offing, proceeded onwards to Sunderland, and so much alarmed the inhabitants of that place, that many of them immediately had their valuable effects either buried in the earth or conveyed up the country. The militia there beat to arms, and with many of the town's people, lined the shore until the next morning; but no descent was attempted, the enemy continuing their course to the southward."

During the evening of the twentieth the *Richard* rejoined the *Pallas* and *Vengeance* off Whitby. Earlier in the day the *Emerald,* a royal frigate of 32 guns, had come into Sunderland from the southward. There her captain was given the news of the squadron off the coast, but decided that it would be better if he carried out his orders to go to Leith. Frigate captains were not going out of their way to meet this pirate, whose terrible exploits were decorating the front pages of the daily journals, making more of a furor than the great armada of sixty-six ships of the line and fourteen frigates under D'Orvilliers.

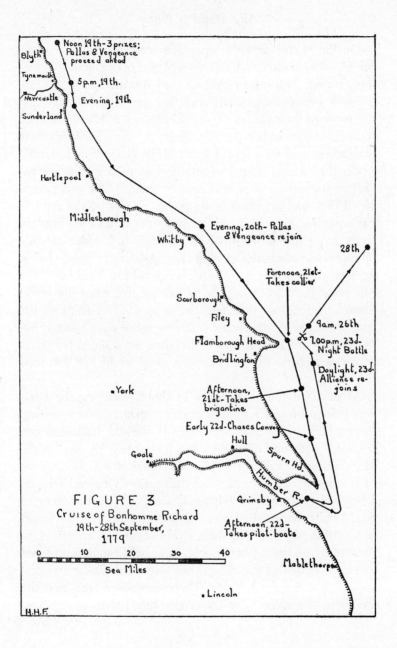

Blyth

Noon 19th–3 prizes;
Pallas & Vengeance
proceed ahead

Tynemouth

5 p.m. 19th.

Newcastle

Evening, 19th.

Sunderland

Hartlepool

Middlesborough

Evening, 20th– Pallas
& Vengeance rejoin

Whitby

28th

Forenoon, 21st–
Takes collier

Scarborough

Filey

9 a.m. 26th

Flamborough Head

7.00 p.m., 23d.
Night Battle

Bridlington

Daylight, 23d.
Alliance re-
joins

York

Afternoon,
21st– Takes
brigantine

Early 22d– Chases Convoy

Hull

Goole

Spurn Hd.

Humber R.

Grimsby

FIGURE 3
Cruise of Bonhomme Richard
19th–28th September,
1779

Afternoon, 22d–
Takes pilot-boats

0   10   20   30   40
Sea Miles

Mablethorpe

Lincoln

H.H.F.

On the twenty-first the squadron reached the rendezvous off Flamborough Head. It proved a most profitable cruising ground. First a brigantine loaded with coal was sunk. Then a convoy appeared over the southern horizon and the *Richard* gave chase. To avoid capture a ship was forced to anchor close inshore off Bridlington. Another brigantine was taken—she was bound from Holland for Sunderland.

On the twenty-second events moved with increasing rapidity; the climax now was near at hand. The great combined fleet had returned to its ports. News of the American squadron—which now for many days had been in plain sight from the shore—had spread far and wide. Public opinion was demanding that the Admiralty take action against the impudent "pirate" who calmly blockaded the east coast ports as though he, not Britannia, ruled the wave. Soon squadrons of fleet frigates, supported by ships of the line, would be on the scene. A few more days must bring the cruise to an end. Yes, the time was short for Paul Jones to perform the great exploit of which he had dreamed for years.

At daylight the commodore is about, scanning the horizon. Soon he sees a convoy coming up the coast rounding Spurn Head. Full sail now—see if the old Indiaman can come up with one of them. No luck; they all run up the Humber. The *Richard* lies to and signals for a pilot. Two of them row out in haste; they think she is a royal frigate. They say that another frigate is anchored up the river to guard the convoy; they even tell the commodore the secret recognition signal. He makes this signal in an effort to draw out the merchant vessels, but their captains are not so easily fooled as are the pilots. Now the *Pallas* has disappeared to the northward. The commodore feels that the shoals in the river offer too many hazards to navigation.

Reluctantly he sails back toward the rendezvous. With him goes the faithful little *Vengeance*. Perhaps the morrow will bring better luck. Let us hope so!

While the two ships sail through the night despatch riders are galloping to London with the news. The seacoast is now thoroughly alarmed and exasperated at the failure of the Admiralty to provide protection for their ports and shipping. Town officials ride off posthaste to make their complaints in person. The London *Evening Post*, under date of September 25, gives its readers a lurid description of events off the Humber: "Two gentlemen of the corporation of Hull reported express at the Admiralty with the alarming account that the celebrated American corsair, Paul Jones, had entered the river on Thursday last and chased a vessel to within a mile of the Pier, where he sunk, burned and destroyed sixteen sail of valuable ships, which threw the whole town and neighborhood into the utmost consternation; as a few men in armed boats might have laid the town in ashes. He had taken nine or ten colliers and other vessels a day or two before he appeared at Hull." These gallant gentlemen certainly did not fail to paint the situation in dark colors.

Next an express comes on from Sunderland: "In consequence of the capture of so many colliers and the interception of trade, the price of coals will be enormous. Instead of having the dominion of the sea, it is now evident that we are not able to defend our own coast from depredations." Here is further proof of the soundness of Robert Morris' ideas on naval strategy. This year coals will be carried to Newcastle!

CHAPTER XI

OFF FLAMBOROUGH HEAD

DAYBREAK of the twenty-third found the *Richard* and *Vengeance* southeast of Flamborough Head. Soon the *Pallas* was made out, and then, to the surprise of all, the *Alliance*. Again the squadron had been concentrated. Lieutenant Lunt was sent off in one of the pilot boats to take the brigantine anchored off Bridlington. Then a large ship was seen coming around the head from the northward and chased.

But now the beaters stir out bigger game. At 12:30 P.M., clouds of canvas cover the horizon to the north-northeast. Forty-one sail are counted. Here, Commodore, is your opportunity. Immediately a signal flutters out from the flagship's yardarm: "General chase!" Let Lunt in his pilot boat follow as best he can. Paul Jones waits for no man on such occasions as this.

It was the great Baltic convoy that Jones had sighted. Its escort was a heavy one; consisted, in fact, of the fine new 44-gun *Serapis* and the 20-gun *Countess of Scarborough,* a chartered privateer manned with a regular naval crew. As early as 11:00 A.M. Captain Pearson of the *Serapis* had learned of the hostile squadron in his path. For then a boat sent by the magistrates of Scarborough came alongside. They said that an American force of two 50-gun ships and a 40-gun frigate were harrying the coasts to the southward. The captain had gallantly replied to the magistrates that "he was, notwithstanding the superiority, not afraid to meet the enemy." Doubtless he was accustomed to the manner in which civilians magnified the forces harrying their coasts.

Immediately the *Serapis* had started to beat to windward to interpose between the convoy and the reported position of the enemy, Pearson signaling his convoy to run free before the south-southwesterly breeze to get under the frigate's lee. But the merchant captains, not knowing the reason for this precaution, which would have delayed their passage, had held to their courses until they reached the promontory. Then, at about 12:30 P.M., they had sighted the American squadron, and had tacked in haste to reach the protection of *Scarborough Castle*. "Upon which," Pearson said, "I made all sail I could to windward, to get between the enemy's ships and the convoy, which I soon effected." At about 1:00 P.M., his masthead lookout sighted the American squadron.

We left that force responding to their commodore's signal for a general chase. "In approaching the enemy," he wrote, "I crowded every possible sail, and made the signal for the line of battle, to which the *Alliance* showed no attention." In the fighting instructions which the commodore had issued, the *Pallas* had been assigned the position in the van, the *Richard* was to be in the center, and the *Alliance* in the rear. Now Landais took station ahead of the flagship instead of astern. Cottineau accordingly had to follow the *Richard*. The *Vengeance* trailed along behind the others. The pilot boat was well astern and could not reach the *Richard* until after the battle had begun; in it were sixteen men, mostly Americans, whose absence further depleted the crew.

It was not until 4:00 P.M., that Pearson could make out the strength of the enemy. Up to this time the *Scarborough* had remained with the convoy; now she was signaled to join the *Serapis*. Pearson brought his ship to and waited for her. At 5:30 P.M. the junction was made and both ships tacked toward the shore on westerly courses.

The scene now was set for the climax of the Paul Jones saga. Four long years had he been preparing for this moment—now at last his hour had struck. Through these waters had Hakon the Brave, Eirik Bloodaxe, Olaf Tryggeveson, and many another sea king sailed their longships— now the last of the sea kings was to receive from the God of Battles his final test. About him stood his faithful officers, his hardy seamen, his French marines. His glance roved from face to face—that glance which one of his Frenchmen said could make any man brave.

> Alack, there lies more peril in thine eye
> Than twenty of their swords.

Perhaps strange thoughts pass through the hero's brain. He is not noted for his religious sentiments, but in such moments as these every man feels the need for support from supernatural power. Maybe from his heart rises a strange prayer, appropriate to some Homeric hero, some Danish chieftain, some Prussian grenadier! Similar, one might guess, to that offered up in such homely sincerity by the rugged Old Dessauer before his last fight. "O Herr Gott," so that old Prussian said, mystically perhaps, "help me yet this once. Or if thou wilt not help me, don't help those scoundrels, but leave us to try it ourselves!"

The commodore showed some vexation that Landais paid so little attention to his instructions. But after all it mattered little where Landais fought—so long as he fought. Perhaps now that the moment of danger had arrived, Landais might be going to play the game. Yes, let him go into action first, if he wished it. Let him take the place of honor in the van; there will be glory enough for all!

But Landais' bellicose attitude wavered as soon as he

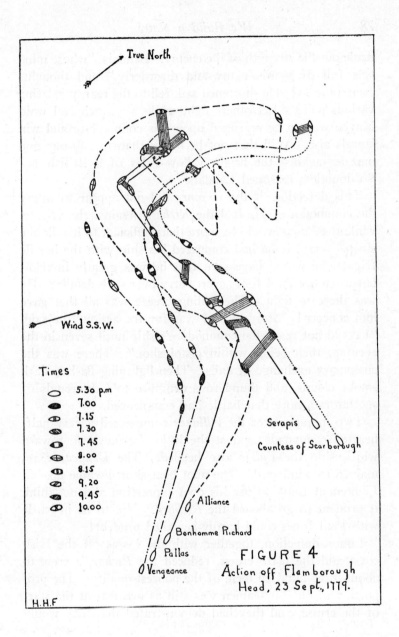

True North

Wind S.S.W.

Times
5.30 p.m
7.00
7.15
7.30
7.45
8.00
8.15
9.20
9.45
10.00

Serapis

Countess of Scarborough

Alliance

Bonhomme Richard

Pallas

Vengeance

FIGURE 4
Action off Flamborough
Head, 23 Sept., 1779.

H.H.F

made out the strength of the enemy. Landais, "whose mind was full of words many and disorderly," and thoughts even more so! He shortened sail, fell to the rear, pondering various plans. Let others fight while we watch and wait. Maybe we can be revenged upon this commodore and win laurels also. Will that not be better than to rub our gun muzzles against the bright yellow sides of a British 44? So doubtless reasoned Landais.

This defection of the *Alliance* did not appear to worry the commodore. He had the *Richard* against the frigate, while the *Pallas* would be more than sufficient to handle the sloop. True, if he had compared his ship with the hostile frigate, he would have seen that he was greatly inferior, but when did Paul Jones ever worry over such details? He was there to fight. The falling breeze was all that gave him concern! "Earnest as I was for the action," he said, "I could not reach the commodore's ship until seven in the evening, then being within pistol shot." There was the customary exchange of hails. Then lightning flashes, dark smoke clouds, and thunderous drumfire told thousands of spectators ashore that battle had commenced.

Two minutes later the *Alliance* commenced a very half-hearted cannonade against the little *Scarborough,* toward which ship the *Pallas* also headed. The *Vengeance* remained to windward. The pilot boat shortly came up, but Lieutenant Lunt, to use his own expression, did not think it prudent to go aboard the *Richard.* No, to be in battle with Paul Jones could hardly be called prudent!

Lunt's defection, together with the losses off the Irish coast and the prize crews, reduced the *Richard's* crew to about three hundred men, of the poorest quality. The proportion of British seamen was still as great as at the start of the cruise, and they had demonstrated that they would

desert at the earliest opportunity; some did in the confusion after the battle. Also, there were on board a great
number of prisoners, said by some to total four hundred;
these might, with the assistance of the British seamen in
the crew, break loose during the battle—as they did. On the
other hand, the *Serapis* had an excellent crew of 305, with
15 lascars in addition. Thus, as regards the human element,
if we except Paul Jones himself, the British had a decisive
advantage.

So much for the men—now for the ships. The *Serapis*
was a new ship on her first cruise; she had been built according to the very latest frigate designs, and had two
covered decks for her battery. The *Richard* had been built
as a merchant vessel and her timbers had been found so
rotten that many of the alterations necessary to convert
her into a man-of-war could not be made. She was twelve
years old and had been laid up for a long time in port. She
was very inferior in speed and maneuverability.

Although Paul Jones would not have taken the trouble
to compare the broadsides of the two ships, let us do so
in parallel columns to see what odds he was so cheerfully
accepting:

Richard			Serapis		
3	18-pounders	54 lbs.	10	18-pounders	180 lbs.
7	12-pounders	84 lbs.	10	9-pounders	90 lbs.
7	9-pounders	63 lbs.	5	6-pounders	30 lbs.
4	9-pounders	36 lbs.			
21 guns		237 lbs.	25 guns		300 lbs.

However, even these totals do not give a true measure
of the superiority of the *Serapis;* for if we subtract the
Richard's 18-pounders, as we are certainly justified in doing,

her broadside is only 183 pounds against 300 for the *Serapis*. Thus from every viewpoint is verified the remark of Paul Jones that the enemy was of "greatly superior force."

British writers urge the point that the presence of the *Alliance* imposed a moral handicap upon Captain Pearson, and that is true. But we leave it to our readers to determine whether Landais' actions during the fight, taken in conjunction with those in the past, did not impose an even greater handicap on the American commodore. Remember that the American frigate had a large proportion of Englishmen in her crew and that many on the *Richard* supposed that they had seized the ship and were fighting on the enemy's side.

CHAPTER XII

THE *BON HOMME RICHARD* AND
THE *SERAPIS*

WHEN firing commenced the *Richard* and *Serapis* were both sailing close-hauled on the port tack. The *Richard* was to windward, i.e., southward, and slightly forward of the port beam of the *Serapis*. Twilight was commencing, but the spectators who crowded the high coast could follow the fight in the bright moonlight.

At the first broadside the *Richard* suffered a disaster which would itself have been sufficient to cause an ordinary captain to yield: two of the three starboard 18-pounders on the lower deck burst. Nearly all their crews were killed or terribly wounded and the force of the explosion burst through the main deck above and tore a great hole in the ship's side. The lower deck ports were closed and Midshipman John Mayrant led out the remaining seamen to reenforce the crews of the guns above. "The battle being thus begun," the commodore wrote, "was continued with unremitting fury. Every method was practiced on both sides to gain an advantage and rake each other; and I must confess that the enemie's ship, being more manageable than the *B.H.R.*, gained thereby several times an advantageous situation, in spite of my best endeavors to prevent it."

Let us see how Pearson gained these advantages. First, it appears that he backed his topsails and killed his ship's headway. Thus he placed the *Serapis* on the *Richard's* quarter in a position where his double-decked battery would be fully effective, while our ship could make little return. When Jones tried to counter by backing his own topsails,

[81]

Pearson tried a second crafty maneuver. Quickly the *Serapis* filled her sails and forged ahead. The plan was to drive her across the *Richard's* bows, rake her fore and aft with several broadsides, and then pass by into the weather position. If Pearson could do this the battle was as good as won for him—but it was a risky maneuver, because if he should foul the *Richard* while trying to pass her bows, then the two ships could be lashed together and his superior handiness would be lost.

No sooner did Jones see the enemy gain headway than he guessed Pearson's plan. He saw its danger to him and also his own great chance. "As I had to deal with an enemy of greatly superior force, I was under the necessity of closing with him, to prevent the advantage which he had over me in point of maneuver." Thus he ordered the sails filled and put the helm up to try to run the *Serapis* aboard. Pearson was alive to this danger; saw that he could not get past the *Richard* without fouling her; so he also quickly put his helm up for an instant and came back to his original course. It had been a close call for him, for he said that the *Richard* had attempted to "run us on board upon our weather quarter, and attempted to board us; but being repulsed he sheered off." Again backing his topsails, Pearson dropped back alongside the *Richard* to the position he had held when the action started. During this maneuvering the *Serapis* had held for a few minutes a position on the *Richard's* bow favorable for her gunnery. Of course, even without such favorable positions gained by maneuvering, the enemy had an overwhelming advantage in the weight and number of his guns. Thus, while Paul Jones had avoided a knockout for a time, impartial judges must award round one to Pearson, in both tactics and gunnery.

It was now nearly eight o'clock. Twilight was ending,

From an engraving after the painting by Eton

Bon Homme Richard AND Serapis

The near vessel on the left is the *Serapis*; beyond her is the *Bon Homme Richard*; in the right center is the *Alliance*, firing into the *Richard*'s bows; in the right background are the *Pallas*, *Scarborough*, and *Vengeance*.

John Paul Jones

From an old engraving by C. J. Notte

PAUL JONES

but a great yellow moon was assisting gunner and mus-
keteer. In one hour's fighting the *Richard* was practically
a beaten ship. "The *B.H.R.*," said the commodore, "had
received sundry eighteen-pound shot below the water and
leaked very much. My battery of 12-pounders, on which
I had placed my chief dependence, being commanded by
Lieutenant Dale and Colonel Weibert, and manned principally with American seamen and French volunteers, were
silenced and abandoned." Colonel Chamillard with his
twenty marines had been driven from his station on the
poop. Yes, round one had been a bloody one for the old
Indiaman. How she could have enjoyed one minute's rest!
But the rounds are continuous in a sea fight. One more
like this would be the end. Blood cannot last against iron
forever!

While under the main tent the show was surpassing all
advance notices, Landais' side show was developing into a
farce. For twenty minutes the *Alliance* conducted some
long-range battle practice. The hits on the target have not
been considered worthy of record by history. We do know,
however, that at length the *Alliance* was hit three times.

True, the range was so great that none penetrated her
hull; but at that Landais decided that it was too short for
prudence. So he made off in haste. See what Jones did
with a French crew and compare it with what Landais did
with an American crew. Then agree that Æsop was about
right when he said: "An army of stags led by a lion is
stronger than an army of lions led by a stag."

This weak conduct of the *Alliance* nearly had some very
bad results. For a real idea came to Captain Piercy of the
Scarborough. "I then made sail," he said, "up to the *Se-
rapi*s to see if I could give you any assistance; but upon coming near you, I found you and the enemy so closely to-

gether and covered with smoke that I could not distinguish one ship from the other; and for fear I might fire into the *Serapis* instead of the enemy, I backed the maintopsail in order to engage the attention of one of the frigates that was coming up." This was the *Pallas*. It was now 7:45 P.M. De Cottineau would put on a better act.

Let us now come back to the chief action, which we left at such a critical stage. The two ships might be likened to boxers entering the second round of a finish fight. The Briton was confident, fresh, and strong, just ready to do his best work. The American was groggy and staggering— out on his feet, but still resolved to fight to the very end. The Briton maneuvered for a knockout blow; the American for a chance to clinch. If he could only turn this boxing bout into a fight-as-you-please wrestle, there might still be a chance. Whether there was a chance or not, Paul Jones would fight and, when nothing more could be done, sink alongside.

As the *Serapis* backed her topsails to drop back abreast the *Richard,* the commodore saw that another chance had come to run the *Serapis* aboard. He put his helm up and sheered down upon the enemy. Slowly the *Richard* increased her headway, slowly she approached the enemy. Too late Pearson saw his danger. Before he could take action his sails were blanketed by the *Richard*. "It was my intention," Jones reported, "to lay the *B.H.R.* athwart the enemie's bow, but as that operation required great dexterity in the management of both sails and helm, and some of our braces being shot away, it did not exactly succeed to my wishes; the enemie's bowsprit, however, came over the *B.H.R.'s* poop by the mizen mast, and I made both the ships fast in that situation."

The British captain little liked the turn events had taken

and had an expedient which he thought might still save him from having to fight at such close range. He let go a bower anchor in the hope that the *Richard's* lashings might carry away when the strain came upon them. But the only effect of this was to break his bowsprit through the *Richard's* mizzen shrouds and bring the ships fairly alongside, bow to stern. Both rode on the *Serapis'* anchor into the southerly wind and tide. It was about 8:15 P.M.

Soon after the ships had been lashed together the bright moonlight disclosed the *Alliance*. She was on the port bow of the *Richard* and just outside of musket shot. Hope rose high—but not for long. For, to the astonishment of friend and foe alike, she raked the *Richard* with deadly cross-bar and grape shot. Several men were killed, some guns dismounted. This was a deadly blow, delivered just when it seemed that events had taken a more favorable turn. Despite Jones's brilliant maneuver, this round also belonged to Pearson. The end seemed near; hope was at its lowest ebb, except in the heart of one man.

For now an awesome impression began to spread through these two ships, locked in deadly fight. One personality grew stronger as defeat came nearer. One man began to dominate friend and foe alike. Let Pearson give his idea of this miracle of psychology. "Long before the close of the action," he stated before the court-martial which acquitted him with honor, "it became clearly apparent that the American ship was dominated by a commanding will of the most unalterable resolution, and there could be no doubt that the intention of her commander was, if he could not conquer, to sink alongside. And this desperate resolve of the American captain was fully shared and fiercely seconded by every one of his ship's company."

Now here were two miracles: one of character, one of

leadership. It is conceivable that one man in a hundred million should have the "unalterable resolution" of Paul Jones. But that he should be able to inspire three hundred men, bound together by no tie other than his own personality, with that same unalterable resolution—that sounds like an old Norse myth or one of the poems of Ossian! Winston Churchill in *Richard Carvel* gives us a vivid picture: "What was it kept the crews at their quarters and the officers at their posts through that hell of flame and shot, when a madman could scarce have hoped for victory? What but the knowledge that somewhere in the swirl above us was still that unswerving and indomitable man who swept all obstacles from before him, and into whose mind the thought of defeat could not enter. His spirit held us to our task, for flesh and blood might not have endured alone."

As the ships came alongside two 9-pounders on the *Richard's* quarter-deck were the only guns of her starboard battery still in action. Mr. Mease, the purser, had commanded there, but he had been wounded and the men had left their posts. The commodore saw that in these two guns and his muskets lay the sole hope of victory. So there he took personal command, rallied a few men, and reopened fire. With immense exertions another gun was moved over from the unengaged side, "so that we afterwards played three pieces of 9-pounders upon the enemy." While one was fired again and again at the mainmast of the *Serapis* with double-ended shot, "the other two were exceedingly well served with grape and cannister to silence the enemie's musketry, and clear her decks, which was at last effected." While these guns were firing, musketry was seconding their efforts. The marines on the forecastle and poop did well in this respect. In the maintop Lieutenant Stack and Midshipman Fanning silenced the maintopmen of the *Serapis* and then fired down upon her decks. Midshipman Coram did the same from his position of vantage in the mizzentop.

But cannon and muskets were not the only weapons used by American seamen and French marines during this dramatic struggle to the death. While locked in close embrace with their foe they resorted to a means of destroying the enemy's ship, which, if successful, would have destroyed their own ship also—fire. "From the great quantity of combustible matters," Pearson stated, "which they threw in upon our decks, chains, and into every part of the ship, we were on fire not less than ten or twelve times in different parts of the ship, and it was with greatest difficulty and exertion imaginable at times that we were able to get it extinguished."

As the fight continued the marvelous ability of Paul Jones as a fighter and leader became every minute more evident. We must go back to Olaf Tryggeveson and read of his epic struggle in the *Long Serpent* at Svold to find a worthy comparison. Midshipman Fanning from his position in the maintop could look down upon this never-to-be-forgotten scene. Let him tell us of it: "I myself was in the maintop at this time, fifty or sixty feet above the quarterdeck, but I could hear distinctly, amid the crashing of the musketry, the great voice of the commodore cheering the French marines in their own tongue, uttering such imprecations upon the enemy as I never before or since heard in French or any other language, exorting them to take good aim, pointing out objects for their fire, and frequently giving them direct example by taking their loaded muskets from their hands into his and firing himself. In fact, toward the very last, he had about him a group of half a dozen marines who did nothing but load their firelocks and hand them to the commodore, who fired from his own shoulder, standing

there on the quarterdeck rail by the maintopmast backstay."
Ah, what a subject for a Meissonier!

But while on the upper decks fortune had taken such a
favorable turn, below decks things were going from bad to
worse. Our starboard side was still toward the enemy and
all the guns of this battery had been silenced even before
the two ships came together. On the other hand, the *Serapis* had been turned so that her fresh starboard battery was
now toward the *Richard*. The ships were so close together
that the British were unable to open their gun ports—so
they blew them off with their own guns. Their shot literally
ripped the *Richard* to pieces. Gaping holes appeared in
her side and decks. The leaks increased and water was
rising in the holds. A round shot wrecked a hand pump
which the carpenter was working to keep down the water.
He shouted out that the ship was sinking. The gunner ran
to the poop to strike the colors. He found them already
shot away. Then he, with the master-at-arms—in the
phraseology of our Navy Regulations—"pusillanimously
cried for quarter."

Now occurred the most famous incident of the battle;
Pearson describes it vividly for us: "Hearing or thinking
that I heard a call for quarter from the enemy, I hailed to
ask if he had struck his colors. I did not myself clearly
hear the reply, but one of my midshipmen, Mr. Hood, did
hear it and soon reported it to me. It was to the effect
that he was just beginning to fight. This I at first thought
to be mere bravado on his part. But I soon perceived that
it was the defiance of a man desperate enough, if he could
not conquer, to sink with the ship alongside." Just picture him as he said it, a very Agamemnon, "his head and
eyes like unto Zeus, whose joy is in the thunder."

There are many versions of this characteristic incident.

While differing slightly in language, they all agree as to the idea Jones meant to express in his dramatic retort. "The English commodore asked me," he wrote to Franklin, "if I demanded quarters, and I having answered him in the most determined negative, they renewed the battle with double fury." Dr. Rush relates that some years later Jones told the story to a party of friends. He then gave as his reply to Pearson the words: "No sir! I will not. We have had but a small fight yet!" This sounds much more like what one would expect from the commodore than the generally accepted version, as told by Dale, "I have not yet begun to fight." A French marine said that Jones's remark was: "I am just beginning to fight." He adds that this was followed by a great oath—which we may well believe.

English seamen who deserted after the fight gave the newspapers an interesting version: "In the engagement between the *Serapis* and Paul Jones, his vessel was so disabled, that the Captain of the *Serapis* called out to Jones to strike, else he would sink him. To which the latter replied, 'that he might if he could; for whenever the devil was ready to take him, he would rather obey his summons, than strike to anyone.'" Please note the compliment in the words, "the engagement between the *Serapis* and Paul Jones." A letter from Amsterdam to an English paper gives the commodore's reply thus: "No sir, I have no thought of it, but I am determined to make you strike!"

All these stories of the incident corroborate each other remarkably; and this certainly is one historical romance which happened just as is popularly believed. Personally, we like best the words, "We have had but a small fight yet!" They sound more like the commodore than the somewhat stilted and theatrical popular version.

During all this time the *Pallas* and *Scarborough* were

having a spirited fight. At about 8:00 P.M. the action had begun. After the *Serapis* anchored, these smaller craft were carried away from her by the southerly wind and tide. After firing her broadside into the *Richard* at 8:15 P.M., the *Alliance* stood down and watched the fight between the *Pallas* and *Scarborough* without venturing within gunshot, or firing a round. De Cottineau did well and his superior weight of metal made the result inevitable. At 9:20 the British ship struck her colors. She had lost twenty-four killed or wounded and had seven guns dismounted. After hailing both ships Landais leisurely beat back against wind and tide toward the *Richard*.

By 9:45 P.M. the *Alliance* was again close at hand. At last Jones "thought that the battle was at an end; but to my utter astonishment he discharged a broadside full into the stern of the *B.H.R.*" According to all the evidence this broadside was fired from a position about thirty-five degrees abaft the *Richard's* beam, from where it could have had little or no effect upon the *Serapis*. There could have been no mistake on Landais' part, for the bright yellow sides of the *Serapis* stood out clearly in the moonlight. "The *Alliance*," according to the charges preferred against Landais, "then passed us at a very considerable distance along the larboard or off side of the *Bon Homme Richard*, and having tacked and gained the wind, ran down again to leeward, and, in crossing the *Bon Homme Richard's* bow, Captain Landais raked her with a third broadside, after being constantly called to from the *Bon Homme Richard* not to fire, but to lay the enemy alongside. Sundry men were killed or wounded by the broadside."

Nor was this the worst. For many of the round shot pierced the *Richard's* hull along and below the water line. Leaks increased; water gained on the pumps. Up and up its level crept along the ship's side. The *Richard* was doomed. Now it was only a question of time before she would sink—but how long would that time be? The master-at-arms again lost his head and let loose the hundreds of prisoners. Through the hatches they poured in a wild panic. Even the commodore now was forced to admit that the situation was "gloomy indeed." But still he would not yield. Assisted by Dale and a few loyal men, he drove back the prisoners at the point of the pistol; told them that the ship would sink unless they manned the pumps, which they did with alacrity. Thus Englishmen kept his ship afloat while other Englishmen in his crew strove with might and main to sink an English frigate. If Paul Jones could inspire loyalty, he could also inspire fear; we read it in every word of a statement of the English seamen who later deserted. "He was dressed," so they said, "in a short jacket and long trousers, with twelve charged pistols slung in a belt around his middle and a cutlass in his hand."

Pearson had almost made up his mind to strike at this time. Probably he would have done so had not one of the prisoners, one-time captain of the *Union* and a most resolute fellow, slipped over to the *Serapis*. He described to Pearson the terrible conditions between decks on the *Richard* so vividly that the British captain decided to carry on.

In fact, both vessels had been fought to a finish. It was now only a question as to which captain would weaken first. One thing was certain: Paul Jones would not yield until the ship sank beneath his feet. But this would soon happen if fortune did not quickly come to his aid. The fickle goddess had tested him with every conceivable form of ill-luck and disaster—now she gave him her favor. It was in an unusual and most decisive manner.

Quite early in the fight our topmen gained what might

be compared to present-day "supremacy of the air." In other words, they had killed or silenced the enemy's topmen. Then they stormed the tops of the *Serapis*. "It was done," says Midshipman Fanning, "by reason of the *Serapis'* yards being locked together with ours, that we could with ease go from our maintop into the enemy's foretop; and so on, from our foretop into the *Serapis'* maintop." Quantities of hand grenades were passed over into the enemy's tops and our young fellows had good practice heaving them down upon such Englishmen as made the best targets on deck— in much the same way as our bombing planes would do today after the fighters had gained the supremacy.

When the most suitable targets had disappeared from the weather deck, it occurred to one of our topmen to try to throw a grenade down a hatch into the upper gun deck. Fanning tells what luck he had: "A single hand grenado having been thrown by one of our men out of the maintop of the enemy, designing it to go among the enemy who were huddled together between her gun decks, it on its way struck on one side of the combings of her upper hatchway and rebounding from that, it took a direction and fell between their decks, where it communicated to a quantity of loose powder scattered about the enemy's cannon." A terrible flame swept the length of the gun deck, exploding other charges of powder here and there. Twenty men were killed outright and some thirty others badly burned. It was the coup de grace. Boarders were called away. As John Mayrant led them over the side, Pearson struck his colors. Paul Jones had won!

CHAPTER XIII

THE EFFECTS OF PAUL JONES'S CRUISES

BUT HIS difficulties were by no means over—and were they ever? The mainmast of the *Serapis,* weakened by many 9-pound shot, crashed down. About one half of the crews of the two ships had been killed or wounded, and the latter of course needed instant attention. Nearly two hundred prisoners had to be secured, in addition to those already on board the *Richard.* The *Alliance* and *Vengeance* made no effort to assist, nor did they try to chase the rich convoy now entirely without naval protection. What a chance they lost!

For the commodore there were other more immediate dangers to be faced. "I had yet," he said, "two enemies far more formidable than the Britons: I mean fire and water. The *Serapis* was attacked only by the first; but the *B.H.R.* was assailed by both." So terrible had been the losses in the *Richard* that the ship must have succumbed to these new enemies had it not been for the working parties which Cottineau sent over from the *Pallas.* All through the night these men kept heaving and straining on the handles of the three remaining pumps; finally they kept the water from rising further. The danger from fire was even more terrible. All night and well into the next day wearied seamen and marines fought it. When it advanced steadily toward the magazine, all hands hurriedly carried the powder up on deck out of its path. Not until ten the next morning were these fires finally extinguished. During this time seven Englishmen of the *Richard's* crew stole a boat and landed

[93]

at Filey. From there fantastic tales spread over the countryside; legends and myths grew overnight; could the devil himself have arrived on the English coast he could not have caused more terror! Ah, what a night!

Terrible in battle, Paul Jones was a generous victor. The man who a few minutes before was hurling terrible imprecations upon the enemy now received Captain Pearson with distinguished courtesy. And, what was far more important, he saw that the British wounded had every attention—which must have been little enough. To Lieutenant Lunt he gave the temporary command of the *Serapis*.

All through the twenty-fourth the squadron kept its position in sight of Flamborough Head. Fortunately the sea continued calm and the breeze light. A careful inspection of the flagship disclosed the unanimous opinion that, if the sea rose, she would sink. As it would be impracticable to bring her to port in such a condition, Paul Jones reluctantly gave the order which breaks a captain's heart—"Abandon ship." At 5:00 P.M. the evacuation of the wounded and prisoners to the *Serapis* commenced; it continued all through the night. "The wind augmented in the night and the next day, on the twenty-fifth, so it was impossible to prevent the good ship from sinking. They did not abandon her until after nine o'clock; the water was then up to the lower deck; and a little after ten I saw with inexpressible grief the last glimpse of the *B.H.R.*"

Now it was evident to all that the cruise was at an end. The great French and Spanish squadrons had retired towards their coasts and soon the East Coast would be filled with British cruisers and ships of the line. The point to decide was where the cruise should end. The commodore advised that they sail boldly through the Narrow Seas and come to Dunkirk. But this was too venturesome for the

other captains; their vote was for the Dutch port of Texel.
Jones felt constrained to yield to their opinion, which did,
in fact, agree with Chaumont's instructions.

The wind was still light and as late as 9:00 A.M. of the
twenty-sixth the squadron was still in plain sight from Bridlington. Just after it went over the horizon there appeared
a detachment of three frigates and four other armed ships
sent out in haste by the Admiralty. These same ships were
sighted also from Scarborough and reported as being eight
or nine in number. From other reports we gather that they
belonged to a still larger squadron which on the twenty-fifth
had passed Harwich eleven strong—one of them being the
Edgar, 74 guns. Some at least of these vessels kept on in
pursuit of Paul Jones until the twenty-eighth, for on that
day a Danish vessel reported that she "saw Paul Jones and
his squadron near the coast of England, and that in three
hours afterward she met the *Winchelsea,* Captain Saxton,
and other frigates, in pursuit of that daring rover."

Also on the twenty-eighth there arrived off Scarborough
the *Prudent,* 64, and four frigates which had come all the
way from Spithead in quest of the American squadron.
The *Emerald* and two other ships had received orders to
"scour the coasts." But her captain evidently decided to do
his scouring in the port of Leith, for he was still there on
the thirtieth when the *Prudent's* squadron came in sight.
"Their first appearance," said a newspaper, "caused a general alarm and the *Emerald* and other ships in the road prepared to engage, supposing them to be enemies." Paul Jones
is far away, but still his influence remains. And even the
Royal Navy is getting jumpy!

It was not only in the North Sea that dispositions were
taken to put an end to Paul Jones's activities. From Plymouth came the word that on the thirtieth the 50-gun ship

Jupiter, four frigates, and a sloop had received orders to take station northward of Ireland to intercept the American squadron, should it use that line of retirement. Off the Scilly Islands the frigates *Milford* and *Crescent* were keeping watch—better, may we hope, than the *Emerald.*

Unaware of the hornets' nest he had stirred up, the commodore made for his port. But the winds continued unfavorable day after day—blew back the squadron into the center of the North Sea. It was not until October 3, ten days after the battle, that he reached the refuge of neutral waters. His arrival in the Texel created a sensation throughout Europe. "For some days after the arrival of your express, scarce anything was talked of at Paris and Versailles but your cool conduct and persevering bravery during your terrible conflict." Thus wrote Franklin from Paris in reply to the commodore's report.

But troubles soon thickened. Sir Joseph Yorke, the British ambassador, insisted time after time that the Dutch surrender Jones as a pirate and criminal of state. One party in Holland would have been glad enough to do so; both parties wanted him out of their waters just as soon as his ship could sail. The French government acted with utmost duplicity and treachery—took away from him the dearly won *Serapis* and *Scarborough.* In order to ease the situation with the Dutch the French ambassador wished the commodore to hoist the French flag over his ships, and to claim that he had commenced his cruise with a French letter of marque instead of an American commission. The ambassador would provide the forged paper. This was abruptly refused. "I am persuaded," Jones wrote to Franklin, "it could never be your intention that the Commission of the American Congress should be over laid by the dirty piece of parchment which I have this day rejected." To another friend he wrote: "They invite me to insult the Stars of America. They are mistaken. The stars of Freedom are but rising here—they are not rich enough to buy 'the Pirate Paul Jones.' "

Crazy Landais had to be relieved of his command and left the fine *Alliance* in such awful condition that it took weeks to get her ready for sea. Pearson, who felt humiliated after being captured by one he considered a pirate, constantly showed his ill humor; he did not think that a proper consideration had been given his rank. The commodore came back strong: "I know not what difference of respect is due rank between your service and ours; I suppose however, the difference must be thought very great in England, since I am informed that Captain Conyngham, of equal denomination, and who bears a senior rank in the service of America, than yours in the service of England, is now confined at Plymouth in a dungeon and in fetters."

Having entered port with over five hundred English prisoners—more than the number of Americans in English prisons—Paul Jones was most anxious to arrange for their exchange. After long negotiations this was arranged with all formality, only to have the French government admit months afterward that there had never been any intention on their part of living up to their solemn promises. How could one combat such diplomatic duplicity on the part of sworn allies? Even at that, one hundred Americans were freed, among them our old friend, Captain Gustavus Conyngham. He joined the squadron at the Texel.

We cannot recount in detail the diplomatic disputes with Dutch and British. Suffice it to say that Jones defeated Sir Joseph Yorke in this test of wits as handily as he had Captain Pearson in the ordeal of battle. With the Dutch he came out exceedingly well and succeeded in staying in port for nearly three months, until conditions were favorable for his exit. This had immense diplomatic results, for soon thereafter Great Britain declared war on Holland, alleging as a chief cause the protection given to the "Pirate Paul Jones and the American Squadron."

On December 27 a southeasterly gale blew off the blockading squadrons. Here at last was a chance to evade them. At 10:00 A.M. the *Alliance* slipped her cable and stood out before the gale. Once the shoals were cleared, the commodore turned to the southwestward; hugging the Flemish coasts, he passed to windward of the watching frigates. The next day he counted the British men-of-war at anchor in the Downs and sailed boldly through the Straits of Dover. During the night the *Alliance* skirted the southern coast of England and the next morning sped by the Isle of Wight "in full view of the enemy's fleet at Spithead." Gustavus Conyngham, as a passenger, enjoyed these adventurous days.

Next the *Alliance* cruised off Finisterre. On January 8 she took a merchant brig and sent her to America with a prize crew. Eight days later the frigate put into Corunna for repairs. There another tumultuous welcome awaited the famous commodore. On January 28 the *Alliance* again put to sea. After cruising off Finisterre with no luck, she was pointed back again toward Groix. There on February 10 she ended her cruise. The last of the sea kings had reached his port.

The effects of Paul Jones's cruise can scarcely be exaggerated. His romantic career and dramatic sea fight caught the fancy of the European public and created an interest which his magnetic and engaging personality still further increased. For a time he was the best-known man in Europe. His name was on every tongue. Even in London a rudely fashioned print of the "notorious pirate" sold at the rate of eight thousand a week. This publicity throughout Europe was of enormous advantage to the United States, and offset the many victories won by the British in America during this critical phase of the war.

France in particular was enthusiastic. The King was delighted to honor the hero of the hour; gave him a specially engraved sword, made him a Chevalier of the Order of Military Merit. The public recognition did much to popularize the war in France and caused it to be prosecuted with greater energy.

We have seen how Holland had been drawn into the war, largely as a result of Jones's diplomatic ability in the Texel. Prussia and Russia came within an ace of following suit, but Old Fritz was too old now for such an adventure.

If the cruise had its effects in Europe, they were even more marked in England. The British press launched violent assaults against their own government. On October 5 the *Public Advertiser* published one which may serve as a sample. "A little American squadron," writes an indignant Briton, "captures a man-of-war and a stout armed ship. He alarms the whole northeast coast; and the town of Hull unguarded and defenseless implores from the Minister the protection of the government. Our ministers stare at one another in a simple astonishment, in a stupid infatuated ignorance. They found themselves bewildered and devoid of all counsel, foreseeing no danger and frightened at every alarm, they flatly give the wretched inhabitants up to despair."

Lord Sandwich, first lord of the Admiralty, was the butt of most of the letter writing. "For God's sake," he wrote to one of his commanders, "get to sea immediately. If you take Paul Jones you will be as high in the estimation of the publick as if you had beat the combined fleets."

Many journals demanded that the burning of American towns should cease for fear that Paul Jones would retaliate against their own seaports.

Renewed impetus was given to American privateering. Since early in 1779 two famous cutters had been at work along the British coasts. They were named the *Black Prince* and *Black Princess,* manned with a few Americans and many English and Irish smugglers out of a job. In eighteen months Franklin said that these vessels between them took 120 prizes, which broke all existing records.

The fear in which his enemies held Paul Jones is demonstrated by the scurrilous references to him in their press. Take the following as an example: "Paul Jones in his action with the *Serapis* conducted himself like the pirate, not the hero. He meanly sued for quarter, when his intentions were murder; thus taking advantage of our Englishman's humanity to make American treachery triumphant. On land the rebels fight from lurking holes and seek the blood of their enemies like cowardly villains. At sea they cry for quarter, to mask the malice of premeditated assassination." Such was eighteenth-century British propaganda.

When Paul Jones came home to America in the *Ariel* he was received everywhere with the highest honors, and assigned to command the *America,* our first ship of the line. He had founded the tradition of the United States Navy— the only asset which our new Navy had when reëstablished in 1798.

Napoleon said: "The great weakness of our navy is that the men who command it are inexperienced in all the hazards of command. I looked unceasingly for the right naval officer without being able to find him. In that profession there is a specialty, a technicality, which put a limit to all my conceptions. No sooner did I propose a new idea than I had Ganteaume and the Navy Department on my back. 'Sire, that is impossible.' And why? 'Sire, the winds do not permit it; and then the calms, and current.' And I was stopped short. If, instead of having to combat obstacles, I had had someone who agreed with me and furthered my views, what results might we not have obtained?"

When in 1792 Paul Jones, still a young man, died in Paris, the commission of admiral in the French Navy lay on his table. Had he lived, who can say how the history of the French Revolution and Empire might now be written? How the boundary lines now might run? Paul Jones and Bonaparte—what combinations of nations could have held a shield against such a two-edged sword?

PART II

We Fight the Mediterranean Pirates, 1801-1805

CHAPTER I

THE REVOLUTIONARY NAVY DISBANDS

ON A September day in 1803 an American frigate bowled along the bluff Spanish coast towards Gibraltar. From her blunt bows curled back a foamy wave. Her hull was black. Around it, halfway up from the water line, ran a broad white stripe, broken by dark, square gun ports. Her spars tapered aloft. Her white canvas billowed out before the fresh breeze. Joshua Humphreys had done his work well. He had made her a picture of beauty unsurpassed on the seven seas—the United States Ship *Constitution.*

Watchers on the Rock might have noted, had they been observant, that from her mizzen truck flew out the broad pennant of a commodore. His name was unknown then; not too well known even now—Edward Preble. But as time passes the conviction grows that he should be classed in the very first rank of our naval commanders, for he was every inch a commodore. His flag flew from a splendid ship, but thus far without a record which lifted her above the average. Edward Preble was to commence that long series of successful cruises and spectacular sea fights which was to endear "Old Ironsides" to every American.

Countless ships for countless centuries had passed those pillars of Hercules; some on errands of peace, but most on the grim business of war. Phoenician traders had sailed out northward to Britain for cargoes of its precious tin. Carthaginian traders under Hanno's command had ventured far down the Atlantic coast of Africa. Scipio Africanus with his legions had come that way to complete the conquest of Spain. Moorish galleys had ferried across to Europe the Moslem horsemen who were to overrun the Iberian Peninsula and fight for Europe on the battlefields of France. Norse sea kings had sailed on through to Sicily and Constantinople. Jacob van Heemskerk and his Dutch seamen had defeated the mighty galleons of Spain under the very shadow of the Rock. De Ruyter had come through to make his last campaign on the blue waters of the Mediterranean. And only five years before the greatest sea captain of them all had hastened by to match his wits with a General Bonaparte and destroy his fleet at Aboukir Bay.

The entry of Edward Preble with a Yankee frigate into the great sea which had supported so many great war fleets doubtless seemed at that time utterly devoid of historic significance. But now, as we look back over a century and a quarter, it takes on new importance. It was to mark the rise of our young Navy to a high plane of efficiency—how high even we ourselves could not guess until nine years later it was pitted against the greatest sea power of history. And, what is more, it should have signaled to watchful eyes the rise of a new sea power, a new world power. It should have indicated, not only to African pirates, but also to great European empires, that the American Republic had become a factor that they would soon have to reckon with on the chessboard of world politics.

We believe that, as much as any other man of that era, it was Edward Preble who gave the United States that initial impulsion along the path of undreamed-of prosperity, unparalled commercial power, and world-wide influence.

But how was it that our naval squadron sailed such distant seas, and on a war mission? Let us go back twenty years and trace the march of events.

During the Revolution our government had devoted money and effort to the establishment of a Navy. We have hinted briefly at its first campaigns along the coast, the good conduct of some captains balancing the inefficiency of others. We have followed in some detail the remarkable campaigns of Wickes, Conyngham, and Paul Jones in British waters. While these were being fought in distant seas many notable exploits were being performed in home waters by our enterprising sea captains—and this despite the poor construction of their ships and the difficulty of recruiting suitable crews.

In January, 1778, Captain John P. Rathburne made a daring cruise in the little *Providence,* one of our luckiest ships. He attacked and captured Fort Nassau in the Bahamas, spiked the guns, and carried away quantities of powder and small arms. Being interrupted by the sloop-of-war *Grayton,* he turned furiously and drove her off; then burned two merchant vessels in the port and sailed away with three others. Quite a stunt for a little 14-gun brig. Next year he returned to the attack and, with the help of two other vessels, took eleven rich prizes during a pleasant cruise off the coast. Quite a captain to do such stunts on the very waves Britannia was supposed to rule.

In 1780 Captain Jonathan Haraden in the *General Pickering* won a famous fight with the privateer *Achilles.* It lasted three hours and was so desperately fought that Farragut said, "I would rather have fought that fight than any ever fought on the ocean." That sentence was a sufficient biography for Haraden!

Captain John Barry in 1781 cruised to France and back in the *Alliance.* On the return trip he was attacked by two sloops-of-war, the *Atlanta* and *Trepassa.* After a hard fight, which looked bad for a time, he took them both—and kept the deck until the fight was done, severely wounded as he was!

Finally, as was inevitable under the circumstances, our poorly constructed, and often even more poorly manned, naval vessels fell one after another a prey to the more numerous and powerful British cruisers. When peace was signed only three remained.

During the last years of the war privateering became much more successful, and many of the best captains of the Navy made highly effective cruises against British commerce. In 1781 our privateers at sea totaled 449. It is estimated that during the war they took three times as many prizes as our naval vessels.

Captain John Manley became a leader in this work. Twice captured, he started out a third time. In July, 1779, he took two privateers and many other prizes in the 18-gun ship *Jason*. Later he fought off successfully the *Surprise* frigate, of 28 guns.

Daniel Waters, in the 16-gun privateer *Thorn,* boldly engaged two armed ships, the *Tryon,* 16 guns, and the *Erskine,* 18. After prolonged fighting both surrendered. But while he was securing the latter, the *Tryon* rehoisted her colors and got away, a trick which must have made our captain boil. When next day he met the *Sparlin,* of 18 guns, he was just in a proper humor, and went for her hammer and tongs. After a lively scrap he had added her to his list. Both prizes came safe and sound into port.

Joshua Barney lived through adventures more exciting than any hero of romance. It is said that he was made prisoner seven times. He lived through two stays in the horrible Mill Prison—but only because he proved so adept at escaping. Several times the British threatened to hang him for piracy, but never quite had the nerve. In the end Barney evened all his scores. In the privateer *Hyder Ali* he took the celebrated sloop-of-war *General Monk*. The

British had an advantage of two to one in all except captains. By masterful maneuvering, Barney won the fight almost before the enemy knew that it had begun. His prize was taken into our service under the name *General Washington,* which certainly was more appropriate than its former name. What would a General Monk be doing over in America? Yes, we learned considerable about privateering in those campaigns; perhaps this experience could be used again. Old Joshua would have been quite surprised if he could have known that many, many years later he was to show the way against the same foe. Then the reader will find him as spry as ever, just as though the sun had stood still at his command for thirty years.

Few of us now realize the weakness of our country during its first years of peace. It could hardly be called a nation. Under the Articles of Confederation there was practically no central authority; each state jealously retained its full sovereign powers. We were little more than an ill-assorted league of nations, with few interests in common, bankrupt, and heavily in debt to foreign powers. Even the common bond of war with the mother country, loose as that was, no longer held. A majority of our leaders believed an army and navy dangerous to the free institutions we prided ourselves on having won. Foreign nations looked on us as we today look on China.

Thus it was by no means strange that the sale of the fine old *Alliance* in August, 1785, marked the disappearance of American men-of-war from the high seas. "With the passing of the ships," wrote Admiral Chadwick, "passed all semblance of naval organization. The Board of Admiralty had really consisted of Robert Morris only, and the Congress of the loosely bound confederation was itself almost moribund. The United States found itself free, but it was

the freedom of disorganization, an atrophy of government."
The Army was more fortunate. It retained an impressive
strength of one captain and eighty-three men. Utopia had
been discovered.

CHAPTER II

WE MAKE THE ACQUAINTANCE OF THE MEDITERRANEAN PIRATES

THE REVOLUTION had almost swept our exuberant merchant shipping from the seas. But now that peace had been won our privateers again became merchant vessels and commenced to ply their trade. As early as 1783 they began to suffer from the depredations of the pirates who swarmed out from their nests along the North African coast. Before the war our ships had enjoyed the protection of the ever-present Royal Navy and the most energetic diplomatic service of the world. Like our Philippine friends today, we could not realize what a blessing this was until we had lost it. Now, of course, such protection was no longer forthcoming. Quite the contrary!

Minister Franklin reported at that time from Paris: "I think it not improbable that these rovers may be privately encouraged by the English to fall upon us and to prevent our interfering in the carrying trade; for I have in London heard it a maxim among the merchants, that, *if there were no Algiers, it would be worth England's while to build one.* I wonder, however, that the rest of Europe do not combine to destroy these nests and secure commerce from future piracies."

Next year the British position was openly, even cynically, stated by Lord Sheffield. In a widely circulated pamphlet aimed at Pitt's bill for free trade with the United States, he wrote: "It is not probable that the American states will have a very free trade in the Mediterranean. It will not be to

[111]

the interest of any of the great maritime powers to protect them from the Barbary States." And he gratuitously added that Americans "cannot pretend to a navy." No longer did Franklin have to guess at the facts. Here were all the cards face upwards on the table, even the joker!

What were we to do? How could we reply to such diplomacy? But first let us see what a nut we had to crack —without any crackers!

The northern coast of Africa, despite poor harbors and atrocious weather, had long fostered sea power. Perhaps the deserts which separated the various state into which it had been divided forced trade routes from the land to the sea. Thus at one time Carthage was the sea power of the Mediterranean. In bitterly contested sea fights, fought on a scale unknown today, Rome wrested the trident from her hand. When Hannibal grappled with Rome on the plains of Italy in that mighty struggle for world supremacy, he fought without the backing of a powerful navy. So like Napoleon and Ludendorff, he lost. Zama—Leipzig—The Second Marne: these were the decisive battles, and all on land. But the inexorable pressure of sea power in each case was the underlying cause of defeat. Roman fleets and legions eventually executed that terrible injunction with which Marcus Cato ended every oration: "Also Carthage, methinks, ought utterly to be destroyed."

Then Romans settled the African coasts, founded prosperous colonies, and connected them to their great empire by sea routes. The famous Roman roads covered the sea as completely as they did the land. In fact, legions and traders traversed the seas with far greater ease and despatch than they did the great stone roads which covered Europe, Asia, and Africa like a gigantic spider's web.

After the downfall of Rome an age of ceaseless warfare

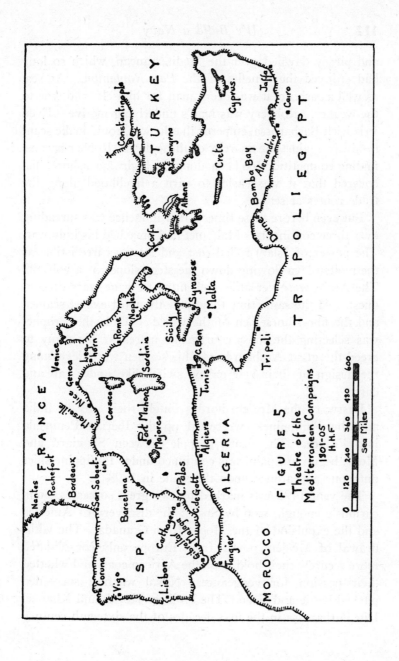

FIGURE 5

Theatre of the
Mediterranean Campaigns
1801-05
H.H.F.

Sea Miles
0   120   240   360   480   600

and piracy dawned over the Mediterranean, which so long had enjoyed the benefits of the *Pax Romanum*. At sea, as well as ashore, it was every man for himself, and woe to the weaker. Robbery was man's underlying motive. Even Friedrich Barbarossa, emperor that he was, could make scant headway against the anarchy of those days. Robber barons, finding competition too keen along the highways ashore, discovered that it was easier to earn a livelihood along the trade routes at sea.

But even before these times a new influence was spreading over three continents. Mahomet had preached his holy war. The power of Islam rolled east and west, as irresistible as the molten lava flowing down the steep slopes of a volcano. The Arabs were versatile, well fitted to wage wars of conquest. At the same time they were the most expert seamen and the finest horsemen of the world. While the Prophet was selecting the most courageous mares of his army to breed the great Arabian horse, his seamen were developing the design of their war galley, swift alike under sail and oars.

Eastward the Moslem hordes fought their way to India and the Philippines; westward up the Iberian Peninsula into France. The death grapple between Spaniard and Moor, begun in Spain, was continued under Philippine skies until our appearance upon the scene in 1898.

The year 1492 was marked by two great successes, both, curiously enough, won by Spain: the discovery of America and the expulsion of the Moors from Granada. The withdrawal of Moslem power from Europe only consolidated more securely their hold upon the African coast and whetted their passion for vengeance. Naval warfare succeeded pitched battle and siege. The brothers Horuk and Khair-el Din Barbarossa in the first decades of the sixteenth century organized great fleets and disputed with Charles V for the command of the Mediterranean. "Go tell your King," said Barbarossa to ambassadors of Emperor Charles V, "he is King of the Land; but I am King of the Sea." Morocco grew into a powerful empire. Algiers, Tunis, and Tripoli became flourishing Ottoman provinces, acknowledging nominal allegiance to the Sultan at Constantinople. Until 1571 the struggle ebbed and flowed. Then at bloody Lepanto Don Juan and Alexander of Parma raised the Cross above the Crescent and ended the efforts of the Turk to hold the Mediterranean in open battle against the combined fleets of Christendom.

Now roving corsairs replaced assembled fleets. Piratical forays and cruises took a heavier toll than battles—and it fell upon peaceful traders, fishermen, and inhabitants of coastal towns. The Mediterranean did not limit their activities. The North and Irish Seas proved fruitful cruising grounds. Even Iceland knew their slanting sails and flashing oar blades. Moro *vintas* harried the Chinese coasts.

Many a great expedition sailed to chastise the "Barbarous Moor." Cardinal Ximenes, Imperial Charles V, Genoese Andrea Doria, English Blake, Dutch de Ruyter, and French Duquesne all tried their hand. As late as 1775 the Spaniards sent out a great armada of 400 ships and 30,000 troops. Many of these expeditions ended in disaster; none gained more than a temporary or partial success. None saw fit to add "Africanus" to his title. All that Charles V could accomplish was to give the Moslem some real good lessons in Christian cruelty; in a later expedition he met a just retribution.

CHAPTER III

DIPLOMACY TACKLES THE PROBLEM

BUT NOW we must again pick up the thread of our tale. Let us see the various measures our statesmen took to handle a problem which had troubled Europe for centuries. In October, 1784, a Moroccan ship captured the brig *Betsey;* this reduced the problem from the general to the particular, from theory to practice. Fortunately the Sultan seems to have had a liking for us. How many Americans know that his country was the first to recognize our independence? He had asked us in most friendly terms for a treaty, but we had shown little interest. Now we woke up to a realization that the Sultan might prove a handy friend to have. We interested the King of Spain in our behalf and soon the *Betsey* was released. Two years later a highly satisfactory treaty was signed. On the whole it was well observed. After the Sultan's death there was some trouble from time to time, but never a very threatening situation. No tributes or ransoms were ever paid and our entire dealings with Morocco for a period of over twenty years did not cost over some $30,000, expended in presents for the Sultan.

The other Barbary states took a different attitude. In 1786 Abdur Rahman, Tripolitan ambassador, grandly stated to John Adams, our minister in London, "that Turkey, Tripoli, Tunis, Algiers, and Morocco were the sovereigns of the Mediterranean; and that no nation could navigate that sea without a treaty of peace with them." And he was right!

Why did Great Britain permit these grandiloquent pretensions when it would have been a simple matter for her to have stamped out such piracy? Because her statesmen were playing a deep game to further the interests of their overseas trade. By giving small annual presents and tributes to the Barbary states they obtained secret passports for their own vessels. Along the margins of these documents were cut series of notches at irregular intervals. Each pirate captain carried a stick in which there were notches at similar intervals. If passport matched with stick then the ship could sail on free from molestation. If not, woe to her crew and passengers, and financial ruin to her owners.

Having thus secured the safety of their own shipping, or the greater part of it, the next step in British diplomacy was evident. "There are not wanting persons in England," Adams reported concerning the same Abdur Rahman, "who will find means to stimulate this African to stir up his countrymen against American vessels."

On June 30, 1785, the ship *Maria* was captured by an Algerine xebec west of Lisbon. James L. Cathcart, a seaman on board, described vividly the workings of the British system: "We were welcomed on board the xebec, by the rais, or captain, a venerable old Arab, who informed me that they were a cruiser of Algiers, that they had come through the straits in consequence of their having concluded a peace with Spain and of the arrival of a British consul, Charles Logie, who informed them that they might take all such vessels that had not passports of a particular cut."

"What do? They have the cannon!" Thus mused the elector of Brandenburg when Gustavus Adolphus demanded passage through his territory. Now a similar situation confronted our government. Would we pay tribute or fight? Staunch John Adams, patriot that he was, did not see how we could fight. "As long," he wrote, "as France, England,

Holland, the Emperor, etc., will submit to be tributaries to these robbers and even encourage them, to what purpose should we make war upon them?" For the time, at least, Adams was right. Our confederation was impotent.

On the other hand, Thomas Jefferson in Paris was strangely belligerent for one who later developed such pacifist tendencies. Being a Democrat in politics, it was perhaps natural that he should conceive the idea of a league of nations to curb the pirates. He thought that all the lesser powers would join; that France, Spain, and Holland would remain neutral or at least passive; and that there was "only England who would give any real aid to the Algerines."

The time proved not to be ripe for Jefferson's scheme. So, fertile in expedients as he always proved himself to be, he evolved another idea: to ransom the prisoners through the offices of a French religious order. He kept this move shrouded in secrecy, "because, this being the first instance of a redemption by the United States, it would form a precedent, because a high price given by us might induce these pirates to abandon all other nations in pursuit of Americans." Verily, diplomacy hath its pitfalls!

Both ministers, while in disagreement over our Mediterranean policy, were united in desiring a navy. "I will go all lengths with you," Adams gave as his opinion, "in promoting a navy, whether it be applied to the Algerines or not." "It is a question," Jefferson replied, "which should be addressed to our honor as well as our avarice; nor does it respect us as to these pirates only, but as to the nations of Europe. If we wish our commerce to be free and uninsulted, we must let these nations see that we have an energy which at present they disbelieve."

While our diplomats in Europe thus correctly analyzed the situation, the ship of state, without a captain at the helm, drifted at the whim of wind and tide. With conflict, bank-ruptcy, and confusion of every kind at home, how could a strong policy abroad be expected? It reminds us strongly of recent conditions in Europe to hear John Jay say that "it would not be right to make new loans until we have at least some prospect of paying the interest due on former ones."

CHAPTER IV

BLACKMAIL

B UT BETTER days were coming. The adoption of our Constitution on September 13, 1789, was an epoch-making event. Now at least we had a goal to strive for, and a plan to reach it. Slowly we began to find our feet and move forward a bit, stumbling in the dark. One thing we quickly recognized: the necessity to rebuild our overseas trade to its pre-war level. Another principle, clearer to our statesmen then than now, was that our goods must be carried in American ships.

Action was surprisingly quick. The charter of our merchant marine was the wise act of July 4, 1789, a second declaration of independence. A tariff on imports was then first established and—listen to this—a discount of 10 per cent from the prescribed duties allowed when the goods were imported in vessels owned and built by American citizens. To specially encourage the trade in tea, the duties on this product when imported in foreign bottoms were fixed at twice the amount charged when carried in American ships. The results were astounding. In six years our overseas trade and merchant shipping increased fourfold.

So far, so good. But our people could not see the next step—the protection of this vital trade by a naval force. Its mushroom growth only increased our Mediterranean problem. Yearly its solution became more and more pressing. Counsel still was divided. The central government had not yet consolidated its powers. A witticism of the day referred to it as a bantam hen sitting on a nest of turkey eggs. The brave pioneers who were fighting their way westward to the Mississippi were incensed at Federal misrule, and justifiably so. John Sevier, founder of the state of Franklin, was being tried for treason. George Rogers Clark, conqueror of Illinois, Indiana, and Ohio with 150 soldiers, hero of Kaskaskia and Vincennes, was fast being driven into open rebellion. Each community looked upon its own interests alone. National unity had not even begun to exist. It is not entirely without justice that the Chinese, when taxed with the anarchy in their country today, point to the early years of our own country for a similar situation.

We must not expect too much of these early statesmen. They had tremendous problems to solve and for most of them history could point no precedents to guide their actions. And remember that the mills of the gods grind slowly. Still progress, if slow, was sure. One after another, time showed us our errors and forced us along different paths. The French Revolution wrecked Jefferson's plan of ransom. We must try something else. On December 30, 1790, Washington referred a report on the situation to Congress. On January 2 the Senate Committee on Mediterranean Trade stated formally its opinion that our shipping could "be protected but by a naval force, and that it will be proper to resort to the same as soon as the state of the public finances will admit."

Apparently this strong stand met little support, even from President Washington. For at his request Congress appropriated in May $50,000 to be used in bribing the pirates to sign a treaty and release the thirteen captives in their hands. Paul Jones was appointed envoy to negotiate the treaty. Perhaps it is fortunate for his reputation that death overtook him before he could appear in this sad rôle. Others delays ensued and it was not until September, 1793, that Colonel Humphreys was appointed to the post.

Meanwhile our ships had been receiving their protection from a strange source—the Portuguese Navy. That little country had been at war with Algiers and her cruisers had kept back the piratical craft from their most profitable cruising grounds. In September, 1793, however, just as Colonel Humphreys was receiving his appointment, peace between Portugal and Algiers was negotiated in a wondrous fashion. According to our colonel, it was signed by Charles Logie, the British consul general at Algiers, without the authorization, or even the knowledge, of the Portuguese government. Our consul at Lisbon complained bitterly to the Queen, alleging that her previous protection had "lulled our citizens into a false security."

And well might he take this strange stand. For now Algerine ships steered boldly into the Atlantic. In October and November alone, they seized eleven American vessels and enslaved their crews of 109 men. A picture of the capture of an American ship may be illuminating. Let John Foss, seaman of the brig *Polly,* paint it for us:

"When she [the pirate craft] came near enough to make us hear, she hailed us in English, asked from whence we came and where bound, which was immediately answered by Captain Bayley. The man who hailed us was dressed in the Christian habit and he was the only person we could see on deck. By the time the brig was under our stern; we then saw several men jump upon her poop to haul aft the main sheet and saw by their dresses and long beards that they were Moors or Algerines. Our feelings at this unwelcome sight are more easily imagined than described. She then hove to under our lee, when we heard the most terrible shouting, clapping of hands, huzzaing, &c., and saw a great number of men rise up with their heads above the gunnel, drest in the Turkish habit like them we saw on the poop.

They immediately hoisted out a large launch and about one hundred of the pirates jumped on board, all armed, some with scimitres and pistols, others with pikes, spears, lances, knives, &c. They manned about 20 oars and rowed along-side. As soon as they came on board our vessel they made signs for us to go forward, assuring us in several languages that if we did not obey their commands they would imme-diately massacre us all. They went below into the cabin, steerage, and every place where they could get below deck and broke open all the trunks and chests there were on board, and plundered all our bedding, clothing, books, charts, quadrants and every moveable article that did not consist of the cargo of furniture. Then they came on deck and stripped the clothes off our backs, all except a shirt and a pair of drawers."

With such hunting as this why should the Dey consider our paltry $50,000? He refused even to receive our envoy. Well had Charles Logie served His Britannic Majesty!

The high-handed actions of the Dey and the reports of cruelty to our seamen had several effects. One of them was good. On Christmas Day, 1793, Humphreys wrote home some advice: "It appears absurd to trust to the fleets of Portugal, or any other nation, to protect or convoy our trade. If we mean to have a commerce, we must have a naval force, to a certain extent, to defend it."

On January 20, 1794, the Ways and Means Committee of the House reported a bill for the construction of six frigates. It was fought through the House and Senate and on March 27 received the President's approval. Soon the sum of $688,000 was appropriated to build the ships.

This bill, like other more recent ones for naval expansion, was passed probably more as a bluff than with any real in-tent to build a navy. For it contained a clause requiring the cessation of work on the frigates immediately upon the signing of a treaty with Algiers.

After this belligerent gesture, pacifism again gained control of the situation. On July 19, 1784, our consul at Algiers was authorized to pay $800,000 to the Dey and to promise annual tribute. This was quite different from the old story of Henry the Fowler, first of the German emperors. When the Hungarians demanded tribute he returned a mangy hound. "There is your blackmail," said he to the waiting embassy, "make the most of it." Would that President Washington had spoken out in the same spirit.

Meanwhile, to have still another string to our bow, we resorted to a humiliating expedient. When in 1794 John Jay sailed for England to make the treaty which bears his name, his pouch bore instructions which will amaze Americans today: "It may be represented to his British Majesty, how productive of perfect conciliation it might be to the people of the United States, if Great Britain would use her influence with the Dey of Algiers for the liberation of American citizens in captivity, and for a peace upon reasonable terms."

And this to the nation which we knew was encouraging, even instigating, piratical attacks upon our ships! Thomas Jefferson is now Secretary of State. He has been getting strange ideas of late; will have stranger ones still before many years pass. No longer is he the stalwart patriot of 1776 or even 1786. Domestic politics and presidential ambitions hold out glittering temptations.

Gouverneur Morris, financier and statesman, has an entirely different idea: "I believe," he wrote in 1794, "that we could maintain twelve ships of the line, perhaps twenty, with a due proportion of frigates and small vessels. And I am tolerably certain that, while the United States of America pursue a just and liberal conduct, *with twenty sail of the line at sea,* no nation on earth will dare insult them. One thing I am thoroughly convinced of, that if we do not render ourselves respectable, we shall continue to be insulted." Here was advice of the soundest, that would have made our country a real sea power. Morris would have built up our overseas trade upon a foundation of solid rock—not a bed of quicksand, into which it later disappeared.

Our negotiations with Algiers do not make pleasant reading. As is usual with blackmailers, the Dey's price rose from month to month and his conduct became more and more insulting. Finally we threw in a 36-gun frigate and the bargain was sealed. Nearly a million dollars more than required to build three *Constitutions,* was the immediate charge against our budget. The continuing charge was an annual tribute of naval stores costing over $25,000. This infamous bargain was ratified by our Senate March 2, 1796. In July the captives, now reduced by death from 122 to 85, were set free. We paid the full ransom for all who had died since the signing of the treaty nearly a year before.

In November a treaty was arranged with Tripoli at a cost of some $60,000 and next August we came to terms with Tunis for about double that price. Both had increased their demands after seeing how easily Algiers had bluffed our envoy. The Senate refused to ratify the Tunisian treaty and William Eaton was sent out to obtain modifications. Finally, in 1800, ratification was accomplished. "The United States set out wrongly," Eaton stated, "and has proceeded so. Too many concessions have been made to Algiers. There is but one language which can be held to these people and that is terror."

In accordance with law Washington now should have ceased the construction of our six frigates, but Congress permitted work on three to be continued. The President now seems to have taken a stronger stand. In his annual message of December, 1796, he stressed the necessity for developing a navy: "To secure respect to a neutral flag requires a naval force, organized and ready to vindicate it from insult or aggression. This may even prevent the necessity of going to war by discouraging belligerent powers from committing such violations of the rights of the neutral party as may, first or last, leave no other option." How well does this wise opinion fit the situation in which we found ourselves in 1914.

Our Navy was singularly fortunate in its first naval constructor. Joshua Humphreys was not only a technical genius, but a farseeing student of naval history. His ideas on cruisers are applicable to this very day.

"If we build our ships of the same size as the Europeans," he wrote to Robert Morris, himself a shrewd strategist, "they having so great a number of them, we shall always be behind them. I would build them of a larger size than theirs, and take the lead of them, which is the only safe method of commencing a navy." And this he did, subject to congressional limitations. In 1797 were launched the *Constellation, Constitution,* and *United States,* all destined to become household words and to fill a niche in history.

Meanwhile—*horribile dictu*—we do not seem to have been very punctual in fulfilling our sacred treaty obligations. On the occasion of the sailing of the 36-gun frigate *Crescent* for Algiers in January, 1798, we read the following in an oft-quoted newspaper: "The *Crescent* is a present from the United States to the Dey as a compensation for delay in not fulfilling our treaty obligations in proper time. The *Crescent* has many valuable presents for the Dey, and when she sailed was supposed to be worth at least $300,000. Twenty-six barrels of dollars constituted a part of her cargo." Thus did we apply the motto blazoned across the pages of our histories: "Millions for defense—but not one cent for tribute." What a strange similarity in the names we gave our ships: *Constellation* and *Crescent*.

CHAPTER V

WE BUILD A NAVY—AND FIGHT
THE FRENCH

THESE BRIBES quieted the African pirates for a time and "all went merry as a marriage bell," until other troubles came to a head. In the spring of 1798 the seizure of our vessels by French privateers and cruisers became a little too frequent. Ambassador Genet also added to the excitement, by putting on the airs of a Soviet commissar! Congress was roused to action. On April 27 we created a Navy Department and appropriated money to recommence work on the *President, Congress,* and *Chesapeake.* In June the *Constellation* put to sea with orders to attack French cruisers off our coast.

Peculiar mob reactions work through the populace of a nation. Our people are highly emotional, easily swayed by currents of feeling. Perhaps we are at the same time the most peaceful and most warlike of all the nations. Patient and long-suffering as we may be, when the spark is struck, our passions break out in a fierce and all-consuming blaze. Here was an example. For years we had stood almost without complaint the depredations and cruelty of the Mediterranean pirates. Now Citizen Genet and the capture of a few ships off our coast set the people into a fury. War spirit blazed so hotly that Congress had to take action. On July 9, it authorized the capture of French cruisers and privateers wherever met.

A week later a new construction program was authorized to bring our fleet to a total of twelve vessels of thirty-two guns or over; twelve of twenty-four guns; and six of eighteen guns. Preparations were made to build six ships of the line. Before July had ended the *United States* and *Constitution* had put to sea and they, together with the *Constellation*, sailed for the West Indies. Twelve smaller vessels completed the squadron. Thus our Navy within a few months of its organization and without opportunity for training was thrown into a campaign against a great naval power.

We must emphasize the point that this was a new Navy, entirely distinct from the Continental Navy of the Revolution. Of this there remained nothing except a few old officers and some rather chequered traditions. But, everything considered, the start was made under favorable auspices. The stimulus of war attracted good men; the officers were selected with considerable care; our merchant seamen were incomparable and their training as man-of-war's men was a much simpler process then than today. Our large frigates were the finest ships afloat and in excellent condition. We had the moral support of the people and, what was most unusual for that era, the financial backing of Congress.

The French squadron in the West Indies seems to have been about equal to ours. There were innumerable brushes between our small craft and the privateers which swarmed from the French islands like bees from a hive—but only two frigate actions. Both fell to the lot of the *Constellation* and Captain Thomas Truxtun. This was a lucky break for our young service, for Truxtun was one of the finest captains who ever trod a quarter-deck, American or otherwise. Not only was he an expert seaman, but, what was even more important, a strict disciplinarian. In those days seamen were a tough lot; even the Americans among them were little actuated by patriotism. James Durand, good

American as he was, was frank about it. "I always obeyed my commanders," he wrote, "although I did it more through fear than anything else." The foreigners were mercenaries, pure and simple. With the able assistance of John Rodgers, William Cowper, and Andrew Sterett, Truxtun had made the *Constellation* known as a crack ship.

On February 9, 1799, she met the French frigate *Insurgente* off the island of Nevis. We had slightly superior gun power; they the larger crew—"everyone burning with ardor for the fight," as Captain Barreaut wrote afterward. It seemed a fair fight, but the gods decided otherwise! As the ships jockeyed for position a violent gust of wind snapped off the *Insurgente's* main topmast and sent its whirling tangle of spars, sails, and ropes down upon the decks.

This stroke of luck gave Truxtun, to use the terms of air combat, superior maneuverability. Naturally he was determined to make the most of it. So expertly did he handle his fast-sailing frigate that after a cannonade of one hour and fourteen minutes the Tricolor was lowered. He had won a notable success with only one man killed and three wounded. Another was killed for leaving his post. "One fellow," said Sterett, "I was obliged to run through the body with my sword, and so put an end to a coward. You must not think this strange, for we would put a man to death for even looking pale on board this ship." Only one such example was needed; never do we hear of its being repeated on this or any other American ship.

There seems to have been considerable bitterness of feeling at this time against the French Navy. When John Rodgers boarded the captured ship he was mightily pleased at what he saw. "Although I would not have you think me bloody-minded," he wrote, "yet I must confess the most

Constellation AND *Insurgente*

From a drawing by Hoff

Enterprise AND *Tripoli*

From a drawing by Hoff

gratifying sight my eyes beheld was seventy French pirates
(you know I have just cause to call them such) wallowing in
their gore." His remark has a similar ring to that of Captain Miller of the *Theseus* while watching the *Orient* blow
up in Aboukir Bay only some six months before. Barreaut
himself hardly obeyed the scriptural command to love one's
enemies. "My honor, my existence," he wrote, "all are
compromised by the duplicity of this infamous government."
All he neglected was an exclamation point!

There was one notable feat in this action which showed
the mettle of our young fellows. Midshipman David Porter
was stationed in the foretop. With him were a few seamen
to handle the sails and snipe the French officers with their
muskets. Early in the action an 18-pound shot shattered
the fore topmast; it swayed against the shrouds and stays
with the roll and pitch of the ship. The huge fore topsail,
bellied out by the trade-wind breeze, threatened every instant to snap the spar and send it crashing down a hundred
feet upon the crowded forecastle. Young Porter knew he
must keep the mast standing. In the din of battle there was
no time to communicate with those below. Up the ratlines
he ran, doubtless with brave unnamed seamen at his heels,
cut the slings and let down the fore topsail yard with a run.
The mast was saved. Truxtun still had his ability to maneuver; he placed his ship where the enemy could not return his
fire and won a battle with only one man killed. We shall
watch David Porter play many a fine rôle in these early
scenes of our naval drama.

After the action John Rodgers, Porter, and eleven seamen
were sent to the prize. A few hours of smooth water was
now much desired; instead a gale broke loose. The *Constellation* separated in the night. Trustun gave up his
prize for lost. And well he might! Two topmasts had

gone over the side; most of the other sails and rigging were
shot away.   Dead and wounded covered the decks; 173
unwounded prisoners still remained on board.   What a task
for thirteen men!   First of all measures must be taken to
prevent the prisoners from recapturing the ship.   They
were forced below and various expedients adopted to keep
them there, including the pointing of a gun, loaded with
grapeshot and cannister, down the only hatch up which they
might escape.   While part of the prize crew, with a whole
armory of weapons, kept constant watch there, the rest
worked the ship as best they might through the gale.   It took
three whole days and nights for weary men to sail the ship into
St. Kitts.   As they neared the island the tall spars of a frigate
could be picked out from the hilly background.   Imagine
their joy when hopes became reality and they knew her for
the *Constellation*.   Truxtun could bring home his prize.

Truxtun and the *Constellation* proved a lucky combination.   For a second time, on February 2, 1800, there came
to both the opportunity to engage a French frigate.   This
time it was the enemy who was superior in gun power.   The
crews were equal in number.   The *Vengeance* was loaded
with valuable stores.   "Everything showed me," Captain
Pitot wrote, "that I must avoid an action in the position I
was in, and must limit myself to the defensive."   Truxtun
forced the issue.

It was eight o'clock at night when the first shot was fired.
Five hours long the thunder and lightning of battle must
have illuminated the western horizon for the startled people
of Guadeloupe. Yardarm to yardarm, Yankee and Frenchman fought it out.   Our gunners aimed at the *Vengeance's*
hull and they hit it 186 times.   What havoc their shot must
have made!   At last every French gun ceased fire; the battle
seemed won.

But meanwhile the *Constellation* had been suffering also. Pitot aimed his guns high up at our spars so he could escape. At last, after his battery had been silenced, fortune gave him her favor. Only then, after the excitement of battle had subsided, was it found that the mainmast of the *Constellation* was about to fall. All shrouds and stays had been cut and nothing could be done. A little midshipman, James C. Jarvis, was in command of the maintop. With him were a few seamen. One of them told him that the mast was about to fall; "If the mast goes," this young hero answered, "we go with it." And so they all did!

An hour elapsed before the wreckage could be cleared away, and the Frenchman escaped. Our losses were heavy but only one-fourth those of the enemy. Dismasted and sinking, the *Vengeance* was glad to reach the refuge of Curaçao.

Truxtun's two victories were a veritable tonic to public opinion. National solidarity grew apace. The Navy belonged to the entire nation; all sections could take pride in its success. Congress honored Truxtun with a gold medal.

These are only the high spots of the campaign. Much hard work had been done which does not appear in the history books. Many notable cruises had been made. Of these we may mention only one. The little topsail schooner *Enterprise*, under Lieutenant John Shaw, was out eight months, fought seven actions, and captured or recaptured nineteen vessels. In all fifty French privateers were taken.

These accomplishments firmly established the reputation and tradition of our young service. They showed our statesmen what a handy instrument a naval squadron was when diplomacy did not gain their ends. Congress in one year appropriated two and a half millions for the Navy.

Meanwhile, our enemy must have been giving serious

We Build a Navy

thought to the situation. First Consul Bonaparte was crossing the Great St. Bernard to fight Marengo. Had he not enemies enough already? Were these American bickerings bringing any glory to his Tricolor? He apparently thought not, for on September 30, 1800, peace was signed on the basis of the *status quo,* all captures being returned. Marvin, in his excellent history of our merchant marine, writes: "Perhaps the greatest and most enduring result of the ocean war with France was its demonstration of the intimate relationship of a merchant marine and a fighting navy. But for our spirited resistance, France in 1798 would have destroyed our West India carrying, and then turned her privateers loose upon our coastwise trade and our profitable traffic with the ports of Britain and North Europe."

CHAPTER VI

THE NAVY MOVES AGAINST THE PIRATES

AFTER peace was declared the usual reaction set in—in this case aggravated by the overwhelming popular vote which carried into power Jefferson and his so-called Republican Party in November, 1800. On March 4, only a few hours before the new President was sworn in, Congress passed, and John Adams signed, a bill for a drastic naval reduction. The number of officers was reduced by one-half, not such an unwise provision, for it allowed some who had been carelessly appointed to be eliminated. The President was empowered to scrap, at his discretion, all but the thirteen best ships and, except for the *Enterprise,* he hastened to exercise this prerogative. This in itself was proper, had he only built a few from time to time to replace them. Of these fourteen vessels he decommissioned all but six. And, worst of all, he suspended the construction of the six ships of the line authorized in 1798. He did appoint a good Secretary of the Navy.

Despite this retrenchment a use for a naval squadron soon appeared. Our Mediterranean trade had grown by leaps and bounds. The Barbary states watched it with jealous eyes, saw it was still without naval protection. Their demands became more and more exorbitant, and they waited only for a pretext to renew their piracy.

In the fall of 1800 Captain Bainbridge brought the annual tribute to Algiers in the frigate *George Washington.* The Dey behaved in the most insulting and threatening manner to him. Only his weakness—or good judgment, if you prefer it that way—and that of Consul O'Brien in complying with the humiliating demand to carry the Dey's tribute to Constantinople, averted open war.   It is fair to say that Bainbridge created a most favorable impression in Turkey and upon his return to Algiers used the influence he had gained at the Sublime Porte with telling effect upon the Dey.

The Bashaw of Tripoli had long been dissatisfied with his treaty.   His blackmail had been small in comparison with that extracted from our scanty moneybags by Tunis and Algiers.   Thus his prestige as a pirate had been sadly lowered: even a pirate has a reputation to maintain.   He did not like the presents sent from over the water.   Uncle Sam seems to have made a failure as Santa Claus.   The Bashaw wanted another Christmas stocking, and he didn't want to wait for next Christmas.   In February, 1801, he demanded a cool quarter of a million with an annual tribute of $20,000, so that he could live happily forever after.   As all this did not happen as quickly as he would have liked he proceeded to declare war and on May 10 reduced the flagpole in front of the American consulate to firewood.   He then sent his two largest vessels to Gibraltar to attack our trade in the Atlantic.

In Tunis only the steady hand of William Eaton, constantly stirring the simmering pot of intrigue, kept it from boiling over into open war.   He seems to have been the inventor of "shirt-sleeve" diplomacy, for on one occasion he horsewhipped a French intriguer through the streets to great effect.

On May 20, 1801, the Secretary of the Navy ordered Commodore Richard Dale, whose exploits we have recounted in a previous chapter, to make a summer cruise in the Mediterranean.   With him were to go the frigates *President, Philadelphia,* and *Essex,* and the schooner *Enterprise.*   If he found upon his arrival at Gibraltar that Tripoli or any other Barbary state had declared war he was to "cruise off that port so as effectually to prevent anything from going in or coming out," and also to "sink, burn, or destroy their ships and vessels wherever you find them." By a peculiarly strict interpretation of his powers Jefferson held that he could not authorize the taking of prizes. He conceived this to be an act of war, which Congress alone could declare. Thus did a later president, during the capture of Vera Cruz, draw a very hazy line between what was an act of war and what was not. In any event Dale was to come home in December. The crews had been enlisted for but one year and it was thought that the Mediterranean would be too dangerous during the winter months.

On July 1, the squadron arrived at Gibraltar. There were found the two corsairs which the Bashaw had ordered to cruise in the Atlantic. The *Philadelphia* remained to keep them locked in port. Bainbridge was captain and his blockade was strict. He had a score to pay off; the pirates decided that it was best not to venture out.

Dale with the *President* and *Enterprise* went to Algiers. The Dey decided that it was just as well that he had not yet declared war. On July 17, the commodore came to Tunis and here the *Essex* joined his flag. The Bey also was much impressed by such a show of force; his demands became less insistent. On the twenty-fourth the squadron was off Tripoli. The *Essex* parted for a European cruise; the *Enterprise* went to Malta. The *President* carried out an eighteen-day blockade and headed in the same direction. On August 16 she reached port. Good news was at hand.

Next to the *Constitution* the little topsail schooner *Enterprise* was the most famous ship of our early naval annals; for twenty-five years she was in full commission—and always lucky. She seemed to gravitate naturally toward the scene of every conflict. More often even than "Old Ironsides" had her battle ensigns flown. We have seen what exploits she accomplished against the French privateers. Now Andrew Sterett was captain, David Porter her first lieutenant; her crew of ninety-four had been well trained to fire her twelve little 6-pounders, to handle sails, and to board. Their schooling had been completed. The final examination of battle was at hand.

Let no one think that the Tripolitans could not fight. William Eaton had long studied their tactical methods. Here is what he tells:

"Their method of attack is uniformly boarding. For this their vessels are peculiarly constructed. Their long lateen yards drop on board the enemy and afford a safe and easy conveyance for the men who man them for this purpose; but, being crowded with men, they throw them in from all points of the rigging and from all quarters of the decks, having their sabres grasped between their teeth and their loaded pistols in their belts, that they may have the free use of their hands in scaling the gunnels or netting of the enemy. In this mode of attack they are very active and very desperate. Proper defenses against them are high nettings with chains sufficiently strong to prevent their being cut away, buckshot plentifully administered from muskets or blunderbusses, and lances. But it is always best to keep them at a distance, that advantage may be taken of their ignorance at maneuvering."

Now Sterett had just met Eaton at Tunis and here the methods of combat of the enemy had doubtless been a subject of discussion. Thus, when on August 1 the lateen sails of a Tripolitan *polacre* came over the horizon, Sterett had his plan of battle made. The enemy craft carried eighty-five men and fourteen guns. Her name was *Tripoli*. First she tried to escape, then to board. But the Yankee schooner was too swift, her gunnery too deadly. For three hours they fought at pistol shot. Twice the pirate surrendered and twice reopened fire. This treachery, however, did him no good. Finally her captain lowered his colors with his own hands and threw them overboard in token that this time surrender was really intended.

When Porter boarded the prize he found it literally shot to pieces. Fifty of her crew lay dead or wounded about her decks. All her guns and equipment were thrown over the side; then with one mast and one sail she was allowed to continue her cruise. Her captain did not receive a cheery welcome from the Bashaw; in fact he was awarded the order of the bastinado.

The *Enterprise* did not have a single man hurt during this long fight, a singular proof of Farragut's remark that the "best defense is a well-directed fire from your own guns." Sterett was delighted with his crew. "It is with heartfelt pleasure that I add," he reported, "that the officers and men throughout the vessel behaved in the most spirited manner, obeying every command with promptitude and alertness." Congress voted him promotion and a sword and gave one month's pay to every man in the crew—a frequent and not, in our opinion, very appropriate reward. But it was better than paying blackmail.

After watering at Malta the *President* returned to Tripoli for a brief blockade, leaving on September 3 for Gibraltar. The *Philadelphia* took over the Tripoli blockade; the *Essex* watched off Gibraltar. In October the *Enterprise* went home. The *Boston* and *Washington* arrived on the station, but the former did not report to the commodore for duty. The latter was used to escort convoys. In December the flagship grounded at Port Mahon, Minorca, and was so severely damaged that her return to the United States was delayed until March, 1802. The *Philadelphia* retired to Syracuse for the winter, and the *Boston,* without orders from anyone, cruised off Tripoli.

While Dale had gained no decisive results, the effects of his cruise were very favorable. The blockade of the Tripolitan ships in Gibraltar, Sterett's fight, and the escort of convoys of merchant vessels, had safeguarded our commerce as never before. The demonstrations against Algiers and Tunis had been effective at least for the time. The smart appearance of his ships and his dignified bearing had raised our reputation in Europe. Our officers had learned much from their association with other navies. His orders, unfortunately, had prevented him from taking the aggressive action against Tripoli which alone could have decided the campaign.

CHAPTER VII

COMMODORE MORRIS FAILS

ENCOURAGED by the good effects of Dale's cruise, the President decided to send a second and greatly reënforced squadron to Europe in the spring of 1802. In February Congress passed a bill which was virtually a declaration of war against Tripoli, giving our naval commanders authority to go the limit in obtaining satisfaction. Thomas Truxtun, who had made such a splendid reputation in the French War, was appointed as commodore, but due to a minor squabble in which neither he nor the Department would give way, resigned his command. While Truxtun doubtless was in the right, he cannot have had much zeal for the service to have thrown up his command for such a reason; his action certainly compares very unfavorably with the conduct of Paul Jones, who was eager to get at grips with the enemy regardless of the conditions. This episode had most unfortunate effects for the country and the Navy, for with Truxtun in command we cannot imagine that the coming campaign would have ended in such a discreditable manner.

Commodore R. V. Morris succeeded to the command. In some respects he had a much better chance than Dale. He was not hampered by restrictive orders, and his crews were enlisted for two years. In other respects, however, he was still greatly handicapped. Sun Tzu tells us how a Chinese army was prepared for a campaign in the fifth century, B.C.; Xenophon describes how Cyrus organized his forces and prepared his supplies for a long march; Herodotus relates the details of the manifold arrangements made by Xerxes to bring his fleet and army into Greece. We fell behind these most ancient standards. Our ships were sent to sea in very poor condition and much time had to be devoted to their repair after arriving in Europe. Their supplies of equipment, food, and water were deficient and the measures for replenishing them grossly inadequate. Thus the new commodore did not get an even break.

The ships of his squadron proceeded singly when ready for sea. The *Enterprise* left in February, the *Constellation* in March, the *Chesapeake,* with the commodore on board, in April; the *Adams, New York,* and *John Adams* followed in order, the last in September. When the *Enterprise* reached the station the *Philadelphia* and *Washington* went home. Sterett joined the *Boston* off Tripoli. Captain McNeill, of that ship, was an erratic fellow, but seems to have been quite energetic. He enjoyed his blockade duty and on a recent occasion had attacked three gunboats close to the shore, sinking one and driving back the others. On another occasion he was not so fortunate, for early in June five "row galleys, with three lateen sails, each having four guns," slipped out past him. We will hear more of these craft.

The *Enterprise* went next to Tunis, where on May 28 the *Constellation* arrived. Captain Murray of that frigate sent Sterett on to Gibraltar with a convoy and joined the *Boston* off Tripoli. McNeill was ordered to go to Malta for provisions and return. But he seems not to have enjoyed the company of his seniors, for he went off on a grand tour of the Mediterranean on his own. In September he turned up mysteriously at Gibraltar, took aboard some sick men from the *Adams,* and hoisted his homeward-bound pennant.

Our naval commanders and consults had been endeavoring for the last year to get all merchant vessels to obey their orders to sail in convoy under the escort of men-of-war. The merchant vessels disliked this system and frequently decided to take a chance rather than delay until the convoy was ready to sail. This recklessness played into the hands of the pirates. On June 10, two of the corsairs that had slipped past the *Boston* came to Algiers for supplies. Then they made for the Spanish coast. On the seventeenth, off Cape Palos, they took the brig *Franklin.*

The prize first was brought to Algiers, then to Tunis; thence on July 19 the corsair slipped into Tripoli with the nine men of the *Franklin's* crew. It was planned to bring the prize in several days later and on the evening of the twenty-first Murray saw several gunboats stealing out to the westward, presumably to escort her into port. On the twenty-second, as day broke, the whole Tripolitan fleet of eight vessels was seen close inshore three miles west of the harbor entrance.

Captain Murray at once headed the *Constellation* in for the enemy squadron. Before he could get within gunshot the galleys had reached the support of the batteries and a large body of troops. But Murray wanted some action to relieve the monotony of the blockade. Despite the danger of wrecking his ship on uncharted reefs he kept on until a mile and a half from the shore line, "our pilot being much alarmed." Batteries and gunboats now opened fire at this long range. "We rounded to in twelve fathoms of water," Murray reported, "and gave them a very severe fire for about half an hour, which must have done them considerable damage. At the same time they had an army of at least 6,000 men drawn up along the beach, which our shot put to the rout." This was a sharp skirmish, but we doubt if as

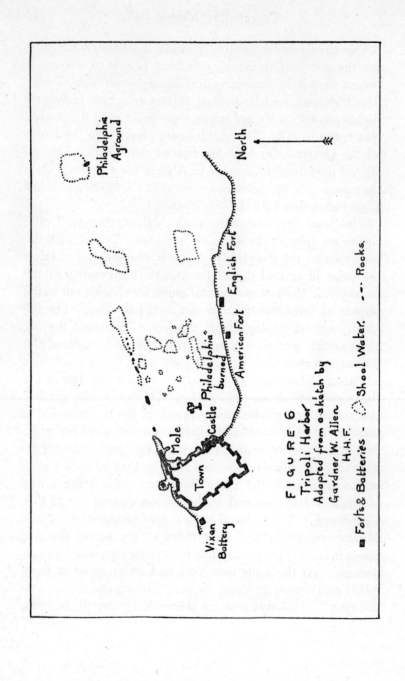

FIGURE 6
Tripoli Harbor
Adapted from a sketch by
Gardner W. Allen.
H.H.F.

■ Forts & Batteries - :: Shoal Water. --- Rocks.

much damage was done as Murray imagined. Wait until we see "Old Ironsides" do some real bombarding.

Early in July, after having watched Tripoli for several months, the *Constellation* sailed to Leghorn for supplies. Murray was much discouraged by his lack of success. He gave it as his opinion that small craft could not be prevented from slipping in and out of port without the use of similar craft by the blockaders.

On May 25, Commodore Morris arrived at Gibraltar in the *Chesapeake*. He found the *Essex* still blockading the Tripolitan ship *Meshuda*. The British kindly permitted Morris to repair his mainmast at the dockyard. When on June 17 this was completed the *Essex* sailed for home. The Sultan of Morocco now began to act in a high-handed manner. He demanded that the *Meshuda* be given to him and that we let wheat be shipped past the Tripolitan blockade. When the commodore refused he declared war. Nevertheless, he was most careful not to commit any overt act. Morris was joined by the *Enterprise* about July 15 and the *Adams* came in from the United States. These reënforcements induced the Sultan to receive back our consul and the usual negotiations commenced. Leaving the *Adams* to assume an attitude of "watchful waiting," the *Chesapeake* and *Enterprise* went off with a convoy along the European coast. On October 12, the *Chesapeake* and *Constellation* met in Leghorn.

When the *New York* arrived in October she had to put into Port Mahon for a refit. When the *John Adams* appeared she had to be recaulked. The *Chesapeake* needed more repairs. The *Constellation* left for home. Our chartered storeships had a contract to deliver their cargoes at Gibraltar and would not enter the Mediterranean.

Finally, by the end of January, 1803, the squadron was

ready for sea. And high time it was. For six months not a single vessel had been at Tripoli. And the sum total of their efforts had been Murray's half-hour bombardment at 3,000 yards range, as far as his guns would shoot. Pretty sad! But the worst was yet to come.

On January 30, Morris felt that it was incumbent upon him to do something. So he sent the *Enterprise* to Tunis and sailed with the *Chesapeake, New York,* and *John Adams* for a grand demonstration off *Tripoli*. He never got there. Gales drove him back. Provisions were exhausted. He sailed for Gibraltar to fill up. En route he stopped at Tunis and Algiers, only to receive the most insulting demands from their beys. Seeing his impotence against Tripoli the insolence of the other states increased.

On March 23, the entire squadron rendezvoused at the Rock. The *Chesapeake* went home. The commodore shifted his flag to the *New York*. Isaac Chauncey was captain and David Porter first lieutenant. Hull relieved Sterett in command of the *Enterprise*. To quiet the Sultan of Morocco we gave him the *Meshuda* and let him ship wheat to Tripoli.

On May 1, the *New York, John Adams,* and *Enterprise* assembled again at Malta; the *Adams* was escorting a convoy. But still delays were in order; the *New York* had to repair the damage caused by a powder explosion; the *Enterprise* was recoppered. Only the *John Adams* was ready for a cruise and on the third John Rodgers sailed with her for Tripoli. For the first time in nine months we had a vessel off the hostile coast.

Rodgers was just in time. He caught the *Meshuda,* under Moroccan colors, trying to gain the port, and brought her to Malta. By this time the other vessels were ready and on the twenty-fourth Morris sailed to establish the

blockade with the *New York, John Adams,* and *Enterprise.*
He had been on the station exactly a year and was taking
a look at Tripoli for the first time!

As the squadron neared the coast a convoy of grain
feluccas, escorted by eleven gunboats, was seen coming
along the shore toward the port. A general chase was signaled but the gunboats escaped under the guns of the batteries and the *feluccas* were beached in the old port. To
protect them, earthworks were thrown up and a large stone
building prepared for defense. The fixed batteries also
partly covered the *feluccas.*

David Porter rowed in close to the beach that night in
a small boat to reconnoiter, but was driven off by musketry
before anything could be learned of the enemy's dispositions.
He now asked for permission to lead a night attack. Morris
instead authorized an attack by day. Porter organized the
expedition and assigned James Lawrence at first lieutenant.

As the boats neared the beach a fusillade of musketry
commenced. The batteries opened up and the splashes of
their shot covered the boats with spray. Oars churned the
water; the boats surged ahead with every stroke; here and
there a man fell wounded, and a comrade took his oar. Then
keels grated on the beach. Led by their officers, the seamen sprang splashing into the shallow water and gained the
short, cutlass in teeth, pike or battle-axe in hand. The
Tripolitans were reputed to like fighting hand-to-hand; now
they had their fill of it. Pike clashed against scimitar, cutlass against musket, pistols barked, muskets roared. The
enemy developed new tactics on the spur of the moment:
they threw sand and gravel into the eyes of our men.

Step by step, led by Porter and Lawrence, our seamen
forced back the enemy; they carried the *feluccas,* as the old
saying goes, "by push of pike." Then, while some held

back the pirates, others kindled fires; soon the grain ships were in a blaze. Now retreat was ordered, but it was more difficult than attack. It was a critical moment. Reënforcements for the enemy were rushing up—cavalry and infantry. The killed and wounded, about fifteen in all, had to be carried off; boats had to be pushed off, turned end for end, and rowed away. Porter fell wounded with a musket-shot through the thigh.

James Lawrence now showed the spirit which later made him a national hero. Under his calm supervision the withdrawal was conducted in perfect order. The boats pulled off to right or left so that the ships' guns could have a clear line of fire. A bombardment commenced. But now the Tripolitans in turn showed their gallantry: rushing out of their earthworks, they put out the fires and saved their ships.

This was a boldly planned and executed attack. Its material results were small, but its moral effects were great. It showed the fighting spirit of our crews; gave the seamen confidence in their officers and themselves. It broke the long period of inactivity; gave all hands something to talk about.

On the twenty-sixth the *Adams* reënforced the squadron to four ships. Two days later an attack was planned on the enemy gunboats. The breeze was light and only the *John Adams* reached her station. Her fire had slight effect. Morris now sailed off in the *New York* for Malta. John Rodgers remained in command.

On the evening of June 21 there were signs of activity in port and Rodgers made his dispositions. He sent the *Enterprise* a short distance to the eastward, the *Adams* to the westward, and sailed the *John Adams* hull down off the port. At six o'clock the next morning the *Enterprise* discovered a large vessel making for Tripoli. Captain Hull made for her. Although the enemy craft was far superior, her captain decided that discretion was the better part of valor and withdrew into a large bay twenty miles from Tripoli. There he anchored with springs on his cables and prepared to fight. A large force of troops on the beach dismounted and got their muskets ready.

Hull saw that Rodgers was fast coming up and lay to for a time to communicate with his superior by flag signals. At eight o'clock Rodgers was close enough to read the flags and then, without waiting for the assistance of the frigate, Hull again headed for his enemy. Before commencing the famous campaign against Croesus, Cyrus convinced his soldiers that he should move against the enemy as quickly as possible, "because the faster we march the less perfected we shall find their arrangements and the greater we shall find their deficiencies." Hull was in the same mood; as he drew near he saw that he was opposed by the largest of the Tripolitan squadron, a vessel with a crew of about two hundred men and twenty-two guns. Nine gunboats were rowing up to her assistance.

The *Enterprise* sailed in between the Tripolitan and the shore and at about 8:30 A.M. commenced firing her little 6-pounders—one battery at the ship, the other on the shore. Thus the action was fought for half an hour until Rodgers opened fire at three hundred yards range. His battery was too heavy for the Turks and after forty-five minutes of firing they abandoned their ship, some in boats, others swimming. They were just in time, for the corsair soon blew up. "The explosion burst the hull to pieces," Rodgers wrote, "and forced the main and mizzen masts one hundred and fifty feet perpendicularly into the air, with all the yards, shrouds and stays belonging to them.

On the twenty-sixth Morris ordered the blockade to be abandoned. He assembled the squadron in Malta and spent the summer in European waters escorting convoys. He was in Malaga when the *Nautilus* brought him orders to turn over his command to Rodgers and return home. His cruise had been almost a complete failure. While handicapped by poor arrangements for repair and supply, he seems to have been convinced of the futility of his campaign and made little endeavor to execute his orders. So disappointed had the government become that Consul Cathcart had been authorized to offer annual tribute to both Tunis and Tripoli, with a bonus of $20,000 to the latter. The Navy had failed!

CHAPTER VIII

PREBLE TAKES COMMAND

FORTUNATELY for us the Tripolitans did not know where to stop. They rejected our offers with disdain. Thus it was decided to give the Navy a final chance. This time we had to make good. First, we needed a commodore. Edward Preble was third from the bottom on the list of captains, but was noted for his energy and forcefulness. He was selected. Second, we needed a properly constituted squadron. The fine frigates *Constitution* and *Philadelphia* were to be its backbone. For inshore work, there had been specially constructed the 16-gun brigs *Argus* and *Siren,* and the 12-gun schooners *Nautilus* and *Vixen.* Third, these vessels had to be properly prepared for a long cruise. This seems to have been at least moderately well done. Fourth, proper captains and officers had to be appointed. The pick of the service was selected. Fifth, the quality of the crews had to be improved. This was done to a certain extent, but the pay was so low that many foreigners had to be used. Sixth, better arrangements had to be made for supply. Syracuse was selected as the squadron base and the contracts with supply ships required the delivery of their cargoes at that port. This time we were to do a good job.

The *Nautilus,* Lieutenant Richard Somers, arrived on the station late in July, 1803. She commenced escort and patrol duty. On September 12, she fell in with the *New York* and delivered to Morris his orders to come home. Next came the *Philadelphia.* On August 24 she anchored under the Rock. Her captain was a veteran of the Barbary coast, William Bainbridge, burning with eagerness to pay off old scores—to deliver his tribute, as he had once said, from the mouths of his cannon. News awaited him that two Tripolitan vessels were cruising off the Cape de Gatt. Sailing up the Spanish coast he found a Moroccan cruiser, the *Mirboza,* of 22 guns and 120 men. With her was the *Celia,* of Boston, which she had just captured. Bainbridge brought both vessels into Gibraltar. Here he was lying on September 12 when Preble appeared in the *Constitution.* Thus we have completed our survey of the events leading up to the main theme of our story—Preble's campaign. Now that we have its historical background we may judge more justly what he accomplished in one short year, for, by a coincidence, it was almost exactly one year later that his flag was hauled down, his life work ended.

Preble was forty-two years old. He had long service in merchant and naval vessels back of him. He believed in stern, almost harsh, discipline; had a hot temper; was forceful and energetic, bold and resourceful; wanted action and demanded results; delighted in accepting responsibility and in running risks; was, in short, a very Wellington of a man. Unpopular at first, as such men are, he came later to be respected, admired, perhaps even loved, by his officers and men. He said afterward that not a duel was fought nor a court-martial ordered during his stay in the Mediterranean.

The commodore had an involved problem to solve. Every Barbary state had been incited by the tragic failure of Morris' squadron. Tripoli was at war. The attitude of Algiers, Tunis, and Morocco was threatening to the last degree. Their rulers were intent on discovering what manner of man the newcomer was. At the first sign of weakness the storm would break all along the African coast. Furthermore, the old squadron, in which two captains were senior to him, was concentrating at Gibraltar. It was permeated with a spirit of failure. His own squadron was only partly assembled. Preble decided to go slow at first. He would wait at Gibraltar and study the situation.

On September 14 the *Vixen* came in from home and the *New York* and *John Adams* from Malaga. On the nineteenth the *Philadelphia* and *Vixen* went off via Malaga and Malta to commence the Tripoli blockade. The next day the flagship ran over to Tangier to see how the Moroccan pot was boiling. While there the *Adams* arrived at the Rock on the twenty-second and Morris sailed in her for home three days later. The *Siren* arrived from home and the *Nautilus* came in.

On October 1, the commodore returned from Tangier. He decided that a demonstration in force was now in order. Rodgers, although senior in rank, agreed to help. On the sixth an imposing force anchored off Tangier: *Constitution, New York, John Adams,* and *Nautilus.*

The Sultan's ardor cooled at the sight of these four fine ships cleared for action. Besides, we held the two trump cards: the *Meshuda* and *Mirboza.* On the twelfth he confirmed the old treaty of 1786. Peace was reëstablished and one potential enemy removed. Back went the squadron to Gibraltar. On the nineteenth the *New York* and *John Adams* hoisted their homeward-bound pennants. Their cruise had been none too happy in the Mediterranean.

CHAPTER IX

THE *PHILADELPHIA* IS LOST

WHILE Preble was making his show of force off Morocco the *Philadelphia* and *Vixen* were establishing a close blockade off Tripoli. It was October 7 when their arduous watch commenced. On the twentieth Bainbridge sent the *Vixen* to cruise off Cape Bon—an ill-fated decision. A succession of fierce gales swept the *Philadelphia* off to the eastward.

On the forenoon of the thirty-first she is sweeping back to her station before a favoring breeze. A small native vessel is sighted close inshore making for the port. All sail is set in chase. Skillfully the Arab captain pilots his craft through rocks and shoals. Bainbridge has neither a pilot nor a chart which makes pretense of accuracy. Still he chases!

At length the Tripolitan has about reached the entrance to the harbor. Bainbridge tacks to the northward—heads off the coast. Now the chase is over, but the captain still keeps his beautiful ship bowling along at eight knots, as Porter later testified. Three leadsmen sing out their soundings as rapidly as they may. Soon their rhythmical cries tell of a rapid shoaling of the water. Bainbridge shouts a hurried order. Too late! With a grinding, grating crash the beautiful frigate drives hard and fast aground. With full momentum she runs for her entire length up the gradual slope of the coral reef. When she comes to a stop her bow has been lifted a good four feet above its normal water line. It is 11:30 A.M.

[154]

Every effort is made to free the ship. First of all, sails are set to drive her ahead over the shoal, then backed in the hope that she will slide off astern. To lighten her bow the anchors are let go and the guns run aft. It is no use, Bainbridge. Your ship is in a giant's grip—you cannot break it!

Tripolitan watchmen have kept a good lookout from their lofty turrets. Soon schooner squadrons sail slowly forth to see how they may annoy their trapped lion. How well, were she there, could little *Vixen* play the rôle of Æsop's mouse! These vessels have each of them, in their bows great brass 29-pounder cannon, not to mention howitzers aft for short-range firing. However, their gunnery is none too good—witness how Andrew Sterett won a fight without losing a man—and they are none too eager to come to grips. Four take station on the ship's port quarter and open a distant cannonade.

Bainbridge replies with the after guns of his port broadside, but finds that the ship has listed that way so far that they cannot be elevated enough to reach the enemy. So he points three long 18's through his cabin ports and they are able to keep the enemy at such a distance that he makes no hits.

Meanwhile Bainbridge, assisted by David Porter and Jacob Jones, has been doing everything his experience can suggest to free the ship. Over the side go all the guns but those in immediate use—a rather questionable measure. And also all the loose equipment and provisions. Even the water is run overboard and the foremast cut away, thus heartening the enemy. Not an inch do these measures move the ship. On the contrary the ebbing tide causes her to keel more and more to port, until her port sills are even with the water.

The schooners now have edged over to the ship's starboard quarter. Here the stern chasers cannot touch them, even though the side is cut away to give them greater arc of train. Their discharge sets fire to the ship. No, it seems that the guns cannot be made to bear. When the pirates see this they come in closer and closer. Five more are on their way to reënforce them. Bainbridge thinks that they fire high to injure his rigging—more probably it is just Tripolitan gunnery. It is about 4:30 P.M. now, but people have more to think about than remembering such things.

Yes, there are other things Bainbridge has been thinking about. Now he calls together his officers; ominous sign, indicative of worse to come—nothing less than surrender. Yes, we must save the lives of our brave men, though yet not a one has been wounded! Porter and Jones—both very young to hold their responsible posts—agree with their captain. He orders the magazine flooded, the small arms thrown overboard, some holes bored in the bottom, then strikes his colors! Yes, October 31 is the black day of the United States Navy!

Over the side pour the pirates. They pilfer watches, rings, purses, snatch lockets from the necks of officers, strip the clothing from officer and man alike. Bainbridge, bare-handed, fights for the locket which hangs about his neck— in it is his wife's picture. Three hundred and fifteen officers and men are led ashore in triumph; ahead of them lie eighteen months of cruel imprisonment. All act well, demonstrate under these adverse conditions how strong have been the links of discipline on board the *Philadelphia*.

Poor Bainbridge was broken-hearted. The brave, though pitiful, letter he sent off to his wife even now brings tears to the eyes. A letter, signed by every officer, and approving completely of his conduct, was presented to him by Porter. This greatly eased his mind and gave him more confidence

for that saddest of all official duties, a captain's report of
the loss of his ship. "When my officers and self," he wrote,
"had not a hope left of its being possible to get her off the
rocks and having withstood the fire of the gunboats for four
hours, and a reënforcement coming out from Tripoli, without the smallest chance of injuring them by resistance, to
save the lives of brave men left no alternative but the distressing one of hauling our colors down and submitting to
the enemy whom chance had befriended."

To Preble he stressed one point even more strongly: "Had
we been able in our situation to have injured our enemy
in the least never would I have surrendered, while such
means were in my power."

But our unfortunate captain still was to receive the cruel-
est cut of all. In a few days the Tripolitans brought the
frigate off the ground, towed her into port, and moored her
under the guns of the Bashaw's castle. Even her guns were
fished up and mounted in place. Gloomy must have been
the thoughts of Bainbridge as he viewed this scene from his
prison window.

Preble was magnanimous to a degree. He wrote his unlucky captain the kindest letter, which did honor to both.
"Recollect that destiny," he wrote, "and not want of courage, has deprived you of liberty, but not of honor. . . . May
you have health and live to enjoy the smiles of the fickle
goddess." Only wait ten years, Bainbridge, and that thread
which the fates have spun for you will take on a brighter
hue! Patience, Captain, better days will come; you will
watch a battered frigate lower its battle flags, and command
a great squadron in these very waters. Better have your
misfortunes at the start, than at the end, of your career.

Let us add that a court of inquiry later declared that
"Captain William Bainbridge acted with fortitude and good

conduct in the loss of his ship . . and that no degree of
censure should attach itself to him from that event." All
historians have accepted that verdict and so do we.

Now, having cleared Bainbridge in due order, let us examine this most important event in an entirely impersonal
manner. Let us see what lessons there are in it for us
today. A reason which makes this imperative is that it exercised an almost decisive effect upon the entire course of
the campaign. Cooper thinks that the Bashaw was well disposed to treat with Preble before Bainbridge and his men
fell into his power, and this seems entirely probable. The
disaster of the thirty-first completely changed his attitude,
for with so many valuable hostages in his hands he was assured of a good treaty whenever he wanted it. Also, it
placed the American commanders under a serious moral
handicap: throughout they were more anxious to free the
prisoners than to get a favorable treaty. We shall see more
of this when the signing of the actual treaty is described.

The initial causes of the *Philadelphia* disaster were very
small indeed. The first was the sending away of the *Vixen*
to Cape Bon. Had she been present, she instead of the frigate would have made the chase inshore. Even had the
Philadelphia still grounded, she could have kept off the
schooners or at least have saved the crew. However, Bainbridge had good reasons for sending the *Vixen* away and
we do not criticize his decision, however unlucky it proved
to be. It should, however, have induced him to exercise
even greater care in navigating such poorly charted waters
as those off the Tripolitan coast.

While chasing the enemy craft he probably was justified
in making his full speed. However, once the chase was
abandoned, this was no longer necessary. At eight knots
no number of the most expert leadsmen could give warning

of rapidly shoaling water in time to prevent the ship from grounding. There are enough necessary risks to run in war without accepting others that are not necessary. True, this was only a small risk—but small things often are decisive in war.

These two initial causes wove a mesh of moral influences about Bainbridge which he could not break. They concentrated his attention on matters of lesser importance and warped his judgment so that correct decision was almost impossible. Had Homer written an epic poem on the subject he would have shown that every step in the chain of events was caused by a deeply laid and cleverly conceived conspiracy of the gods to bring fame to Stephen Decatur and we would agree that poor Bainbridge had been but a plaything in their hands.

No plot of the gods could have been better conceived to break a captain's spirit than the grounding of the *Philadelphia*. First, it was absolutely unexpected and came with tragic suddenness. One minute Bainbridge was in command of a fine, speedy ship; the next he had only a hopeless wreck. Second, it was an act of God which had robbed him of his ship, not of man. Even Homeric heroes were disheartened when the gods fought against them. When mighty and victorious Patroclus, wearing the unmatched helmet and armor of Achilles, was struck by the sword of far-darting Apollo, his spirit broke. "Blindness seized his heart and his shining limbs were unstrung, and he stood in amaze." Then it was easy for mortal hands to strike the death blow. Can we blame William Bainbridge, who was no demigod, but just an average good naval officer, if he too was disheartened by this cruel blow of fate? Third, to a captain his ship is everything; it is alive, has a spirit and a soul. When it is wrecked his heart is broken; for a time his own life stands still. He cannot reason logically or judge correctly. His mind is warped.

These influences induced Bainbridge to concentrate every effort on getting off his ship. Probably had his brain been working normally he would soon have seen that with an ebbing tide it was useless to try to lighten his ship over four feet forward and two aft. But having grounded his ship, all he could think of was to get her off. His failure still more discouraged him and led to the final surrender.

Not until the enemy threatened was attention given to resistance, and then it was subordinated to freeing the ship. The throwing over of guns, provisions, and water, and the cutting away of the foremast, disheartened his men and encouraged the enemy—paved the way for surrender. No thought was given to two most important matters: first, the tremendous advantage the enemy would receive by obtaining 315 hostages, including such a well-known commander as himself, and twenty-one other officers. Second, the necessity for increasing the reputation of the service throughout Europe and for creating a profound moral impression upon the enemy by a determined, or even desperate, resistance. Instead, attention was concentrated upon saving the lives of his men—an entirely secondary consideration, particularly as years of cruel slavery was an alternative hardly preferable to the chance of death in brave fight.

One thing is absolutely certain: the surrender was decidedly premature. The mere fact that the Moors had fired for four hours without wounding a man was an argument for continuing resistance, not for surrender. When it is considered that the surrender meant practically the loss of the war, it must be agreed that it should not have been resorted to until every desperate expedient had at least been attempted. It seems certain that it would have been easy to have held out until after dark, and with few, if any, losses. That would have given a 12-hour respite in which anything might have happened: a foreign man-of-war, belonging to a nation at war with Tripoli, might have arrived; the *Vixen* might have returned; a gale might have driven off the enemy or freed the ship. We are by no means certain that some form of resistance was impossible. With twelve hours three hundred men must certainly have found some means to point three guns at the enemy. Then there was the possibility of a night attack upon the enemy in boats—or as a last resort an attempt of part of the crew to escape in boats. Certainly there would have been ample time to see that the ship was completely destroyed, if that had been decided upon. Again, those Arabs were no supermen; the Lord only knows what mistakes they might have made. One thing is certain: they would have waited for many days before they tried to board. Fortune loves to change her interest from side to side. But, as Sophocles said, "Fortune is not on the side of the faint-hearted."

Above and beyond all this the degree of resistance made was unworthy of Americans. It is true that then we had no naval tradition—but Germans also had none when they entered the World War. Yet they knew how to die! True, for Bainbridge there are many good excuses. But how we wish that he had stood forth there and spoken to his comrades, in the words of Beowulf:

> Each of us must his end abide
> in the ways of the world; so win who may
> glory ere death! When his days are told,
> that is the warrior's worthiest doom,

Or that some young fellow, perhaps David Porter or Jacob Jones, had volunteered to attack the enemy in boats at night, that "speedily we may learn whether we are to win glory from others, or other men from us."

True, ultimate defeat could scarcely be avoided. But defeat with honor may help rather than retard our cause. "There are some defeats," Montaigne said, "more triumphant than victories." And we could have made this one. Ten years more and David Porter in distant seas would do so. His lesson, we think, is the only compensation our Navy received from this black day—October 31. But of this enough. Let events march again.

After having quieted the Moroccan situation Preble spent several weeks at Gibraltar taking on supplies. On November 1 the *Argus* came in; her captain, Decatur, exchanged commands with Hull of the *Enterprise,* which alone of Morris' squadron had remained in Europe. The *Siren* was sent to Leghorn with a convoy. The *Enterprise* escorted a storeship to Syracuse. On the thirteenth the commodore himself, with the *Constitution* and *Nautilus,* sailed via Algiers for Malta. In high hopes was he—wanted much to finish his job quickly and get his treaty. News traveled slowly, but sooner or later it always reached its destination. On the twenty-fourth, while off the coast of Sardinia, Preble hailed H.M.S. *Amazon.* From her he received "the melancholy and distressing intelligence of the loss of the U.S. ship *Philadelphia.*" Here is a problem for you, Commodore, one to test all your intelligence and stoutness of heart! Now, like Old Fritz, "you must oppose to ill fortune a brow of iron.

After touching at Malta for a few hours the *Constitution* came into Syracuse on November 28. Immediately Preble began to lay his plans for the destruction of the *Philadelphia.* Suggestions came from an unexpected source. Mr. Nissen, the Danish consul at Tripoli, had shown Bainbridge a method of using lime juice as invisible ink with which to write between the lines of innocent-appearing letters. "By chartering a merchant vessel," Bainbridge wrote to Preble on December 5 with his lime juice, "and sending her into the harbor with men secreted, and steering directly on board the frigate, it might be effected without any or a trifling loss. It would not be possible to carry the frigate out owing to the difficulty of the channel." An excellent plan, but one much more easy to suggest than to execute. "For," as the Corinthians said, "the execution of an enterprise is never equal to the conception of it in the confident mind of its promoter; men are safe while they are forming plans, but, when the time for action comes, then they lose their presence of mind and fail." Perhaps, however, we could find a young fellow who would know what to do when the time for action came.

CHAPTER X

ENTER STEPHEN DECATOR

FIRST Preble must make a reconnaissance; see how the situation looked. Accordingly, on December 17 the *Constitution* and *Enterprise* sailed. Off Tripoli the latter made a lucky capture—the Tripolitan ketch *Mastico*. With her Preble returned to Syracuse. He decided to use the *Mastico* to board and destroy the *Philadelphia*. His choice fell upon Stephen Decatur to do the work. It could not have been more fortunate.

The *Philadelphia* was moored close under the guns of the Bashaw's castle. Her port broadside pointed toward the entrance, her guns ready for instant discharge. Guns ashore to the number of 115 bore upon her at point-blank range. About her lay at anchor a brig of 10 guns, two schooners of 8, and two galleys. The other schooners were drawn up on the beach. Few would wish to risk even the rocks and shoals which guarded the harbor entrance, not to mention the perils of boarding a fully armed and manned frigate in the center of an enemy port. That would be an enterprise of almost unparalleled audacity. Never was there to be a better illustration of the motto of Commander Rizzo of the Italian motor boats: "Remember always to dare!"

But it was the very difficulty of the plan that fired Decatur's imagination. He was one of Plutarch's heroes come to life. Had the old biographer been able to write a life of our young captain, he would have said of him, instead of Flaminius: "But being ever thirsty after honor, and passionate for glory, if any thing of a greater or more extraordinary nature was to be done, he was eager to be the doer of it himself."

On January 31 Decatur was ordered to prepare the little 60-ton ketch for a 35-day cruise. Preble appropriately commissioned her in the Navy under the name *Intrepid*. Her crew were quickly enrolled: Lieutenants James Lawrence, Joseph Bainbridge, Jonathan Thorn, Surgeon Herrmann, Midshipman Thomas Macdonough, and sixty-two men, all from the *Enterprise;* Midshipmen Izard, Rowe, Laws, Davis, and Charles Morris from the *Constitution;* and Salvador Catalano, a Sicilian pilot. In all there were seventy-four officers and men.

Preble's instructions were precise. "It is my order," he wrote, "that you proceed to Tripoli, in company with the *Siren,* Lieutenant Stewart, enter the harbor in the night, board the *Philadelphia,* burn her and make good your escape." Thus were tabulated, in logical order, the steps to be taken, and in language in which no loopholes could be found! If the attack had been a complete failure, as it might well have proved, the entire responsibility would have fallen squarely upon the shoulders of the commodore. He would have been ridiculed throughout the country for having sent a handful of men on such an errand; accused of having sent young officers and their men to death while he remained in safety. On the other hand, should the enterprise succeed, all the honor would belong to Decatur.

Many an officer in such a situation would have shifted the responsibility to the shoulders of the subordinate by the insertion of evasive phrases; have left it to the judgment of the subordinate whether the conditions for attack were favorable. Such phraseology creates doubts in the mind of the junior, and no young fellow with doubts in his mind will burn his *Philadelphia*. Once it is decided to undertake an enterprise, the order to carry it through must be hard and fast. That eases the mind of the man on the spot—lets him concentrate his thoughts on times and methods, which may well be left to him. In our opinion, Preble's moral courage in ordering the attack was as worthy of praise as Decatur's physical bravery in actually making it. He deserves an equal share of the credit. We think that this was very generally, and rightly, conceded. It showed a healthy disposition to reward the man who risked the "hazards of command."

In accordance with the custom of the time the instructions as to the methods to be used in the attack were detailed. It was hoped that before destroying the *Philadelphia* her guns might be used to bombard the castle and the shipping in port. It was suggested that after reaching the frigate the *Intrepid* might be used as a fireship while the party retreated in small boats. "On boarding the frigate," the order concluded, "it is probable that you may meet with resistance. It will be well, in order to prevent alarm, to carry all by the sword. May God prosper you in this enterprise." It was unwise to mention so many details—to some of which Decatur paid no attention.

"A bad beginning maketh a good ending," runs an old proverb; and so it was in this case. The *Intrepid* left Malta on February 3; stormy weather delayed arrival at Tripoli until the evening of the seventh. The sufferings of the party were extreme. The ketch was only two-thirds as large as a submarine chaser; the latter's complement is twenty-four; the *Intrepid* had seventy-four. Our chaser crews thought that they suffered great discomfort during the World War. What would they have said to sleeping on the *Intrepid's* water casks, eating decayed provisions, and avoiding, as well as they might, "the attacks of innumerable vermin which our predecessors the slaves had left behind them"?

Decatur was anxious to make the attack as soon as possible, while the spirits of his men still were high. So he sent Midshipman Morris and the pilot off in a small boat to reconnoiter the entrance. They brought back the word that the waves were breaking so high over the bar that passage was impossible. Before day broke a fierce gale had lashed the waters into foam. Our seamen of classic bent might have consoled themselves with memories of how the legendary fleet of Aeneas had been tossed, by an equally wild storm in these same waters. They had, however, no Venus to intercede with Neptune, and had to wait for a full week before the windbags of Aeolus had been emptied. The *Siren's* log tells us what an effective series of gales and storms the wind god loosed on this occasion.

It is not so difficult to perform a bold feat when the first wave of enthusiasm runs high; when we have had a good night's sleep and a fine breakfast; and when comrades are watching our efforts. It is an entirely different matter to carry through a desperate venture in dead of night with men who have been exhausted mentally and morally, as well as physically, by a two weeks' battle against a succession of Mediterranean storms. It is then no longer a case of momentary enthusiasm, but cold-blooded and constant courage, of Nordic rather than Latin variety.

On the sixteenth the *Intrepid* and *Siren* were again off Tripoli. Midshipman Anderson and nine men came over from the latter in a cutter to be towed astern. This reënforcement must have had a cheering effect upon our weatherbeaten adventurers. At last the sea was smooth, the wind lulled slowly to a calm. As night came on, a young moon, the enemy's emblem, diffused a gentle light over the waters.

Wary Odysseus might have turned back his prow at sight of such an omen, but not all the gods on Olympus would have turned back Stephen Decatur that night.

Slowly, silently steals the *Intrepid* toward the entrance. This cold wintry night there are no vessels on patrol; only irregular ranks of cruel, jagged rocks keep watch. The moonlight discloses these ever-present sentinels. The ketch passes through!

Quietly upon deck stand Decatur, the pilot, and ten seamen, disguised as Sicilians. Close down behind the bulwarks crouch the rest of the crew. Ahead looms up the great hulk of the *Philadelphia*. Her foremast has not been replaced, but the main and mizzen masts, with their networks of rigging, trace a spider web against the dull glare of the city. Fifteen gaping gun ports are dotted with the muzzles of frowning 18-pounders, loaded, shotted, and ready to be touched off. High overhead towers the black mass of the Bashaw's castle, its embrasures filled with cannon.

Five times strikes the frigate's bell. It is ten-thirty. Her sentinel hails. Long has our leader thought of this thrilling moment, often has he rehearsed with his pilot the rôles they are to play. Well the pilot knows his lines—audaciously will he say them. Catalano answers the hail. He has lost his anchors. May he not secure to the frigate for the night? Now the ketch is but forty yards off; what will be the answer? It is "Yes!" Lawrence lowers a small rowboat. With a line from the *Intrepid* he pulls for the frigate's bow, secures his end to the fore chains under the foremast. At the other end crouching seamen haul away.

The Moors are courtesy itself. One of their boats rows out toward the ketch with a second line. Such politeness had not been counted on. Like many a last-minute complication, it holds the possibility of disaster. But there are quick wits on the *Intrepid*. Midshipman Anderson shoves off in his boat, meets the Tripolitans half way and takes the line from them with such thanks as he or his men may be able to utter. Soon the *Intrepid* has two lines.

Watchers on the frigate must wonder at the hidden power which draws the little ketch steadily upon her prey. Soon they make out that there are anchors on her bows. Then they see a crowd of men upon her decks. A wild yell, "Americanos!" breaks the silence of the night. Decatur answers with "Away boarders!" Another pull and the *Intrepid* is alongside, in perfect safety under the line of long gun barrels. Then ensues a confused din, a wild scramble for the honor of being the first to scale the enemy's side. Decatur trips over his scabbard; Morris passes him; over the high bulwarks, sword in teeth, he disappears. Officers, midshipmen, seamen crowd after him.

Surprise has won the day—it is complete. There is no resistance on the upper decks. The enemy dive over the side or scuttle below. Wild Americanos or hungry sharks —what a Scylla or Charybdis to choose between. Now every man to his appointed task. Lieutenant Thorn with fourteen people holds the ketch alongside; Anderson with nine captures the boats tied up under the frigate's stern; Decatur with seventeen keeps the upper decks; Lawrence with the rest dashes below. Preble's injunctions are specific: "Be sure to set fire in the gun-room berths, cockpit, storerooms forward and berths on the berth deck." Lawrence himself with twelve men is given the berth deck; Bainbridge with eleven the wardroom; Morris with eight the cockpit.

There is many a fight with Turks skulking in the semi-darkness. Some twenty of them are killed before the ship is cleared. In less than twenty minutes the ship is everywhere ablaze. Now as the flames shoot up the Tripolitan guns ashore and afloat add to the beauty of the pyrotechnic display.   Back spring the Americans into their craft. Flames are roaring out through gun ports—almost reach to her rigging.   Lines are cut by battle-axe and cutlass, just in time.   The ketch drifts clear.   Out ring three cheers above the crackling roar of fire and the thunder of cannonade; our leader must send his foe this last defiance.

The roaring flames now have lighted the harbor, turning night into day.   The little *Intrepid* is in clear sight of enemy gunners; their shot converge on her from every direction.   Out are run the sixteen great sweeps; strong men, willing galley slaves for an hour, double-bank their handles; their long blades churn the water into foam. Away races the little craft through the shell splashes.

At the very last an unexpected danger threatened.   Midshipman Charles Morris thus describes it: "We were in great danger from the ship, whose broadside commanded the passage by which we were retreating and whose guns were loaded and were discharged as they became heated.   We escaped these also, and, while urging the ketch onward with sweeps, the crew were commenting on the beauty of the spray thrown up by the shot between us and the brilliant light of the ship, rather than calculating any danger that might be apprehended from the contact.   The appearance of the ship was indeed magnificent.   The flames in the interior illuminated her ports, and ascending her rigging and masts, formed columns of fire, which, meeting the tops, were reflected into beautiful capitals; whilst the occasional discharge of her guns gave an idea of some directing spirit within her."

During the entire enterprise only one American was wounded.   The *Intrepid* was hit but once, by a shot which pierced a sail.

Meanwhile Lieutenant Charles Stewart had approached the entrance. It had been arranged in advance with Decatur that the firing of a rocket from the *Intrepid* was to be the signal for sending in reënforcements. Soon after the ketch left him Stewart hoisted out the launch and barge. In the former he placed Lieutenant Caldwell, Midshipman Dorsey, and twenty seamen; in the latter Mr. Brooke, Mr. Budd, and eight seamen. The *Siren's* log reads: "At ½ past 10, Lieutenant Decatur made the signal for a reënforcement of officers and men in boats; answered it; about ten minutes after which the Frigate *Philadelphia* in the harbor of Tripoli burst into a flame fore and aft; the castle and batteries then commenced the fire on the *Intrepid*, all around the frigate in every direction."

When the *Intrepid* reached the *Siren's* boats near the entrance, she stopped. All hands watched the great frigate drift from her moorings toward the shore. At about 12:30 A.M. her magazine exploded. Her masts fell. Her hull sputtered beneath the waters. "At half past midnight," continues the log, "the launch and barge returned and were welcomed with repeated cheers. Hoisted in boats. At 1 A.M. spoke the *Intrepid* and took her in tow."

Thus ended what Lord Nelson called the most bold and daring act of the age. When, three days later, the *Intrepid* sailed through the American squadron in Syracuse Harbor, each ship gave her a deafening salute of cheers. As for you, Decatur,

> Thyself has now
> fulfilled such deeds, that thy fame shall endure
> through all the ages.

Yes, Decatur's reputation was made. Congress promoted him to be a captain at twenty-five. The other officers and men received an entirely inadequate and inappropriate reward: two months' extra pay. But what our young officers prized most was the reputation won among their comrades. Decatur's exploit was the spark which kindled an ambition for distinction in many a hero's heart.

CHAPTER XI

PREBLE ATTACKS

DURING all the winter the blockade was maintained by our brigs and schooners. Their captains were animated by a spirit of real aggressiveness and they weathered the March gales, eager to get a chance at the enemy. The *Siren* captured a large armed brig, manned by eighty men. Preble commissioned her as the *Scourge* and mounted sixteen 6-pounders aboard her.

Preble made extensive preparations for attacking Tripoli. Passive blockade was to be replaced by aggressive attack. This was easier to decide than to accomplish. All history, including recent Gallipoli fighting, has shown that a naval force without the support of troops has little chance of making an impression on a strongly posted enemy ashore. Preble was not strong enough to make a landing attack; Porter's enterprise had shown that the few sailors and marines the squadron could land would not be able to maintain themselves ashore permanently. He might attack the gunboats which patrolled the harbor entrances. This required small light-draft schooners. So Preble borrowed six from the King of Naples. They were flat-bottomed boats of twenty-five tons, suitable only for harbor defense, but he had to use what he could get. A long 24-pounder was mounted in the bow of each.

Bombardment was a second idea. For this he had the *Constitution*. To increase her gun power six long 26-pounders were obtained from Naples and mounted on the weather deck amidships. To supplement the effect of her horizontal fire with high-angled vertical fire he obtained two bomb vessels, also from the obliging king. Each carried a long brass mortar, throwing 13-inch bomb shells. For each of the gunboats we must have thirty-five men, for the bomb vessels forty. Here was another problem. We borrowed ninety-six Neopolitan sailors, and provided the remainder from our larger ships.

A third possible method of attack was the use of fire ships. For this purpose we had the *Intrepid* and such smaller craft as we might capture from the enemy.

By July 25 the entire squadron was concentrated before Tripoli: *Constitution, Siren, Argus, Nautilus, Vixen, Scourge,* and *Enterprise,* six gunboats, two bomb vessels, and the *Intrepid.* Officers and men amounted to 1,060. It was estimated that the Bashaw had about 25,000 troops and seamen under his orders.

Plans were issued and preparations made for a general attack. The commodore was determined that this was to be no distant cannonade. The *Constitution* was to engage the batteries at point-blank range. The gunboats were to attack *au fond*—to the finish.

Early on the morning of August 3 the Bashaw saw that the storm was about to break over his head. He advanced nine large gunboats outside the line of reefs east of the entrance; five took station under the batteries to the westward; five more, with two large galleys, remained in reserve in the harbor. Each of these gunboats had three guns, one a large one, and twenty-four to forty men—real fighters noted for boarding.

At 2:00 P.M. the flagship displayed the signal to attack. Our six gunboats had been detailed to attack the nine Tripolitan vessels outside the line of reefs. Somers, being to leeward, could not beat his boat up against the easterly

From the painting by John W. Jarvis

EDWARD PREBLE

From a painting by M. Carné

PREBLE'S FIRST ATTACK ON TRIPOLI

The *Constitution* (large ship right center foreground) leading the attack on Tripoli, August 3, 1804.

breeze. Blake misunderstood the signal and did not join his comrades. Bainbridge had his lateen yard shot away and could fire only from a distance. Three against nine were big odds. But, thought our young fellows, the bigger the odds, the greater the glory. And they had Stephen Decatur to lead them. He, like the Spartans, was "not wont to ask how many, but where the enemy were!"

Decatur led the charge. He made for the nearest enemy, a large vessel, armed with a great 29-pound cannon and two howitzers. Her crew were thirty-six.

Decatur holds the fire of his great gun until he is close down upon his foe, until he can "see the whites of their eyes." Then, "Fire!" A deafening roar shakes his little craft from stem to stern. A hail of grapeshot and cannister sweeps the enemy's decks. The two ships rub together and the boarders are away. For a few minutes the fight is furious. Then the Turks give way. Their craft is carried by push of pike. Not a man escapes. Sixteen are killed, fifteen wounded; five receive quarter.

Meanwhile Sailing Master Trippe is having a bad quarter of an hour. After an exchange of gunfire he runs his gunboat alongside a large enemy craft whose armament and crew are similar to Decatur's opponent. Boarding is the order of the day; Trippe thinks that it is a good way for Americans, as well as Tripolitans, to fight! He springs on the enemy's decks. Midshipman Henley and nine seamen are after him; before more can follow the vessels drift apart. Here is a situation—one worthy of Decatur himself. Trippe sees that audacity is his only hope. In strategy Paul Jones had proved that, being too weak for defense, it was necessary to attack. Trippe is to show that this principle has wider applications. He singles out the enemy captain and attacks him with his pike. The latter seems to be a good swordsman, for he rains blows on Trippe's chest and shoulders—wounds him eleven times in all. But at length one good thrust of his pike evens up matters—and then some. At the same instant Marine Sergeant Jonathan Meredith bayonets another Moor about to cut down his captain from behind. Their leader lost, the Tripolitan resistance weakens; they give in. Fourteen of them have been killed, seven wounded; unwounded prisoners are fifteen. Besides their captain, three of our men are wounded.

Lieutenant James Decatur, brother of Stephen, engaged successfully a third enemy gunboat, but when attempting to board was shot through the head. Stephen was towing off his prize when the news of his brother's death reached him. According to this report James had been treacherously shot after the enemy had surrendered. Stephen was so infuriated that he cast off his prize and made full sail for an enemy craft, the one he thought his brother had fought. It was one of the smaller enemy vessels, with a long 18-pounder, two howitzers, and twenty-four men. Sailing alongside, Decatur leaped upon the enemy's deck; young Macdonough and nine seamen followed.

The enemy's captain was a gigantic man. Fiery Decatur pushed at him with his pike, but missed his thrust. The Turk wrested this weapon from his hand. Decatur now drew his sword, but his luck was no better. His blade broke off short against the pike and its point scratched his breast. He sprang upon his enemy and grappled. They fell upon the slippery deck, the Turk on top. As they struggled for life another Turk swung his scimitar at the captain's head, but Seaman Daniel Frazier,* both his arms already

*The usual account credits Reuben James with saving Decatur's life; we have followed Gardner W. Allen.

so wounded that he could not hold a weapon, received the blow full upon his own head. The Turk now tried to hold Decatur with one hand while with the other he reached for his knife. Here was Stephen's last chance. He also reached down, pulled a pistol from his waistcoat pocket, fired full into the Turk's back just as the knife was descending toward his own chest. After passing through the body of his opponent the pistol ball lodged in his own coat. A close call. Their captain killed, the Turks were beaten; seventeen were dead, four wounded; only three prisoners were unwounded. Four of our men were wounded, brave Frazier no less than ten times. This was real schooling for a young navy, and taught the Tripolitans something of their own game also. Boarding tactics were never so popular thereafter.

Richard Somers, the bravest of the brave, had not been able to join Decatur. So single-handed he attacked the enemy craft west of the entrance. "By this time," he reported, "there were five of the enemy's gunboats of the lee line under way, advancing and firing. When within point-blank shot I commenced firing on the enemy with round shot and grape. They still advanced to within pistol-shot, when they wore round and stood in for the batteries. I pursued them until in musket shot of the batteries, which kept up a continual fire of round shot and grape." That was how Somers fought!

The *Constitution* followed Somers close under the batteries west of the entrance and engaged them heavily as she stood back and forth along the coast. The commodore reported: "We were several times within two cables' length of the rocks and three of their batteries, every one of which in succession we silenced so long as we could bring our broadside to bear upon them. But the moment we passed a battery it was reanimated, and a constant heavy fire kept up from all that we could not point our guns at." This reads like a description of one of the Dardanelles bombardments; batteries are easy to silence, but difficult to damage permanently.

Twice the Tripolitan gunboats in reserve tried to come out. But each time the brigs and schooners, assisted by the flagship when necessary, "kept their flotilla completely in check." The bomb vessels kept busily at work scattering their huge shells over the town; unfortunately there were many "duds."

At 4:30 P.M. the wind shifted and withdrawal was signaled. The flagship covered the retirement in great style. "Tacked ship," Preble laconically recorded in his journal, "and fired two broadsides in stays, which drove the Tripolitans out of the castle and brought down the steeple of a mosque."

It had been a real fight; Preble had proved himself a leader of the first order. Our losses had been very slight: one killed and thirteen wounded. On the decks of the three captured vessels we counted forty-seven killed, twenty-six wounded, twenty-three prisoners. There were certainly heavy losses on the other vessels. Ashore the Tripolitans also suffered severely. "A number of the guns in the battery were dismounted," Bainbridge wrote, "the city considerably injured and many of the inhabitants killed." The three captured gunboats were commissioned in our squadron.

But do you think that Preble was contented? Admiral Gleaves tells how, after the battle, Decatur came aboard the flagship to make his report. Approaching the commodore on the quarter-deck, he said: "Sir, I have the honor to report that I have captured three of the enemy's gunboats." "Three, sir," Preble answered, "where are the rest of them?

Why have you not brought them all out, sir?" Later, however, when writing his official report and personal journal, Preble expressed complete satisfaction with the manner in which his subordinates had conducted the attack.

On the seventh the attack was renewed. The gunboats, now nine in number, stood in close to a 7-gun battery west of the entrance. They engaged it at close range with their heavy guns. The *Siren* and *Vixen* kept within close support to attack the Tripolitan gunboats should they come out; their short carronades were of no use in bombardment. As it was blowing fresh toward the shore, Preble deemed it wise to keep the *Constitution* at rather long range. The *Enterprise* and *Nautilus* kept by her, ready to engage the enemy gunboats should opportunity offer. Both sides meant business; the action was sharp. "The 7-gun battery," Preble reported, "in less than two hours was silenced, except one gun. I presume the others were dismounted by our shot, as the walls were almost totally destroyed."

You can't make an omelet without breaking eggs. Similarly you cannot bombard shore batteries at point-blank range in flimsy little gunboats without being hit in return. The enemy used hot shot. One of them landed in the magazine of *Gunboat No. 9*, captured four days before from the enemy. The explosion killed Lieutenant Caldwell, Midshipman Dorsey, and eight men; six more were wounded. Midshipman Spence was loading the bow gun at the time. Like that brave officer in charge of the *Borodino's* after turret in the Sea of Japan, like that heroic captain of the *Gneisenau* at the Falkland Islands, this young hero was set on firing one last shot at the enemy before his ship sank. So he completed his loading—not such a simple operation as it is now—aimed his gun, and fired. Then his crew gave three cheers as the boat sank under their feet. All the survivors, including the wounded, were saved. The story of this little craft makes a bright page in our naval annals.

Nor were these all the losses: *Gunboat No. 4* was pierced by a 24-pound shot; *No. 6* had her yard shot away; *No. 8* lost two men killed. "We threw forty-eight shells and about five hundred 24-pound shot into the town and batteries," the commodore reported. "All the officers and men engaged in the action behaved with the utmost intrepidity. At half past six all the boats were in tow and the squadron standing to the northwest." The honors of the day had been even. The Tripolitans had given us a good party.

Next day the *John Adams* arrived from home, the first of a powerful reënforcing squadron. She brought unwelcome news to the squadron: Commodore Barron was coming to take over the command. The Secretary of the Navy, in expressing entire confidence in Preble's work, explained that he was sending out four frigates and that there were only two captains in the Navy junior to Preble. Too bad —for Preble and for the Navy. "When the race is on," Xenophon said, "it is not the time for any chariot to change horses." Had the sailing of the new ships been delayed until after news of Preble's bombardments arrived at home, probably some method could have been found to retain him in command. But when Barron sailed, Preble's fame rested only on his pacification of Morocco and the *Philadelphia* episode.

Although deeply disappointed at the news that he was to lose his command, Preble resolved to make the most of the few days remaining to him. He decided, probably in view of the losses received in the last bombardment, to attack at night. On the evening of the ninth he boarded the *Argus* for a reconnaissance. Hull went in close to the entrance and drew a heavy fire from the batteries. Practice seems to have improved the Tripolitan gunnery, for a round shot struck the *Argus* three feet above the water line. It broke the plank half through and ripped off the copper sheathing under water. It was a close call.

A long stretch of bad weather now intervened. It was not until the twenty-fourth that the first night attack was made. It seems to have taken the enemy by surprise, for though it lasted four hours, it drew no reply. It seems that the firing was at long range and that the damage inflicted on the enemy was slight.

Four days later a second attack was delivered. By this time our gunners seem to have learned the technique of night firing and the enemy made heavy weather. At 3:00 A.M. eight gunboats anchored close in to the reefs. The brigs and schooners kept under way in supporting distance. The *Constitution* kept station two miles off Fort English. In a heavy bombardment which lasted for two hours and a half the gunboats eased off four hundred round shot, not to speak of grape and cannister. At 5:30 A.M. dawn streaked the east and thirteen Tripolitan gunboats came out to fight. Here was the *Constitution's* chance. Preble sailed her to within five hundred yards of the rocks and covered them with his broadsides. One vessel was sunk and two more went ashore in sinking condition. He then lay to within musket shot of the batteries for forty-five minutes and deliberately fired nine broadsides into the town and castle. Despite prolonged fighting at close range, the casualties of the entire squadron were only four. The losses of the enemy were reported by neutrals to have been heavy. This time the honors were ours. The stock of piracy now was not paying such high dividends.

On September 3 a final night bombardment again disturbed the slumbers of the Bashaw and his followers. At

3:30 A.M. the bomb vessels anchored within easy range of the town and commenced firing. Simultaneously a brisk gunboat action flared up. But before our vessels could board, the enemy gunboats withdrew through the line of reefs and took station under Fort English. We followed. Four gunboats engaged the enemy craft. Four others, supported by the five brigs and schooners, attacked Fort English and the battery just west of it. The range was so short that, for the first time, carronades could be used for bombardment. Tripolitan troops along the beach covered our craft with musketry. The bomb vessels seem to have been in a bit too close, for the batteries concentrated a heavy fire on them. One of them was hit and in danger of sinking. "To draw off the enemy's attention and amuse them whilst the bombardment was being kept up," the *Constitution* sailed into grapeshot range and fired eleven broadsides. At 4:30 A.M. a northerly wind came up and the signal to withdraw was hoisted. Again we had scored heavily, without a single casualty to our crews. As the *John Adams* was not yet ready for service, her captain, Isaac Chauncey, had commanded the *Constitution* during the night attacks. He won the commodore's warm commendation.

CHAPTER XII

RICHARD SOMERS FINISHES IN STYLE

N OW THE season of good weather was drawing to an
end and Preble decided to execute a daring plan for
which long preparation had been made. Centuries before,
when Alexander of Parma built his great bridge across the
Schelde to cut off Antwerp from the sea, an Italian resident named Gianibelli had presented to the Dutch commandant a remarkable scheme: to explode a powder magazine, built into the hull of a ship, against the bridge. So well
had the plan worked that the bridge was wrecked and a thousand Spaniards mangled to death. Preble now had a similar
idea: the *Intrepid,* so lucky in her first attack, was to be exploded in the midst of the harbor of Tripoli.

A large magazine was built below decks. In it were
packed one hundred barrels of powder. Over them were
150 bomb shells with numerous round shot and pieces of
pig-iron ballast. When word of the plan leaked out through
the squadron, officers and men hastened to volunteer for
the perilous duty. Lieutenant Richard Somers, as brave a
man as ever wore our uniform, or any other, was given
the coveted command. With him were to go Midshipman
Henry Wadsworth and ten seamen—heroes all. The men
disposed of their effects as a sign that they did not expect
to return. When doubt arose as to whether the fuse might
burn too long, Somers declared that he needed none at all.
Said Callicratidas: "Sparta will not miss one man!"
Neither, thought Somers, would the United States.

The night of September 4 was set for the attack. At

[183]

sunset the commodore sent over Midshipman Joseph Israel
with a last message. This young hero pleaded so hard to
be allowed to accompany the expedition that Somers gave
permission. By 8:00 P.M. it was completely dark and the
Intrepid set sail for the entrance. The *Argus, Vixen, Nautilus,* and *Siren* slowly followed toward their appointed stations off the western entrance. The plan was to gain a
position in the center of the harbor, ignite the combustibles
on the upper deck, light off the fuse, and abandon ship in
two small boats which towed astern. In the fifteen minutes
which the fuse would burn the crew might gain a good distance from the fire ship. The fire would prevent the enemy
from boarding while the fuse was still burning; also it
would deceive them as to the true nature of the ship.

There was a good breeze from the eastward. The night
was pitchy black, with a mist rising from the water. Soon
the ketch was lost to sight, except to a few people on the
inshore vessels who followed it with their night glasses.
Every man in the squadron was on deck, with eyes glued
to that dim outline which marked the city. An unparalleled
drama of glory and death was being played before their
eyes. Most eagerly of all watched those two close friends
of gallant Somers: Stephen Decatur and Charles Stewart.
Only a few minutes before they had pressed his hands
in silent good-bye. He had spoken quietly and seriously
with these comrades—with no epigram to be passed into history. But his whole courageous manner spoke more truly
than words that line which Beowulf said: "I seek doom of
glory, or Death shall take me."

Imagine Preble following the hands of his watch, as
it ticks away relentlessly those last great minutes in the
lives of heroes. Now it is nine o'clock—now nine-thirty.
Seven minutes more; did ever hands move so slowly about

RICHARD SOMERS

From an engraving by D. Edwin after the painting by G. Stuart

ISAAC HULL

a watch's face? Then there is a sudden burst of gunfire; in several minutes it reaches the violence of drum fire. Then in the direction where the *Intrepid* was last seen a light appears—seems to be a lantern. A mighty and blinding flash of light rises to the heavens; a thunderous and deafening roar is heard. Then silence, darkness, mystery. Now *Argus,* search with your hundred legendary eyes. You, also, *Vixen, Nautilus,* and *Siren!* But you will find nothing. Somers and his comrades will not return. "The paths of glory lead but to the grave!"

What had happened? We may only guess. The clues as to the fate of Somers and his people are very meager and inconclusive. Next morning the *Intrepid's* mast was seen on the rocks at the western entrance. One of the galleys on watch there had disappeared and two others were drawn up on the beach for repairs. Two bodies were taken by the enemy from the wreck of the *Intrepid,* which seems to have been on the northern side of the rocks; one was found in one of her boats which floated ashore; ten more were washed ashore, one of which was thought to be the remains of Somers. There in some forgotten spot he now lies buried.

> We carved not a line, and we raised not a stone,
> But we left him alone with his glory.

How did Somers and his men die? Cooper gives the evidence in great detail, and draws his conclusions. Mighty inconclusive they are, too. Allen does the same. So do other writers of lesser note. The truth is that nobody knows; one guess is as good as another. But Preble in his official report tells us a pretty story; from it there has sprung a legend in keeping with Somers' knightly character. If it may not be actually true, it could have been true. We rather like it better than the inconclusive conclusions of better writers, and propose to tell it to you.

Let us try to reconstruct the scene on the *Intrepid's* deck. Somers had two very difficult problems: first to pass through the openings in the reefs on a dark night without the aid of navigational lights; second, to avoid the three rowing galleys which patrolled the entrance. Had he analyzed these problems in cold blood, he must have admitted that only by extraordinary good fortune—or, if you prefer, providence guiding the destinies of mankind—could he even enter the harbor. There was hardly a chance in ten for success; but then the same might have been said of Decatur's exploit. None of these considerations seems to have affected Somers' confidence. And to him "to do or die" meant no idle boast, but grim reality.

As the *Intrepid* reached the entrance two gunboats appeared. Right well they knew the *Intrepid* by this time. No person on board could answer their challenge in their own tongue. Chance for deception did not exist. One of the galleys came along side; the other drew close. Thirteen men could not hope to repel so many boarders. The game was lost!

Two alternatives there were: surrender the great store of ammunition to the enemy or blow it up. One of these did not exist for Somers; his decision had long been made. *Le vin était tiré, il fallait le boire*—the wine had been poured, it must be drunk. As his little crew tried to hold off their enemies for a time, Somers ran below and threw a lantern into the powder! Thus did the little *Intrepid* finish in a style worthy of her name and the flag she bore. And that's the legend!

Thus ended Preble's campaign—with a failure, just as it had begun with one. The season was now too late for the little harbor gunboats; ammunition remained sufficient only for three ships; the reënforcing squadron and the new commodore were close at hand. On the seventh the *Constitution, Argus,* and *Vixen* took up the blockade; the rest sailed off for Syracuse. Three days later Commodore Barron arrived with the *President* and *Constellation* and assumed the command.

Among the many letters of congratulation which Preble received was a unique tribute from the Pope: "The American commander, with a small force and in a short space of time, has done more for the cause of Christianity than the most powerful nations of Christendom have done for ages." Congress voted Preble a gold medal. His countrymen received him home with every honor. The Navy had come into its own again! Preble's fame, like a rolling snowball, grows with time.

CHAPTER XIII

WILLIAM EATON CONQUERS THE DESERT

THERE is an epilogue to our tale. A new character, an understudy as it were, entered upon the stage and took for himself the leading rôle of the final act. Yes, in Barron's flagship traveled one of the unique characters of history, General William Eaton, United States naval agent to the Barbary regencies. This was the same fellow we have listened to from time to time from Tunis, where he had been practicing his "shirt-sleeve" diplomacy. Years ago Eaton had decided that the only thing which would influence the Tripolitans was *terror;* now he was to test his own ideas. Eaton was every inch a fighter—had been a captain in the Revolutionary Army. He had a fertile brain, too, for it was he who had devised, and was to execute, a plan which was to prove just as effective as Preble's cannonading. "I have often regretted," Preble wrote to him, "that you did not leave the United States with me. An earlier acquaintance might have given greater reputation to our arms." Well for Tripoli they did not advance together upon her.

Eaton hoped to transfer the scene of fighting from sea to land. He would attack with an army. But whence, one might ask, would the army come? Eaton would furnish it—with a little money and a few supplies. Barron authorized Eaton to try his hand and on November 17 sent him in the *Argus* to Alexandria. After a long journey up the Nile, down again, over the desert he came to the village of Demanhour in the province of Behera. And there he found the object of his search, Hamet Karamanli, second son of the former Bashaw of Tripoli.

[188]

Yusuf, the present ruler, was a first-class villain. In 1790 he had murdered his eldest brother. In 1796, when his father died, he drove off Hamet and seized the power. Hamet had made several attempts to regain his birthright, but in 1804 had given up hope and come to Egypt.

Eaton urged Hamet, with promise of American assistance, to commence a new campaign. Finally they reached an agreement. A motley force of some four hundred souls was collected near Alexandria. For sinews of war Eaton had but four thousand Spanish dollars. With this insecure backing he assumed in due form the office of commander in chief. His first objective was the large city of Derne. It lay on the coast five hundred miles east of Tripoli and six hundred miles west of Alexandria. That six hundred miles was the blazing Lybian desert. Part way over this waste of sand Alexander had marched to visit the temple of Jupiter Ammon; Eaton proposed to go the whole route! All he asked was that two field pieces, one hundred muskets, an equal number of marines, and $10,000 be brought to him at Bomba Bay, sixty miles east of Derne. As Hull sailed off with this modest request, Eaton gave the order to march.

Thus did William Eaton set out to conquer a country, with the help of God and a few marines. He had First Lieutenant O'Bannon, one sergeant, and six privates. The Navy was represented by Midshipman Peck. This, with Eaton himself, made ten Americans in all. But it takes only a little leaven to make a big loaf. In addition, there were twenty-eight European artillerymen, forty Greek cutthroats, and enough Arabs to bring the total to four hundred. This included the men and women who led the 107 camels and an unrecorded number of asses.

On March 8 the campaign opened—the march commenced. On April 15 Bomba Bay was reached; thirty-seven terrible days at an average of fifteen miles each. As a military exploit it has seldom been equalled. We say this advisedly. When Alexander made his march Aristobolus said that rain fell to show that the gods were propitious. We hear also that two ravens—some say serpents—pointed out the route for him. Eaton had no such divine assistance. Provisions and equipment were lacking; water very scarce; so also courage, except in the breast of the commander. For there never was such a show of leadership, such a marvelous combination of tact and threats, pleading and bulldozing, rewards and punishments. Scarce a day passed without mutinies, demands for money and food, wholesale desertions, and wild panics. The camel drivers deserted *en masse* with their animals. Starvation and thirst became constant companions. Eaton wrote: "We have experienced continual altercations, contentions and delays among the Arabs. They have no sense of patriotism, truth or honor; and no attachment where they have no prospect of gain, except to their religion, to which they are enthusiasts. Poverty makes them thieves and practice renders them adroit at stealing."

Hamet was no help, except as a figurehead. He wavered as the wind blew. But William Eaton was inexorable, inflexible. He refused to weaken, to give up the enterprise. His campaign has many striking points of similarity with that of Paul Jones, and he himself was much the same kind of a fellow. Several times he quelled a mutiny in person, "a column of muskets aimed at my chest." Still he kept on and when he brought his force to Bomba Bay it numbered some 1,200 souls, over 650 of whom were fighting men. But now there was not a ship in sight, nor any water! Signal fires were lighted on a high hill. Perhaps *Argus,* with her hundred eyes, will see them. Yes, next morning

prayers rose to many different gods. A ship was in sight.
It was the little *Argus!*

Isaac Hull brought cheering news: the *Hornet* was coming with supplies. Two days later she was in port. Her
sailors hastened to bring on shore 1,088 pounds of bread,
1,240 of beef, 785 of pork, 6 of butter, 295½ of cheese,
11 gallons of molasses, and 63½ of spirits. Actually some
of these provisions may have been landed later, as Eaton
signed a receipt on May 31 in full for all stores received
to that date; and that receipt was for the stores above
listed. Other items were of still more importance: water
and seven thousand Spanish dollars. There is no mention
of the one hundred muskets or the marines to shoot them.

Considerably cheered by this practical demonstration of
Uncle Sam's support, the army marched again westward on
April 23. It covered in two days the sixty miles to Derne.
Eaton had fallen upon his enemy, as Suvaroff used to say,
"like snow on the head," a particularly appropriate expression in this instance, for his arrival must have been about
as unexpected as a snowstorm in the Sahara.

Isaac Hull with his little squadron seems to have been
left behind by Eaton's rapid marching. On the twenty-sixth
the *Nautilus* was sent to join the army and anchored off
its camp some two and a half miles east of the town. At
9:00 A.M. of the twenty-seventh the *Argus* and *Hornet,*
then some ten miles east of the city, sighted the *Nautilus*
and made all sail for her. At 10:30 A.M. *Hull* spoke her
and heard from Captain Dent that Eaton proposed to attack
the city and wished two field pieces as soon as possible.
They, with other stores, were placed in the Argus' boat and
sent in.

"We found that it was impossible to land the guns," Hull
reported, "without hauling them up an almost perpendicular

rock twenty feet above the boat; but with the perseverance of the officer and men sent on this service they effected the landing of one of them, by hauling it up the steep rock; Mr. Eaton, finding that we should lose time in landing the other, sent it off again, informing me that he should march for the town as soon as he could mount the field piece that he had on shore."

The town of Derne was surrounded by an old wall. Some distance outside, possibly a quarter of a mile, was a battery whose eight guns faced the sea. Between the battery and the city wall were houses, gardens, and old walls. As Eaton's force advanced, the enemy retired to these points of vantage, lined the city wall, and strongly manned the battery—which is also called a fort in Hull's report. The commodore had arranged to give the land forces the full support of his little detachment.

At 2:00 P.M. Eaton with his little group of seventy foreigners attacked from the eastward, opening fire with musketry and his lone cannon. At the same instant Lieutenant Evans brought the *Hornet* in gallant style to within one hundred yards of the battery. There he anchored with springs on his cables and commenced a heavy fire. The *Nautilus* and *Argus* anchored east of the *Hornet* and about one-half mile from the shore. They divided their fire between the battery and the town. For an hour the Arabs fought their battery well and kept up a heavy fire on the ships. Then their guns became silent one after another and the gunners were seen slinking off into the houses and gardens in rear.

The vessels then directed their fire along the beach to clear the path for Eaton and his men. By this time the rammer of the field piece had been broken; a number of the men had been wounded by musketry from the houses outside the wall. Hamet and his Arabs had gone off to attack the city from the other side, where they could fight more after their own fashion, or not at all, if that seemed preferable. Eaton ordered an advance on the battery and on came his little band. The enemy's musketry increased; a ball passed through Eaton's wrist. Still he led, nobly seconded by his marines and Greeks, and well supported by the ships' cannonade. "About half an hour after three we had the satisfaction to see Lieut. O'Bannon and Mr. Mann, Midsn. of the *Argus,* with a few brave fellows with them enter the fort, haul down the enemy's flag, and plant the American ensign on the walls of the battery."

Finding the guns charged and ready for firing, our people pointed them on the town and commenced firing. By four o'clock the town was completely in our possession. One of the most interesting campaigns in history had been won.

The ships sent ashore their boats with ammunition for the battery and brought back the wounded. One marine, John Wilton, had been killed, and two wounded. Nine Greeks—who seem to have fought right well—and one Maltese also were wounded. "Mr. Eaton gave the necessary orders at the fort, and went into the town to see everything quiet during the night; at ½ past 5 he returned on board to get his wound dressed, having received a musquet ball through his left wrist."

Next day another hostile army appeared outside the walls. For a month and a half the campaign continued. But now, incited by success, his Arabs fought well, and Eaton had an answer to every move of the enemy. The Tripolitans raised the siege and withdrew. Now to bring his squad of marines—only five now unwounded—"to the walls of Tripoli."

CHAPTER XIV

"OPEN COVENANTS OPENLY ARRIVED AT"

NOW the tide of success is at its flood. Not only is Eaton performing wonders at Derne, but a most formidable naval force is assembling in Tripolitan waters. President Jefferson has been acting with unusual vigor. After hearing of the loss of the *Philadelphia* he has written a note to Congress in a way we much approve. "This accident," he has said, "renders it expedient to increase our naval force and enlarge our expenses in the Mediterranean." And so he has done.

But now other influences begin to show their baneful effects. Commodore Samuel Barron stays at Syracuse, a very sick man. With him is Consul General Lear, who has powers to make a treaty. Barron seems to have been easily influenced by Tobias Lear. And Lear hates to think of winning a peace at the cannon's mouth. A recent Democrat was not the first to conceive the brilliant idea of a peace without victory. It has been intimated also that he is none too friendly with our friend William Eaton, that first exponent of "shirt-sleeve" diplomacy. He has never looked with favor upon that campaign toward Derne—with still less now it has ended so well. He thinks also that it is rather costly, some $20,000 having already been paid; almost as much as a year's tribute to Algiers. It will be cheaper to pay our money direct to the Bashaw than to Eaton's army.

It is true that his instructions from Secretary Madison express a strong hope that he will conclude a treaty "without any price or pecuniary compensation whatever," such being allowed only in case of some naval disaster. But this seems to the consul general only "diplomatic eyewash." No, it must not be taken too seriously. Nor must such minor considerations as "points of honor, taken in the abstract."

After long discussions with Lear at Syracuse, Samuel Barron sent off his peacemaker in the *Essex* to Tripoli. With him went a letter to John Rodgers, then blockading in the *Constitution*. In it Barron, on the plea of ill health, turned over the command to that officer with an injunction to carry through his peace policy, which Lear would explain in detail. Rodgers had previously expressed the opinion that negotiations should not commence until "our whole force was drawn up before the enemy's walls." Now he was placed in a most embarrassing position, particularly as Barron had reserved the right to resume the command should the campaign be prolonged. Only once did he speak out. Lear records what he said: "At breakfast this morning Commodore Rodgers observed that, if the Pasha would consent to deliver up our countrymen without making peace, he would engage to give him two hundred thousand dollars instead of sixty thousand, and raise the difference between the two sums from the officers of the Navy, who, he was perfectly assured, would contribute to it with the highest satisfaction."

There was also a point of ethics to be observed. To make a treaty without the knowledge of your ally is not done in the best diplomacy. No effort was made to consult in any way with Eaton or Hamet. It was in this connection that Barron wrote to Lear: "I must contend that the liberty and perhaps the lives of so many valuable and estimated Americans ought not to be sacrificed to points of honor, taken in the abstract." Lear agreed!

The Bashaw was really worried. Derne was in the hands of the enemy. Summer was at hand, and well did he remember the buffets he had received last summer. When he learned that he could treat with Tobias Lear, and not an American commodore, he gladly indicated his willingness to commence negotiations. On June 3 the treaty was signed. All prisoners were to be freed, including the *Philadelphia's* crew. No American vessels were to be captured nor Americans enslaved in the future. Tribute in every form was to cease. For these terms we paid the sum of $60,000. Undoubtedly, had Lear restrained his inordinate passion for peace, we could have obtained these same terms, or better, without the payment of a cent. Encouraged by Preble's victories, the country had made a great effort and a strong force was fast being assembled. Within a few weeks Rodgers would have had six frigates, four brigs, two schooners, one sloop, two bomb vessels and sixteen gunboats. The bomb vessels and nine of the gunboats had been specially constructed by Preble after his return to the United States and would have been most effective for bombardment.

Could not Lear have waited long enough to let the Bashaw look at this concentration of force before his harbor? Might we not have let him listen once to its drum fire and hear the masonry falling about his ears? Rodgers seems to have made no protest; seems to have been worried over what might happen to our prisoners in Tripoli. Bainbridge, who wanted years before to deliver tribute from the mouths of his cannon, threw his influence on the side of Lear. A Roman named Regulus once acted a part near these very shores which excites our admiration to this day. Taken prisoner by the Carthaginians, he was sent to Rome to urge the conclusion of peace. Instead he strongly urged that war be continued, and returned of his free will to Carthage to meet a cruel death. Alas, Bainbridge was no Regulus.

There seems to have existed a curious weakness on the subject of these *Philadelphia* people. It was an old Roman policy never to be influenced in the slightest degree by any consideration of what might befall Romans in the possession of the enemy—and it was one of the cardinal principles of war. In the Civil War we acted in accord with it when we refused to exchange prisoners. It would have been better had we forgotten the existence of these people from the *Philadelphia,* who had fallen into the enemy's power under none too honorable conditions. Still, everything considered, the terms of our treaty were certainly better than any obtained by a European power. The $60,000 were far below the demands of the Bashaw several years before.

Would that we could end the story of Lear's peacemaking here. We had not done so badly for ourselves. Apparently it was considered proper to pay our Arabian allies back with some of their own treachery, which is what we did. Even now, after a century and a quarter, it brings a blush of shame to the cheek. We were to *persuade* Hamet, who knew nothing of these negotiations, to evacuate his captures for no consideration other than the release of his family, held prisoner by the Bashaw for many years. The crowning shame was a secret article which permitted this restoration to be delayed four years. Here was an example of "open covenants openly arrived at."

On June 11 the *Constellation* brought the bitter news to Derne. Eaton had just won his campaign; the enemy had withdrawn. Naturally he was infuriated; but what could he do? Hamet and his suite, twenty-five foreign artillerymen, and forty Greeks were embarked. The remainder of the expedition and the poor people of Derne, whom we had induced to revolt, were left to the tender mercies of Yusuf Bashaw. The treaty contained no provision whatever in their favor. Once its terms were known, the injustice done to Hamet was recognized and his interests were cared for as well as they deserved. As to what happened when Yusuf Bashaw reoccupied Derne we have no knowledge and no desire to press such inquiries too closely. It is alleged that the Bashaw pardoned the indiscretions of his rebellious subjects.

William Eaton, picturesque adventurer, had caught the eye of our public and upon his return was received with high honors. The rest of his years—which were not many—were embittered by controversies with Lear over the Tripolitan treaty. The Bashaw loyally kept his word for many years. Edward Preble and William Eaton had taught him some lessons in Yankee warfare which stuck in his memory for a long time.

The Tripolitan treaty had one good effect: it allowed Rodgers to deal with threatening conditions in Tunis. By August 1 he had concentrated five frigates and five smaller craft off that port. When the Bey complained that the assembly of our whole squadron off his city was an act of hostility, Rodgers replied that a frigate, a brig, two bomb vessels, and eight gunboats would arrive shortly to further augment his squadron. Lear was the official diplomat, but now Rodgers was running the show, and laying down the law in no uncertain terms, both to Lear and the Bey. In a letter to Lear concerning the Bey the commodore spoke out of turn in a way we much admire: "I have only to repeat that if he does not do all that is necessary and proper, *at the risk of my conduct being disapproved by my country,* he shall feel the vengeance of the squadron now in this bay."

The Bey gave in and offered to send an ambassador to the United States. The squadron remained in port until September to prevent any backsliding. Then the *Congress* embarked the embassy and Rodgers sailed off. The other consuls at Tunis were astonished. "No other nation," they said, "has ever negotiated with the present Bey on such honorable terms." This ended our trouble with Tunis.

We never came to a real show-down with Algiers. Here we were still suffering from the weakness of our original treaty. Only to Algiers had we promised annual tribute and this caused constant bickering. We had never come to blows with these people and they had not learned our prowess in a sea fight. Due to the threatening war with England our squadrons were needed nearer home and our Mediterranean forces gradually decreased to zero. Conditions grew worse and worse, particularly as Algiers itself was in a most unstable condition, dey after dey being assassinated by his own soldiers. By poetic justice, Consul General Lear was left to fight our battles with Algiers— without naval support. Finally in 1812 he was thrown out bag and baggage. In his final report he inserted a significant sentence: "If our small naval force can operate freely in this sea, Algiers will be humbled to the dust." And so it happened when Stephen Decatur returned with a squadron in 1815. But that is another story.

PART III

Our Cruisers Keep the Seas, 1812-1815

CHAPTER I

THE WAR OF 1812

AT LAST the day has come. Long and eagerly awaited has it been by American seamen. For many years the cup of hate and bitterness has been filled to overflowing. A tall-sparred frigate plows her bluff bows through the purple water of the Gulf Stream. From her mastheads lookouts report a tiny speck upon the clear distant horizon. Larger and higher it grows—becomes a second frigate, equally large and beautiful. Across one of her topsails is painted a cryptic phrase, "Not the Little Belt," with little meaning to us now, but full of grim significance in the year of our Lord 1812. From her peak flutters a white ensign, barred with red—the proud emblem of the Royal Navy.

On the first ship there is a muffled roll of drums, a brief hurrying of men about the decks, a period of well-ordered activity—then quiet, silence. "Silent is the path of duty for every well-drilled man!" Up to her mastheads creep three balls of bunting, which at a quiet word of command break out into stripes of red and white, stars of white against a blue field—battle ensigns of the United States. *Constitution* and *Guerrière* have met. A great moment of history is at hand!

In order to appreciate the significance of this historic fight we must see how it was that the United States and Great Britain found themselves a second time at war. Independence is a great prize, but hard to win. Swiss mountaineers first learned that. Dutch burghers and seamen

[203]

fought thirty years to win a freedom which, though actual, their enemy still would not formally acknowledge. Eight years of fighting sufficed for us to gain formal independence. Thirty more years of nominal peace and three more of war were necessary before our freedom became an acutal fact.

We have seen the rapid expansion of our merchant marine and overseas trade during the nineties and the early years of the nineteenth century. We have seen the covert methods by which Great Britain used the African pirates as instruments to check our commerce with Europe, and how Preble and Eaton checkmated these intrigues. Now again commenced the death grapple between Napoleon and England. This gave our merchants their opportunity and they seized almost all the carrying trade of Europe. Such rapid expansion of foreign trade and merchant shipping was without precedent in history. But it was only a mushroom growth. For a time France and England, in their own interests, tolerated this invasion of their waters by a foreign shipping, but not for long.

Centuries before, Raleigh had said: "Whosoever commands the sea, commands the trade." England had made it her cardinal policy to command the sea; why, then, should she permit us to command the trade? She didn't!

There were two good methods for striking down our overseas trade and at the same time furthering their naval and commercial campaigns against the French Emperor. First, they searched our ships and impressed such seamen as they desired to man their own vessels. Second, they seized the ships on the pretext that they were trading with the enemy.

There is an official count of 6,257 men impressed by British men-of-war. Could a complete record have been made,

it would undoubtedly have been two or three times larger.
Let Seaman James Durand tell us how impressments were
made:

"About 11 o'clock at night there came alongside a boat
belonging to the *Narcissus* frigate. They boarded our brig
and they came below where I was asleep. With much abuse,
they hauled me out of bed, not suffering me to put on or
take anything but my trousers. In this miserable condition
I was taken on board their ship, but did not think to be destined there for a term of seven years. Had I known my
destiny that night I would have instantly committed the
horrid crime of self-murder."

Moses Smith tells another story:

"A colored seaman belonging to New York had been
pressed into the English service, and when the *Adams* was
lying off their coast, he got an opportunity to come on board
of her as one of a boat's crew, sent with an officer on some
errand. Thinking now his time had come to escape from
the British, he determined if possible not to return. Accordingly, as he stood upon the deck of the *Adams,* he suddenly
seized a boarding axe, and in the presence of the crew, cut
off the fingers of his right hand at a single blow. Then,
with his left hand holding up the bloody weapon, he ex-
claimed, 'Now let the English take me, if they want me.'
However, disabled as he was, they took him back."

Admiral Chadwick states that the British seized 917
American ships in ten years. New York was blockaded by
two of their frigates. A midshipman on board one of them
wrote:

"Every morning at daybreak we set about arresting the
progress of all the vessels we saw, firing off guns to the
right and left to make every ship that was running in heave
to or wait until we had leisure to send a boat on board to

see, in our lingo, what she was made of. I have frequently known a dozen and sometimes a couple of dozen ships lying a league or two off the port, losing their fair wind, their tide, and, worse than all, their market for many hours, sometimes the whole day, before our search was completed."

The crowning insult was the capture by force of the U.S.S. *Chesapeake,* 38 guns, by H.M.S. *Leopard,* 54 guns, on June 22, 1807. Twenty-one of her crew were killed or wounded and four alleged deserters taken off, one of whom was hanged. Captain James Barron, the unlucky commander of the *Chesapeake,* was suspended from duty for five years for failure to prepare for action as soon as he read the order of the British commander. He was able to fire but one gun in answer to the cannonade of the *Leopard,* whose surprise attack was quite in keeping with her name. The British captain was highly commended by his admiral: "You have conducted yourself most properly. I hope you mind the published accounts as little as I do. We must make allowances for the state of the populace in a country where law and every tie, both civil and religious, is treated so lightly."

Jefferson was a good note-writer. He could pen some rough phrases, make some good arguments. Plenty of Treasurer Gallatin's hard-saved dollars were used for the purchase of note paper and ink—to little purpose. Monroe in London clearly saw that note-writing would do little to remedy the situation, just as our leaders came to a similar decision in 1917. Madison wrote: "Nothing will be obtained without some kind of pressure, such a one as excites an apprehension that it will be increased in case of necessity, and to produce that effect it will be proper to put our country in a better state of defense by invigorating the militia system and increasing the naval force."

Such language to Jefferson was comparable only to the waving of a red cloth before the eyes of a bull. During the Tripolitan War he had behaved with considerable firmness, but once peace had been concluded, his pacifist tendencies had regained control. Horace long ago had stated as an axiom that: "In peace, as a wise man, he should make suitable preparation for war." Remembering this, the commonwealth of Venice had chiseled into the walls of her armory a motto: "Happy is that city which in time of peace thinks of war." George Washington had recently somewhat altered these epigrams and expressed the idea with renewed force to Congress. Jefferson had more enlightened ideas than the Father of our Country. And as for building a naval force which could be used for exerting some kind of pressure—it could not even be thought of! Like Mr. Hughes, he had a horror of building up what that statesman recently called "provocative armaments." So Jefferson allowed three frigates to rot away, canceled the building of six ships of the line, and limited his construction of seagoing craft to two sloops of 18 guns, the *Wasp* and *Hornet*. In 1806 there was in commission a magnificent fleet of one frigate and two smaller craft.

In the place of these useful naval vessels he decided to build 257 coast-defense gunboats. On February 10, 1807, he made this proposal to Congress. Listen to the arguments he used to defend this raid upon the Treasury: "It must be superfluous to observe that this species of naval armament is proposed merely for defensive operations; that it can have but little effect toward protecting our commerce in the open seas, even on our own coast; and still less can it become an excitement to engage in offensive maritime war, towards which it would furnish no means." Here is the theory of "non-provocative armaments" in a nutshell. Mr.

Hughes missed a point in not quoting from Jefferson to support his theory.

Well, the boats were built, even improved, if such were possible. Jefferson tried to, at least. "Believing," he wrote to a friend, "that gunboats are the only water defense which can be useful to us and protect us from the ruinous folly of a navy, I am pleased with everything which promises to improve them." Here is an example of amateur strategy—with all its perils.

David Porter hit the nail on the head with some caustic criticism, which he expressed after the follies of Jeffersonian naval policy had been conclusively demonstrated: "The vital error, if not criminal neglect of the government, is in not introducing the naval element into the Navy Department. Experienced officers would have avoided the terrible mistakes which have been committed within my recollection, and we would have had now such a respectable force of frigates that Great Britain would not have dared to go to war with us, for fear of having her commerce destroyed—thirty frigates on our side would make her respect us."

The British seized upon our weakness and played with us. "There is here an opinion," wrote Monroe from London, "which many do not hesitate to avow, that the United States are by the nature of their government, incapable of any great vigorous, or persevering exertion." Do you blame them?

But now Jefferson conceived a really clever idea. "This exuberant commerce brings us into collision with other powers in every sea and will force us into every war with European powers." Yes, right for once, Mr. President. Well, then, the answer is simple, so simple that no one has ever even thought of it: prevent any of our ships from going to sea! Then no ships can be seized, no seamen impressed. Thus the embargo. We suspect that one of Mr. Jefferson's motives in issuing this decree was to find some use for his gunboats; instead of protecting our ships on the high seas, now our Navy must guard the harbors and prevent any of them from going out. Alas, even for this the gunboats proved of little use. "For enforcing the embargo," we have it from Treasury-Watchdog Gallatin himself, "gunboats are better calculated *as a stationary force,* and for the purpose of stopping vessels in certain places, than for pursuit."

Unfortunately for Jefferson, the problem was not quite as simple as it seemed, as old Philip II of Spain found when he issued a decree canceling all his debts. "Direct action" sometimes has its complications. Our foreign trade in one short year fell from $246,000,000 to $79,000,000. An English traveler wrote from New York: "The port, indeed, was full of ships, but they were dismantled and laid up; their decks were cleared, their hatches fastened down, and scarcely a sailor was to be found on board; the grass had begun to grow upon the wharves." The embargo was violated then as much as the prohibition law is today. The New England states were on the point of secession. "The excitement in the East renders it necessary," said Senator Williams of South Carolina, "that we should enforce it by the bayonet, or repeal." Thus pacifism had brought us to the verge of civil war—strife in its most terrible form.

The country was in a ferment. Mr. Giles of Virginia made an impassioned oration in the Senate. "Sir," he shouted, "when the love of peace degenerates into fear of war, it becomes of all passions the most despicable."

Such of our ships as escaped our own Navy first, and the British Navy second, fell a prey to the French Emperor.

At one time he seized 134 vessels and all their cargoes, a loss of over $10,000,000. For this sum alone we might have built Morris' twenty sail of the line.

At last it became apparent that, despite all our horror of war, it was rapidly becoming a certainty. In 1811 occurred the famous incident of the *President* and the *Little Belt*. The country's reaction to it was disgusting. One half the press made Rodgers a national hero for beating a ship of one-fourth the size of his frigate. The other half roasted him for returning the enemy's fire.

In December, 1811, a special committee of Congress recommended the immediate construction of twenty frigates. "The important engine of national strength and national security," so ran its wise report, "which is formed by a naval force, has hitherto been treated with a neglect highly impolitic, or supported by a spirit so languid, as, while it has preserved the existence of the establishment, has had the effect of loading it with imputations of wasteful expense, and comparative inefficiency." A few months later David Porter stated the case more specifically. "I really wish," he wrote, "that Congress could scrutinize into the expenditures of monies appropriated for the navy—5 expensive navy yards, for the repairs and supplies of 5 frigates, 3 corvettes, and 5 brigs and schooners is shameful—not one million is spent on our ships."

Nevertheless on January 27, 1812—only five months before war was declared—the House of Representatives disapproved by a vote of 62 to 59 the construction of the new ships. "I perceive," Porter wrote, "death to our hopes of an increase of the navy." This has quite a familiar sound! Truly must these politicians of 1812 have rejoiced, as did others in 1917, that we had gone into war unprepared.

Our naval forces consisted of seven frigates and ten

smaller vessels, amounting in all to 15,300 tons, with a total of 442 guns. The British had 1,048 vessels, of 860,990 tons and 27,800 guns. By these standards of comparison we were inferior to the enemy in the ratio of about 1 to 60. But this was not the worst: of the seven frigates, only three were immediately ready for sea; two would be ready in several weeks; two more would require six or seven months. One corvette was not used during the entire war and the other was not ready for a year and a half. The administration of the Navy Department was rotten to the core! As an example, it was seriously proposed to lay up our ships and keep them in port during the war. A fiery protest arose against this cowardice. Charles Stewart and William Bainbridge fortunately were in Washington at the time and their energetic action caused this idea to be dropped.

Opposed to this inefficiency was the great Royal Navy—invincible for centuries—assured by long series of victories of its almost undisputed right to the command of the seas.

> Ye mariners of England
> That guard our native seas;
> Whose flag has braved, a thousand years,
> The battle and the breeze.

These were the warriors against whom our few poorly prepared craft must be pitted—and they had almost as many lieutenants as we had seamen.

But once we could get our ships at sea, away from the inefficient control of the shore establishment, we too had our advantages: we had unquestionably the finest officers and men then in the world; and our three large frigates and two new sloops were among the finest ships afloat.

To have declared war when our vessels were so poorly prepared proved not only the criminal neglect of the Navy

Department, but the gross inefficiency of our State Department and President Madison, who should have waited until the Navy was ready.

It was the more remarkable because of the rather good coördination which existed between the State and War Departments in regard to the Detroit campaign.

CHAPTER II

RODGERS LEADS OFF

IN ORDER that we may follow clearly the naval campaign on the high seas it may be appropriate for us to place before the reader a list of our seventeen naval vessels, with a brief statement as to their location and condition of readiness for war on June 18, when war was declared. Here it is:

Constitution, 44 guns; at Annapolis shipping new crew; ready for sea July 12.

President, 44 guns; at New York; ready for sea.

United States, 44 guns; at sea en route to New York from the southward.

Congress, 38 guns; at sea en route to New York from the southward.

Constellation, 38 guns; at Washington out of commission; ready January, 1813.

Chesapeake, 38 guns; at Boston out of commission; ready December, 1812.

Essex, 32 guns; at New York Navy Yard under repair; ready for sea, July 3.

Adams, 28 guns; at Washington out of commission; ready January, 1814.

John Adams, 28 guns; out of commission; not used during the war.

Wasp, 18 guns; at sea returning from Europe.

Hornet, 18 guns; at New York; ready for sea.

Argus, 16 guns; at sea en route to New York from the southward.

Siren, 16 guns; at a southern port, ready for sea.

[213]

Vixen, 14 guns; at a southern port; ready for sea.

Nautilus, 14 guns; at sea en route to New York from the southward.

Enterprise, 14 guns; at a New England port; ready for sea.

Viper, 12 guns; ready for sea about June, 1813.

On June 21, Commodore John Rodgers, who commanded the squadron at New York, heard that war had been declared. We have traced the career of this able officer from his first cruise on the *Constellation* to his forceful demonstration before Tunis. Since that time he had been coming rapidly to the fore and had a reputation of the finest among his brother officers. Only last year the clash between his frigate and the *Little Belt* and the subsequent wrangling had increased his profound hatred of everything British—a sentiment which his enemy reciprocated. Now, like the fighter he was, the old commodore was ready to spring from his corner at the stroke of the gong.

First, he called his crew to quarters—spoke a few words from the heart: "Now lads," he said, "we have got something to do that will shake the rust from our jackets. War is declared! We shall have another dash at our old enemies. It is the very thing you have long wanted. The rascals have been bullying over us these ten years, and I am glad the time has come when we can have satisfaction." These brief sentences, devoid of all eloquence, expressed to perfection the sentiments of officers and men, on this and every other ship. All were glad that the day had arrived!

By the twenty-first the concentration in process when war was declared had been perfected. All but the *Essex* were ready in the lower harbor. The commodore's broad pennant flew from the fine 44-gun frigate *President;* in company were the *United States,* 44 guns, *Congress,* 38, *Hornet,* 18, and *Argus,* 16; every one old friends of ours.

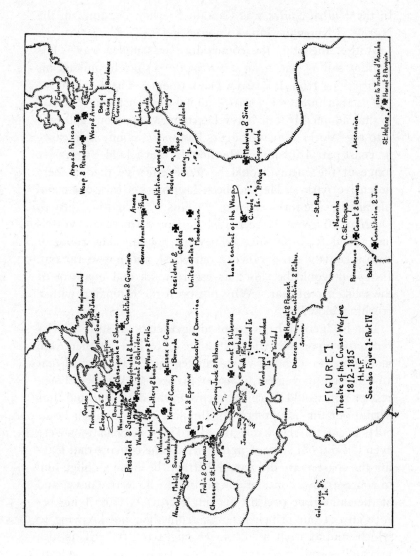

FIGURE 7.
Theatre of the Cruiser Warfare
1812-1815
H.H.F.
See also Figure 1 - Part IV.

In the *United States* was Captain Stephen Decatur; in the *Hornet,* Lieutenant James Lawrence.

Within the hour the commodore was under way. His prompt sailing had a most fortunate result: he missed his instructions from the Navy Department. These called for the establishment of a patrol along the coast, very similar to that adopted by our Navy Department upon our entrance into the World War. Rodgers had more ambitious ideas— no coast patrol for him. He thought that a bold, aggressive lunge at the enemy would be more effective than a mere defensive parry. He had been keeping his ears open and his intelligence service at work. This was what he learned: On May 20 a very large British convoy of merchant vessels had sailed from Jamaica homeward bound. The route of such a convoy ran parallel to our coast, and not so far out. Its speed would be slow; its escort weak and unaware of the existence of war. Why not open the campaign with a crushing blow?

But Rodgers did not count altogether upon such a lucky *rencontre* upon the wide Atlantic. He had another even more important end in view—a deep one. He believed that an offensive movement, whether favored with material success or not, would force the enemy to the defensive and thus permit our far-flung merchant shipping to regain their home ports in safety. He wrote afterward: "My calculations were even if I did not succeed in destroying the convoy, that leaving the coast as we did would distract the enemy, oblige him to concentrate a considerable portion of his active navy, and at the same time prevent his single cruisers from lying before any of our principal ports, from their not knowing to which, and at what moment, we might return." This idea was an inspiration of genius and stamps Rodgers as the leading strategist of our early Navy. The plan itself and the unusual promptness of its execution has escaped the commendation of historians which it so richly deserves.

At 3:00 P.M. of the twenty-first the squadron passed Sandy Hook and at six the *Hornet* discharged her pilot. "At 6:00 P.M.," her log reads, "called all hands to muster, when Captain Lawrence informed the ship's company that war was declared against England and was received with three cheers." Off into the night sailed four ships against those great fleets of the Royal Navy which boastfully claimed the sovereignty of the seas. Good luck to you, Rodgers! Alas, you will not have it!

Standing off in a southeasterly direction, the commodore sighted an American brig early on the twenty-third. She reported having seen the convoy four days before, four hundred miles off the Capes of the Chesapeake. This was only three hundred miles from the squadron's present position. Course was set northeast to intercept.

Only a few hours later, at 6:00 A.M., a large ship was sighted and the squadron made full sail in chase. The fast-sailing *President* drew ahead of her consorts and gained on the strange sail. She was the fine frigate *Belvidera* and it seemed that fortune was about to reward Rodgers' boldness with a striking success. In this perilous situation Captain Byron, the enemy's experienced commander, was resolved to try every expedient to escape or at least make a strong resistance. While throwing over quantities of supplies to lighten his ship and increase her speed, he shifted two long 18-pounders and two 32-pound carronades so that they could point out his stern ports.

By 4:30 P.M. the *President* was within gunshot and Rodgers himself aimed and fired the starboard forecastle 24-pounder—the first shot of the war! The corresponding gun on the main deck below next spoke out and Rodgers fired his gun a second time. All these three shot struck the *Belvidera* in the stern, killing or wounding nine men. The next time the main deck gun was touched off a terrific explosion shattered it into a thousand pieces. Sixteen men were killed or wounded. The deck above was blown upwards and Rodgers went down with a broken leg.

This misfortune had a doubly bad effect: men do not load and fire their guns with alacrity when they are liable to blow up in their faces; and the directing influence of the commodore was lost. Finally, Byron thought it a good time to open up with his stern chasers; and his fire was so accurate that six more people fell killed or wounded on the *President's* forecastle. The *President* then yawed off to the right and discharged her broadside, and it was a very poor one. Also the maneuver lost her much valuable ground. Byron now continued to lighten his ship; Rodgers, at the start of a long cruise, could not throw any of his provisions or gear; thus the *Belvidera,* after several hours of intermittent firing, drew out of gunshot. At midnight the chase was abandoned. This first brush with the enemy reflected little credit upon us; Byron, on the other hand, had done a fine piece of work.

Early the next morning, the twenty-fourth, as he lay on his bed of suffering, the commodore again set the course for the estimated position of the convoy. Actually it was now 450 miles east of him under the weak escort of three men-of-war. On the twenty-ninth, on the western edge of the Newfoundland Banks, an American schooner reported having sighted the convoy two days before in latitude 43°, longitude 55°, steering eastward. On July 1, a great quantity of refuse was seen. On the second the brig *Tionella* was taken; on the fourth the *Portland.* Eight days later the *Hornet,* in latitude 45° 30', longitude 23°, captured the letter

From a painting by C. R. Patterson   Shown in the Winter Exhibition of the National Academy, 1924

"AMERICA'S ANSWER, 1812"

Squadron of Commodore John Rodgers, U. S. S. *President* in the foreground.

From an old painting

CHASE OF THE *Constitution*

of marque *Dolphin*. She reported having seen the convoy only the previous evening; it consisted of eighty-five merchant ships, escorted by one ship of the line, one frigate, and one sloop. This news increased Rodgers' eagerness and for four more days he sailed on under a press of sail. Then, at the entrance to the English Channel, the commodore realized that his opportunity had passed. Reluctantly he gave the word to turn back. On the sixteenth he took the letter of marque *John*. On July 21, he passed Madeira and made for Cape Sable by way of the Azores. On August 31 he came into Boston, having gathered in four more prizes en route. During seventy days of cruising surprisingly few enemy craft had been sighted. His material spoils were few: one ship, four brigs, and two schooners; one American vessel was recaptured. "It is truly an unpleasant task," Rodgers reported, "to make a communication so barren of benefit to our country."

True it is that, if we measure Rodgers cruise by such narrow standards, it was singularly unproductive of results. War, however, is not merely a business of inflicting material damage on the enemy; it is a matching of wits, a battle of wills. Often an enterprise which fails from the viewpoint of tactics has an immense strategic effect; sometimes a cruise without a battle has a greater influence upon the course of a naval campaign than one marked by a successful sea fight. Such was the cruise we have just described. Let us see how this came to pass.

On June 26, the *Belvidera* came into Halifax with her stirring report. Admiral Sawyer at first was not inclined to take it seriously. He thought that it might be merely another *President-Little Belt* affray. A few days later, however, news came of our declaration of war. On July 5, a powerful British squadron sailed from Halifax. We had gained the initiative by two weeks: Rodgers was then in mid-Atlantic. The British squadron consisted of the *Africa,* 64, *Shannon,* 38, *Belvidera,* 36, and *Aeolus,* 32. The senior commanding officer, Captain Broke of the *Shannon,* decided to proceed to New York, our principal naval base. On the ninth, off Nantucket, the *Guerrière,* 38, joined him and five days later he arrived off Sandy Hook. Here Broke learned for the first time the power of Rodgers' squadron and decided, just as Rodgers had predicted, that his force must be kept concentrated, to avoid being beaten in detail. Thus he kept in one body before New York, allowing our returning merchant vessels to enter all other ports without risk of capture.

On July 16, Broke scored a minor success off New York when the *Shannon* ran down and captured the little 14-gun brig *Nautillus,* one of our old Tripolitan friends. Early the next morning fortune gave him a real opportunity— to capture the *Constitution.*

This fine ship had been in continuous commission since the Tripolitan wars, for a long period under Isaac Hull. One June 20, the news of war found her at Annapolis enlisting a new crew. At 5:00 P.M. the declaration of war was read to the crew at quarters. The log quaintly describes the scene: "The crew manifested their zeal in support of the honor of the United States by requesting leave to cheer on the occasion." On July 12, she put to sea with a new crew, composed largely of green men and merchant sailors. On the seventeenth at dawn she ran into Broke's squadron. At first it seemed that escape was impossible. Moses Smith gives us a little scene on the quarter-deck:

"Hull called Lieutenant Morris to him and said calmly, 'Let's lay broadside to them, Mr. Morris, and fight the whole! If they sink us, we'll go down like men!'"

"Mr. Morris now spoke to Captain Hull: 'There is one thing, sir, I think we'd better try.'

" 'What's that?' replied Hull.

" 'Try to kedge her off,' said the lieutenant.

" 'We'll try it,' responded the captain. 'But I imagine you'll fail. The water's too deep here; we've at least forty fathoms.' "

The Yankee trick worked and a little ground was gained. A thrilling chase for three days followed. At last, on the twentieth, American seamanship proved its superiority. The *Constitution* came clear. Six days later she anchored in Boston.

This chase had drawn Broke away from the New York blockade. He did not return. Broke had a hard decision to make. He knew that by scattering his squadron off our ports he could make prizes by the hundred. But, on the other hand, another large Jamaican convoy was coming up the coast. Suppose Rodgers should fall upon it, capture it *en masse*. The very fact that Rodgers accomplished no striking success in the early part of his cruise was a blessing in disguise, for it gave Broke no indication whatever as to his whereabouts, the American squadron might turn up anywhere at an instant's notice. The responsibility was too much for the British commander; he raised the blockade of our coast and headed for the convoy. On July 29, he met it 250 miles southeast of Halifax. Imagine his relief to find it intact! It was still in the danger area, so Broke escorted it for five hundred miles of its homeward voyage. Then on August 6 he heard that Rodgers had commenced his return voyage.

This news allowed Broke to end his concentration. He ordered the *Africa* to proceed with the convoy as far as longitude 45° and then make for Halifax. The *Guerrière*,

being in need of repair, was ordered there direct. With
the rest of his squadron Broke started to beat back against
the prevailing westerly winds toward New York. He did
not arrive until September 10. Thus during the first eighty
days of the war the British had blockaded only one port,
and that for about three days. Therefore Rodgers was
amply justified in adding to his official report the following
statement: "The only consolation I individually feel on the
occasion is derived from our knowing that our being at sea
obliged the enemy to concentrate a considerable portion of
his most active force, and thereby prevented his capturing
an incalculable amount of American property that would
otherwise have fallen a sacrifice."

President Madison in his annual message of November
14, 1812, supported this view: "Our trade, with little exception, has reached our ports, having been much favored in
it by the course pursued by a squadron of our frigates under
the command of Commodore Rodgers."

CHAPTER III

PORTER MAKES A PRACTICE CRUISE

THE *ESSEX,* Captain David Porter, was to have ac-companied Rodgers, but was not then ready for sea. On July 3, Porter shoved off from the navy yard at New York in none too pleasant a mood. For some reason, economical or otherwise, the Navy Department had mounted on the *Essex* a curious armament. Whereas the principal battery of a frigate always consisted of long guns, 18- or 24-pounders, the *Essex* was given but six long twelves, the rest of her battery consisting of carronades, useful only at point-blank range. Porter protested against an arrangement which would make him hopeless in a long-range fight, but the Department was adamant—as was Mr. Hughes a few years ago in refusing to allow the elevation of the guns on our older battleships.

But Porter was resolved to make the most of a bad situation. As he had to fight at close range there might well be an opportunity to board. Farragut, then a midshipman on board, wrote: "Every day the crew was exercised at the great guns, small arms and single stick. And I may here mention the fact that I have never been on board a ship where the crew of the old *Essex* was represented but that I found them to be the best swordsmen on board. They had been so thoroughly trained as boarders that every man was prepared for such an emergency, with his cutlass as sharp as a razor, a dirk made by the ship's armorer out of a file, and a pistol."

Porter set his course to the southeast. Early in the morning of the eleventh he was in latitude 33°, longitude 66°.

At 2:00 A.M. the dim outlines of ships were made out in the dull moonlight. They were evidently a convoy sailing along in very irregular formation. Porter bore down on a ship at a distance from the others and made it his prize. It proved to be a British transport with 197 soldiers on board —a fine capture. From them Porter learned that the convoy consisted of seven vessels which were transporting 1,300 troops from Barbados to Quebec; it was escorted by the *Minerva* frigate, of the same rate as the *Essex*. Before another vessel could be attacked day broke and the convoy assembled in haste about the frigate. Due to his weak battery Porter did not think he should carry the enterprise further. While this judgment doubtless was correct, we confess to a wish that he had attacked.

The *Essex* continued her cruise along the coast, taking prize after prize. In a month she made more captures than had Rodgers' whole squadron. On August 13 Porter sighted a vessel which later proved to be the sloop *Alert*, of twenty short 18-pounders and one hundred men. On this craft he worked a time-honored trick; he closed his gun ports and pretended to be an innocent merchant vessel —like the mystery ships of the World War. By this means he lured the enemy under his guns. As his gun ports opened the British put up a good fight—even gave three cheers. But this availed little, for in eight minutes their colors came down. The heavy shot from the *Essex's* carronades had splintered her hull so effectively that seven feet of water was found in her hold. Porter seems to have directed his gunners to aim at the water line, for only three Britons were wounded.

By this time Porter had made ten prizes and taken 423 prisoners. He allowed the *Alert* to take the latter into St. John's, Newfoundland—the ship then to surrender herself

at an American port. On September 4 there was a brief
encounter with the *Shannon* and on the seventh Porter
ended his cruise in the Delaware River. It had been good
practice for the famous cruise which he was soon to commence.

CHAPTER IV

THE *CONSTITUTION* AND THE *GUERRIÈRE*

WE REMEMBER how the *Constitution* had come into Boston after her close escape from Broke's squadron. Now Hull was anxious to be at sea again. He feared that orders were coming to give his coveted command to another—in fact, they had already left Washington. So on August 2 he gave the order to weigh anchor. For two weeks Hull cruised off Newfoundland and Nova Scotia with excellent success. Many prizes were taken and burnt; numerous American craft were warned to make for the nearest port. On the eighteenth an American brig said she had just been chased by the *Guerrière*. At 2:00 P.M. the next day she was sighted, latitude 41° 42′, longitude 55° 48′. And here we are back again at the beginning of our tale.

The famous duel between the *Constitution* and the *Guerrière* certainly cannot be compared to the many set battles between great fleets which have made naval history. It certainly has lost nothing in the telling by American historians. Still, it is often that small events have a wide influence. Valmy is called one of the decisive battles of the world; so is Saratoga. Neither would be classed as more than a skirmish had it occurred during the Napoleonic wars. With the possible exception of the fight between the *Monitor* and *Merrimac*, this frigate action may be called the most decisive engagement ever fought between two vessels.

To Great Britain, then engaged in a death struggle with Napoleon, our little war was nothing more than a side show. British statesmen doubtless had estimated what effect it

From the painting by Thomas Birch

Constitution AND *Guerrière*

From an engraving by B. Tanner after the original painting by Thomas Birch

United States AND *Macedonian*

might have while pursuing their course of military necessity. Germans made similar estimates of our power a century later; they might have profited by a study of our naval history of this period. The chief concern of our enemy was whether war might interfere with the supply of Wellington's army in Spain, a task performed almost exclusively by American merchant vessels. It did not occur to them that our frigates would put to sea, or, if they should, that they could last long against the British cruisers that covered the ocean. According to Roosevelt, the Royal Navy had fought about two hundred single-ship actions in the last twenty years where there was approximate equality in power, i.e., neither ship had a superiority of over 3 to 2. In these actions only five British vessels had been captured. With such a record back of them it was only natural that the British captains should give scant consideration to our young Navy.

It is true that by British tonnage measurements the *Constitution* was 1,426 against 1,338 for the *Guerrière*. Also we had gone to the 24-pounder gun while the British retained the 18-pounder. This gave us an advantage in weight of metal thrown by one broadside of 100 to 70. However, the British still believed that the 18-pounder was the better gun for frigates and that we had weighted down our ships with too heavy a battery. Again, our hulls were built very strongly—were one inch thicker than those of British 74's. Here again our British friends believed that we had made our ships so heavy that they would be dull sailers. They showed not the slightest concern over these American advantages, and the *Belvidera* incident had only served to confirm their impressions. Captain Dacres of the *Guerrière* had challenged the *President* or any other American 44 to meet him in single combat. He had bet Captain Hull, so the story goes, a perfectly good hat that he would beat the *Constitution.* Dacres said before his court of inquiry: "And I am so well aware that the success of my opponent was owing to fortune, that it is my earnest wish and would be the happiest period of my life, to be once more opposed to the *Constitution,* with them under my command, in a frigate of similar force to the *Guerrière."* All the propaganda of our frigates being disguised ships of the line was a later concoction, disseminated after we had proved in three battles the advantage of the 24-pounder and thick sides, as well as the efficiency of our officers and crews.

Now let us come back to the fight itself. The *Guerrière* was to leeward; the *Constitution* stood down for her before the fresh northwesterly breeze. Both ships stripped to topsails, the usual fighting canvas. At 5:00 P.M. gunshot was reached and the *Guerrière* kept before the wind; Dacres wore his ship from time to time to bring alternate broadsides to bear; as often Hull yawed to a parallel course to avoid being raked. For one hour this continued, the occasional broadsides of the enemy being answered by a few shots from our bow chasers. At six Dacres decided to end this maneuvering and get to business. He headed directly before the wind. To increase speed and come alongside quickly, Hull set his foresail and main topgallant sail. Zero hour was about to strike. What could Yankee seamen do against the might of Britannia?

Moses Smith, sponger of No. 1 gun, describes how "Old Ironsides" went into action: "Hull was now all animation. He saw that the decisive moment had come. With great energy, yet calmness of manner, he passed around among the officers and men, addressing to them words of confidence and encouragement. 'Men,' said he, 'now do your duty. Your officers cannot have entire command over you now. Each

man must do all in his power for his country.' The Stars
and Stripes never floated more proudly than they did at
that moment. All was silent beneath them, save the occasional order from an officer, or the low sound of the movement of our implements of war. *Every man stood firm to
his post!"* Stand by! Stand by!

By 6:05 P.M. the *Constitution* was two hundred yards on
the *Guerrière's* port quarter. Hull then yawed off slightly
away from the enemy, throwing his broadside full upon
her. The guns were fired in rapid succession from forward
aft as they bore on the target, so rapidly that it sounded
like a rippling broadside. "We instantly followed the thunder of our cannon with three loud cheers, which rang along
the ship like the roar of waters, and floated away rapidly
to the ears of the enemy."

The cannonading was terrific. Our gunners, in the heat
of battle, looked well to their aim. "This," says Smith,
"was the pride of American seamen!" With her extra canvas the *Constitution* slowly crept up on the enemy. By
6:20 P.M. she was abeam. Then with a splintering crash
down came the *Guerrière's* mizzenmast. "Huzza, boys!
We've made a brig of her!" The mast, its sails, and rigging checked the enemy's headway. Here was Hull's
chance. Spinning his wheel to the right, he charged across
the *Guerrière's* bow and raked her with his starboard
guns. Down came her main yard. Then there was a brief
lull in the fight as the *Constitution* shot by and her guns
would no longer bear. Seaman Daniel Hogan climbed to
the dizzy height of the fore truck to replace the battle
ensign which the enemy had shot away.

By this time the *Guerrière's* wreckage had checked her
headway and she pointed south. After passing by on a
westerly course Hull wore his ship and headed eastward

across the enemy's bow. His port battery was manned
and cast loose. A second time he raked the *Guerrière*. But
here he made his one mistake: he had steered so close that
before the *Constitution* could get past, the two ships came
together. The bowsprit of the *Guerrière* passed diagonally
across his quarter-deck from port to starboard and became
entangled with his rigging. His bow swung to the right and
the two ships lay in almost a straight line, the starboard
bow of the enemy rubbing against his own port quarter.
Boarders were called away; looked into the whites of each
other's eyes across the bulwarks. A storm of musketry broke
out. Topmen fired down upon the crowded decks. Lieutenant William Bush of the marines fell dead. Lieutenant
Charles Morris, who first had scaled the *Philadelphia's* side,
was severely wounded, as also was Sailing Master John
Aylwin. At 6:30 P.M. the ships came clear just as the
Guerrière's fore and main masts plunged over her side. The
fight was won. Twenty-five minutes had sufficed for Yankee gunners to dismast a British frigate.

Seeing that the battle was won, Hull sailed off to repair
his rigging, so as to be ready for another fight. At 7:00
P.M. he went back and received the surrender of the enemy.
The British casualties were seventy-nine to our fourteen.
Our gunners had fired 953 rounds from their guns, or at
a rate of 38 per minute; rather fast shooting, it would
appear.

The prize was so completely wrecked that she could not
be brought to port. She was set on fire. Brave Dacres
stood by the *Constitution's* rail to watch her end. Flames
and smoke rose from her shattered decks. Her guns were
discharged as the fire reached them.

"Presently," writes Moses Smith, "there was a dead silence; then followed a vibratory, shuddering motion, and

streams of light, like streaks of lightning running along the sides; and the grand crash came! The quarter-deck, which was immediately over the magazine, lifted in a mass, broke into fragments, and flew in every direction. The hull, parted in the center by the shock, and loaded with such masses of iron and spars, reeled, staggered, plunged forward a few feet, and sank out of sight." A sad omen it must have seemed to Dacres. A new sea power had arrived!

The results and influences of this brief engagement in mid-ocean were tremendous. It awoke the Royal Navy from its self-satisfied contentment—just as Coronel was to awaken it a century later. Said the London *Times:*

"It is not merely that an English frigate has been taken, after, what we are free to confess, may be called a brave resistance, but that it has been taken by a *new enemy,* an enemy unaccustomed to *such triumphs, and likely to be rendered insolent and confident by them.* He must be a weak politician who does not see how important the first triumph is in giving a tone and character to the war. *Never before in the history of the world did an English frigate strike to an American."*

In extenuation of this forgetfulness, we should remember that memory courses were not then available for busy editors.

In our country the effect was magical; where before political strife, sectional differences, and commercial rivalries competed in bringing our people to the verge of civil war and secession, now a wave of the wildest enthusiasm spread like a forest fire; for here was a deed of which every man from Maine to Louisiana could be proud. "Thank God for Hull's victory," was a watchword which passed from mouth to mouth. It gave a great impetus to naval opera-

tions and fired our captains with impatience to get to sea
and bring the enemy under their guns. It also encouraged
swarms of privateers to cover the seven seas to attack the
enemy's most vital trade routes. Jervis is reported to have
said to his flag captain as he sighted the Spanish fleet off
Cape St. Vincent that a victory was very necessary to England at that instant. Certainly Hull might have made a
similar remark before engaging the *Guerrière,* and with
equal justice. Our country needed a victory then as it
never has before or since. Napoleon said that in war the
moral was to the physical as three to one; in this case it
was many times more.

CHAPTER V

BARNEY LEADS OUT THE PRIVATEERS

AS SOON as war was declared it became evident that in face of the overwhelming power of Great Britain it would be extremely difficult, if not altogether impracticable, for our merchant shipping to continue its usual cruising for commercial gain. It was natural, therefore, that the owners of merchant vessels should turn to privateering, partly through patriotism, but mostly, it must be confessed, through desire for financial gain. However, most of our best ships were in distant waters so our first privateers were generally slow, of inferior or obsolete design, with an extemporized battery and hastily increased crew.

The British, even before our entry into the war, had used the convoy system for their West India trade. On the other hand, off the Nova Scotia and Newfoundland coasts their shipping sailed singly without escort and the concentration of their naval forces under Broke to watch for Rodgers prevented them from giving it proper protection either by escort or patrol. This gave an exceptional opportunity to our privateers, inefficient though they then were. Mahan estimates that before the end of September over two hundred prizes had been taken; one hundred and fifty on the Nova Scotia-Newfoundland cruising ground, twenty-five off our own coast, and twenty-five in the West Indies. On the debit side of the ledger many of the privateers were themselves taken—no less than twenty-four during July and August in Nova Scotia waters alone. But the balance certainly was highly in our favor.

Perhaps you would be interested in taking a cruise with

[233]

Joshua Barney on the schooner *Rossie,* the most famous of our early privateers. This old Revolutionary commodore had followed the sea for over forty years. His capture of the sloop-of-war *General Monk* had made him famous. Though now an old man, he had lost nothing of his energy and cunning, and wanted to get into the ring once more. The *Rossie* hailed from Baltimore, a port noted for its fast-sailing schooners. She carried 14 little guns and 120 men—an extra large complement for manning prizes. On July 12 she sailed; three days later reached the open sea and bowled along northeastward past the purple Gulf Stream.

In the first week at sea six American vessels were warned of the war. On the twenty-third a British frigate got close enough to ease off twenty-five shot at the *Rossie* and nearly ended her career before it started. In another week the cruising ground east of Halifax was reached and then a rushing business was done. Let us glance through Barney's log and see how a privateer worked:

"July 30, chased by a frigate; outsailed her. July 31, took and burnt the ship *Princess Royal.* August 1, took and manned the ship *Kitty.* 2, took and burnt the following: brig *Fame,* brig *Devonshire,* schooner *Squid;* and took the brig *Two Brothers*—put on board her sixty prisoners, and sent her to St. John's, to be exchanged for as many Americans. 3, took and sunk the brig *Henry* and the schooner *Racehorse;* burnt the schooner *Halifax,* manned the brig *William* (arrived) and gave the *Two Brothers* to 40 prisoners, and sent them to St. John's on parole. 9, took the ship *Jeanie,* after a short action, she mounting 12 guns; sent her for the United States (arrived)."

Twelve ships in eleven days—pretty good work. Perhaps, too, some American seamen gained their freedom if prisoners were exchanged. Now as Barney went down the

American coast his captures ceased. Before arriving at Newport he spoke nine American vessels returning to port. There on August 30 the old fellow ended his cruise. Again he was a national hero. As Hull had led the way for our naval captains so Barney had set the fashion for the privateer skippers—and aroused the cupidity of the shipowners. That has often, we must confess, proved a powerful influence in war as well as peace. To profiteer at the expense of the enemy seems an excellent measure to encourage. Alas, we fear that these and other persons still had sufficient time and opportunity to profiteer at the expense of our own sailors and soldiers.

During this first period of privateering other well-known and successful privateers were the *Dolphin, Globe, Highflyer, Yankee, Paul Jones, Comet, Nonesuch,* and *Saratoga.* These little craft gave officers and men their schooling for later more extended and scientific cruises.

CHAPTER VI

THE *UNITED STATES* AND
THE *MACEDONIAN*

THE CRUISES of Rodgers, Hull, and Porter, and the numerous captures made by our privateers showed the British that the American problem was not going to be so simple as they had at first expected. The loss of the *Guerrière* was a blow at their naval prestige which must be countered. As usual, when once aroused as to the seriousness of the situation, their measures were most energetic; they did not send a boy to do a man's errand. The Jamaica, Leeward Islands, and Halifax stations were on September 26 consolidated under the command of Admiral Sir John Warren. His force was increased until at the end of the year it reached the formidable total of eleven sail of the line, thirty-four frigates, twenty-eight sloops, and eighteen smaller craft. In addition, about seven of the line and as many frigates were stationed about the Azores, Madeiras, and St. Helena as a result of Rodgers' passage through those waters.

In the same way our Navy was stimulated to greater efforts by its first successes. During the autumn and early winter no less than six forces commenced cruises on the high seas:

Port of sailing	Date of sailing	Commander	Vessels and rates	Remarks
Boston	Oct. 8	Rodgers Smith	*President,* 44 *Congress,* 38	Joint cruise against trade

Boston	Oct. 8	Decatur	*United States,* 44	Captured *Macedonian*
		Sinclair	*Argus,* 16	Independent cruise
Delaware	Oct. 13	Jacob Jones	*Wasp,* 16	Captured *Frolic*
Boston	Oct. 26	Bainbridge	*Constitution,* 44	Captured *Java*
		Lawrence	*Hornet,* 18	Captured *Peacock*
Delaware	Oct. 28	Porter	*Essex,* 32	Pacific cruise
Boston	Dec. 17	Evans	*Chesapeake,* 38	Independent cruise

On October 8 Rodgers and Decatur sailed from Boston with their combined squadron of four ships so as to afford each other mutual support against blockading forces. "I feel a confidence," wrote Rodgers to the Department, "that with prudent policy, we shall, barring unforeseen accidents, not only annoy their commerce, but embarrass the commanders of their public ships, equally to the advantage of our commerce and the disadvantage of theirs." Two days after sailing the squadron chased the *Nymphe,* 38, without success, and next day the *United States* and *Argus* parted company.

Rodgers kept on toward the Great Bank of Newfoundland. There on the eighteenth he made a rich prize: the Jamaica packet *Swallow* with $200,000 in coin on board. On the thirty-first, in latitude 32°, longitude 33°, he gave chase to three sail: the *Galatea* frigate and two merchant vessels. The *President* gained rapidly on the *Galatea,* but when night came on the chase was lost. Unlucky Rodgers! The *Congress* took one of the merchant vessels, the whaler *Argo.* After this failure the detachment kept on to the Cape Verde Islands; then Rodgers turned about and came home via Bermuda. The two frigates sailed into Boston just in time to hear the new year come in.

The material results of this cruise were most meager—only nine prizes. Still the indirect effects were most important: it led the enemy to a wide dispersion of effort and held off much of his force from our waters, thus confirming those ideas of Robert Morris which we have discussed in an earlier chapter. The Admiralty reported to Warren:

"Rear Admiral Beauclerk with two of the line, two frigates, and two sloops, is stationed in the neighborhood of Madeira and the Azores, lest Bainbridge should come into that quarter to take the place of Commodore Rodgers, who was retiring from it about the time you state Commodore Bainbridge was expected to sail. Commodore Owen, who had preceded Admiral Beauclerk in this station, with a ship of the line and three other vessels, is not yet returned from the cruise on which the appearance of the enemy near the Azores had obliged their Lordships to send this force; while the *Colossus* and *Elephant,* with the *Rhin* and *Armide,* are but just returned from similar services." This reads like the dispositions taken against Count von Spee's squadron in 1914. A small squadron at large upon the high seas invariably ties up a vastly superior force of the enemy until it is brought to action.

While Rodgers had always advocated squadron cruises, Decatur believed that single ships scattered over a wider area could do more injury to the enemy. Therefore, as soon as he parted from Rodgers, he in turn sent off the *Argus* on an independent cruise. Captain Arthur Sinclair headed his swift little craft for Cape St. Roque, the easternmost point of Brazil, a cruising ground later frequented by Semmes in the *Alabama* and Köhler in the *Karlsruhe.* The focal points of the trade routes remain always the same.

Only a few days after leaving the *United States* the *Argus* made an unpleasant rendezvous, with two sail of the line and four other vessels. She had need of all her speed now. Being heavily laden for a long cruise, much of her equipment had to be cast over the side, including anchors and boats. Thus lightened, the *Argus* held her own for three thrilling days and nights. Sinclair showed his skill by actually taking and manning a prize while his pursuers were in sight. Finally he distanced his pursuers and reached his cruising ground. From Cape St. Roque he worked his way up the South American coast as far as Surinam and then sailed toward Bermuda. After ninety-six days at sea the little *Argus* ended her cruise at New York. Six valuable prizes were made.

Meanwhile Decatur in the *United States* had kept on toward Madeira. October twenty-fifth, in latitude 29°, longitude 29° 30', a large frigate was sighted. She was the *Macedonian,* a fine ship with a crack crew; or at least so she was thought before the fight. The ships compared with each other exactly as had the *Constitution* and *Guerrière*. Whereas Hull had decided to force the issue to a quick decision by fighting at pistol shot, Decatur now planned to fight at long range and gradually wear down his opponent. It is interesting to note the cold-blooded, even scientific, manner in which he went about his business— a man who only nine years before, was a reckless dare-devil with no thought in his mind but boarding.

Decatur handled his ship with remarkable skill; his gunners loaded with rapidity and aimed with splendid accuracy. It was then the pride of American seamen that every shot be well aimed. They put over one hundred shot into their enemy's hull, brought down his mizzenmast and shot off both fore and main topmasts. It was a wonderful exhibition of gunnery. On the other hand, Captain Carden handled his ship so poorly that part of the time his guns could not bear. His gunners put on a poor show indeed and made few hits. In an hour and a half they had had enough; our victory was as decisive as any might wish.

As the tactics were so different, it may prove interesting to compare the results of this fight with those of Hull's battle. Decatur had taken ninety minutes to win, against twenty-five for Hull; he had inflicted 104 casualties on the enemy against 79 for Hull; this was counterbalanced by the smaller material damage he had caused. Neither American ship had received any material injury worth mentioning and the personnel losses were equally small: fourteen on the *Constitution* and eleven on the *United States*. Thus the results of two radically different tactical methods were identical. We confess a preference for Hull's "downright fighting," as against Decatur's skillful maneuvering and long-range gunnery. Other things being equal, it was certainly more spectacular and created a more vivid moral effect. It is amusing to read the accusations of trickery and unfair tactics made against Decatur by an enemy seeking an excuse for defeat. Before the battle of Arbela it was suggested to Alexander that he make a night attack on the Persian camp. He declined, in his own words, "to steal a victory," wishing to convince his enemy once and for all that even with everything in his favor he could not stand against the Macedonians. Perhaps this same idea actuated Hull in deciding to beat the British at their own game, a point-blank gun fight, yardarm to yardarm.

As his prize was in fairly good condition, Decatur decided to bring her into port. On December 4 the *Macedonian,* under her new colors, came into Newport. The *United States* went on to New London. Lieutenant Hamilton hurried by post to Washington with the report of the action and the captured colors. Imagine how the news spread as his horses galloped along the old Boston post road. He came to the capital just as a ball to our naval officers was in progress. His appearance on the ballroom floor with the British man-of-war ensign over his arm was the first intimation Washington had received of Decatur's victory. A dramatic moment it must have been!

CHAPTER VII

THE *WASP* AND THE *FROLIC*

ON OCTOBER 13 the 18-gun sloop *Wasp* left the Delaware Capes. Jacob Jones was her captain, and a good one, too. On the sixteenth he ran into a heavy gale; well we know them. If now they batter a 1500-ton destroyer about and smash in her bridge windows, what must they then have done to a little sloop. In fact, on this occasion, gigantic waves smashed the *Wasp's* jib boom and washed two seamen overboard. The next evening at 11:30, in latitude 37°, longitude 65°, a number of ships were made out in the dim light. Were they part of a merchant convoy or a squadron of men-of-war? Jones determined to find out, so he tracked them until morning. Imagine how eagerly he and his men watched for the first streaks of dawn in the east. At last straining eyes made them out to be six merchantmen, four heavily armed, and a British sloop-of-war. The lay could not have been better.

The vessels in sight were part of a convoy of fourteen vessels from Honduras. The *Wasp's* gale had scattered it over the face of the ocean. The *Frolic* sloop, Captain Whinyates, had lost her main yard and had several sails blown to ribbons. On the seventeenth the sloop collected six merchant vessels and lay to to repair damages. Early on the eighteenth the *Wasp* came on the scene and Whinyates stood down to fight. First he showed Spanish colors as a ruse—just as British merchantmen used our colors during the submarine campaign. When he saw that the *Wasp* was not deceived he hoisted his battle flags. The British had ten guns in the broadside to our nine; our crew was a little larger. The ships were equal in material power; results would judge their efficiency.

The sea was rough; the little craft rolled and pitched about in lively fashion. It was a bad day for gunnery, so Jones decided to fight alongside his foe. On he came before the fresh breeze; no firing until he could see the whites of their eyes. Then at sixty yards hell broke loose. Never was such a terrible hail of shot poured from the muzzles of a sloop's carronades. The *Frolic's* hull was smashed by the low-velocity shot, her decks literally swept as by a broom. After forty-three minutes of firing she was a helpless wreck, drifting in the trough of the seas. The ships came together; away went our boarders; resistance there was none, nor could there be. Out of 110 officers and crew only 20 remained unwounded. The *Wasp* had lost only ten men, but her rigging had been shot to pieces. It had been a wonderful fight.

But fortune does not always favor the brave, or even the skillful. A great ship came over the horizon, the *Poictiers*, 74 guns. Now was seen the value of the *Frolic's* resistance. Let it be a lesson to every naval man! Neither ship could move; victor and victim alike fell into the hands of the new entrant upon the scene. This misfortune did not dim the honors won by Jacob Jones and his crew. When they arrived home after exchange an enthusiastic reception awaited them. Congress voted $25,000 in prize money for these heroes of the hour.

CHAPTER VIII

BAINBRIDGE WINS HIS VICTORY

THE CAPTAINS who had the ill luck to be stationed ashore when the war commenced naturally were desirous of gaining commands at sea. After her victory the *Constitution* became the most desirable command in our entire service. "Captain Hull," says Lossing, "with noble generosity and rare contentment with the laurels already won, gave up the command of his frigate for the sole purpose of giving others a chance to distinguish themselves." His successor in command was one of our old and most unlucky friends, William Bainbridge. The old fellow came forward for a last cruise to round out his none too successful career and it is a pleasure to record the accomplishments of "Old Ironsides" under his efficient command.

On October 26 Bainbridge sailed out from Boston. With him was the 18-gun sloop *Hornet,* still under eager young Lawrence, "Captain Jim," as he was affectionately known throughout the service. David Porter was ordered to join the commodore with the *Essex* at one of a number of designated rendezvous. Bainbridge's plan, as communicated to Porter, was to proceed first to Porto Praya in the Cape Verde Islands; then on about November 27 he was to sail for Fernando de Noronha, a small rocky island two hundred miles off the Brazilian coast. He expected to leave this second rendezvous by December 15 and to cruise south along the Brazilian coast until January 15. Later he proposed to carry out his orders to operate in the St. Helena area against the British East India trade.

The *Constitution* made such speed that she got far ahead

[244]

of schedule. Instead of waiting at Noronha until December 15, she was at Bahia on the thirteenth. As Noronha was a Portuguese possession the commodore pretended that his ships were British cruisers. In accordance with a pre-arranged plan he left for Porter a letter addressed to the captain of H. M. S. *Southampton.* This was written so as to convey information to Porter, but phrased so as to mean nothing should the letter fall into the hands of the enemy. Between the lines in sympathetic ink were orders for Porter to go to Cape Frio, near Rio de Janeiro.

At Bahia Bainbridge found the British sloop *Bonne Citoyenne,* which was somewhat superior to the *Hornet* in both armament and crew. She had on board an immense sum of money—said to be fifty thousand pounds—for transport to England. Our two ships blockaded the port until the twenty-sixth. The commodore then left the *Hornet* off the port while he cruised offshore along the trade routes. Fortune at last gave a boon to unlucky Bainbridge—sent a fine frigate into his arms!

This happened on the twenty-ninth. At nine o'clock in the forenoon two sails were made out. One was the large frigate *Java,* 38 guns, Captain Lambert; the other was the ship *William,* recently made prize. Neither captain had any thought of dodging the issue; each made ready to fight to the end; fighting canvas was spread and battle ensigns broken at every masthead. Bainbridge kept his royals spread to increase his speed in the light breeze. Lambert ordered his prize to make for Bahia.

The *Constitution* had a superiority in weight of broadside of 10 to 9 and slightly the larger crew. Englishmen had never worried at odds such as these, and Lambert saw his opportunity to avenge the *Guerrière.* At 2:10 P.M. the fight opened with desultory firing at long range, but in a few minutes the distance was down to two hundred yards. Then the real business of the day commenced. It was as finely contested a frigate action as ever was fought. Both captains maneuvered their ships with remarkable skill— tacked, wore, sailed on the wind and free, turned to right or left, and backed or filled their sails as occasion demanded. First one ship would gain an advantageous position, then the other, like two skilled wrestlers each in turn gaining a hold, only to have it broken by his opponent.

All this time the guns' crews were fast at work, rushing from one battery to the other as their captains tacked or wore. It was a grim hard work hauling at the gun tackles, ramming powder and shot, and slewing around the clumsy gun carriages to bring the enemy into the line of sight. The roaring of the guns was deafening; acrid smoke clouds swept along the decks; perspiration streamed from bodies stripped to the waist. Other men on deck strained and hauled on the braces, lifts, halliards, and sheets; swinging about the yards and setting sail under the direction of the sailing master and captain. Clouds of splinters flew over the decks.

For a time the battle is closely contested, but its issue is never in doubt. For Yankee gunners are the best in the world, and they have *iron sides* to protect them: twenty inches of stout oak beams. They cannot be beaten. Slowly but surely their superiority in gunnery—and also, we must state, in weight and metal—wears down the enemy. One after another the *Java's* spars crash down. Heroic Lambert fights well, but is killed. Lieutenant Chads already wounded, continues the fight in most gallant fashion, but cannot do the impossible. Nearly half of his crew is out of action, but still he fights.

The *Constitution* also has had her losses. Bainbridge himself has been severely wounded, but still keeps the deck,

still retains his command. For he is determined to have this
victory. Gallant Lieutenant Aylwin falls mortally wounded.
Already in the *Guerrière* fight he had earned a wound stripe
—and Isaac Hull's warm commendation. He had been
promoted to lieutenant and now commands the forecastle
guns. But this is his last fight. Well, he has seen two
British frigates lower their battle ensigns. His life has
been well spent. Over thirty others lie dead or wounded
about the decks or under the surgeon's knife in the cockpit.
An omelet cannot be made without breaking eggs, nor can
British frigates be won without losing men.

For two long hours the battle rages. Then Chads can
do no more, nor could any other. He surrenders. Here
is a fight in which there is honor enough for all, vanquished
as well as victors. And Bainbridge, after such buffets of
fate as few have received, at last has won his victory.

The losses have been heavy: 34 on the *Constitution* to
150 on the *Java*. Bainbridge, despite the slanders of William James, does all he can to alleviate the suffering of the
wounded. He is thanked by the British officers for his
kindness. The *Java* is a total wreck and has to be destroyed.
This much have the British accomplished—and we think it
a very worth-while accomplishment, too. If we wanted a
Java, we would have to build one.

The *Constitution* returned to Bahia. As she passed in
the *Hornet* saluted her with three thunderous cheers. What
music to a seaman's ears! Disturbing though it must have
been to Captain Pitt Barnaby Green of His Majesty's good
ship *Bonne Citoyenne*.

The prisoners were sent ashore on parole—the arrangements for exchange seem to have been very amicably arranged all through this war. We always had a good balance
in our favor. An examination of the shot holes through

the *Constitution's* hull showed that her sides were not as stout as had been thought; in fact they were rotten in places. So Bainbridge decided to go home—perhaps a bit too quickly. But let the old fellow enjoy his triumph. Before leaving, the commodore instructed Lawrence to continue the blockade of the British sloop. He gave the *Hornet* to Lieutenant Shubrick, a remarkably fine officer. Already he had seen two sea fights, and soon would see another!

"Old Ironsides" reached Boston on February 27. There a great reception awaited the commodore. He marched through the gaily decorated streets, arm in arm with Hull and Rodgers. Fifes and drums play "Yankee Doodle." It's a big Navy Day. Three frigate victories in as many months! Now the Navy rides on the top of the world. What is this order the Admiralty sends out: no more American 44's to be engaged by single British frigates. Ha, a mean trick the Yankees have played us—sending out disguised ships of the line. Pretty good disguise, don't you think, to have remained undetected for over a dozen years and to have lost Captain Dacres a hat!

CHAPTER IX

THE *HORNET* AND THE *PEACOCK*

WELL, LET'S come back to the Bahia blockade. Captain Jim for some time had been trying to get a fight out of the *Bonne Citoyenne*. Captain Green had not liked to venture out while the *Constitution* was about. Now she was gone, it was necessary to get another excuse. That was easy: he had to protect his treasure. How convenient that money proved! But if he wanted to fight could he not have intrusted it to his Portuguese friends for a few hours? That surely would be enough to lick the *Hornet*. Lawrence kept up the blockade for two weeks after Bainbridge left, getting much pleasure out of the situation. Then he was nearly caught himself, for down swooped the *Montagu*, 74. The *Hornet* in turn sought refuge in Bahia.

Lawrence now was in a fix. He knew how much consideration an English captain would give to Portuguese neutrality and saw his cruise about to end. After dark he made sail, crept slowly out of the entrance, and ran the blockade. Then he started up the coast and on February 4, took the merchant brig *Resolution* with $25,000 in specie on board. On the twenty-fourth he approached the mouth of the Demerare River and chased a merchant vessel. At anchor off the entrance he sighted a sloop-of-war, the *Espiegle*, 18.

This was game more to his liking. Prize money meant nothing to this young hero. He was fired by a passion for distinction. With Porter he had landed on the Tripolitan coast and fought hand to hand. With Decatur he had scaled the *Philadelphia's* side. In command of a little gunboat he had bombarded the Tripolitan forts at point-blank range. Now he must take a British man-of-war. His crew had been trained with great care, and to the fighting edge. Had not a British sloop refused to fight them for two weeks? They also wanted no prize money. They wanted to fight.

Before the *Hornet* could round the intervening shoals another sail came in sight. This was the 18-gun brig *Peacock*. A whole covey had been flushed. Which one he fought made no difference to Captain Jim. "The fresher fish, the better fish!" So said old Field Marshal Schwerin as he moved to the attack with his Prussians at Prague, and so thought Lawrence off the mouth of the Demerara! He bore down under press of sail for the *Peacock*. The *Espiegle* was anchored six miles off—might be attracted by the sound of the guns. Better get this *Peacock* quickly, Captain Jim!

At pistol shot the fight began. How those Hornets fought. This was not a fight, but a massacre! "My clerk," Lawrence said, "reported the time of the action as eleven minutes, but I thought fifteen minutes short enough, so I made it so in my report." When the *Peacock* surrendered over forty of her crew had been killed and wounded and she hoisted the signal of distress, her ensign with union down. Boats were lowered immediately to save her crew but she sank so quickly that nine of them, with three Americans were drowned. Lawrence had lost one killed and two wounded by the enemy fire and had two men burned by the bursting of one of his own carronades. The *Hornet's* hull was practically undamaged, but her sails and rigging had been somewhat cut up. When was there ever a victory like this?

Apprehensive that the *Espiegle* might come out, Lawrence

made haste to repair his damages and by nine that night was ready for a new fight. At 2:00 A.M. he got under way for home.

"On mustering next morning," he reported, "found we had 277 souls on board, including the crew of the American brig *Hunter,* of Portland, taken a few days before by the *Peacock.* And, as we had been on two-thirds allowance of provisions for some time, and had but 3,400 gallons of water on board, I reduced the allowance to three pints a man, and determined to make the best of my way to the United States."

On March 19 the *Hornet* dropped anchor off Martha's Vineyard. Thence she sailed to New York via Long Island Sound.

The report of her quick victory created a sensation, even among the enemy. A Halifax newspaper made the following comment relative to the sudden sinking of the *Peacock:* "If a vessel had been moored for the sole purpose of experiment, it is not probable that she could have been sunk in so short a time. It will not do for our vessels to fight theirs single-handed." Brave and chivalrous Lawrence became a national hero and the toast of every wardroom— the inspiration of every midshipman, a Hercules to many a young Theseus! Many a young fellow commencing his naval career must have felt as Theseus did on rolling back the stone, bringing out his father's sword and commencing his journey to Athens. "For he, it seems," says Plutarch, "had long since been secretly fired by the glory of Hercules, held him in the highest estimation, and was never more satisfied than in listening to any that gave an account of him; especially those that had seen him, or had been present at any action or saying of his."

Lawrence's reputation for chivalry was enhanced by his

kindness to the poor officers and men of the *Peacock,* who had lost all their clothing and gear. All the surviving officers addressed him a note of thanks, saying "we ceased to consider ourselves prisoners." Like the old heroes of Ossian, a fierce joy of fighting changed instantly to kindness and generosity once the issue was decided.

It may be interesting to present a condensed account of New York's reception for the Hornets. Admiral Gleaves quotes it from the *Evening Post:*

"On Tuesday, April 6, agreeable to a vote of the Common Council, a dinner was given to Captain Lawrence of the *Hornet* and his gallant crew. The dinner was given at that splendid edifice, Washington Hall. The seamen came in barges from their ship and landed at White Hall at half past two o'clock. They marched, attended by the elegant band of the 11th Regiment of the First Brigade of Artillery, through Pearl Street and Broadway to Washington Hall, cheered in every street they passed by the huzzas of their grateful and admiring countrymen. After the meats were removed, a visit was made them by the members of the Common Council, accompanied by Captain Lawrence. At the sight of their gallant commander they rose, cheered him with three times three, in a style that evinced it came from their hearts. In the evening the theater was brilliantly illuminated, and the proprietor having politely set aside the pit for the gallant tars of the *Hornet,* they went from their dinner table to the theater at six o'clock; the piece set for the evening being of a naval character the men were highly amused and entertained."

James Lawrence is now at the height of his fame. He is promoted to be captain and his joy has no limit when he is offered the *Constitution.* Eagerly he looks forward to the performance of new exploits with that fine ship.

But Mars is a hard master, and a most treacherous one. See how he raises a Hannibal, a Marcus Antonius, a Bonaparte, a Ludendorff to the pinnacles of success, only to cast them down ruthlessly into the depths of defeat.

Truly did the Danish chieftain say to Beowulf:

> The flower of thy might
> lasts now a while; but erelong it shall be
> that sickness or sword thy strength shall minish,
> or fang of fire, or flooding billow,
> or bite of blade, or brandished spear,
> or odious age; or the eyes' clean beam
> wax dull and darken: Death even thee
> in haste shall o'erwhelm, thou hero of war!

Yes, war is a hard game. It is a cruel fate that the Norns have spun for our brave young captain. One by one its steps unfold, each one leading inexorably to the next. The *Constitution* is being repaired, will not be ready for some months. The *Chesapeake* is ready now but her captain is sick. He must be replaced and who is more available than Lawrence. Our captain, brave though he be, does not relish service on such an unlucky ship. He would prefer to remain on his little *Hornet*. But the orders stand and must be obeyed. Once the decision is final, Lawrence accepts it loyally, is confident in his ability to meet any situation. And, should the Fates prove unkind, Captain Jim will know how to finish in style. Doubtless he knows the old Japanese verse:

> Man has to die once and once only;
> He should make his death glorious.

He will know how to act it, too, when the time comes.

CHAPTER X

PORTER SWEEPS THE PACIFIC

MEANWHILE Porter in the *Essex* had been making a cruise of his own. On November 27 he ran into Porto Praya and took on supplies. Next he set his course for the second rendezvous, Noronha. On December 11 he made a lucky strike: the packet *Nocton* with $55,000 in specie. Two days later he dropped anchor off Noronha. Hearing that two British ships had sailed thence a few days before and had left a letter addressed to Sir James Yeo of the *Southampton,* Porter pretended to be that officer and obtained the letter. Here is how it read:

My Dear Mediterranean Friend,
Probably you may stop here. Don't attempt to water; it is attended with too much difficulty. I learned before I left England that you were bound for the Brazil coast; if so we may meet at St. Salvador (Bahia) or Rio de Janeiro. I should be happy to meet and converse on our old affairs of captivity. Recollect our secret in those times.

Your friend of His Majesty's ship *Acasta,*

KERR

The last sentence indicated a further message in sympathetic ink. When heat was applied to the paper other words stood out:

I am bound for St. Salvador (Bahia), thence off Cape Frio, where I intend to cruise until the first of January. Go off Cape Frio, to the northward of Rio de Janeiro, and keep a lookout for me.

Tripolitan captivity had its advantages after all.

The discovery of the *Bonne Citoyenne* had kept the *Con-*

[254]

stitution at Bahia and the action with the *Java* on December 29 resulted in her return home. Thus Bainbridge failed to keep his engagement. On the twenty-sixth Porter arrived off Cape Frio; he cruised between there and St. Catherine, taking the schooner *Elizabeth* on the twenty-ninth. When the commodore failed to appear Porter came to a bold decision: to round the Horn and sweep British whalers from the Pacific. After watering at St. Catherine he headed south on January 26 along the trail blazed by Drake and Anson, to link his little *Essex* with the *Golden Hind* and *Centurion.*

On February 14 Porter rounded the Horn, passed Staten Island and Orange Bay—names which reminded our adventurers of old Dutch explorers. On March 5 a brief stop was made at the deserted island of Mocha; on the fifteenth the *Essex* dropped anchor in Valparaiso. Here cheering news came on board: Chile had gained her independence from Spain. This changed a hostile port to one which for the time at least professed neutrality; stores could be bought with the money so conveniently furnished by the *Nocton.*

After supplies had been replenished Porter put to sea. On March 25 he heard that the Viceroy of Peru had sent out an armed vessel to attack American ships, and that this vessel, the *Nereyda* 16 guns, had captured the whalers *Walker* and *Barclay* off Coquimbo. Sailing north over the ground where later Graaf von Spee fought brave Cradock, Porter soon came up with the *Nereyda*. Releasing the Americans on board and throwing over her guns, he sent her back to the Viceroy with a sharp protest against his piratical behavior. Near Callao the *Barclay* was retaken. Her master said that the Galapagos Islands were the base and resting place for British whalers.

On April 17 the islands were made, but not the sharpest

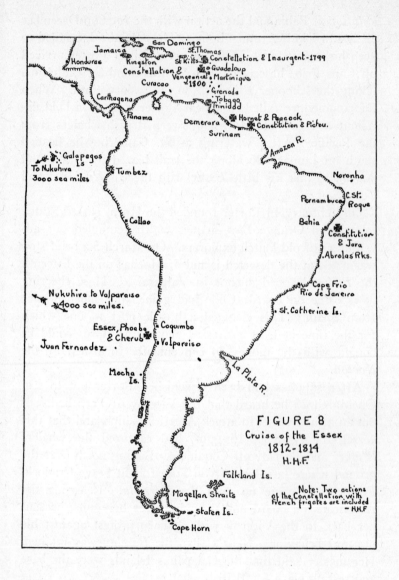

Jamaica
San Domingo
St. Thomas
Honduras
Kingston
St. Kitts
Constellation & Insurgent - 1799
Constellation &
Guadeloup
Vengeance Martinique
1800
Curacao
Grenada
Carthagena
Tobago
Trinidad
Panama
Hornet & Peacock
Demerara
Constitution & Picton.
Surinam
Amazon R.
Galapagos Is
Noronha
To Nukuhiva
Tumbez
3000 sea miles
C. St.
Pernambuco
Roque
Bahia
Callao
Constitution
& Java
Abrolas Rks.
Cape Frio
Nukuhiva to Valparaiso
Rio de Janeiro
4000 sea miles.
St. Catherine Is.
Essex, Phoebe
Coquimbo
& Cherub
Juan Fernandez
Valparaiso
La Plata R.
Mocha
Is.

FIGURE 8
Cruise of the Essex
1812 - 1814
H.H.F.

Falkland Is.

Note: Two actions
of the Constellation with
Magellan Straits
french frigates are included
Stafen Is.
- H.H.F
Cape Horn

From the original painting by John W. Jarvis

DAVID PORTER

PORTER'S SQUADRON LEAVING TUMBEZ BAY

lookout could disclose a single vessel. The landing party, however, made a cheering discovery: in a letter box were messages addressed to the captains of British vessels. The *Essex* lay in ambush, like a lion waiting at the water hole for its prey to appear. They were not long delayed in coming. On the twenty-ninth three fine ships stood in: the *Montezuma, Georgiana,* and *Policy.* All were taken; the *Georgiana* was converted into a cruiser, her battery increased to 16 guns. Lieutenant Downes broke his colors on May 8 and with a crew of forty-one from the *Essex* sailed off on an independent cruise.

Now the prizes came thick and fast: Porter took the letters of marque *Atlantic* and *Greenwich;* Downes the armed vessels *Hector, Catherine,* and *Rose.* The latter craft was sent away to St. Helena with the prisoners, who already were becoming a problem. On June 19 the entire detachment assembled at Tumbez in the Gulf of Guayaquil. Now the *Georgiana* was converted to a storeship. Downes commissioned the *Atlantic* as the *Essex Junior.* Sixty men and twenty light guns made her a splendid cruiser.

Porter had won his own promotion—commodore he was, with a fine squadron of nine vessels. On July 9 he sent off the *Essex Junior* with five prizes to Valparaiso. With the *Essex, Georgiana,* and *Greenwich,* he once more headed for the Galapagos. Again luck favored him, for on the thirteenth he got his grip on the *Charlton,* 10 guns, the *Seringapatam,* 14 guns, and the *New Zealander,* 8 guns— all fine prizes. Prisoners again were mounting up; the *Charlton* took them off to Rio de Janeiro. The *Georgiana* sailed home with a cargo of oil valued at $100,000. The battery of the *Seringapatam* was increased to 22 guns.

After making these dispositions the voyage to the Galapagos was resumed. On August 4 they came over the horizon and a long wait commenced. It was not until September 15 that the next and last prize was made, the *Sir Andrew Hammond,* 12 guns. The taking of these twelve prizes practically swept the British merchant flag from the Eastern Pacific.

Downes now rejoined the commodore, with bad news. The large frigate *Phoebe* and two smaller men-of-war were en route to the Pacific. The Chileans were showing a pronounced leaning toward our enemies. It was necessary to refit the ships. The squadron got under way for a long cruise, to the Marquesas in mid-Pacific. Six ships in all now, they left the Galapagos on October 2. On the twenty-fourth they arrived at the fine port of Nukuhiva.

Here, instead of peace and quiet, the war spirit also reigned. In order to refit his ships, Porter had to ally himself with the nearest tribes and conduct arduous mountain campaigns against the others. A breastwork of water casks was named Fort Madison in honor of the President. Here on November 19 the commodore hoisted the American flag and took formal possession of the island in the name of the United States. The *New Zealander* was sent home; the *Seringapatam, Greenwich,* and *Hammond* were moored close inshore under the fort.

On December 12 the *Essex* and *Essex Junior,* having completed their refit, set sail for Valparaiso. Here along the route later traveled by Graf von Spee on a similar errand we must leave our adventurers for a time. Leaving a secure base behind him, Porter was deliberately seeking out his enemy; despite his weak battery, he was fully confident that his fine crew would bring him success. Alas, the gallant *Essex* was going to her last fight. Let us hope that, as their little ships plowed their way through the placid waters of the Southern Pacific, no presentiment of their heroic, though untimely, fate disturbed the thoughts of our brave seamen. Soon David Glasgow Farragut, aged ten, will learn a lesson he can never forget: how Americans can fight, even after hope of victory has vanished. Perhaps in later years his experience on that terrible day will be used to the advantage of his country, to win victories worth many an *Essex!*

CHAPTER XI

THE ROYAL NAVY TIGHTENS ITS GRIP

ON DECEMBER 17 Captain Evans put to sea from Boston in the *Chesapeake*. He made a prolonged cruise in the Atlantic. Here are the milestones on the track he followed: Cape Verde Islands, Surinam, Windward Islands, Porto Rico, Santo Domingo, Bermuda, and back into Boston on April 9. The *Chesapeake's* poor luck was proverbial—only six prizes were made in all these months. Evans went ashore sick—would never command again. Lawrence would take his ship on her last cruise.

The government had been so delighted with the accomplishments of our Navy in the early months of the war that on January 2, 1813, Congress authorized the construction of four sail of the line, six large frigates, and six large sloops-of-war. None of these vessels was completed during the war except three sloops: *Wasp, Peacock,* and *Frolic.* As vessels of the sloop type could be built quickly and break the blockade at will, it seems that it would have been better policy to have concentrated most of our efforts on their construction.

During 1812 the British had not yet been able to organize a strict blockade of our coast. But as Warren's force increased and the European situation was eased by the failure of Napoleon's Russian adventure, he was instructed to make more aggressive action. Since October a detachment of three brigs had been watching Charleston; now they were strongly reënforced. On February 4 a powerful squadron of two sail of the line, three frigates, and three smaller vessels entered the Chesapeake, and were just in time to stop the luckless *Constellation* and lock her up in Norfolk. A force of similar composition anchored in the Delaware. Large squadrons took and constantly maintained their blockading stations off New York and Newport. Boston was guarded by the *Shannon* and *Tenedos*. Smaller craft were daily in sight off Portsmouth.

Now we began to feel the iron grip of sea power on our throats. Our large bays and sounds rendered our coast extremely vulnerable to naval blockade and attack. Our foreign trade became practically nonexistent. Even our coastal trade was ruined, and as roads were poor and transportation on shore very difficult, this practically cut off one part of the country from the other. It became increasingly difficult for privateers to leave and enter our ports or to send in their prizes. Even our men-of-war could not, in many cases, break the blockade. The fine frigate *Constellation* was held close in Norfolk without the slightest chance of gaining the sea. In fact, Charles Stewart had to protect his ship from cutting-out attacks. The *United States* and *Macedonian* would be blockaded in Long Island Sound for the rest of the war; two of our frigates would be captured in leaving port; another by an enemy expedition into our own territory. Readers will, in due course, become acquainted with the details of these disasters.

Nor were these the worst. The orders of the Admiralty were "to destroy and lay waste all towns and districts of the United States found accessive to the attacks of the British armaments." The Chesapeake Bay area offered a great opportunity for such attacks and the little town of Hampton was sacked in a fashion which even the British admit was "revolting to human nature." Our national capital even was to suffer from enemy occupation.

While it was evident that our cruiser warfare must be

seriously handicapped by the tightening death grip of the
Royal Navy, preparations were pushed for a new and ambitious series of spring cruises. These were as follows:

Port of Date of sailing sailing	Commander	Vessels and rates	Remarks
Boston April 30	Rodgers	*President,* 44	Independent cruise
	Smith	*Congress,* 38	Independent cruise
Boston June 1	Lawrence	*Chesapeake,* 38	Captured by *Shannon*
New London June 1	Decatur	*United States,* 44	Driven back into New London by B r i t i s h squadron.
	Jacob Jones	*Macedonian,* 38	
	Biddle	*Hornet,* 18	
New York June 18	Allen	*Argus,* 18	Captured by *Pelican*

On the last day of April John Rodgers commenced his
third cruise in the *President.* The *Congress* being ready
at the same time, they sailed in company so as to give mutual
support against the blockading detachment. Boston was a
most difficult port to blockade and Rodgers had no difficulty in slipping out without fighting. He states that encounter with the *Shannon* and *Tenedos* was expected, and
later most vigorously denied British reports that he had
avoided action with these ships. When two days out he
chased the 18-gun brig-sloop *Curlew* without success. On
May 3 he sighted two men-of-war, which he took to be
La Hogue, 74, and *Nymphe,* 38. However, by this time
the commerce-raiding complex had won him to her in-

fluence and he was not taking any too good a look at strange men-of-war. The following emasculating instructions issued by the Secretary of the Navy also had doubtless done their share in this remolding of his character: "It is not even good policy to meet an equal, unless in special circumstances where a great object is to be gained without a great sacrifice. His commerce is our true game, for there he is indeed vulnerable." Fortunately, most of the captains found occasions for evading this plausible but pernicious doctrine.

On May 8 the *President* and *Congress* separated. The latter followed the Cape Verde-Surinam-Bermuda route recently so unsuccessfully covered by the *Chesapeake*. Her luck was even worse, for in seven months of weary cruising Captain Smith could report only three prizes. On December 14 he came into Portsmouth with this bad news to tell. His Christmas could not have been merry.

The very poor results won by the *Chesapeake* and *Congress* clearly proved that in areas where the convoy system was used our frigates could do little to injure the enemy. However, it must be remembered that the mere fact of having to use the convoy system imposed a most serious disadvantage upon the enemy. Ships must delay their sailing for long periods to wait for the convoy to be formed—and when formed it made slow progress across the oceans. Large numbers of men-of-war were required to escort the convoys and heavy supporting squadrons had to be stationed in the Azores and at St. Helena. The remedy was almost as bad as the disease. Thus by merely showing themselves along the trade routes our frigates accomplished something.

Rodgers, in discussing plans of operation before the war, had made a very interesting statement: "It is very generally believed that the coasts of England, Ireland, and Scotland are always swarming with British men-of-war, and that their commerce would be amply protected. This, however, I well know by my experience, in my voyages when a youth, to be incorrect; and that it has always been their policy to keep their enemies as far distant from their shores as possible, by stationing their ships at the commencement of a war on the enemy's coasts, and in other distant situations, and thereby be enabled to protect their commerce in a twofold degree." This entirely correct statement he could have confirmed by a study of Paul Jones's campaigns.

The poor material results of Rodgers' last two voyages now induced the commodore to make a direct attack upon enemy shipping in its home waters, where the compulsory convoy law did not apply. Unfortunately Rodgers was no longer the man to execute his own well-conceived plan. He was not a Paul Jones—or even a Porter. More like Pericles was he becoming every day. The very words with which Plutarch described the great Athenian might be applied to John Rodgers, at this state of his career, without the change of a punctuation mark: "In his military conduct, he gained a great reputation for wariness; he would not by his own good will engage in any fight which had much uncertainty or hazard; he did not envy the glory of generals whose rash adventures fortune favored with brilliant success, however they were admired by others; nor did he think them worthy his imitation."

With this prelude let us accompany Rodgers on his cruise. On May 8 he parted with the *Congress* in latitude 39° 30′, longitude 60°. Fortune did not meet him off the Newfoundland Banks; he sailed to find her off the Azores. Thence on June 6 he headed for the British Isles on the track of a convoy. Although he never could reach it, four stragglers were made prizes between the ninth and thirteenth: the brig *Kitty*, packet *Duke of Montrose*, letter of marque

Maria, and schooner *Falcon.* Not thinking it proper to risk his large ship in the narrow waters of the English Channel, he decided to proceed north-about into the North Sea along the track of Paul Jones. "To my astonishment," he reported, "in all this route I did not meet a single vessel until I made the Shetland Islands, and even there, nothing but Danish vessels trading to England under British licenses."

On June 27 the *President* put into Bergen, Norway, for provisions, but all she could get were sixteen barrels of rye meal and some cheese. So on July 2 she put to sea again, accompanied by the privateer *Scourge.* At the Orkney Islands it was learned that a large convoy would leave Archangel for England about the middle of July, and that its escort would be two sloops. Rodgers headed for North Cape to intercept this rich prize. On the twelfth he took the brig *Jean and Ann* and on the eighteenth the *Daphne.* The next day Rodgers sighted two sail, which were thought to be a ship of the line and a frigate. These vessels now chased him for eighty hours of continuous daylight, "during which time, owing to different changes of wind in their favor, they were brought quite as near to us as was desirable."

Now this sounds really exciting—until we read what the British accounts of this bizarre chase say. They prove that the ships which chased the *President* were the 12-pounder frigate *Alexandria,* 32, and the *Spitfire,* a sloop of 16 guns. With the assistance of the *Scourge*—if, indeed, it should be needed—Rodgers could have taken these ships with ease. The joke is on our commodore—such as it is—and our British friends are entitled to their laugh.

Having thus lost his chance for the Archangel convoy, the commodore took station in the northern approaches to the Irish Sea. There, between July 25 and August 2, three prizes fell into his hands: the ship *Eliza Swan,* bark *Lion,* and brig *Alert.* Then, "finding that the enemy had a superior force in that vicinity, I found it expedient to change my ground." Running down the Irish coast to Cape Clear, he headed for the Newfoundland Banks. There he took the brigs *Shannon* and *Fly.* One of them said that a ship of the line and frigate were near at hand. That started him off again.

On September 22 the *President* reached Nantucket Shoals. There Rodgers did quite a clever stunt, luring under his guns the schooner *Highflyer,* 6 guns. She was the tender to the British commander in chief and had on board confidential papers of great value. One showed the dispositions of the British blockading forces. After studying these Rodgers decided to run into Newport, and there he arrived on the twenty-seventh. His prizes totaled twelve. He reported: "During my cruise, although I have not had it in my power to add any additional luster to the character of our little Navy, I have nevertheless, rendered essential service to my country, I hope, by harassing the enemy commerce, and employing to his disadvantage, more than a dozen times the force of a single frigate."

While this is very true, we feel that he could have accomplished much more by more venturesome conduct. In failing to enter the English Channel he lost a great chance, for when the *Argus* and *Wasp* later entered this most fruitful cruising ground they did not encounter even a frigate. It seems that Rodgers was too much impressed by the possibility of superior forces coming over the horizon. An alternation of daring and caution is the secret of cruiser warfare: a quick dash close into the enemy's waters, several days' busy work, then a rapid shift to a new station —that is the combination.

CHAPTER XII

"DON'T GIVE UP THE SHIP"

ON MAY 20 James Lawrence assumed command of the unlucky *Chesapeake* in the Boston Navy Yard. Admiral Gleaves has done a public service in dispelling many of the myths which have arisen concerning this ship and her crew. Lawrence found the ship in good material condition and ready for sea. While young, new to their posts, and somewhat inexperienced, the officers were good, though not quite up to the high average of our service. The crew, while having some vacancies, were generally satisfactory. There were later found to be thirty-six English deserters on board and twenty-two joined the British service at Halifax, but an examination of the muster roll shows few names of a distinctly foreign aspect. There was some dissatisfaction about the payment of prize money, but this seems to have been adjusted. Perhaps the ship's unlucky reputation was the biggest handicap with which Lawrence had to contend. Given a month's time on the high seas he would have made the *Chesapeake* into a good ship; in three a crack one.

On May 30 the frigate left the yard and anchored in President Roads. Early on the morning of June 1 a large frigate was seen off the port. A gun flashed, a smoke puff covered her side. Thus did the knights-errant of 1812 send their challenges. Lawrence fired a gun in reply and hoisted his flag—"Sailor's Rights and Free Trade"—at his foremast. So did he indicate his acceptance.

The frigate off the port was the *Shannon*, similar in every respect to the *Chesapeake*. She was a fine ship and had had but one captain for her entire seven years of service,

Sir Philip Bowes Vere Broke. One of the outstanding officers of the British service Broke had made the *Shannon* the crack frigate of the Royal Navy. Her crew was organized with a perfection rarely found and unusual attention had been given to the rapid and accurate service of their guns. For some time he had been trying to engage one of our frigates and while in company with the *Tenedos* had challenged the *President* and *Congress*. Now he had deliberately sent the *Tenedos* away as he thought that this would give him a better chance for a fight. Enemy though he was, Americans admired him for his ability as a fighter and for his chivalrous conduct. After the exchange of gun shots which we have witnessed, Broke, in order to be surer of a fight, went below and wrote his famous challenge.

In this he assured Lawrence that he would take every precaution lest other vessels should interfere with their duel. His letter is worthy of careful study, because I am not so sure that, in a future war with a chivalrous enemy of unequal strength, challenges to actions between equal forces may not again come into vogue. An important moral advantage can undoubtedly be gained by the issue of challenges which an enemy does not accept. The conclusion of Broke's letter we consider very fine: "You will feel it as a compliment if I say that the result of our meeting may be the most grateful service I can render to my country; and I doubt not that you, equally confident of success, will feel convinced that it is only by repeated triumphs in even combats, that your little Navy can now hope to console your country for the loss of that trade it can no longer protect."

Broke sent the letter ashore by a fisherman. It never reached Lawrence.

Captain Jim was no man to wait for formal challenges. The sight of an enemy frigate off our coast was challenge enough for him. God grant that no officer who wears our uniform will ever need more. While his crew was preparing to get under way, he wrote to the Secretary of the Navy and his brother-in-law. "An English frigate," he said to the latter, "is close in with the lighthouse, and we are now clearing ship for action." Let American officers take that for their motto!

At noon the anchor came out of the mud; the *Chesapeake* commenced her last cruise! Broke stood out to sea to get plenty of fighting room, which neither he nor Lawrence needed. What did two duelists ready to shoot at five paces need of a wide meadow? At about 6:00 P.M. the ships were nearing each other for their death struggle. Broke could have tried to rake the *Chesapeake* as she came down before the wind, but he did not. Lawrence later could have raked the *Shannon* at point-blank range. No! Some other captain could have done so, not Lawrence!

Instead, just at the last moment, he luffed into the wind to a parallel course. His crew, electrified at his refusal to "steal a victory," cheered three times. Those spontaneous cheers were worth more than a raking broadside! As the *Chesapeake* was standing down to fight, Broke spoke to his crew the simple words that veterans understand: "Don't try to dismast her, fire into her quarters; main deck into the main deck; quarter-deck into the quarter-deck. Kill the men and the ship is yours." This time it was Greek meet Greek!

Slowly the *Chesapeake* crept up on the *Shannon's* starboard quarter. The range was at pistol shot. Just as the two ships came nearly abreast the after gun of the *Shannon's* main battery broke the silence. Drumfire began. The effect of those first broadsides was terrible beyond words to describe. It is said that one hundred men on the *Chesapeake's* upper decks were put out of action at the first discharge of the *Shannon's* battery. The enemy's loss was almost as great. Lawrence was shot through the leg with a pistol shot, but supported himself against the compass binnacle and continued to direct the fighting with perfect calmness. Splendid young Ludlow, first lieutenant at only twenty-one, fell mortally wounded, as did Lieutenant Edward Ballard and Lieutenant of Marines James Broom. Sailing Master White and Boatswain Peter Adams, who had served on the *Constitution,* were killed. Six midshipmen were killed or wounded. The tiller ropes were shot away and the wheel smashed to bits. Three helmsmen, one after the other, were killed at their posts. The unfortunate loss of so many officers and the damage to the wheel were almost decisive. The ship came up into the wind, and her port quarter came against the *Shannon's* starboard side amidships. Here only our aftermost guns could bear, while the enemy's entire battery raked us with terrible effect.

But worse was to come. Both captains saw the opportunity to board; both gave the order to call away their boarders. "All great events hang by a single hair," said Napoleon. And here was an example. The bugler of the *Chesapeake* had deserted his post and, when he could be found, was too scared to blow the call. Broke got his boarders ready, sailors and marines. Most gallantly he led them over the rail. The few men on the Chesapeake's quarter-deck ran forward in panic. Lawrence fell, mortally wounded, with a musket shot in the groin. Brave Chaplain Livermore stood alone on the quarter-deck and fired his pistol full at the British captain, and had his arm nearly cut off in return. The fight had been decided—eleven minutes was all!

There was still some real fighting on the forecastle, in which Broke himself was terribly wounded and nearly lost

From an engraving after the painting by Alonzo Chappel

JAMES LAWRENCE

From an engraving after the painting by J. C. Schelky

Chesapeake AND *Shannon*

his life. There was also some resistance on the main deck, where our losses had not been heavy. The guns still were firing. Lawrence, who had been carried below to the cockpit, while waiting his turn for the surgeon, kept issuing his orders. "Go on deck, and order them to fire faster and to fight the ship till she sinks; never strike; let the colors wave while I live." Again and again he kept repeating that the ship must be fought till she sank. At last, when he knew that the day was lost, he kept saying: "Don't give up the ship. Blow her up!" The most terrible agony man could suffer, mental and physical, could not break the spirit of this hero of heroes.

While the loss of the captain and nearly all the officers and the fact that the ship was boarded before the people on the gun deck knew what had happened had much weakened the resistance, still it was very honorable. This is demonstrated by the fact that out of a complement of 340 no less than 146 had been killed or wounded. The British suffered a loss of eighty-three.

Lawrence lived four days of indescribable agony, knowing that death was certain. In moments of delirium he still kept saying "Don't give up the ship!" His bearing was godlike—sublime even to the very end. Calling about him his few surviving officers, he told them his plan of battle and discussed with them calmly the reasons for its failure. "It was thus," said Washington Irving, "he devoted the last of his moments to usefulness and instruction, teaching his friends how to improve upon his precedent, showing the survivors the way 'out of the wreck to rise.'"

Our hero, as his end drew near, still composed and quiet amid agonies of suffering, might have repeated to his friends those immortal words of the Irish chieftain Cuchullin:

"My days are with the years that are past: and no morning of mine shall arise. They shall seek me at Temora, but I shall not be found. Cormac will weep in his hall and say 'Where is Tura's chief?' But my name is renowned! My fame is in the song of bards. The youth will say in secret, 'O let me die as Cuchullin died; renown clothed him as a robe; and the light of his fame is great.' Draw the arrow from my side; and lay Cuchullin beneath that oak. Place the shield of Caithbat near, that they may behold me amidst the arms of my fathers."

In Trinity Churchyard, in the heart of the world's greatest city, rests the hero. Brave Ludlow is with him. On his simple monument should be carved the lines of the old poet—for no other epitaph suits him so well: "He, of all heroes I heard of ever from sea to sea, of all the sons of earth, most excellent seemed."

And now, Captain Jim, good-bye! Sleep well, brave comrade!

Some writers have accused Lawrence of recklessness, have blamed him for engaging under what they consider unfavorable circumstances. As we said, Admiral Gleaves has shown that the conditions were not nearly so unfavorable as most writers have believed. And the fact remains that the two ships were equal in material strength. To decline battle meant an open acknowledgement of the inferiority of our officers and crew. There is in a naval service an indefinable moral influence which must be given priority over everything else. The prestige and reputation of the service must be maintained at all costs. It can never be maintained in our service if American captains refuse to fight hostile ships of equal strength. We must charge to profit and loss our *Chesapeakes*. Yes, even our Lawrences! Just as did King Henry when news came from Chevy Chase of Percy's death:

"Now God be with him," said our king
"Sith it will noe better bee;
I trust I have within my realme
Five hundred as good as he!"

In war there is no time for lamentation; it is better that warriors' thoughts be turned toward reprisal.

From another viewpoint too continuous a series of victories is not always good. We were getting a bit too cocky, becoming a trifle overconfident ourselves. After describing how Marshal Traun had maneuvered him all over the map, Old Fritz added a pregnant sentence: "Bad is often better for princes than good; and instead of intoxicating them with presumption, renders them circumspect and modest." The same holds true for navies.

CHAPTER XIII

WE LOSE THE *ARGUS*—BUT WIN THE *BOXER*

THE SAME day the *Chesapeake* was lost we suffered another defeat which does not appear with nearly enough prominence in our histories. Decatur had assembled a powerful squadron at New York: the *United States, Macedonian,* and *Hornet*. With it he attempted to break out through the eastern entrance to Long Island Sound. A superior blockading squadron met him and drove the two frigates into New London, where they were blockaded for the duration of the war. This was a very serious defeat.

On June 18 the brig-sloop *Argus* sailed from New York with Mr. Crawford, the newly appointed minister to France. This little craft had been one of our old Mediterranean friends—Isaac Hull had captured her. Now she was starting on her last cruise under our flag. On July 11 she landed her distinguished passenger at Lorient, having taken but one prize en route. Captain William H. Allen, late of the *United States,* was enjoying his first command, earned by his splendid work in the *Macedonian* fight. He seems to have been studying Revolutionary history, reading the exploits of Wickes, Conyngham, and Jones. He decided to do what Rodgers had planned: attack trade in the Channel after the incoming convoys had broken up. He had extraordinary luck. Twenty prizes, worth two and a half million dollars, fell into his hands in thirty-one days. All this without sighting a single British man-of-war. He had located the vulnerable spot in Britannia's armor.

"It seems harder," Xenophon says, "to find a man who

can bear good fortune well than one who can stand against misfortune." So it was now. The crew were wearied by their hard work; Captain Semmes of the *Alabama* tells us how arduous it is to make prizes. There seems to have been no time for gunnery training. Easy plunder and dreams of fabulous prize money planted the privateering habit, a desire to take prizes rather than fight men-of-war. Liquor allowed to be taken on board from a captured wine ship seems to have been too freely dispensed. The fighting edge was lost.

On August 14 a heavy sloop-of-war appeared. She was the *Pelican,* Captain Maples, of considerably superior weight of broadside: 280 pounds to 210. The *Argus* was a fleet little craft; could easily have escaped. But pride in his ship and service induced Allen to fight a battle for which he was ill prepared. He fought his ship most skillfully and gallantly—a very Lawrence! But after only four minutes a round shot carried off his left leg; he fell dying on his own quarter-deck. Raising himself on his elbow the hero continued to direct the fight until he fainted from loss of blood. Lieutenant Watson was knocked out by a grape-shot. Midshipmen Delphy and Edwards fell. Second Lieutenant U. H. Allen took over command, and fought the ship with remarkable skill. He even gained a chance to rake the enemy. But the crew failed to second his efforts. In fact, their gunnery was wretched, and they soon left their stations. When the ships came together the *Argus* was taken by boarding. This breakdown of discipline in battle is, so far as we know, the only case of its kind in our naval annals. How unfortunate that it should be connected with the name of William H. Allen, one of our very finest and most efficient officers. But if he made mistakes, he paid for them with his life. It is human to err, but godlike to die as he did! But let us remember, for future reference only, that when cruising against trade our crews must never lose the fighting edge. They must always be ready and eager for battle. Blakely was to show how this should be done: his Wasps would avenge the *Argus* many times over.

Readers must be wondering why they have heard nothing of the little *Enterprise* for so many pages. They will now hear the story of her past pitched battle. On September 1, she left Portsmouth, N.H. Four days later, off Portland, Me., she met the British brig *Boxer*. The ships were a good match. Lieutenant William Burrows had commanded the *Enterprise* but a short time. His men did not entirely approve of the time he took to maneuver for the weather gauge and began to have some apprehensions. So they sent back the junior officer of the forecastle to let the captain know that they wanted to fight. They were quickly reassured. The battle was one of the most gallantly contested of the war. Captain Blyth of the *Boxer* was killed outright. Brave Burrows was terribly wounded in the body by a cannister shot. Though suffering agonies as he lay on the quarter-deck, he kept continually cheering on his crew, repeating over and over again that the colors must never be struck. Captain Jim had not died in vain. What a fashion he had set! Let's keep it forever. Lieutenant Edward McCall took command—and also the *Boxer*. Before he died, Burrows received his enemy's sword. "I am satisfied," he said, "I die contented!" Yes, we had captains in those far-off days. Men who knew how to win—and to lose!

Midshipman John Aulick was given command of the prize. Both vessels returned to Portland. There, side by side, the two captains lie at rest.

CHAPTER XIV

OUR PRIVATEERSMEN LEARN THE GAME

A S THE war progressed privateering took on an entirely different aspect. No longer were there large numbers of prizes within easy distance of our coast. On the contrary, our waters were swarming with hostile men-of-war of all types. The uselessness of sending out slow, poorly equipped, and hastily manned vessels soon was demonstrated. It was also seen that the personality of the captain was of decisive importance. There were no regulations or traditions of a regularly organized military service to support his enforcement of discipline. A great majority of the prizes were made by a very small number of vessels, a fact which soon became apparent in the German submarine warfare a century later.

Our merchants saw that if they were to make money in privateering it would be necessary to concentrate their energies and capital on a few carefully prepared vessels. The first requirement was an able, energetic, and forceful captain—a leader of men. The second was a carefully recruited crew; if possible the men should have a financial interest in the ship. The third was a ship fast enough to escape from men-of-war and run down merchant vessels, large enough to make distant and prolonged cruises, with a battery sufficient to overpower the defensive armament of merchant vessels and beat off small men-of-war.

Privateers usually were brig-rigged, mounted a long 24-pounder pivot gun in the bow, and a broadside of long 9's or short 12's. They carried a large crew, about one hundred men, to provide for manning prizes. The return of our best merchantmen to their home ports during the summer of 1812 provided a great number of vessels well suited for conversion into privateers.

Salem developed into a great privateering, as it had been a commercial, port. In the fall of 1812 the ship-rigged *America* was converted there for distant privateering cruises. During the war she was out four times, for a total of sixteen months. Her favorite cruising ground was between the English Channel and the Canary Islands. She took forty-one prizes in all, twenty-seven of which reached port. The *America* earned one million dollars over all expenses.

The *Yankee* first sailed out of Bristol, R.I., in the fall of 1812. She took eight prizes off the African coast. These vessels carried in all 196 men and 62 guns. Their cargoes were valued at nearly one-third of a million. The *Yankee* kept cruising all through the war. She is credited with forty captures.

Late in December the *Comet* shot forth for a second cruise under Captain Boyle, the greatest of our privateer captains. Boyle conducted his campaign as a naval captain would have done. From January 9 to 14 he waited off Pernambuco for three British merchantmen. On the afternoon of the latter date he saw them standing out, escorted by a Portuguese brig which carried twenty short 32's, a battery much heavier than the Comet's. There was prolonged maneuvering until 8:30 P.M. By this time Boyle seems to have evaded the brig, so he engaged all three merchant vessels at close range in the bright moonlight. This must have been a great fight. Finally one of the merchantmen surrendered. The *Comet* lowered a boat to take possession and then engaged the Portuguese man-of-war until midnight when the moon went down. Boyle found that his prize was the *Bowes,* a fine large ship. The remaining vessels, with their protector, were glad to regain the port. Our Portuguese friend would think a long time before again getting into someone else's war.

A few days later Boyle was rewarded by meeting the Scotch ship *Adelphi,* which he took after a chase. However, now conditions were reversed: the *Comet* had to sail her best to show her heels to the *Surprise* frigate. On February 6 Boyle took the brig *Alexis* and attacked a convoy of nine vessels standing out from Demerara. A brig attached to the escort offered fight and Boyle promptly forced her to surrender. The next prize was the Liverpool packet *Dominica.* After sending her off, the *Comet* in turn was chased by the man-of-war *Swaggerer.* So little did such a chase concern the Yankee skipper that he took and manned the schooner *Jane* while his pursuer was still in sight. While homeward bound off Porto Rico a famous action was fought with the British merchant ship *Hibernia,* said to measure eight hundred tons and carry twenty-two guns. For eight hours these two craft fought it out tooth and nail, trying every expedient two skillful skippers could conceive. Right manfully their crews stuck to their guns— quite worthy of man-of-war traditions. The *Comet* lost three killed and eighteen wounded; the *Hibernia* eight and thirteen. At last each had had enough. By common consent they called it a draw—went off on their ways. This was only the beginning of Boyle's career. We shall hear some stirring tales of him in later years. A real sea captain he was; would have looked well in a master commandant's uniform on the quarter-deck of a *Hornet* or *Wasp.*

On February 8 the little letter of marque *Lottery* was standing down Chesapeake Bay, out of Baltimore for Bombay. Only a few days before a squadron of four British vessels had anchored in Lynnhaven Bay near the capes. Their mission was to close the Chesapeake. When they saw the *Lottery* standing past in the light airs then prevailing they sent their boats to attack her, nine of them with two hundred men. The *Lottery* was armed only for defense, six 12-pounder carronades. She had only twenty-five men, but one was John Southcomb, her captain. It would have been no disgrace for a merchant vessel as weak as the *Lottery* to have surrendered to such a superior force without resistance. But even a merchant vessel, thought Southcomb, must do something for the honor of her flag, which, in fact, was the same as that carried by our naval vessels. So he fought to the last, until nineteen of his twenty-five men were killed or wounded. Mortally wounded, this heroic captain was brought to the *Belvidera* and, like a very Richard Grenville, died on his enemy's deck. Captain Byron, an officer noted for his chivalrous conduct, treated the dying captain with every kindness and honor. The British themselves lost thirteen men in this sharp fight.

It must be realized, of course, that there were few privateers whose crews could be inspired to fight with the spirit of the *Comet* and *Lottery*. "The privateers," Roosevelt says, "were of incalculable benefit to us and inflicted enormous damage on the foe; but in fighting they suffered from the same disadvantages as other irregular forces; they were utterly unreliable. A really brilliant victory would be followed by an extraordinary defeat." As an example he cites the conduct of four privateers, manned by 160 men and mounting 30 guns, which on March 16, 1813, were boarded and captured by five ship's boats, carrying only 5 guns and 105 men.

In the summer of 1813 many privateers were following the *President* and *Argus* into the profitable cruising grounds around the British Isles. The *Yankee,* having returned from her successful cruise off the African coast, commenced operations off Ireland and in six weeks took four prizes valued at $200,000. Two fast brigs, the *Scourge* and *Rattlesnake,* commenced a cruise in the North Sea which netted them twenty-two captures. Norway permitted them to sell their prizes in her ports. While returning to the United States the *Scourge* alone took ten additional vessels.

Another privateer, the *True Blooded Yankee,* was fitted out in Brest. In thirty-seven days off the Irish coast she is said to have taken twenty-seven prizes. In addition she raided a Scottish port, *à la* Paul Jones, and burnt several ships. On the Portuguese coast the *Leo* gathered in seventeen prizes and the *Lion,* fifteen. They nearly wrecked Wellington's service of supply. The *America* made another of her fine cruises from the English Channel to the Madeiras.

During the twelve-month period beginning October 1, 1812, our privateers took about four hundred prizes, the greater part toward the end of that period. From the first of October, 1813, to the end of the year, their captures averaged nearly fifty a month. These figures remind us of the losses caused by German submarines. They were almost as disconcerting a surprise to the British as the defeats of their frigates and sloops by our naval vessels. If they were harrying our coasts, we were paying them back in their own coin. Few wars turn out according to plans and estimates. Overwhelming strength does not always win, as now our enemies were learning to their surprise.

CHAPTER XV

RODGERS CRUISES AGAIN

THE FIRST two years of war had been fought with fencing foils. The last one was to be a duel with broadswords with razor edges. The campaigns of Germany and Spain had crumbled away the power of the great Emperor. Enormous armies were converging upon his handful of veterans and new levies. Soon the end would come. Ambitious statesmen began to look about for new worlds to conquer, new continents where their veteran fleets and armies might continue their victories. The war with the United States gave them the very opportunity they desired. Here was a chance to retrieve the blunders of 1781, to avenge the surrenders of Saratoga and Yorktown. No French allies would we have this time. Well might they hope to limit our republic to a narrow zone along the coast —to win the rest of the continent for their empire. Thus the year 1814 was one of the most momentous in our history. At last we were aroused and ready to fight for the tremendous stakes which our Democratic politicians had thrown so nonchalantly upon the gambling table. Well for us that there emerged a Perry, a Macdonough, and a Jackson to guard our frontiers at their most vulnerable points.

While formidable armaments were gathering to attack us on three frontiers—Canadian, Atlantic, and Gulf—the prospects for cruiser warfare looked anything but bright. Our sensational victories of 1812 had roused the Royal Navy to fury. It had turned the tables upon us in 1813. Broke received higher honors and greater publicity for taking the *Chesapeake* than if he had annihilated a great French fleet. Even our cruises against trade, with the exception of the

[282]

Essex and *Argus,* had been singularly unprofitable. The one bright spot was the discovery of our enemy's weakness in his home waters. This we were ready to exploit. On the other hand, our privateer warfare had been reduced to almost an exact science. Tremendous losses were being inflicted upon the enemy, and they were increasing month by month. Therein lay our best chance to act on the aggressive, to exert strong pressure upon the enemy. They were getting pretty weary of all this fighting, for with but a short intermission Britons had been at war for over twenty years. If we could demonstrate that they could do nothing on the northern frontier and at New Orleans during the coming campaign, perhaps they would call it a draw and go home.

Notwithstanding its recent reverses, the Navy was eager to attempt longer and better cruises on the high seas. We had learned some valuable lessons from the *Argus* and *Chesapeake* episodes and were determined to come back strong in the last rounds. Our three new sloops were nearing completion and could be used to good purpose.

During the winter and spring of 1814 the following cruises commenced:

Port of sailing	Date of sailing	Commander	Vessels and rates	Remarks
Providence	Dec. 5	Rodgers	*President,* 44	Independent cruise
Boston	Jan. 1	Stewart	*Constitution,* 44	Independent cruise
Washington	Jan. 18	Morris	*Adams,* 28	Independent cruise
Portsmouth, N.H.	Feb. 2	Bainbridge	*Frolic,* 18	Taken by *Orpheus*
New York	Mar. 12	Warrington	*Peacock,* 18	Captured *Epervier*

On December 5 indefatigable John Rodgers commenced his fourth war cruise in the *President*. With customary good luck he ran through the blockading squadron off Narragansett Bay with little difficulty. He sighted one man-of-war, but did not think it prudent to look at her too closely. He then recaptured the American schooner *Comet* from her prize crew. Rodgers had a long series of encounters with vessels which he did not think wise to press home; every ship which came over the horizon he believed to be of superior force. The habit of excessive caution was becoming more and more pronounced. "It would appear," his biographer Paullin admits, "that the commodore was more cautious than some of his naval colleagues, and that in one or two instances his caution led him into error and lost him a capture."

After leaving the active zone off our coast the *President* sailed for a position five hundred miles east of Barbados. On January 5 Rodgers took the *Wanderer,* from London for Jamaica; and four days later the *Edward*. He waited about until the sixteenth for the convoy from which these two ships had straggled, but you know without telling that he never found it. Convoys never had the slightest affinity for John Rodgers. Next he pointed for Cayenne. Thence northward he followed the coast line. Entering the Caribbean between Grenada and Tobago, he sailed out through the Mona Passage, all this without taking a single prize. Traversing the Old Bahama Channel, the *President* came into the Florida Straits. The schooner *Jonathan* now brought the prizes to four, but it was the last. Hitting the coast at St. Augustine, the commodore came north in the Gulf Stream. Then began another series of distant contacts, which were not pushed home enough to make out the strength of the enemy. Off Sandy Hook Rodgers declined an opportunity to engage the 38-gun frigate *Loire,* thinking her a ship of the line. His cruise had been a failure; his war career had ended. On February 19, the *President* anchored in New York.

Field Marshal von Hindenburg explains the seeming inconsistencies of Rodgers' career: "Many a time has the soldier's calling exhausted strong characters, and that surprisingly quick. The fine intellect and resolute will of one year give place to the sterile imaginings and faint heart of the next. That is perhaps the tragedy of military greatness."

Since her return from the *Java* battle the *Constitution* had been having her rotten timbers replaced with strong new oak. It took ten months to complete the job, a fact which does not speak well for our system of navy-yard repairs. Charles Stewart received the command of this fine ship and put to sea on New Year's Day, 1814. He decided to follow the rout taken by the *President.* Early in February he arrived off Surinam. On the fourteenth he took the 16-gun schooner *Pictou* and a letter of marque under her escort. After a few other captures Stewart proceeded north through the Caribbean. On the twenty-third he chased the 36-gun frigate *Pique,* but she escaped under cover of darkness, an unusual piece of bad luck for "Old Ironsides." Running northward along the coast, Stewart was driven into Marblehead by two 38-gun frigates, the *Junon* and *Tenedos.* This was the only one of the *Constitution's* four war cruises which did not result in a striking success.

On January 18 the 28-gun corvette *Adams* escaped out of the Potomac River and through the Capes of the Chesapeake—quite a piece of work. We remember the old *Adams* in the Mediterranean, and also her captain, Charles Morris, first over the *Philadelphia's* side and recently promoted as a result of his success as first lieutenant of the *Constitution.*

Alexander Wadsworth, also from "Old Ironsides," was his first lieutenant. Morris was eager for a success in his first command, but his ship was very slow and of an odd size; no sloop would fight him and every frigate was too heavy. Still he was out to do his very best, and did as well as could have been expected. He set his course eastward along the thirtieth parallel of latitude and made two small prizes in crossing the Atlantic. On March 4 he was off the African coast, watching for British prizes where Carthaginian Hanno made the first known voyage of discovery. Off Cape Mount he took a small sloop and a week later off Cape Palmas the brig *Roebuck* of London. On the twenty-fifth the *Adams* made contact with a convoy, but the escort was too powerful. After touching at the Canaries and Cape Verde Islands, Morris sailed along the equator toward the West Indies. On May 1 he put into Savannah for supplies. The convoys had proved too well escorted for his little ship and Morris had not taken her into waters where the enemy's trade sailed singly without escort. Probably he considered his ship too slow and unhandy for such close work.

CHAPTER XVI

A DEFEAT—AND A VICTORY

DURING 1813 work had been progressing on three fine sloops-of-war: *Frolic, Peacock,* and *Wasp.* The *Frolic* was the first to be ready. Early in February she put to sea, under command of Master Commandant Joseph Bainbridge. Now luck never had any affinity with Bainbridges in our Navy. You may remember that our present commanding officer was the young fellow whose lateen yard had been shot away in the great Tripolitan gunboat action. Now his luck was no better. The Caribbean was the cruising ground assigned to him. After taking one ship, a large privateer from Carthagena, his cruise ended abruptly. It was in this wise: On April 20 he was in latitude 24° 10′ and longitude 81° 25′ when his lookouts made out two ships, the 36-gun frigate *Orpheus* and the 12-gun schooner *Shelburne.* The *Frolic* does not seem to have been as fast as the vessels of her design usually were—or the *Orpheus* must have been much faster. We know of no case but this where our sloops could not show their heels to any British frigate. For thirteen hours Bainbridge resorted to every known expedient to distance his pursuers. He threw overboard a great quantity of stores and equipment, his anchors, and finally even his guns, but it was no use. The enemy came into gunshot and he surrendered without resistance. A court of inquiry acquitted with honor officers and crew. The loss of this fine ship was a real disaster.

We fear that our account has recently not maintained its interest. But we must chronicle our bad days with the good. The Navy had to take its bad breaks in 1814—the reader must take his too.   Our team had been fumbling the ball; punts had been bouncing over their heads; our offensive had been smeared; we were struggling to hold our enemy on the ten-yard line.   But better days were coming; our defense tightened up; our offensive got started; we again aroused the public by a last-quarter rally—won an unbroken series of victories as fine as those achieved in the first months of the war.

Master Commandant Lewis Warrington was the man who started the rally.   He commanded the *Peacock,* named after the *Hornet's* prize.   On March 12 he sailed from New York for St. Mary's, Georgia, with a cargo of war stores.   After several exciting chases Warrington reached his port and discharged his cargo.   He ran down the Florida Straits and took station off Great Isaac Island. After cruising there for a week with no luck, during which time he heard that the Jamaica convoy was to have a heavy escort, he stood north in the Gulf Stream.   On April 29 he sighted four sails off Cape Canavarel.   These were the 18-gun sloop *Epervier* and three merchant vessels under her escort.

Captain Wales, commanding the *Epervier,* ordered his convoy to proceed, while he interposed between it and the *Peacock.*   There was some maneuvering for an advantageous position, which gained nothing for either captain. Soon they agreed to fight.   At 10:12 A.M. the two little ships passed close aboard on opposite courses and fired their guns as they bore.   The *Epervier* then tacked and continued the fight on parallel courses.   Our fire was deadly—forty-five round shot smashed into the enemy's hull; his head sails were shot away; his spanker boom cut in two.   Unmanageable lay the *Epervier.*   Her fire was both slow and wild —a terrible exhibition for a navy which claimed the sovereignty of the seas. Not a single shot hit the *Peacock's* hull. That was shooting into the air with a vengeance. But at that the British had luck on their side. One of the few shots which hit struck the *Peacock's* foreyard and this spilled the breeze from her foresail and fore topsail. In the light airs then prevailing this injury prevented Warrington from maneuvering for a favorable position; it was a gun-fight pure and simple. Forty-two minutes was enough to decide the issue.

"In fifteen minutes after the enemy struck," Warrington reported, "the *Peacock* was ready for another action in every respect but her foreyard, which was sent down, fished and had the foresail set again in forty-five minutes; such was the spirit and activity of our gallant crew." Two men very slightly wounded were his only casualties. When our people went on board the enemy they found twenty shot holes within a foot of her water line—rather good target practice for short carronades. These holes were soon plugged; rigging was made shipshape; Warrington went off with his prize. Specie to the amount of $120,000 was found aboard, a welcome booty for an impoverished government.

The next day as the two vessels proceeded northward, two frigates were made out in the north. Was the *Wasp* and *Frolic* episode about to be repeated? Not if Warrington could help. He ordered the prize to edge in close to the neutral coast of Florida—not that any reliance could be placed on its neutrality—while he attracted the attention of the enemy and drew them to the southward. By rare good luck, or poor judgment, both enemy ships elected to chase the *Peacock* and Warrington distanced them when he had drawn them far enough from his prize. It was a clever strategem. On May 1 the *Epervier* came into Savannah,

followed three days later by the *Peacock*. Warrington had
made a splendid cruise. In those days, with British men-of-
war literally swarming off our coast, it required real skill to
cruise about among them for fifty days, capture a ship of
nearly equal power, and bring her safely into port. It was
time for a victory and Warrington won it. We needed
all the encouragement we could get in those dark days.

CHAPTER XVII

THE *WASP* CAPTURES THE *REINDEER*

DURING the spring of 1814 four cruises commenced:

Port of sailing	Date of sailing	Commander	Vessels and rates	Remarks
Portsmouth	May 1	Blakeley	*Wasp*, 18	Took *Reindeer* and *Avon*
Savannah	May 8	Morris	*Adams*, 28	Independent cruise
Boston	June	Parker	*Siren*, 16	Taken by *Medway*
Savannah	June 4	Warrington	*Peacock*, 18	Independent cruise

Master Commandant Johnstone Blakeley is one of our unsung heroes; his exploits were done far from home; the accounts of his victories hastily and briefly written. He never came home to attend gala receptions, to be honored with the freedom of cities, to receive a sword from Congress. No, Blakeley never came back, nor did the *Wasp*. Bright as a comet was her short career across the sky of history—her end as mysterious.

On May 1 the sloop-of-war *Wasp* left Portsmouth, N.H., on the finest cruise of the war. Readers may remember another sloop which had put to sea from this same port some thirty-odd years before. Blakeley was bound on the same mission: to attack the enemy in his own waters. His ship and crew were quite different from those with which Paul Jones had sailed. A few words about them may be of interest.

[291]

There can be no doubt but that the *Wasp* was, for her size, one of the finest ships which ever put to sea—we think the very finest. She had just been completed; this was her first cruise. She was very large for a sloop, 509 tons burden. She was ship-rigged, had fine sailing qualities, and was very fast. Along her weather deck were lined twenty 32-pounder carronades and two long 12's, which, allowing for the light weight of our shot, could throw a broadside of 315 pounds. The *Wasp* was a perfect combination of speed and power.

So much for the ship—now for the men. In those days our officers set a remarkably high standard, and the *Wasp's* people were high above their average. At that time Blakeley himself had performed no outstanding exploits, but this condition he soon rectified. Two of his lieutenants, James Reilly and Frederick Baury, had seen two frigate actions on the *Constitution*. The third, T. G. Tillinghast, had won a name for himself in the desperate *Enterprise-Boxer* battle. The crew reached the unusual number of 173, and every man was specially selected and an American citizen. While somewhat green in the ways of men-of-war, they were the finest possible material.

It was not until June 2 that the first prize was taken, a vessel twelve days out from Cork to Halifax. On the thirteenth Blakeley seems to have reached his station in the English Channel, for the taking of a second prize, from Limerick for Bordeaux, is then recorded. Now great activity commenced. Sails were seen on all sides, pouring in and out of this funnel to North Europe and the British Isles. Most of the ships proved to be neutral, but in two weeks six good prizes were picked up. Five were burned and the other was used to take prisoners into a British port. During this time Blakeley did not forget the moral taught by the *Argus;* he kept his ship and crew in readiness.

From an old woodcut

Wasp AND *Reindeer*

The Engagement Between the *Essex* and H. M. Ships *Phoebe* and *Cherub*

At daylight on June 28 the *Wasp* was in latitude 48° 36′ and longitude 11° 15′. Two sails were sighted; while chasing them a third appeared. At 10:00 A.M. this vessel hoisted British colors. For nearly four hours Blakeley maneuvered before hoisting his. Then he fired a gun as a challenge. This was readily accepted. Our opponent was the brig-sloop *Reindeer,* one of the finest ships in the Royal Navy. Captain William Manners was an officer of distinguished ability and spirit. His crew was known as the "Pride of Plymouth." Unfortunately the vessels were most unequally matched. We had an advantage of 3 to 2 in both weight of broadside and number of men. We regret that this could not have been an equal match, to give a practical test of British and American efficiency at its best.

After prolonged maneuvering Blakeley presented the weather gauge to the enemy. He wanted to fight, was confident in his crew, though he probably would have some superiority in battery—he could not know that the *Reindeer* would have only 24-pounders against his 32's—and was willing to give an advantage to the enemy rather than waste more daylight in maneuvering. He laid the *Wasp* close-hauled on the starboard tack and waited for the *Reindeer* to commence the action.

Slowly the brig crept up on the *Wasp's* starboard quarter, where our guns could not bear. At 3:17 P.M. Manners commenced firing with a shifting 12-pounder carronade mounted on his forecastle. He knew his inferiority and wished to get every advantage for his men. At a distance of sixty yards this gun was discharged five times. Blakeley praised "the cool and patient conduct of every officer and man, while exposed to the fire of the shifting gun of the enemy, and without an opportunity of returning it." Nine long minutes these Wasps stood to their guns, silent, patient, waiting for their turn. Their captain had an idea, but he wanted to draw the enemy in a bit closer. Then, at 3:26 P.M., he luffed the *Wasp* into the wind. Ready now Wasps! Fire as the guns bear! See if any British brig can stand against you!

Thus the action begins. From aft forward the starboard guns roar, discharging such round shot, cannister, and grape as could be kept from falling out of their muzzles. For a few minutes now the *Reindeer* cannot shoot, but by luffing the *Wasp* has lost her headway. Soon the brig comes up on her beam and fires. There is even danger that she may pass ahead and rake us. But not while Blakeley is by the wheel. He lets the *Wasp's* head fall off slowly from the wind, draws aft his sheets, and makes sail on a parallel course. A clever maneuver!

Now it is broadside to broadside—range twenty yards. One of our New York policemen could almost "put a shot" across that distance. For ten minutes the fire is tremendous. To heavier weight of battery we add a marked superiority in gunnery. Only six times is the *Wasp* hulled; the *Reindeer* is literally cut to pieces in line with her gun ports. Captain Manners is twice terribly wounded, but still cheers on his crew. Nobly do they stand to their guns amid dead and dying.

Brave Manners sees that this cannot last; his ship is being wrecked; his own life blood flowing away. His only chance is to board; not much of one, 'tis true, but he'll try. He has the weather position; puts his helm up; brings the breeze on his quarter. Soon his port bow bumps against the starboard quarter of the *Wasp*. Now is his chance!

"But the Carolina captain," says Roosevelt, "had prepared for this with cool confidence; the marines came aft;

close under the bulwarks crouched the boarders, grasping in their hands the naked cutlasses, while behind them were drawn up the pikemen. As the vessels came grinding together the men hacked and thrust at one another through the open port holes, while the black smoke curled up from between the hulls. Then through the smoke appeared the grim faces of the British sea dogs, and the fighting was bloody enough; for the stubborn English stood well in the hard hand play."

Manners sees that he has no chance—will try anyhow. Sword in hand, he springs into the fore rigging; with him are the remnants of his crew with pike and cutlass. But this is no *Chesapeake* to board. Steady stand the Wasps. They fight like the old musketeers and pikemen of Gustavus Adolphus. No boarding to be done here. On the contrary, their musketry sweeps the *Reindeer's* decks. Down from their perches in the tops and rigging other Wasps fire. Manners falls back dead with two musket balls through his head. This is too much even for British courage. They break away. Now the Yankees try their hand; over the bulwarks they pour, sweeping the decks. The captain's clerk surrenders the ship; he is the only officer unwounded!

The *Reindeer* had lost over half her crew: sixty-seven killed or wounded. Our losses too were severe: twenty-six in all. The prize was a complete wreck and had to be burned, giving thus to many brave sailors a viking funeral. On July 8 Blakeley put into Lorient to refit his ship and rest his crew. His work was but half done; soon we will return to a second cruise and follow the Wasps to their end.

CHAPTER XVIII

THE LOSS OF THE *ADAMS* AND *SIREN*

YOU may recollect that Charles Morris had put into Savannah for a breathing spell. After only a week's stay he stood out again on May 8. His first cruise had been anything but successful; now he would try again and in a different area. On the twenty-fourth he made contact with a large convoy; but see what its escort was: one sail of the line, two frigates, and three brigs. What chance for a little corvette? That was a problem somewhat different from a demonstration off Morocco. After wasting some time and supplies off the Newfoundland Banks, the *Adams* went for the Irish coast. Off the mouth of the Shannon she celebrated the Fourth of July—doubtless principally with extra allowances of grog. Here the cruising was good and several prizes were taken. On the fifteenth in latitude 44° and longitude 10° the 36-gun frigate *Tigris* entered the picture and chased the little *Adams* for a whole day. A real close call it was. A few days later Morris had a similar experience with two frigates. As a steady diet this was not so good. Provisions were getting scarce and scurvy breaking out; not all was glory in those days. Ten prizes were all he had been able to collect in his two cruises.

Nemesis had blundered several times, but still he kept inexorably on the trail of the *Adams*. In a dense fog she piled up hard on the Maine coast. After floating her off Morris retired twenty-seven miles up the Penobscot River to Hampden. A British squadron of two of the line, three frigates, three sloops, and ten troopships was then operating off the Maine coast under Rear Admiral Griffeth. With a

[296]

strong expedition of 1,500 sailors and soldiers he went up the river. No Andrew Jackson appeared to check his advance. Morris had only 150 men in his crew. Hastily collected militia gave him little support. After making such resistance as was possible, which was very little, Morris fired his ship and withdrew overland to Portland.

Early in the war the little 16-gun brig *Siren* had made a short cruise in the Gulf of Mexico under Master Commandant Joseph Bainbridge. This ended in Boston. After Bainbridge had been transferred to the ill-fated *Frolic,* George Parker, who had been first lieutenant of the *Constitution* in the *Java* fight, assumed command. Early in June he commenced a cruise toward the African coast, with the privateer *Grand Turk* in company. Off the Canary Islands Parker died and Lieutenant Nicholson continued the cruise. When chased by a frigate he resorted to a clever ruse. As it came dark he threw over some casks to which lanterns were attached; then, extinguishing his own lights, he made a radical change of course. By daylight the enemy was nowhere to be seen. Next he had a fight in the Senegal River with a ship and fort. Then he took and destroyed the ships *Barton, Adventure,* and *Siren.* On July 12 contact was made with the *Medway,* 74. After being chased eleven hours, Nicholson had to surrender. Before doing so he had thrown over all his cables, anchors, guns, and ammunition.

None of our little brigs had accomplished much. They were too small to fight and except for the *Argus* too slow to run away. We have told how the *Nautilus* and *Argus* were taken. To avoid the charge of omitting American defeats, let us add here that the 12-gun brig *Vixen* and the 10-gun sloop *Viper* had been captured early in the war by British frigates. These little fellows, who had done so well in the Tripolitan campaigns, had now all gone, saving always the lucky little *Enterprise,* which would again return to the Mediterranean with a triumphant American squadron.

Readers will remember how the *Peacock* put into Savannah after taking the *Epervier.* Warrington waited in port a month. On June 4 he followed the *Adams* to the Newfoundland Banks. Thence he sailed for the Azores along the track later followed by our NC seaplanes. Next he headed up for the Irish coast and followed the route of the *Bon Homme Richard.* Skirting the Hebrides, the *Peacock* showed her feathers as far north as the Faroe Islands —past which the *Seeadler* sailed forth on her historic cruise a century later. Unfortunately, Warrington did not now enter the North Sea, where the *Scourge* and *Rattlesnake* had raised such havoc. Instead he retraced his steps and continued on to the Portuguese coast, the profitable cruising ground where the *Lion* and *Leo* had been attacking Wellington's line of communications. He cruised back and forth between Finisterre and Ortegal for a week and then sailed southward. On September 2 he reached the Canaries. Thus far his cruise had met with considerable success: thirteen prizes, of which eleven had been burned and two used to send in their crews. The rest of Warrington's cruise— Cape Verde Islands, Surinam, Barbuda to New York— resulted in the making of only one prize. Leaving Barbuda on October 12, the *Peacock* came into New York on the twenty-seventh. Soon we will hear of her final cruise into far-distant waters.

CHAPTER XIX

THE *WASP* AND THE *AVON*

MEANWHILE Blakeley had been giving the *Wasp* a thorough refit in Lorient. It is rather surprising that this should have been permitted, for now Napoleon had fallen and the Bourbon monarch owed his throne largely to British influence. Before the *Reindeer* was sunk, her shifting 12-pounder carronade had been removed. Blakeley now mounted this on his forecastle, increasing his weight of broadside to 327 pounds. His crew he brought to the strength of 160 by recruiting privateersmen out of a job in French ports. On August 27 the *Wasp* again put to sea for another stroke at British commerce in the approaches to the Channel.

In the first three days two prizes were taken and burned. Then on September 1 was sighted a convoy of ten merchant vessels under escort of the ship of the line *Armada,* a great two-decker of 74 guns. Here was a set-up which had daunted the greatest commodore of them all. But Blakeley had a much better ship than the slow-sailing *Ranger* and his perfectly trained sailors were beyond comparison with Paul Jones's mutinous crew. Hovering eagle-like for a time over his prey, our fleet-winged sloop swooped down upon the brig *Mary,* loaded with cannon, muskets, and other valuable military stores. Blakeley took off her crew and burned her to the water's edge—all this before the liner could interfere. Wonder what story her captain told the Board of Admiralty!

This was to be the *Wasp's* busy day. The capture of the *Mary* was only the prelude to another even more exciting *rencontre.* At 6:30 P.M. four scattered sail were made out to leeward. Neither their rate nor flag could be made out in the fading light, but that only added to the zest of the adventure. Three of them looked to Blakeley like men-of-war. In fact, they were all brig-sloops of the standard type, inferior to the *Wasp* in weight of broadsides in the ratio of 5 to 6.

Blakeley decided at once to attempt something against them. The cool, scientific way in which he went about his business is even now an object lesson to naval officers. We wish John Rodgers might have watched him from a good point of vantage, note book in hand! "First weigh, then venture," was Moltke's motto. We know not if Blakeley ever said it, but now he was to act it in a manner upon which not even the German field marshal could have improved. The ship to windward was a brig of about the *Wasp's* size. If she could be separated from her consorts, they would have a difficult task in beating to windward to come to her assistance. Under cover of darkness Blakeley prepared to execute this daring though well-calculated plan.

At 7:00 P.M. the stranger made night signals. These disclosed her British nationality to Blakeley. She was, in fact, the brig-sloop *Avon,* Captain the Honorable James Arbuthnot, doubtless some ancestor of that brave admiral who took the *Defense* and *Warrior* on their death ride at Jutland. He accepted the challenge of the American ship and made ready for battle. His course was southwest; the fresh southeasterly breeze came over his port side.

The night came on dark; the ships rolled heavily in the long seas—just what Blakeley needed to capitalize his superiority in gunnery. He eased down on his enemy under fighting canvas. Battle lanterns lighted the decks. Their glow shone through a single line of gun ports and upwards upon slender spars, deep-bellied sails, and a dim spider web of rigging. Guns had been loaded and cast loose. Round shot, grape, and cannister lay piled beside them; a few charges of powder lay ready for the first broadsides. Guns' crews stood grouped about their stubby carronades. Marines lounged easily in ranks behind them. Powder monkeys knelt beside their ammunition. Everywhere reigned silence —grim silence. Save that they had no flutes to play the hymn to Castor as they went into battle, that splendid band of seamen remind us of Plutarch's Spartans: "It was at once a magnificent and terrible sight to see them march on to the tune of their flutes, without any disorder in their ranks, discomposure in their minds or change in their countenance, calmly and cheerfully moving with the music to the deadly fight. Men in this temper were not likely to be possessed with fear or any transport of fury, but with the deliberate valor of hope and assurance, as if some divinity were attending and conducting them."

By 9:30 P.M. the *Wasp* is close down upon the Avon's port quarter. Hails are exchanged, but probably not understood. Blakeley's shout of "Heave to" receives no answer by word or action. Now then, Wasps, stand by! Open with the shifting carronade. At 9:29 its first round is fired. Arbuthnot is ready; has a surprise too—a long 6-pounder for a stern chaser. He answers back with this, as well as with several of his after 32-pounder carronades of the port battery.

This is only a brief skirmish to develop the enemy— Blakeley does not intend to fight thus. As long as he remains to windward there is nothing to prevent his foe from running down before the wind toward his friends if he should find he is getting the worst of it, which Blakeley shrewdly suspects will be the case. He must interpose be-

tween the *Avon* and her consorts before forcing the action
—fight from the leeward position. Incidentally this maneuver will give him a chance to pour a raking fire into the
soft stern of his foe—what Lawrence had refused to do.
Conditions now are different; this is not a challenge fight;
other enemy ships are close at hand; anything is fair on this
dark night. So Blakeley puts up his helm, brings the wind
on his port quarter, sails under the *Avon's* stern. Here is
your chance, Wasps! They take it, and their big 32-pound
shot splinter and smash their way through the brig's stern
and port quarter. By 9:35 the *Wasp* is on the *Avon's* starboard beam. Now the fight begins in earnest.

The Wasps surpassed themselves. Blakeley had trained
them to fight under any conditions, night as well as day.
Even the roll and pitch of the ship seems to have affected
their gunnery little, the darkness not at all. They loaded
with unequalled speed, fired with deadly accuracy. What a
scene their glowing battle lanterns must have disclosed.
First the *Avon's* gaff was shot through; then her mainsail
fell over the after guns; her hull was pierced and splintered;
several shot entered below the water line, making jagged
holes difficult to plug; guns were dismounted; man after
man fell killed or wounded; her mainmast crashed down.
"At 10 o'clock," Blakeley reported, "believing the enemy to
be silenced, orders were given to cease firing, when I hailed
and asked if he had surrendered. No answer being given
to this, and his fire having recommenced, it was again returned." At 10:12 Blakeley hailed a second time. This time
the answer had to be affirmative, for now the *Avon* was a
helpless wreck with forty-two of her crew out of action.

This last resistance of the British captain saved his ship
from capture. "In the act of lowering the boat," Blakeley
reported, "a second brig was discovered, a little distance

astern and standing for us. Sent the crew to their quarters, prepared everything for another action, and waited his coming up—at 36 minutes after 10 discovered two more sail astern standing toward us. I now felt myself compelled to forego the satisfaction of destroying the prize." Never mind, Captain, you have already!

Blakeley made his decision just in time. He was in no shape for two more fights similar to the one he had just fought. True, his hull had been hit only four times and his personnel loss had amounted to but three. But the high pointing of the Avon had shot up his rigging very completely and smart maneuvering would have been impossible. As it was, the big *Castilian* fired a broadside at the *Wasp*. Fortunately not a single shot hit. She then went to the assistance of her consort, which sank soon after her crew had been removed. Blakeley never knew the name of his foe, but the distress guns which punctuated the night at frequent intervals must have shown him how complete his success had been.

This exploit we consider one of the finest in our naval annals. Blakeley's handling of the *Wasp* was a masterpiece of skill and judgment, of daring and efficiency. Officers and crew behaved in a manner beyond all praise. Here was cool and steady Nordic courage at its very highest.

The next day was spent in repairing damages. Then the *Wasp* worked her way southward, taking and burning three prizes. On September 21, latitude 33° 12′ and longitude 14° 56′, the brig *Atalanta,* 8 guns, was taken. This prize was so valuable that she was sent for Savannah; there she arrived in due time, bearing Blakeley's official report of the *Avon* action and news of his successful cruise.

On October 9, latitude 18° 35′ and longitude 30° 10′, the Swedish brig *Adonis* was spoken. On her were Lieutenant McKnight and Master's Mate Lyman of the *Essex*. They transferred to the *Wasp*. A sad decision, for this was the last news ever received of this splendid, but ill-fated, little craft. Her end will ever be one of the mysteries of the ocean. In commenting upon the cruise of the *Wasp*, Roosevelt says: "She was as good a ship, as well manned, and as ably commanded as any vessel in our little Navy; and it may be doubted if there was at that time any foreign sloop-of-war of her size and strength that could have stood against her in fair fight."

CHAPTER XX

PRIVATEERING GROWS APACE

AS THE war progressed the operations of our privateers became more and more effective. During the one-year period commencing October 1, 1813, it has been estimated that they made six hundred captures. Of these, two out of every three were made in foreign waters, mostly off the English coasts. The captains had gained experience; the best seamen in the country had been attracted by the opportunity for financial gain; shipowners saw their chance to keep their vessels in operation at a profit and to keep intact their organizations until peace permitted a return to normal activities.

The most successful cruises of the privateers were widely heralded throughout the country by an enterprising press, whose reporters, then as now, were not above a bit of exaggeration where it improved the story and appealed to local pride. These stories encouraged greater confidence, resourcefulness, and daring among our privateersmen, introduced the element of competition, and developed a pride of accomplishment which in many cases was as great an incentive to good conduct as the more material gain. While they did not usually seek action with vessels of the Royal Navy, they frequently defended themselves in the most creditable manner and often attacked merchant vessels of much superior power.

Readers may remember that we promised some further account of Captain Thomas Boyle. After his highly successful cruises in the *Comet* he was offered the command of the fine brig *Chasseur*. This vessel soon proved herself well worthy of her name. During her career she hunted down and seized some thirty prizes. In the summer of 1814 she made a cruise of three months about the British Isles and took eighteen prizes. Our captain had a sense of humor too. Reprisals are a well-recognized means of hitting back at the enemy. So Boyle sent on a proclamation to London declaring "all the ports, harbors, bays, creeks, rivers, inlets, outlets, and seacoast of the United Kingdom of Great Britain and Ireland in a state of rigorous blockade." Joking aside, we think his blockade a rather effective one!

August 5, 1814, found the little schooner *Decatur,* of Charleston, five hundred miles north of St. Thomas. She carried 7 guns, of which one was a long 18-pounder mounted forward on a pivot. Her crew totaled 103 and, curiously enough, were mostly French. On that day Captain Diron sighted a large merchant vessel, escorted by the schooner *Dominica* of the Royal Navy, which carried 15 guns and 88 men. Diron adopted the tactics of the old buccaneers—boarding. Twice the royal schooner foiled his attempts by skillful maneuvering, and shot up the *Decatur* badly. Again Diron came in close and fusilladed the enemy with his muskets. This time he got alongside; his Frenchmen clambered up over the *Dominica's* bulwarks and cleared her decks in really desperate hand-to-hand fighting. The British had no less than sixty casualties; the *Decatur* herself had nineteen. Such a hot fight as this would have done credit to a vessel of our regular Navy. On the twentieth Captain Diron brought the *Dominica* and another prize into Charleston. A real reception must have awaited him.

The *Saucy Jack* was another famous Charleston privateer. On April 30 she was tossing in the strong northeast trades which pour through that natural funnel, the Windward Passage. Along came the large merchant vessel *Pelham,* 540 tons, 10 guns, and 40 men. The privateer was a much smaller vessel, but she had twice as many men. After fighting for two hours the privateersmen carried the *Pelham* by boarding. A lively scrap it must have been, for the British lost fifteen of their forty men and in turn inflicted eleven casualties on the *Saucy Jack.* After bringing this fine prize into Charleston the privateer again returned to her hunting ground in the West Indies. This time she was not so fortunate, for the British tried one of those ruses which so exasperated German submarine commanders a century later. At daylight of October 31 the privateer ran alongside a very innocent-appearing merchant vessel, only to have lines of soldiers appear over the bulwarks and let off a volley or more of musketry. Twenty-three men fell in this ambush and the *Saucy Jack* made haste to get clear of such an early edition of the mystery ship.

On November 29, the *Kemp* stood out of Wilmington. Two days later she made contact with a convoy of eight merchant vessels, escorted by a frigate. Our wily privateersman kept maneuvering about the merchant vessels until the British captain gave chase. The *Kemp* led him on until both vessels lost the convoy. Night came on. The privateer easily gave her pursuer the slip and headed back toward the estimated position of the convoy. By rare good fortune she made it out just as day broke. The frigate was nowhere in sight. By 2:00 P.M. the *Kemp* came into close action with the eight vessels. After half an hour's cannonading six of them surrendered. But the *Kemp's* net could not hold all her fish. While two ships and two brigs were being manned the other two vessels were able to make sail and get away. The prizes were found to be carrying rich cargoes of coffee and sugar, commodities then very scarce along our closely blockaded seacoast.

One of the most successful of the New York privateers was the fast brigantine *Prince de Neufchatel*. She was a splendid craft of 310 tons and 17 guns; when she left port her crew numbered 150 men. During the cruise she was chased seventeen times, showing what a sporting proposition privateering cruises were becoming. Many prizes were made. So many were manned and sent into port that her crew was reduced to forty men. Other prizes were stripped of their most valuable goods and then burned, a procedure which was becoming more common as the blockade of our coast tightened up. On October 11 off Nantucket the frigate *Endymion,* 40 guns, was encountered. Although his crew was only a handful, Captain Ordronaux was determined to fight to the finish to save his ship. The goods in his holds, valued at one-third of a million dollars, provided another strong incentive. At 8:30 P.M. the wind dropped, the sea calmed. The *Endymion* lowered out five cutters, manned them with 111 men, and sent them off against the becalmed privateer. Here was a chance for some rich prize money. As the boats came close the *Neufchatel* gave them some salvos of grapeshot, which sank one of them. First blood for us. The other boats got alongside. Their crews clambered up the sides. Here the boarding nettings delayed them. There was close fighting hand-to-hand as they tried to cut their way through; musket and pistol at first, then pike and cutlass. Some of the boarders actually reached the *Neufchatel's* deck, but here they were all cut down. After this repulse the British drew off, leaving one of their boats alongside the privateer. Of his forty men Captain Ordronaux had lost thirty-one. The British losses amounted to between seventy-five and ninety-three.

CHAPTER XXI

THE END OF THE *ESSEX*

SOME may remember that in December, 1813, Commodore David Porter sailed from the Marquesas for Valparaiso with the *Essex* and *Essex Junior.* On February 3 he reached that port. Five days later the British frigate *Phoebe,* 36 guns, and the sloop *Cherub,* 18 guns, arrived upon the scene. They stood into the port and sailed down upon the *Essex* as if to attack her at her moorings. The *Phoebe,* however, after a menacing approach, fell into a position where she was at Porter's mercy. Captain Hillyar hastily shouted over that he had not acted with hostile intent. Porter had every reason to doubt this statement, but chivalrously withheld his fire. While our captain had ample justification for commencing an action, he deliberately refused to take advantage of his enemy's mistake, even though it gave him an opportunity to fight at the close range where his unusual battery of carronades would have been highly effective. Hillyar, when later he met Porter ashore, thanked him for his chivalrous conduct and assured him that he would never violate the neutrality of the port.

After filling with stores the two British ships sailed out and commenced a close blockade of the *Essex.* Several times Porter stood out with the intention of bringing on a single combat with the *Phoebe,* but each time Hillyar declined the challenge and kept within supporting distance of the *Cherub.* This was a proper precaution on his part, for he had the most urgent orders to put a stop to Porter's cruise in the Pacific. He could not afford to indulge in any Broke chivalry. The capture of the *Shannon* by Lawrence would have meant nothing more than another blow at British pride; the capture of the *Phoebe* by Porter would have ruined British prestige all through South America and have given us the command of the Pacific for another long period. Hillyar's attitude, however, was a remarkable compliment to our young service and Cooper is correct in saying that "no incident of the war so unanswerably shows the character obtained by the American Navy, at this time, as the fact that a 36 declined meeting a 32, in single combat." Gallant Porter deserved, if ever captain did, a victory to complete his cruise, to earn his triumph. Alas! "What gifts hath fate for all his chivalry?"

On March 28 a southerly storm commenced. The *Essex* parted one of her anchor cables. The other anchor began to drag. Porter thought it a good time to proceed to sea, lead off the enemy ships and let the *Essex Junior* escape. Just as he was clearing the entrance a heavy squall snapped off his main topmast, drowning several topmen. Thus crippled, the *Essex* could neither escape, regain the port, nor contend with her enemies on anything like equal terms. Porter ran in and anchored within pistol shot of the shore, some three miles from the city of Valparaiso. Here of course the right of neutrality protected him with the same force it would have had in Valparaiso Harbor. Furthermore, Porter had the express promise of the British captain, given because of Porter's chivalrous conduct, that he would respect the rights of neutrality. Porter relied upon the word of an English officer and gentleman. But this, when put to the test, proved a weak reliance!

Hillyar attacked. A century later British cruisers attacked the German light cruiser *Dresden* as it lay at anchor in Chilean waters. His precedent, it seems, was thought a good one.

The opposing forces on that fateful March day were as follows:

	Essex	*Phoebe* and *Cherub*	
Long guns	6 12's	30 18's	and 2 9's
Short guns (carronades)	40 32's	34 32's	and 8 24's
Crews	255	500	

The *Essex Junior* mounted such small guns, long 6's and short 18's that it would have been useless for her to have taken part in the fight, especially as the enemy were between her and the *Essex*.

It requires only a glance at the above table for the reader to determine what tactics the British commodore should follow. The Essex being crippled, he could choose his range, fight a deliberate action at moderate range for his long guns and thus eliminate the *Essex'* heavy battery of carronades. And that is just what he did. And, we must admit, he made a very seamanlike and skillful job of it. Unfortunately, three times springs on the *Essex'* cable were shot away. It was thus impossible to reply to the *Phoebe's* fire until three long 12's were run out the cabin ports. These were served so well that after half an hour's firing the British ships drew out of range temporarily to repair damages. They then took station on the starboard quarter of the *Essex,* where not one of our guns could reach them. After standing this punishing fire for a time, Porter got under way with his flying jib and made a most gallant effort to board the *Phoebe.* Despite the numerous injuries aloft which the *Essex* had by this time received, she was able to fire her carronades for a few minutes. The British vessels, however, soon drew out of carronade range, keeping up a terribly effective fire from their long guns.

After having fought for nearly two hours Porter saw that his ship was doomed. He determined to run her ashore and destroy her with fire. For a time it seemed as if he would succeed, but when within musket shot of the beach the wind shifted and blew off shore. Undaunted by this Porter again made such sail as he could for the enemy. "I still hoped to be able to board him!" But again it proved of no avail. Next an attempt was made to anchor, in the hope that the tide might carry the enemy out of range before they did likewise. But the anchor cable parted. To add to our difficulties the ship caught on fire; quantities of powder about the decks blazed up. When the fire was extinguished the long 12's were again manned to continue the fight. Master John Cowell fell mortally wounded, but continued to direct his men until he fainted away from loss of blood.

The end was drawing near. One hundred and twenty-four officers and men had been killed or wounded, with many others drowned. About one of the 12-pounders fifteen heroes lay dead. Besides the captain, there was only one officer, Acting Lieutenant McKnight, fit for duty. The long guns had each been fired over seventy-five times; and seven of their shot had pierced the hull of the *Phoebe* below the water line. Lieutenant John Downes, of the *Essex Junior,* had rowed out under a heavy fire to get his last instructions from his commodore. He could do nothing for the *Essex,* so Porter sent him back to defend his own ship.

To Porter the gods had granted neither of those boons for which brave old Antigonus had prayed at Ipsus: "Either victory or death without knowledge of defeat." Only two alternatives now remained: to destroy his ship, which would involve the death of all his wounded heroes, or surrender. For a time he seemed resolved on the former. But at last, like Sir Richard Grenville, he gave in to the pleadings of his people and yielded to the foe.

Captain Hillyar treated the prisoners with great consideration. He allowed them to return home in the *Essex Junior* in exchange for an equal number of British prisoners in our hands. In his official report he said that the defense of the *Essex* "did honor to her brave defenders and most fully evinced the courage of Captain Porter and those under his command."

We always can learn more of value from a defeat than from a victory, and we owe a sacred obligation to those brave men who fell on the decks of the *Essex* to learn in a way never to be forgotten the lessons they taught us. The first lesson is the incalculable value of upholding the honor of the service by a resistance, even against hopeless odds and when there is no hope of victory, until there is absolutely nothing more that can be done to injure the enemy.

Farragut as a very young midshipman fought in the *Essex*. As he in later years began a desperate undertaking often must he have looked back upon that first terrible ordeal of battle: those splintered spars and shattered sails, those battered bulwarks, those bloody decks, covered with smashed gun carriages, wreckage from aloft, and bodies of the dead. That day he learned of what Americans were capable, even when victory was impossible and they knew it. That knowledge, gained at such a price, later enabled him to open the Mississippi and to command Mobile Bay. That price in human life was a heavy one, but it went far toward establishing one of the great traditions of the Navy, just as the defense of the Alamo did for the Texans. In both cases the initial loss was many times over repaid by the moral effects it created—effects which remain to this day and will remain so long as the nation exists.

In later years Farragut gave it as his opinion that Porter should have attempted battle under way or have run his ship ashore. But Porter undoubtedly refrained from taking either of these measures through reliance on Hillyar's promise not to attack him in neutral waters. Under the conditions, Porter had good reason for his bitter statement:

"I now consider my situation less unpleasant than that of Commodore Hillyar, who, in violation of every principle of honor and generosity, and regardless of the rights of nations, attacked the *Essex* in her crippled state within pistol shot of a neutral shore, when for six weeks I had daily offered him fair and honorable combat."

Many writers, among them Theodore Roosevelt, have excused Hillyar on the ground that he acted in the interest of his country, though to the detriment of his personal reputation. In later years, however, our fiery ex-President denounced the Germans most heartily for their violation of Belgian neutrality, an act certainly more susceptible of defense than Hillyar's attack on the *Essex*. The only possible excuse for violating the laws of war thus flagrantly is that the existence of a nation is at stake, and Hillyar certainly could not allege such a reason. With him it was merely a case of military expediency, not by any means necessity; and he violated not only the laws of war but "every principle of honor and generosity."

The chief interpreter of British naval thought in recent years was Sir Julian Corbett. He was knighted for his shrewd comments on naval occurrences. He did not describe, so far as we know, the Valparaiso incident. But his comments on another similar event in the Seven Years' War may be thought significant: "When England is scolded for her treachery on this occasion, as she still is, it would be more charitable to remember the temptation to which she was exposed by the incredible simplicity of her adversary. The wonder is that so great a chance was not seized with greater violence."

The question of expediency against justice is an old one. It was a much debated subject even in the time of Thucydides. At one time the Corinthian ambassadors made a notable statement to the Athenians. "Do not say to yourselves that this is just, but that in the event of war something else is expedient; for the true part of expediency is the path of right." That, we think, is a correct principle of statesmanship, except possibly in some tremendous national crisis, which no one may judge in advance. However, there are still great naval powers which act now, as in the past, upon the principle of military expediency. Should our naval commanders ever—may God forbid!—find themselves confronted with a situation similar to that which David Porter had to face a century ago off Valparaiso, it would be well for them to recall just what happened then and be guided accordingly. Then we will not again find ourselves in the unfortunate position of those Mamertines to whom Pompey made his famous reply: "What! Will you never cease prating of laws to us who have swords at our sides?"

There is still a further point we must make in connection with the surrender of the *Essex*. Porter made a defense which was unusually desperate for the time, and, as we have shown, gained great honor for the service thereby. But times have changed. War has grown more grim, more heartless, and it makes more demands upon naval officers than it did a century ago. Now, in cases of defeat, no thought can be given to saving the lives of the wounded; the ship must at all hazards be kept from falling into the hands of the enemy. There is no surrender now in a naval battle. The Russians and Japanese set the style—Germans and British most nobly kept it. We Americans cannot afford to confess to an inferiority in the military virtues.

Our soldiers proved that they knew how to die as well as those war-hardened veterans of the Prussian Guard. What soldiers can do, so also can sailors. In our regulations there should be a most drastic and categorical prohibition of the surrender of any naval vessel until its loss by sinking or grounding has been made a certainty.

CHAPTER XXII

STEWART CAPTURES THE *CYANE*
AND *LEVANT*

A S THE winter months approached, our Navy made preparations for a new series of ocean cruises. These commenced as follows:

Port of sailing	Date of sailing	Commander	Vessels and rates	Remarks
Boston	Dec. 17	Stewart	*Constitution,* 44	Captured *Cyane* and *Levant*
New York	Jan. 14	Decatur	*President,* 44	Captured by squadron
New York	Jan. 23	Warrington	*Peacock,* 18	Cruised to East Indies
		Biddle	*Hornet,* 18	Captured *Penguin*

On December 17 the *Constitution* ran the Boston blockade. Stewart went past Bermuda and Madeira, then combed the Bay of Biscay to good effect. After holding station for some time off Lisbon "Old Ironsides" was pointed southwest for Madeira. On February 20, when that island group bore west-southwest, distant 180 sea miles, her customary luck brought her into contact with the strong corvette *Cyane,* 34, and the heavily armed sloop *Levant,* 21 guns. Together they mounted 55 guns to the *Constitution's*

[317]

52 and threw a slightly greater weight of metal. This gave
them a formidable strength on paper, but actually almost
all their armament consisted of carronades, which could not
be compared with those terrible long 24's which filled the
Constitution's gun-deck ports. Also they had not her famous iron sides. Still the two Britons formed column
and most gallantly accepted Stewart's challenge.

Stewart might have fought at long range where the British carronades could not reach him, but night was coming
on and immediate decisive action was necessary if he were
to take both ships—he needed two this time to make up for
his failures during the last cruise. "At 5 minutes past 6,"
he wrote, "ranged up on the starboard side of the sternmost ship, about 300 yards distant, and commenced the
action by broadsides, both ships returning our fire with the
greatest spirit for about 15 minutes." Stewart's tactics
have a lesson for us: when you are anxious to engage and
night is approaching, do not waste time in getting all the
conditions in your favor; fight with the situation as it is.
Otherwise you will not capture your *Cyane* and *Levant,*
but have only a Jutland to explain.

After this first burst of cannonading great smoke clouds
obscured the view and gave the British ships a few minutes'
respite. Stewart now commenced a series of beautiful
maneuvers and raked each enemy in turn. They separated
and made off. Stewart ran down upon the crippled *Cyane.*
"We ranged upon her starboard quarter within hail, and
were about to give her our starboard broadside, when she
struck her colors, fired a lee gun and yielded." By eight
in the evening she had been manned by a prize crew and
Stewart was off after the *Levant* to complete his victory.

Captain Douglass had now repaired his damages and,
instead of trying to escape, sailed back to assist his con-

sort. Much as we admire his gallantry, we must say that it amounted to recklessness on this occasion. At 8:30 he ran full into the *Constitution*. He turned about and tried to escape. But within an hour "Old Ironsides" had opened with her bow chasers and at 10:00 P.M. the white ensign came down. "At 1 A.M.," Stewart reported, "the damages of our rigging were repaired, sails shifted, and the ship in fighting condition." Our people well knew the importance of being ready for action on an instant's notice. The misadventure of the first *Wasp* under Jacob Jones's command had taught them that.

It is true that the *Constitution* had a marked superiority of force in this combat and we can claim no special credit in winning it. Still the taking of two ships in such a spectacular manner at a cost of only fifteen casualties was a good day's work and showed that "Old Ironsides" under her new captain had maintained her former high standard of efficiency. Napoleon said that Frederick's tactics at Leuthen were "a masterpiece of maneuver." One would be justified in saying the same of Captain Stewart's in this engagement.

The *Constitution* with her two prizes made for the Cape Verde Islands. On March 10 they dropped anchor in Porto Praya. The frigate's crew was distributed over all three vessels to effect repairs and 120 prisoners were paroled ashore. The next day three large frigates—two were 50-gun ships—suddenly appeared off the port in a fog. Stewart knew what regard the British were accustomed to pay to the observance of neutrality. If they had attacked the *Essex*, what would they do to the *Constitution*, which three times had humbled their pride? Effective resistance was out of the question; her crew could not be reassembled before the enemy would be upon her. Stewart hoisted the signal to get under way and ordered the smaller vessels to follow him to sea. It is said that all his squadron were under way in ten minutes.

The three Britishers followed in full chase. There was small chance that they could overtake the *Constitution,* but it seemed certain that both other ships, injured as they still must have been, would be recaptured. The *Cyane* was in the rear and was rapidly being overhauled. Stewart ordered her to separate. Such was the respect for our frigate that all three British vessels kept on after her. This allowed the *Cyane* to escape; on April 10 she came into New York. Next Stewart ordered the *Levant* to tack. By this time our enemies seem to have given up hope of running down the *Constitution;* they would have to take what they could get. To make sure of the little sloop all three of them tacked after her. Lieutenant Ballard was in command of the *Levant.* He could not have been in a more awkward situation. If he kept at sea capture was certain. His only hope, and a very slim one, was that his enemies might observe Portuguese neutrality. So he headed back and made the port. There he let go his anchor within 150 yards of a Portuguese fort in the hope that this might deter the British from attacking him. Very much the contrary—for the paroled prisoners seized the fort and opened fire on the *Levant* with its guns. The *Acasta,* 40, and *Newcastle,* 50, soon joined in the target practice. Their fire was ludicrously wild. In fifteen minutes they did not injure a single man on the *Levant,* but levelled a good part of the town. Ballard then surrendered, unfortunately without scuttling his ship, which certainly should have been done. "On the 12th, at 6h 30m," writes William James in the most matter of fact way, as though he were telling of an everyday occurrence, "Sir George Collier went on shore to communicate with the governor, in consequence of the damage done to the houses of the town by the shot of the *Acasta* and *Newcastle.*" James makes no comment upon this phase of the episode, but writes bitterly of the *Constitution's* escape, "the most blundering piece of business recorded in these six volumes." Poor Sir George never lived it down; ten years later he committed suicide.

The *Constitution* landed her remaining prisoners at Maranho, Brazil. Thence she sailed for Porto Rico, where Stewart learned that peace had been signed. When she sailed into New York in the middle of May, "Old Ironsides" received a splendid welcome from this, her last war cruise. To this day she holds first place in the hearts of Americans.

CHAPTER XXIII

THE LOSS OF THE *PRESIDENT*

THE NAVY Department, in view of the slight successes recently won in Atlantic cruises, had been planning an expedition into the distant East Indies. The sudden arrival of a squadron in this area so vital to British trade might result in successes surpassing even those of Porter in the South Pacific. The convoy system had not yet been organized effectively in the Indian Ocean, and the great East Indiamen were then the richest prizes afloat. Stephen Decatur, renowned for his Tripolitan exploits and his victory over the *Macedonian,* was selected as commodore. His broad pennant flew from the *President,* 44, in which we have followed the fortunes of John Rodgers for four long cruises. In January, 1815, he was joined by two fine sloops: the *Peacock,* Captain Warrington, and the *Hornet,* Captain Biddle, who had been first lieutenant of the *Wasp* under Jacob Jones. A storeship, the *Tom Bowline,* completed the squadron.

New York was a very difficult port from which to run the blockade. Decatur had already tried getting out through Long Island Sound, with the most unfortunate results. The exit to the southward was no easier. Its approaches then were not so well dredged as they are now and it was a simple matter for the British to watch its one channel, which does not appear to have been any too well charted or buoyed. Even when through this channel, the Long Island and Jersey coasts limited the courses of outgoing vessels to a sector of some ninety degrees. Should the blockaders be blown off by a northwest storm they would still have but a short line to patrol. All through those terrible winter months a powerful British squadron maintained the blockade: *Majestic*, 56, *Endymion*, 40, *Pomone*, 38, and *Tenedos*, 38. Good captains commanded these ships, good seamen manned them.

Yes, Decatur had a most difficult problem to solve. His previous failure increased his eagerness to culminate his war career with a striking success. But the fates decreed otherwise. We were to have a new and most striking illustration of the bruising pressure of an overwhelming sea power. Even Stephen Decatur, our bright Roland of the Seas, was to fall before its might; and not, we must sadly confess, in the knightly manner his previously gallant career had led us to expect.

On January 14 a gale blew off the British squadron; here was the chance. The sloops were not ready for sea. But the *President* weighed anchor and stood down the Main Ship Channel. The pilot grounded her on the bar, and there she bumped and pounded for several hours. Her hull was damaged and her masts sprung so as seriously to reduce her speed. A westerly wind prevented return so Decatur made full sail to the southeastward. Soon darkness covered him and all seemed well. But, no! In the early morning the unlucky *President* ran full into the midst of the British squadron. The hunter now was hunted!

It is just one hour before daybreak on the fifteenth when the first contact is made, so the enemy have a full period of daylight in which to make their chase. It was in these same waters that Isaac Hull in the *Constitution* had distanced a British squadron early in the war. But now a tenacious enemy gain, yard by yard, foot by foot, upon our splendid *President*. Inexorable as time they come on, like four great hounds in chase of a lone black wolf. At 2:30 P.M. the

Endymion opens up with her bow chasers. For three hours Decatur stands this harassing fire. Finally he can stand it no longer; soon a shot will bring down a spar and end everything.

Darkness is coming on. Perhaps if he can beat his fastest hunter, or even cripple him, he can distance the others. So he stands at bay, turns quickly down upon the *Endymion*. His guns are loaded with bar and chain shot. They are aimed high at her spars and sails. Close action begins!

The action is sharp indeed, our gunnery as good as ever. The *Endymion's* sails at length are "cut from the yards"; so they themselves admit. But in turn, the *President* has suffered heavily. The British have obeyed the injunctions of Broke to shoot into the hull and kill the men. Lieutenants Fitz Henry Babbitt and Archibald Hamilton—the same who took the colors of the *Macedonian* to Washington—have been killed. And many others. The ship, however, is little damaged and Decatur again makes sail. For a time it appears that he has escaped but at length the hunters again appear. On come the *Pomone* and *Tenedos,* followed by the great *Majestic,* 56 guns. The two former gain rapidly. At 11:00 P.M. the *Pomone* opens fire. All hope of escape is at an end. All Decatur can do now is to finish in style. But no! Splendid Decatur, daring, eager in attack, a very *beau sabreur* of the seas, gives up the ship!

It is true that the *President,* which already had suffered severely, had no chance of defeating two more frigates, each almost equal to her in size. And, if they needed assistance, there was the great *Majestic.* Still, we are decidedly of the opinion that the surrender of our fine frigate, yet capable of prolonged resistance, was premature. While it has been said by Roosevelt that the surrender reflected no discredit upon the Navy, he adds that it likewise reflected no credit. It demonstrated that, at this stage of his career, Decatur fell far short of being a Lawrence or a Porter. He knew how to win but not how to lose.

A great captain must mix boldness with caution, but Decatur had mixed them the wrong way. We could wish that he had used more caution in running the blockade, more boldness when brought to bay. As long as he could inflict any further losses upon the enemy and delay their return to the blockade it was his duty to have continued the fight. He might thereby assist the remainder of his squadron in breaking the blockade.

But there was another and more far-reaching reason why he should have made a more determined resistance: the enhancement of the prestige and honor of our service and our country. Reputation is the most precious asset in this world, whether in civil life or in a military service. In defeat, even more than in victory, it must be maintained. We have seen how the heroism of Lawrence and the desperate defense of the *Essex* had enhanced the reputation of the Navy in defeat, raised us even in the estimation of the foe. Decatur now had an opportunity to perform an exploit which would have rung around the world; one which would have made a profound impression upon our poor divided people and the war-wearied enemy. He failed to seize it!

To do so would have cost the lives of brave men. But success in war, material and moral, must be paid for in the lives of men. That is one of the rules of the game. A commander cannot be influenced by a desire to save his men as long as his ship can fight. Nor would a properly disciplined crew wish their commander to be concerned with their lives in the heat of battle. Rather would they follow

the example of those companions of King Harold Hard-
raade, of whom Arnor wrote the immortal lines:

> The gallant men who saw him fall
> Would take no quarter; one and all
> Resolved to die with their loved king
> Around his corpse in a corpse-ring.

It is not pleasant to make such comments about such a
brave man and splendid captain as Decatur. We have given
him the highest praise, and shall do so again. All great
leaders have had their moments of weakness; this was his
bad day. But even here he had suffered no disgrace, for
a court of his peers honorably acquitted him of blame. We
have held him to a high standard, which he himself was
among the first to set. Certainly it would have added to
the prestige of his country and his own fame had Decatur
died gallantly on the deck of a battered frigate rather than
from the pistol of a brother officer. Then, lying mortally
wounded, he said: "I wish I had fallen in defense of my
country!" What sadder words were ever said?

Also, had his ship been fought like the *Essex*, we could
walk with higher heads along the Thames Embankment past
that old ship which bears across its stern those ironic words:
H.M.S. *President*.

Incidentally, though it has little bearing on the subject,
we can hardly recommend the way in which Decatur's court
presented its findings. In it one may find such self-satisfied statements as this: "In this unequal conflict the enemy
gained a ship, but the victory was ours." Let us hope the
U. S. Navy gains no more such victories! It reminds us
too forcibly of some remarks Thucydides made of the
Corinthians:

"They refused to acknowledge defeat on the same ground
which made the Athenians unwilling to claim the victory.

For the Corinthians considered themselves conquerors, if they were not severely defeated; but the Athenians thought that they were defeated because they had not gained a signal victory."

The Secretary of the Navy published his comments of the action, saying "that further resistance would have been unjustifiable, and a useless sacrifice of the lives of brave men." That is an excellent way in which to encourage your captains to fight courageously! But let us pass to a more cheerful subject.

CHAPTER XXIV

THE *HORNET* TAKES THE *PENGUIN*

UNAWARE of the fate of the *President,* the *Peacock, Hornet,* and *Tom Bowline* continued their preparations for a distant cruise. On January 22 another northwest gale blew off the blockaders; the next day our little detachment put to sea and got clear without even sighting an enemy. They headed for Tristan da Cunha, the appointed rendezvous. After a few days the *Hornet* parted company. The other two vessels made the rendezvous on March 18, but a gale blew them off. On the twenty-third the *Hornet* arrived. Not a sail was in sight.

Captain Biddle decided to wait for his consorts and in order to do so with more comfort he sailed for the northern end of the island where there was precarious holding ground for his anchors. Before he could let go, a tiny speck appeared on the horizon to the southeast. It was a sail. Probably it would turn out to be the *Peacock;* it might be an enemy merchantman, even a man-of-war. To be prepared for any eventuality Biddle made sail and stood down the western side of the island, doubtless to prepare an ambush for the stranger.

As the *Hornet* rounded the southern end of the island the strange sail was still in view, coming on steadily for the Yankee sloop. She was not the *Peacock,* not the *Bowline,* not a merchantman. She certainly was not avoiding the issue, seemed entirely confident in her strength. Hornets had better be ready! They have a reputation to live up to—a tradition to maintain. It is now two years since their famous battle with the *Peacock,* but probably there

[328]

still remain some old topmen and gunners who fought under Captain Jim. The yarns of those old days have doubtless improved with time; we doubt if the *Peacock* now lasted even for the eleven minutes recorded so accurately by the captain's clerk. Now these old-timers must make good; show how they did it two years ago. The young fellows doubtless had become a bit tired of these boastings; they would show now what they could do; would shoot straighter than these old gunners; handle their sails more smartly. Who knows, perhaps they might even beat that eleven-minute record. Well, at any rate, let's try.

Still the stranger came on, seemed looking for a fight. Our captain reported: "At 1:40 P.M., being within nearly musket-shot distance, she hauled her wind on the starboard tack, hoisted English colors and fired a gun. . . . The satisfaction which was diffused throughout the ship when it was ascertained that the stranger was an enemy's sloop-of-war, and the alacrity with which every one repaired to quarters, fully assured me that their conduct in the action would be marked with coolness and intrepidity." Biddle, a splendid officer, was taking his ship into battle for the first time. What a reassuring effect must the high spirit of his crew have had upon him in this moment of awesome responsibility. Had Tolstoi seen his report he would have cited it as another instance where the mass spirit of an organization rather than the will of its commander directed the course of battle. Incidentally, no one has written so well on the psychology of war as Tolstoi—he surpasses even Ardant du Picq.

The British vessel was the strong sloop-of-war *Penguin,* Captain Dickenson, practically equal in fighting strength to the *Hornet,* 274 to 279 pounds of metal in the broadside. She had been searching for an American privateer, the

Young Wasp, which had been attacking East Indiamen, but a Yankee sloop-of-war would do just as well, if she could be taken!

When the enemy showed his colors, Biddle broke his battle flags and let go a broadside. The cannonade grew fast and furious. The wind was about north; both vessels were making westerly courses on the starboard tack, converging somewhat towards each other. The *Penguin* was to windward. The swell was long and the ships rolled deeply; accurate gun-pointing was difficult. These were the conditions under which we had won our most decisive victories; the more difficult the conditions for shooting, the more was our superiority in gunnery emphasized. In fifteen minutes it became evident that we would win with ease in a purely gunnery battle. Captain Dickenson saw that his only chance was to board. He had the weather position, so threw his helm up, sailed free, and stood down upon the *Hornet.* Being mortally wounded, he was no longer able to personally supervise the maneuver, but his first lieutenant, McDonald, executed his orders to perfection. Biddle reported: "As soon as I perceived he would certainly fall aboard, I called the boarders, so as to be ready to repel any attempt to board us. At the instant every officer and man repaired to the quarter-deck, where the ships were coming in contact, and eagerly pressed me to permit them to board the enemy; but this I would not permit, as it was evident, from the commencement of the action, that our fire was greatly superior both in quickness and effect." Fortunate is the captain who has thus to restrain the impetuosity of his crew. Fortunate the crew which has a captain able to make correct decisions so coolly in the heat of action.

The *Penguin's* bowsprit came over the *Hornet's* starboard side between the main and mizzen masts. As the *Penguin* pitched forward, her bowsprit came down on the *Hornet's* side and broke off. This parted her forestays, and her foremast came crashing down. The wreckage caught in the *Hornet's* mizzen rigging and broke the spanker boom. Our musketry swept the enemy's decks and prevented him from even trying to board. Believing that he heard calls for quarter, Biddle ordered all fire to cease and sprang upon the taffrail. Two marines on the *Penguin's* forecastle leveled their muskets and fired at him at point-blank range. One missed—the other wounded him severely in the neck. The action was renewed; our sloop drew clear, commenced wearing to bring her port broadside to bear. The *Penguin* had had enough. Her battle ensign came fluttering down. "From the firing of the first gun," said Biddle, "to the last time the enemy cried out he had surrendered, was exactly twenty-two minutes by the watch." Well done, Hornets! And you also, Captain Biddle, well done!

The *Penguin* had made a most gallant resistance; brave Dickenson had fought well. His ship was a perfect wreck; 14 killed and 28 wounded were his losses out of a total of 132 officers and men. Our losses were trifling: 2 killed and 9 wounded, mostly by musket balls when the ships were alongside. The hull had not been hit by a single round shot, but there were considerable injuries aloft. The victory had been one of the most decisive on record. Even James, a partisan British historian, is forced to admit that he "cannot offer the trifling disparity of force in this action as an excuse for the *Penguin's* capture. The chief cause is . . . the immense disparity between the vessels in . . . the effectiveness of their crews."

On the twenty-fifth the *Peacock* and *Tom Bowline* reappeared. The latter was sent off to Rio de Janeiro with the prisoners. A great quantity of the *Penguin's* stores were shifted to the *Hornet* and she was then scuttled. After waiting in vain for Decatur until April 12 the two sloops sailed for the East Indies. On the twenty-seventh at 7:00 A.M., when in latitude 38° 30′ south and longitude 33° east, a sail was chased. This unique pursuit was continued until 3:22 P.M. of the twenty-eighth, when the *Peacock* suddenly signaled that the stranger was a ship of the line. In fact she was the 74-gun ship *Cornwallis* and her captain, having lured the *Hornet* to within eight miles of him, tacked about and made all sail in chase. The sloop was weighted down with the *Penguin's* stores and the liner gained rapidly; during the night Biddle threw overboard a great quantity of excess gear.

Still the *Cornwallis* gained; by 7:00 A.M. of the twenty-ninth she was within gunshot of her prey; her bow chasers spoke out in turn, firing thirty rounds in all. Fortunately for us her gunnery was of the worst; not a shot hit its mark. "As his shot went over us," Biddle reported, "I cut away the remaining anchor and cable, threw overboard the launch, six more of our guns, more of our shot, and every heavy article that was at hand." Thus lightened, the *Hornet* drew ahead; by nine o'clock she was out of gunshot. All hands breathed easier. But not for long, for soon the liner again commenced to gain. By eleven she was close at hand. "I now therefore threw overboard all our remaining guns but one long gun, nearly all our shot, all our spare spars, cut away the topgallant forecastle, and cleared everything off deck, as well as from below, to lighten us as much as possible."

Despite these measures the great liner drew closer and closer. By noon she had reduced the range to three-quarters of a mile—very moderate gun range. Again her bow chasers opened up. The Hornets gave themselves up for lost. With only one gun left they could not make even a show of resistance for the honor of her flag. What an end for Captain Jim's old ship! Doubtless many a strange prayer passed the lips of grizzled old seamen, victors of two sea fights. Picture officers and men watching those smoke puffs against the liner's bows, holding their breath as the solid shot whistle overhead or splash alongside. Shot after shot miss, but can not keep on missing forever. See! The liner yaws off to one side; gradually her great broadside comes into view. There are her two full decks of long guns, 32's and 24's. Now a double row of smoke puffs appears: she has fired a broadside. A numerous salvo of shot hurtle toward their little target, followed by a thunderous roar. Again and again her broadside fires; but the bark of this British bulldog is worse than his bite. Only three shot find their mark and they do little damage. Perhaps after all sea-god Neptune will help his gallant Yankee seamen, answer their unorthodox prayers. Sure enough, the liner's yaws have lost her ground; Aeolus sends the little *Hornet* a favorable wind. See, she draws away, foot by foot, yard by yard. By 2:00 P.M. the *Cornwallis* is out of range, ceases fire in disgust. Better get in a little target practice if you want to catch these Yankee ships.

Still the liner plugs along—will not give up. It is not until the afternoon of the thirtieth that her topsails drop below the horizon and the Hornets can congratulate themselves on their miraculous escape. No use, though, to continue her cruise with only one gun; even a merchantman could beat her! So Biddle reluctantly turned about. Not thinking it prudent to make directly for the American coast in his defenseless condition, he headed for Brazil to get the news. When he arrived at San Salvador (Bahia) on June 10 he heard that peace had been declared.

Meanwhile Warrington kept on in the *Peacock* for the
East Indies. He took four great East Indiamen. By June
30 he was in the Straits of Sunda. There he encountered
the East India Company's brig *Nautilus* of 14 guns. Her
captain hailed that peace had been signed. Believing this
to be a customary British ruse, Warrington demanded unconditional surrender. This demand the British captain refused to accede to until two broadsides had convinced him
that resistance was useless. Warrington later released his
prize. He has been criticized for opening fire, even by
Roosevelt, but when we consider the many breaches of in-
ternational law which the English committed during this
war, we believe that his suspicions of a ruse in this case were
amply justified.

CHAPTER XXV

PRIVATEERING DELIVERS THE PUNCH

DURING the fall of 1814 the successes of our privateers increased by leaps and bounds. The conclusion of peace with France and the serious losses received by our sea-going Navy allowed the British to give them practically their exclusive attention. But even this advantage did not allow the British Navy to give anything like suitable protection to their merchant marine. Englishmen perhaps had those days in mind when in 1927 they demanded cruiser construction. It is estimated that in the five-month period from September 30, 1814, to the end of the war our privateers took no less than four hundred prizes. British merchants, believing that the conclusion of the Napoleonic wars would give renewed impetus to their trade, found conditions becoming worse than ever before. The *Naval Chronicle,* a British service journal, admitted that: "The depredations committed on our commerce by American ships of war and privateers have attained an extent beyond all former precedent. The insurance between Bristol and Waterford or Cork is now three times higher than it was when we were at war with all Europe. The Admiralty have been overwhelmed with letters of complaint or remonstrance."

Mahan adds: "This weighty blow to the pride and commerce of Great Britain was not dealt by the national government; for the national government had gone to war culpably unprepared. It was the work of the people almost wholly, guided and governed by their own shrewdness and capacity; seeking, indeed, less a military than a pecuniary result, an indemnity at the expense of the enemy for the loss to which

[335]

they had been subjected by protracted inefficiency in administration and in statesmanship on the part of their rulers."

Among the most effective privateers during this period of the war were the *Monmouth,* which took twenty-three prizes off Newfoundland; the *Lawrence,* which came into New York on January 25, 1815, after having made thirteen captures; and the *Amelia,* which returned to Baltimore with a record of ten.

On the twenty-sixth of September, 1814, the privateer brig *General Armstrong* made herself more famous than the Secretary of War whose name she bore. Under Captain Samuel C. Reid she was anchored at Fayal in the Azores, near the place where Sir Richard Grenville, later nobly assisted by poet Tennyson, made the *Revenge* famous in naval history. The *Armstrong* had a crew of ninety men and a battery of one long 24-pounder and eight long 9's. Early in the afternoon a British squadron en route to New Orleans came in for a few days' rest. It consisted of the *Plantagenet,* 74, *Rota,* 38, and *Carnation,* 18. Captain Lloyd of the *Plantagenet* thought it would be a simple matter to take the privateer. The letter of a British eyewitness ashore, appended to the account of James Durand, recently published by the Naval Order of the United States, gives a graphic description of the epic struggle which took place, well worthy of comparison with that made by the *Revenge* against her fifty-three Spanish enemies.

About nine in the evening four boats rowed in from the British vessels to cut out the privateer. The moon was full and spectators ashore could see every detail of the fight. With admirable calmness Reid held his fire, several times warning off his enemies. "They, notwithstanding, pushed on and were in the act of boarding before any defense was made on the privateer. A warm contest ensued on both

From an old painting

SAMUEL C. REID

From an old engraving

H. M. PACKET *Hinchinbrook* AND THE U. S. PRIVATEER *Grand Turk*

sides. The boats were finally dispersed with great loss."
Thus ended the first lesson!

Captain Reid now got up anchor, brought his schooner
under the very guns of the Portuguese fort, and moored
his ship parallel to the shore. The governor sent a warm
protest to the British captain. He found that, as Lysander
said, "the law spoke too softly to be heard in such a noise
of war." "Van Lloyd's answer," says our English eyewitness, "was that he was determined to destroy the vessel
at the expense of all Fayal and if any protection should be
given her by the fort, he would not leave a house standing
in the village." That has a real pleasant ring to it, don't
you think? Well, Captain, you have poured your wine—
now drink it! Perhaps it will be bitter!

At midnight fourteen cutters left the British squadron.
They formed in order and rowed toward the schooner. According to our eyewitness, they were manned by four hundred officers and men. In them were the first four lieutenants of the *Plantagenet* and *Rota* and the first officer of
the *Carnation*. This time the British meant business, as
they came on with their "No quarter!" shouts.

But Samuel Reid meant business too! As he made his
last preparations, his men insisted that he take off the conspicuous uniform hat which he wore. To please them he
pushed on a tall hat—looks like a present-day opera hat in
his portrait—which was even more conspicuous. Yes, Reid
was ready.

> Wakeful, ready, with warrior's wrath,
> Bold he bided the battle's issue!

On came the boats. Says our witness: "When they got
within gunshot, a tremendous and effectual discharge was
made by the privateer which threw the boats into confusion.

They then returned a spirited fire, but the privateer kept up so spirited a discharge that it was almost impossible for the boats to make any progress. They finally succeeded, however, after immense loss, to get alongside of her and attempted to board her at every quarter, cheered on by the officers with a shout of 'No quarter,' which we could distinctly hear as well as shrieks and cries."

Well did our privateersmen stand to their nettings with musket, pike and cutlass, "and their hearts were steadfast and lusted for battle." For full forty minutes the tide of battle ebbed and flowed. Then the enemy withdrew—such of them as could. Rarely have they ever suffered such a bloody defeat. Four boats were sunk; others drifted ashore; only one officer escaped unwounded. They admit a loss of thirty-four killed and eighty-six wounded. Our British witness states that their killed exceeded 120 and their wounded 90, that for three days they were burying the bodies which washed ashore. Reid placed their killed at 120 and the wounded at 130. "Captain Lloyd is badly wounded in the leg," he reported. "It is said, however, by the British that the wound was occasioned by an ox treading on him." Rather a delicate touch, don't you think? In all this fighting our loss was but two killed and seven wounded, reported by Captain Reid officially and confirmed by our Englishman ashore.

Next morning the *Carnation* came in and commenced a gunnery duel at close range. The privateersmen still continued to fight with the greatest gallantry and to the surprise of all hands beat off their much stronger opponent, with one of her topmasts and yards shot away, her rigging much cut up, and her hull splintered by several shot. "The Americans, now finding their principal gun and several others dismounted, deemed it folly to think of saving the privateer against so superior a force. Therefore they cut away her masts to the deck, blew a hole through her bottom, took out their small arms, clothing, etc. and went ashore. I discovered only two shot holes in the hull of the privateer, although much cut up in the rigging." This is what Ballard should have done to the *Levant*.

Being unable to use the prize, thus damaged, the British set her on fire. Next Captain Lloyd demanded the surrender of the Americans and threatened to come ashore with five hundred men to seize them. Our men then retired into a strong convent and prepared to defend it to the last. The people ashore, including many Englishmen, were incensed at the conduct of the attacking squadron, which already had resulted in the destruction of many houses and the killing of a woman. The governor stuck to his guns and Lloyd backed down. The tremendous losses he had received delayed the sailing of his squadron for ten days and thus Reid contributed indirectly to Andrew Jackson's brilliant victory at New Orleans.

Other accounts of this noted action differ somewhat in details from that given above. It is said that there were seven instead of fourteen boats in the second attack, but the loss of 120 which the British admit officially would seem excessive for such a small number.

We have followed Captain Boyle on his first cruise in the brig *Chasseur* to British waters and seen how he established his blockade of the enemy coasts. After a refit he set out for the West Indies. His battery had originally consisted of sixteen long 12-pounders, but when chased by the *Barossa* frigate he had thrown overboard ten of them to avoid capture. After this narrow escape the *Chasseur* continued her hunt, gathering in twelve prizes. From one of them she took eight long 9's. There were no shot available to fit these guns, so Boyle was reduced to the expedient of ramming home one 6-pound and one 4-pound shot in each, a measure which scarcely contributed to accuracy in gunnery.

On February 26 Boyle was six miles off the Cuban coast and twenty miles east of Havana. At eleven in the morning he sighted a schooner and gave chase. At 1:00 P.M. the stranger hoisted British colors and fired a stern gun. Our people could see only three gun ports on her port side and thought that they had to deal with but a weakly armed merchant vessel. At 1:26 the privateer ranged up on the enemy's port beam at pistol shot. Both vessels were on the starboard tack, the privateer to leeward. The wind was fresh from east-northeast, the sea moderate.

Readers remember what a cruel surprise the little *Saucy Jack* received from a mystery ship loaded with soldiers. Now the *Chasseur* was to have a similar experience. Suddenly, and to Boyle's complete surprise, the schooner opened seven more gun ports on her port side, hoisted the white ensign, and let go a broadside of round shot and grape.

Here was a pretty mess; poor Boyle must have cudgeled his brain for a few moments. What should he do? Here is how he reasoned: "I should not willingly, perhaps, have sought a contest with a King's vessel, knowing that is not our object; but my expectations at first were a valuable vessel and a valuable cargo also. When I found myself deceived, the honor of the flag intrusted to my care was not to be graced by flight." Bravo, Boyle! Now go and fight him!

The *Chasseur* had much headway on and ran past her opponent; the British captain put his helm up and tried to run under her stern. Boyle countered by luffing into the wind. He shot across the schooner's bow and gained the weather position. Both captains now eased off and ran before the wind. Ten minutes of heavy cannonading convinced Boyle that he could not win that way, so he ran the schooner aboard. His boarders sprang over the side. The enemy surrendered. The prize proved to be the schooner *St. Lawrence,* Lieutenant H. C. Gordon, a regular cruiser of the Royal Navy. She was formerly the American privateer *Atlas* and now carried one long 9 and fourteen short 12's, a battery considerably superior to the makeshift armament of the *Chasseur.* The casualties were heavy for such small craft: twenty-three for the *St. Lawrence* and thirteen for the *Chasseur.* This was a fitting exploit to conclude the long privateering career of Captain Boyle. A very real sea captain he was—may his memory long remain in the hearts of American seamen!

While the efficiency of our privateers had greatly increased, we must expressly state that we have selected some of the most creditable of their exploits to describe. Roosevelt wrote: "Captain Southcomb of the *Lottery,* Captain Reid of the *General Armstrong,* Captain Ordronaux of the *Neufchatel,* and Captain Boyle of the *Chasseur,* deserve as much credit as any regularly commissioned sea officers. But it is a mistake to consider these cases as representing the average; an ordinary privateer was, naturally enough, no match for a British regular cruiser of equal force."

The great increase in the effectiveness of privateering during the last six months of the war induced the Navy Department to propose a plan for constructing and operating vessels of the privateer type. On November 11, 1814, Congress authorized the construction of twenty small vessels to mount from eight to sixteen guns. It was planned to operate them in two squadrons under Porter and Perry. The close of the war prevented us from making this most interesting experiment, which resembled so closely many aspects of the German submarine warfare. Perhaps there is still merit in this old idea. Had the Germans had free access to the ocean there is little doubt but that squadrons of armed merchant raiders, like the *Moewe* and *Wolf,* would have taken heavy toll among British merchant vessels, until a convoy system for all the Seven Seas could have been organized.

There can be no doubt but that our naval exploits on the high seas during this war contributed much toward the comparatively favorable terms of the peace treaty. They raised our Navy to a place in American hearts which it has never been able to regain. They moved even our bitterest enemies to outspoken admiration. An Englishman, Michael Scott, in 1830 expressed this idea with admirable clarity:

"I don't like Americans; I have no wish to eat with them, drink with them, deal or consort with them in any way. But let me tell the whole truth—nor to fight with them, were it not for the laurels to be acquired by overcoming an enemy so brave, determined, alert, and in every way so worthy of one's steel as they have always proved. In the field of grappling in mortal combat on the blood-slippery quarter-deck of an enemy's vessel, a British soldier or sailor is the bravest of the brave. No soldier or sailor of any country, saving and excepting always those damned Yankees, can stand against them."

PART IV
We Hold Our Lake Frontier
1812-1815

CHAPTER I

THE WAR ON THE NORTHERN FRONTIER

HAVING covered in some detail our cruiser warfare on the high seas, it now becomes our task to picture those even more momentous campaigns along our northern frontier, during which our naval forces played so decisive a rôle.

It may be recalled that the date of our declaration of war was June 18, 1812—three years to a day before Waterloo. Although the whole world had been at war for twenty years, and conflict with Great Britain had been developing for at least ten, our country was completely unprepared, morally as well as physically.

For the last three administrations Jefferson and Madison had been genially wrecking our military and naval services. Since 1801 these master politicians had been reducing our national debt, largely at the expense of the naval and military establishments. "The interest on the savings," Mahan pungently declared, "was received at Detroit, on the Niagara frontier, in the Chesapeake and the Delaware."

However, it was not entirely a question of money. The military services could undoubtedly have been organized on a far more efficient basis had the administration shown a proper interest in their development or even permitted the responsible officers to go ahead. The truth is that Jefferson, forgetting that we owed our independence to military and naval power, hated, even feared, the regular Army and Navy. Once war was declared, however, the arch pacifist changed overnight to an ardent militarist. "The acquisition of Canada this year, as far as the neighborhood of

Quebec, will be a mere matter of marching." This brave prediction bears a certain resemblance to the statement of another Jeffersonian Democrat who considered it a simple matter to raise a million armed men overnight.

The prediction of the gallant ex-President reminds us greatly of a paragraph from the facile pen of Colonel Ardant du Picq: "When in complete security after dinner, in full physical and moral contentment, men consider war and battle, they are animated by a noble ardor that has nothing in common with reality. But oblige them to march for days and weeks to arrive at the battle ground, and on the day of battle oblige them to wait minutes, hours to deliver it. If they were honest they would testify how much the physical fatigue and mental anguish that precede action have lowered their morale, how much less eager to fight they are than a month before, when they rose from the table in a generous mood." Unfortunately, Jefferson did not submit himself to the test of marching to Quebec; had he been given this opportunity perhaps he might have revised his opinions.

Not even responsibility bore its weight upon the resident of Monticello. This rested on the weak shoulders of his henchman, poor note-writing Madison. Gerald W. Johnson writes: "A bewildered and apprehensive President he was, facing a war he was in no wise prepared to fight, and which relatively few of his own countrymen seemed disposed to help him fight. In front of him Old England, grimly clearing for action, was hardly more dreadful to contemplate than was New England behind him, howling bloody murder and threatening to bolt to the enemy camp. War abroad, sedition at home, no army, no navy, no money, no men— he was a bewildered and apprehensive President indeed."

We have seen how poorly prepared our Navy was on the

ocean. On the lakes along our northern frontier we were even worse. Our only naval vessel in these vital waters reposed on Lake Ontario. Our Army was little better. Of the 10,000 troops authorized as the permanent strength of the regular Army there were available ten days before war was declared only 6,734. Of an additional 25,000 specially authorized in January the Secretary of War guessed that he might have about 5,000 enrolled. There were, of course, militia in numbers which appeared formidable on paper, but they were of no use in the field unless a genius at mutiny-quelling should be sent by Heaven to command them.

The distribution of these troops for a war on the northern frontier does not seem to have been arranged by a Moltke. Detroit was secured by a huge field army of ninety-four, Fort Mackinac by an army corps of fifty-seven. The discipline and training of our troops were at the lowest ebb. The officers were remarkable for their incompetence. Save only Harrison, there was no general worthy of the name. He had beaten Tecumseh the year before at Tippecanoe and now was not employed in an important command. Down in Tennessee there was, it is true, a certain major general of militia, but he had been a defender of Aaron Burr and was anything but *persona grata* to the Virginia dynasty then on the throne. Gerald W. Johnson tells us, and we believe him: "Washington had no eyes for studying men. It was still obsessed with the notion that the only proper way to conduct a war was to turn armies over to ossified old dug-outs, relics of the Revolution, forgetting the obvious truth that the very fact that a man was a good soldier thirty-five years ago is proof positive that he is too old to take command today."

Fortunately for us the Napoleonic wars had concentrated almost the entire military power of Great Britain in Europe.

Our declaration of war surprised the British almost as much as it did our own people. In all Canada they had but 4,500 regular troops. However, their efficiency was far greater than our ill-trained recruits and, what is really worthy of note, they had a general. In fact, we think that he was the only general of the first year of the war who really knew his job. It is a real satisfaction for the historian to find one such fellow, even if he wears a red coat. His name is Isaac Brock, lieutenant governor of Canada. Even in these busy days he is worth study by Americans. We hope readers will enjoy the manner in which he played the lead in the first act of our drama.

The British had another advantage which must be strongly emphasized: they had the practically undisputed naval command of the Lakes. As we shall describe later in more detail, they had no less than twelve naval vessels on the Great Lakes; these proved a mighty support to Brock's slender and widely scattered detachments.

In 1812 there were extremely few roads along our northern frontier; such as existed were almost impracticable for wheeled traffic during much of the year. Under such conditions lakes and navigable rivers provided the only suitable lines of communication for trade and warfare. All the British settlements on the Great Lakes depended upon the St. Lawrence River for supplies from eastern Canada and the home country. It should therefore have been evident that our most effective way of exerting pressure upon the enemy was to establish ourselves in force at some point on this river. Brock saw this clearly. "Should the communications between Montreal and Kingston be cut off," he wrote from the West, "the fate of the troops in this part of the province will be decided."

By an unusual coincidence, not only did an operation

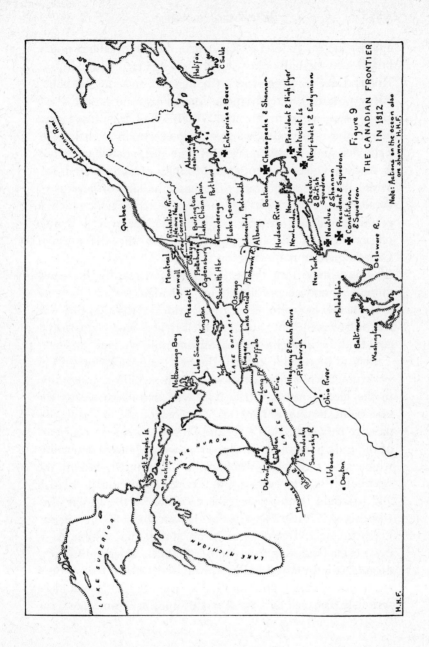

Figure 9

THE CANADIAN FRONTIER
IN 1812

Note: Actions on the ocean also
are shown.—H.H.F.

H.H.F.

against the St. Lawrence River promise the greatest results, but it was actually the easiest to execute. The Hudson River, Lake George, Lake Champlain, and the Richelieu River provided a ready-made line of transportation direct from New York to Montreal. This had been used time after time in previous wars and was certainly well known. Schuyler and Montgomery had travelled northward along it toward Quebec; Gentleman Johnny Burgoyne had followed it to the southward. Perhaps the lack of success of these ventures had given this route a reputation which it certainly did not deserve. Even after the war a British officer sent by Wellington to examine the defenses of Canada gave it as his opinion that "the Montreal frontier is the most important and at present confessedly the most vulnerable and accessible part of Canada."

A further point in favor of an attack along this line was that this was the only area in which British naval superiority could not be brought to bear on our military enterprises.

Instead of moving toward the key point of Montreal our government concentrated its striking forces for an operation in the Detroit area. Now it is true that Detroit was the key point in the northwest. It controlled the navigable passage between Lakes Erie and Huron. Lying in the heart of the Indian country, its possession would largely determine which side the tribes would join. Tecumseh, beaten the year before at Tippecanoe, was a potential ally of the British and it would be most desirable to overawe the Indians before his skillful intrigue could deliver them to the enemy. Unfortunately, Detroit was in an almost inaccessible position; even from our most outlying Ohio settlements it was distant two hundred miles through trackless forests and swamps. Furthermore, any move in its direction would be seriously menaced by British naval superiority on Lake Erie.

Not only would success in the Detroit area be comparatively unimportant when compared with the capture of Montreal or the seizure of a position astride the St. Lawrence River, but it would be many times more difficult to gain.

Another key point in the northwest was Fort Mackinac, on an island near the passage between Lakes Huron and Michigan. This was important also because of its influence upon the Indians.

While Brock stressed the primary importance of the St. Lawrence position, he realized that Detroit and Mackinac were also essential to the defense of western Canada. As early as February he declared his "full conviction that unless both Detroit and Mackinac be in our possession at the commencement of hostilities, not only Amherstburg, but most probably the whole country, must be evacuated as far as Kingston." This, later events showed, was somewhat of an exaggeration.

CHAPTER II

THE DETROIT OFFENSIVE

S O KEENLY did our government have its eyes on Detroit that it committed an act without precedent, so far as we know, in our history. It deliberately planned to secure Detroit and the surrounding area by massing an army there before the declaration of war. This was, for us, a most remarkable combination of strategy and policy—the very keynote to success in war. Long before we declared war the plan was broached to Governor Hull of Ohio and he was offered the command of the troops to carry the scheme into execution. Not only that, but Hull wrote back to the War Department a most able estimate of the whole situation. In it he stated that to maintain his communications in Detroit it was essential that we have naval superiority on Lake Erie. This was in March; for once we seemed to be looking into the future, preparing our plans for war in time.

So far, so good. But here the good was to end. Hull accepted his general's commission; came on to Washington to discuss his letter and how the campaign was to be fought. Here Madison the Unready commenced to make his ill-omened influence felt. "I was twice at the President's with General Hull," General Porter later testified, "when the subject of a navy was talked over. At first it was agreed to have one; but afterwards it was agreed to abandon it, doubtless as inexpedient." There is a blow at your fine plan, General Hull, from which you can scarcely recover! There is an example of the "Perils of Amateur Strategy."

Yes, Madison, the easiest way is the easiest—for a time. Building a navy on Lake Erie will take some trouble. You will have to use some of those troublesome regular officers; it will cost you some money. How much easier to let Hull muster in his militia for a few months and march through Canada. The ex-President of illustrious memory has shown how easy it will be to overrun the whole country as far as Quebec. Surely there will be no difficulty in mopping up that sparsely settled territory about Detroit.

Hull has fought in the Revolution. Perhaps he is not any too sure of these militia; perhaps he may have quoted Washington's damning denunciation of them. "Experience," once said our old general, "which is the best criterion to work by, so fully, clearly, and decisively reprobates the practice of trusting to the militia, that no man who regards order, regularity, and economy, or who has any regard for his own honor, character, or peace of mind, will risk them upon this issue." What the issue was we do not remember, but it certainly could not have involved a problem more difficult than this Detroit campaign. Well, then, Hull, if you have some doubts, we will give you the Fourth United States Regiment. True, it is not exactly at full strength—but when was any United States Regiment? Now, we have had enough discussion, go about your business! Win your marshal's baton—or perhaps the thanks of Congress! We hope readers will excuse these imaginings. Now for a few facts.

In accordance with the President's decision, no attempt was made to build a naval force on Lake Erie. Hull acted with due speed and mustered in three regiments of Ohio militia at Dayton. Thence he marched to Urbana. Here the Fourth United States Regiment joined his army. Off he struggled on his 200-mile trek through wilderness and swamp to Detroit. He was well on his way when war was declared on June 18. Perhaps we have painted the situation

too blackly. Maybe, despite all mistakes, he will accomplish
something. Brock, too, has his troubles.

Yes, for him also the situation looks dangerous. He
knows he will be outnumbered for a year at least. But he
has some advantages on his side; two stand out at first:
naval superiority and a good intelligence service. Perhaps
we should add his own genius.

On June 27 Brock, at York (now Toronto), heard of
our declaration of war. He received this news through his
intelligence service even before it was known to Americans
in the vicinity. He immediately warned Colonel Proctor
at Fort Malden, opposite Detroit, also Captain Roberts at
St. Joseph's Island, opposite Mackinac, and ordered both to
commence hostilities. Apparently he did not attempt to direct them from a distance, but left the conduct of operations
to their initiative.

Word travelled slowly in those days. It was not until
July 8 that Captain Roberts received the news. He decided
to attack Fort Mackinac. His naval force consisted of the
brig *Caledonia*, of 2 guns. As we had nothing, this little
craft was just as effective as a squadron of ships of the line.
She escorted and carried a British force of 46 regulars,
260 militia, and 715 Indians to Mackinac. When this
expedition arrived on the seventeenth our little garrison of
fifty-seven, unaware even of the existence of a state of war,
had to surrender without resistance. The President's reference to this initial disaster was quite amusing. "We have
just learned," he said, "that the important post of Michili-
mackinac has fallen into the hands of the enemy, from what
cause remains to be known."

He learned in due time of the causes—or at least we hope
he did. There were several which will be apparent to readers. The principal one was that the enemy had naval su-

periority. This little campaign is as striking an example
of the importance and dominance of sea power as the great
naval campaigns which culminated in Trafalgar and Tsu-
shima. Had we possessed the *Caledonia* instead of the British, it requires no proof that her two guns or even musketry
could have dispersed Roberts' flotilla of bateaux and canoes
with hardly an effort, thus not only protecting Mackinac,
but giving us the complete control of the lake. Of course
we assume that other British vessels would not enter Huron
from Erie. Naturally we would have to attend to them
with another naval force on that lake—as later Perry did.

Proctor was not as aggressive as Roberts. He was certainly superior to our garrison of ninety-four at Detroit,
and had the support of a strong naval force on Lake Erie.
This consisted of the *Queen Charlotte*, 17 guns, *Lady Prevost*, 13 guns, *Hunter*, 10 guns, *Little Belt*, 2 guns, and
Chippeway, 2 guns. Proctor seems to have missed an opportunity here to win a success for his chief: he decided to
remain on the defensive and hold Fort Malden, using his
naval superiority to wear down Hull's approaching forces.

For Hull now was close at hand. But what a march
he had made! The sufferings of his troops were almost indescribable. Once they had openly mutinied and refused
to march into more torture, and we cannot blame militiamen
for such natural tendencies. As we have said before, the
handling of militia is a profession of its own, requiring
heights of leadership never demanded of an Alexander or
a Napoleon. What George Rogers Clark did with his Kentucky "Long Knives" seems to us one of the miracles of
history; the same might be said of Andrew Jackson and
his Tennessee militia. But Hull was no Jackson, to seize
an unloaded musket from the hands of a soldier and threaten
to shoot down the first man who left the ranks. No, he

was just General Hull. So he had the Fourth Regiment march up and compel the militia to march under threat of opening fire upon them.

On June 30 his army reached the Maumee River. While his men could still keep going, the baggage animals were absolutely exhausted. For this reason the supplies were loaded on the schooner, *Cuyahoga* and sent direct to—no, not Detroit, for the *Cuyahoga* was captured by the brig *Hunter* and brought into Fort Malden. Thus early did naval superiority on Erie begin to make itself felt. Now the loss of the baggage was bad enough, but it was not the worst. Hull's son, serving as aid, had thought to save himself some work by adding to the *Cuyahoga's* cargo a trunk containing the complete files of the army. He did not know that war had been declared, but Proctor did. Thus there fell into the latter's hands not only Hull's orders for the campaign, but the exact strength of his army. This vital information was sent posthaste to Brock. Rarely has a general been presented with such an advantage by his enemy.

On July 7 Hull reached Detroit. His total strength, including the garrison, amounted to 2,200. On the twelfth he crossed into Canadian territory and advanced toward Fort Malden. This was the key point; in addition to being the only military stronghold for hundreds of miles, it was the naval base for the British Erie squadron. Proctor had in all but 200 regular troops, 475 militia and 270 Indians. Hull thus had overwhelming forces. His grumblers, once on enemy territory, had forgotten their hardships. Their spirit was high and they demanded to carry the fort by assault.

Thus far Hull had done well—we have no complaint against his leadership. A Clark or a Jackson is not to be found in every campaign. All he needed was one last push with all his strength and an astounding success was within his grasp. He would have been more famous than his relative, Isaac Hull, of the *Constitution*. But, at this decisive stage of the campaign, the general showed himself wholly unfit to command an army. On July 22 he stated that "it is in the power of this army to take Malden by storm, but it would be attended, in my opinion, with too great a sacrifice under the present circumstances." Alas, General, the future holds even larger sacrifices for you.

The refusal to authorize the assault proved the turning point of the campaign. The army sat down to make a regular seige. Naval power began to cause its disintegration and ruin. Brock sent down a reënforcement of fifty regulars by water from Long Point. The *Queen Charlotte* anchored in the Detroit River, where she could command the route along which the siege guns must be advanced—they never reached their positions. Proctor used his command of the lake to send raiding parties over to the American shore; there they cut to pieces Hull's precarious lines of communication, as did Lawrence and his Arabs to the Turks in Arabia. Soon Hull heard that further British reënforcements were expected. He had had enough. On August 8 he recrossed to the American shore. He was a ruined commander of a beaten army.

As we have seen, Brock had given himself two tasks: first, to defend the St. Lawrence from Montreal to Kingston; second, to attack and seize Detroit and Mackinac. Now, to his great surprise, he found himself relieved of his first task by our failure to attack him in his most vulnerable sector. Instead he saw that we were preparing an advance over the Niagara frontier. Here we were attacking his very strongest front. Not only did he have two strong defensive works in Fort George and Fort Erie, but it was evident that an invading army could accomplish nothing of strategic importance unless it advanced up the Niagara peninsula as far as the Long Point-Burlington road under the handicap of British control of the lakes on either flank. He estimated, and correctly, that General Dearborn, the American commander in this sector, would not attack for some time, although he had a formidable force, on paper, of 1,200 troops.

As soon as he received news of Hull's unexpected strength in the important Detroit sector, Brock decided on a Tannenberg stunt—with Dearborn going to sleep peacefully *à la* Rennenkampf, while Hull found himself in the ill-fated shoes of Samsonov. On July 20 news of Hull's invasion of Canada told him he would have to hurry. His plan was a daring one, but as he said—with a Hindenburg ring—"the state of Upper Canada admitted of nothing but desperate remedies."

Its execution reflected even more credit upon the British general than its conception. The Indians, influenced by Hull's force, refused to join him. The militia said, and rightly in a way, that they could not leave their homes while the attitude of the redskins was uncertain. By the twenty-fifth Brock had almost given up hope. But, as Napoleon was wont to say, all great events hang by a single hair. What this was you could never guess. It was the arrival on the twenty-ninth of news that Fort Mackinac had been captured. Inspired by this comparatively unimportant success in a distant theater the militia said they would fight anywhere in their province. Brock started one hundred of them off by road to Long Point. On the sixth he followed in person with two hundred militia and forty regulars by boat over Lake Ontario to Burlington and thence by road to Long Point. There on the eighth his detachment embarked in boats, bateaux, and canoes. On the thirteenth it was received at Fort Malden with a *feu de joie* of musketry. Witness another trump card which control of the Lakes placed in the hand of our enemy.

Now Brock had no time to lose. He must finish off Hull quickly so as to get back against Dearborn. On the sixteenth he crossed the Detroit River. He had 330 regulars, 400 militia, 600 Indians, and five guns. He found against him an army that had beaten itself. Hull's indecision and unfitness to command, internal dissensions, sickness, losses in the constant guerrilla warfare, and the necessity of detaching troops to guard the insecure line of communications: all these had reduced the forces in Detroit to 1,000 men. Even now, if these brave frontiersmen had had a determined leader, they might have beaten Brock or at least have held him in check until Dearborn could begin his campaign. But they had only poor Hull and they let Hull surrender. Without firing a shot he surrendered all the forces under his command and all his detachments, even those entirely out of reach of the enemy. It was worse than Dupont at Baylen —probably the most disgraceful page in American history. August 16 is certainly the "black day" of our Army.

Among the rich spoils of war was a brass cannon; on it British officers read with delight: "Taken at Saratoga on the 17th of October, 1777." Ha! Thus do we pay back these quarrelsome Yankees! But, my British friends, be circumspect in your present elation. Your Brock has already approached the end of his gallant career. Then there will be only Proctor, who is no Brock. No, not by any means! Perhaps this cannon may change hands again before many campaigns.

The brig *Adams* also fell into the hands of the enemy. She was armed and renamed the *Detroit:* proved a welcome reënforcement to British naval commanders.

In his court-martial Hull brought forward a most curious argument, which, out of his own mouth, proved his incapacity for military command. He said: "I shall now state what force the enemy brought, or might bring, against me. I say gentlemen, 'might bring,' because it was that consideration which induced the surrender, not the force which was actually landed on the American shore on the morning of the sixteenth. It is possible I might have met and repelled that force; and if I had no further to look than the event of a contest at that time, I should have trusted to the issue of a battle." Apart from the utter fallacy of such a theory under any conditions, British forces at Detroit must have diminished rather than increased.

In justice to Hull we must admit that he had one point in his favor—the insecurity of his communications. Naval command of Lake Erie would not only have made this problem a simple one, but would have prevented Brock from carrying through his brilliant combination. With our fleet in superiority on the lake, even Hull, incapable as he was, must have won the campaign. Madison frankly admitted his blunder: "The command of the Lakes by a superior force on the water ought to have been a fundamental part in the national policy from the moment the peace (of 1783) took place." Too late he recognized that a navy was essential.

Just as Brock was arriving at Malden on August 8 General Dearborn signed an armistice for the Niagara front. Immediately after the fall of Detroit on the sixteenth, Brock, who of course knew nothing of this cession of hostilities, embarked part of his troops and hurried back to Fort George. Proctor at Detroit was ordered to remain on the defensive.

These initial successes had placed the British commander

in a very strong position. Although inferior in number of troops, the command of the Lakes gave him a line of excellent lateral communications all the way from Montreal to Mackinac. Thus he could shift his forces at will to meet the attacks of our armies. In other words, he had what military writers term interior lines, an advantage used by the Germans in the World War to such telling effect. "Already," Mahan comments, "at the most critical period, the use of the water had enabled Brock, by simultaneous movements, to send cannon from Fort George by way of Fort Erie to Fort Malden; while at the same time replacing those thus depleted by others brought from Toronto and Kingston."

CHAPTER III

THE NAVY ENTERS THE CAMPAIGN

ON LAKE ONTARIO the declaration of war found us with one naval vessel, the brig *Oneida,* commanded by Lieutenant M. T. Woolsey. She mounted eighteen 24-pounder carronades and operated from Sackett's Harbor, a very small but well-protected port at the eastern end of the lake. Commodore Earle, a Canadian officer, commanded a powerful squadron of six vessels, viz.: *Prince George,* 21 guns, *Prince Regent,* 16, *Earl of Moira,* 14, *Duke of Gloucester,* 10, *Simcoe,* 8, and *Seneca,* 8. We had a certain advantage in the quality of personnel; our officers and crew belonged to the regular Navy; those of the enemy vessels were Canadians and at first were distinct from the Royal Navy.

The Canadians opened the campaign on Lake Ontario with a naval bombardment of Sackett's Harbor. Woolsey had made what preparations he could to withstand the powerful enemy squadron. He had moored the *Oneida* so that one of her broadsides would bear on the approaching enemy; the guns of the other broadside he mounted in a battery ashore. In another location he mounted an old iron 32-pounder. As no shot could be found to fit this gun, her crew wrapped pieces of carpet around 24-pound balls so that they would fit the bore more tightly. Our guns were mounted on a high ridge along the shore which gave them the advantage of a plunging fire. For two hours the hostile squadron endeavored to silence our batteries, with no success whatever. On the other hand, our fire seems to have been little more effective. There is an old yarn to the effect that a British 32-pound shot fell near our battery and that

[362]

the gunners, delighted to get one good ball that would fit their gun, returned it with such good effect as to kill or wound several men on the hostile flagship. Earle then withdrew.

Woolsey next took over the merchant schooner *Julia* and armed her with a long 32-pounder and two long 6's. Appointing a crew of volunteers to man her, she was sent to Ogdensburg down the St. Lawrence River to protect six American schooners blockaded there by the enemy squadron. The armistice between Dearborn and Prevost permitted all these vessels to be brought up to Sackett's Harbor and Oswego. In this respect it proved very advantageous to us.

The President, at last convinced as to the necessity for naval forces on the Lakes, decided to make an effort on a large scale to gain their command. On September 3 Captain Isaac Chauncey, commandant of the New York Navy Yard, was ordered to take charge of the operations on Lakes Erie and Ontario. Chauncey was one of the senior officers of the Navy and had a high reputation in the service. He had commanded the *Constitution* during the bombardments of Tripoli and won the warm commendation of Commodore Preble.

On September 7 Chauncey sent on Lieutenant Jesse D. Elliott to report to General van Rensselaer, who commanded in the Niagara sector. There he was to commence the building of a squadron sufficient to gain the command of Lake Erie. On the fourteenth Elliott arrived at Buffalo and commenced preparing a navy yard behind Squaw Island on the Niagara River, three miles down stream from Buffalo. On the twenty-second Chauncey sent ninety seamen from New York to report to Elliott. Sailing Master Dobbins proceeded to Erie with orders to build four gunboats there.

On October 8 two British men-of-war appeared off Fort

Erie, across the river from Buffalo. One was the brig *Detroit,* which had been captured when Hull surrendered; the other Elliott thought was the *Hunter,* 14 guns, but actually it was the *Caledonia,* which had played so decisive a part in the taking of Mackinac. Elliott gazed longingly at these two fine ships and at length came to an interesting decision. "Having been on the lines for some time," he wrote, "and in a measure inactively employed, I determined to make an attack, and, if possible, get possession of them. A strong inducement to this attempt arose from a consideration that with these two vessels and those which I have purchased and am fitting out, I should be able to meet the remainder of the British forces on the Upper Lakes."

Just as he had arrived at this conclusion he was cheered by hearing that the ninety seamen from New York were close at hand. At noon a tired lot of sailors arrived at the little village. Among them were twenty pistols, but not a single cutlass or battle-axe. Elliott applied to General Smyth for assistance. Captain Towson, Second Regiment of Artillery, was detailed by the general to collect a party of fifty soldiers and to bring along such weapons as he could find for the seamen. He wrote to Colonel Winder, commanding the Fourteenth Regiment: "Be pleased to turn out the hardy sailors in your regiment, and let them appear, under the care of a non-commissioned officer, in front of my quarters, precisely at 3 o'clock this evening. Send also all the pistols, swords, and sabres you can borrow at the risk of the lenders, and such public swords as you have."

By 4:00 P.M., two boats had been made ready and a party of 124 seamen and soldiers had been selected, stationed, armed, and instructed in their duties. "Under circumstances very disadvantageous," Elliott reported, "my men scarcely having had time to refresh themselves after a fatiguing march of five hundred miles, I put off from the mouth of Buffalo Creek at 1 o'clock in the morning and at 3 I was alongside the vessels." Elliott's boat ran alongside the *Detroit* and his men sprang up her sides. So completely were the Canadians taken by surprise that in ten minutes all resistance had ceased. At a loss of only one killed and one wounded our enterprising lieutenant, with tired men and borrowed weapons, had made prisoner fifty-nine officers and men and had released thirty American prisoners on board. The battery of the prize was found to be six long 6-pounders.

The second boat was commanded by Sailing Master George Watts, "who performed his duty in a masterly style." The *Caledonia* apparently had been put on her guard by the uproar on the *Detroit* and the twelve officers and men of her crew were prepared to give Watts a warm reception. It seems that they had no time to use their great guns, but even with musket and pike they had an excellent chance of defending their high ship against a more numerous force in a single small boat. But Watts and his people were out to win and though they suffered five casualties they carried the brig by storm. "In a word, sir," Elliott wrote with justifiable pride, "every man fought as if with their hearts animated only by the interest and honor of their country." Thus did the Navy make its début in northern waters.

To capture the two ships was only half of Elliott's problem. Now he had to extricate them from a dangerous position under the enemy's guns. The wind was very light and as soon as anchors were weighed the ships would be swept down by a murderous current toward Niagara Falls in such a way that their crews would hardly appreciate its scenic beauties. Watts cut the *Caledonia's* cable and worked her over to the American shore. There he beached her under our batteries at Black Rock. Elliott was not so lucky, for the *Detroit* was swept toward the Canadian bank; he had to anchor her again four hundred yards from the batteries of Fort Erie. As day broke a heavy fire was directed upon her. Elliott mounted all six of his guns on the side that would bear and fought back as long as his ammunition lasted. Attempts to run hawsers to the American bank proved futile and, seeing that he would ultimately be sunk in his present position, Elliott cut his cable and drifted ashore on Squaw Island. He then abandoned ship and rowed to the American bank with his prisoners. The guns of both armies now opened up on the unfortunate *Detroit* and destroyed her. We recovered four guns from the wreck.

The *Caledonia* was salvaged and duly commissioned in our Erie squadron. In her were found furs valued at $200,000. While Elliott did not gain all he had hoped for in this gallant enterprise, he had certainly opened the naval campaign with a striking success. Its moral effect was greater than the material results gained. "This event is particularly unfortunate," Brock wrote to Prevost, "and may reduce us to incalculable distress. The enemy is making every exertion to gain a naval superiority on both lakes; which, if they accomplish, I do not see how we can retain the country." He wrote to Proctor at Detroit, saying that he would have to do without the provisions ready at Fort Erie to be shipped in the *Detroit*. But poor Brock's worries were soon to cease. In a combat at Queenston he died gallantly at the head of his men in the moment of victory. A great man passed!

Elliott had little luck at Black Rock. He had the *Caledonia* as a nucleus for his squadron and commenced arming six schooners. However, he had selected as a shipyard a place that was within musket shot of the Canadian bank. The carpenters had little liking for a job where they lived under a continual fusillade and finally refused to work any longer. The vessels were hauled up a creek; the Erie campaign was over for the year.

CHAPTER IV

CHAUNCEY WINS LAKE ONTARIO

MEANWHILE Chauncey had sent on toward Sackett's Harbor a force of 140 ship-carpenters; parties of seamen and marines amounting to seven hundred in all; one hundred cannon of various size, together with powder, shot and other naval stores. On September 26 he started from New York and on October 6 arrived at Sackett's Harbor. The season was far gone, but perhaps something could still be done. At least he could show the Army that the Navy was commencing to do business.

Elliott was ordered to Oswego to fit out the four schooners which the *Julia* had escorted up from Ogdensburg. Two more of them were being armed at Sackett's Harbor and these, with the *Oneida* and *Julia,* would give the commodore a squadron of 8 vessels, mounting 40 guns, and manned by 430 seamen and marines. The Canadian squadron had about 80 guns, but they were smaller and served by less efficient crews.

Chauncey was at his best as an organizer—it was quite a feat to organize a squadron in one month's time. Yet we find that on November 6 he stood out with the *Oneida* and six schooners. His plan was to intercept the Canadian squadron as it returned from Niagara to Kingston. He took station off the False Ducks to wait in ambush. The enemy seem to have been taken by surprise, for their vessels came straggling along like a regiment of militia on the march. On the eighth contact was made with the first, the flagship *Royal George,* of 21 guns. She was forced to withdraw in haste into the Bay of Quinte. Chauncey followed her into the bay and took a trading schooner.

Early the next morning the *Royal George* withdrew under cover of the Kingston batteries. The American squadron followed, engaging her and the guns ashore for an hour and forty-five minutes. It was a lively combat. "The *Royal George*," so the commodore reported, "must have received considerable injury in her hull and in men, as the gun vessels with a long 32-pounder were seen to strike her almost every shot, and it was observed that she was reënforced with troops four different times during the action." Just as we seemed on the point of a decisive success a strong westerly wind sprang up and Chauncey felt constrained to order a retirement. His losses had been only nine killed and wounded. As he drew off another trading schooner was made prize near the harbor entrance.

Now Chauncey had shown very commendable energy in fitting our his squadron, training his crews, and attacking the enemy in his own base. However, even this early he disclosed a failing which was to prevent him from ever becoming a commander of the first class. This fight was typical of all Chauncey's battles; all were highly successful during their first phases, but just as a decisive success appeared inevitable, there was always some reason why he could not deliver the coup de grace. He had not that characteristic so essential to a great commander, the willingness to hazard everything on a single roll of the dice; no, not even when the dice were loaded and he could not lose. Thus he missed being a great commander and our Navy missed many a decisive victory on Lake Ontario.

On the tenth our squadron was again on the open lake and there sighted the armed schooner *Simcoe*. Three gunboats made sail in chase, drove her over a ledge of rocks, and punished her so heavily that, according to Lossing, she sank before reaching port. On the evening of the twelfth a heavy gale drove the squadron into Sackett's Harbor. "I think I can say with great propriety," Chauncey reported to the Secretary of the Navy, "that we have now the command of the lake, and that we can transport troops and stores to any part of it without any risk of an attack from the enemy."

Yes, Chauncey in this six-day cruise had certainly won the temporary command of the lake for us, but unfortunately there remained only two more weeks of navigation. Then ice forced both squadrons into winter quarters. Just four days before operations came to a close our rapidly expanding navy yard at Sackett's Harbor completed the fine corvette *Madison,* armed with twenty-four short 32-pounders. "She was built," Chauncey said, "in the short time of forty-five days; and nine weeks ago the timber she is composed of was growing in the forest." This showed American initiative and energy at its best. In those days our shipbuilders were without their equal in the world. Perhaps other days like those may come!

Had President Madison realized the importance of naval power on the Lakes in March, or even June, instead of in September, the war might well have taken a different course. It is entirely possible that decisive successes might have been won along the northern frontier in the first campaign.

After Hull's surrender at Detroit General Harrison assumed command of our troops in Ohio. He commenced an offensive into the Maumee-Sandusky region. Here Indian warfare reached its height of horror, for British officers exercised little restraint over the ferocity of their allies. Harrison suffered a disastrous check at Frenchtown, where one of his detached columns surrendered to Proctor. This was on January 22, 1813. We spare the reader the gruesome details—they are not pleasant to write about. Harrison now settled down to wait until the Navy had its turn on Lake Erie.

Having got things moving well on Ontario, Chauncey went over to stir up things on Erie. As a promoter he was unequalled. First he looked over the situation at Black Rock and found it anything but good. Not only were its workmen required to dodge musket balls from the Canadian bank, but even when the vessels were completed it would be necessary to drag them up the river three miles against a four-knot current, during which time they would have the entire British army using them as targets. Nevertheless, to a certain extent, it was necessary to take things as he found them; so he directed that their reconstruction be expedited. When the time came he would find a way to get them to the lake.

Next, the commodore rode on to Erie and found that Dobbins had two schooners well under way. This port impressed Chauncey very favorably and he decided to build there two 300-ton brigs. By Christmas the collection of their material had commenced. Most of the equipment was assembled in Pittsburgh from Philadelphia and Washington. Thence it was barged along the Allegheny and up one of its tributaries, from which a good road, only twelve miles long, led to Erie. This line of communications was far superior to that from New York to Sackett's Harbor.

While Chauncey was thus concerned with questions of material, he did not forget that men are more important than the ships they fight. Most important of all was the officer who was to command the Erie squadron. Although both lakes were under the commodore's supervision, it was evident that the Erie command would be practically independent; he must select an enterprising young fellow to exercise it. His choice fell, fortunately, for all concerned, including the Navy, upon Oliver Hazard Perry, then in command of a flotilla of Jeffersonian gunboats based upon Newport.   On January 21 Chauncey made his formal request and on the seventeenth of the next month Perry received with delight his instructions to proceed to Lake Erie.   He must have been raised to the seventh heaven when he learned that he could take with him 150 picked men from his gunboat flotilla.

Sending on his sailors in advance, Perry left Newport on the twenty-second and arrived in Sackett's Harbor on March 3.   Because of a rumored attack on that base Chauncey kept him there for a time.   It was not until the twenty-fourth that he inspected his vessels at Black Rock.   After infusing some of his ginger into the workmen there, Perry hurried on to Erie.   Arriving on the twenty-seventh, he found that two schooners were nearing completion and that the keels of two brigs, one schooner, and one sloop had been laid.   He heard that the British were building a large ship-rigged vessel to reënforce their squadron.

Erie was absolutely defenseless against a British attack; even landing parties from their squadron could have carried it by storm.   The burning of his ships on the stocks would have sounded the death knell to Perry's aspirations for naval success on the lake; would have ended Harrison's hopes to regain Detroit and carry the war into Canada. Perry did what he could to provide some defenses and obtained four small cannon and a few muskets.   He asked the Erie militia to help him out; their colonel was willing enough, but when he ordered guards posted about the building ways at night, the soldiers demurred.   "I told the boys to go," the old fellow said to Perry, "but the boys won't go!"   It must have been cold on those winter nights.

For a long time Proctor contemplated an attack, but kept

waiting for reënforcements. The capture of York, as will be related later, delayed their arrival. So he turned upon Harrison instead; on May 1 he shut him up in Fort Meigs. He annihilated a relieving detachment of nine hundred, but could not quite get the fort. Still he had crippled our army for a long time. Fortunate it was for us that he had not kept to his first objective, Erie and those wooden skeletons which were fast taking on the appearance of ships. They, not Harrison's stockades, were the "wooden walls" to bring us victory.

CHAPTER V

WE CAPTURE YORK

WE HAVE hinted at certain operations on Lake Ontario and it is proper that we should describe them at this time, for they influenced to a predominating degree the Erie campaign. On February 10 General Armstrong, the new Secretary of War, had issued his instructions to General Dearborn for the coming campaign. He recognized the immense importance of Montreal, but believed that the time had passed when its attack was practicable: he thought that too many reënforcements had come from over the water. The Secretary, therefore, ordered the concentration of two armies: one of 4,000 at Sackett's Harbor; the other of 3,000 at Buffalo. The first force, under Chauncey's escort, was to seize Kingston and York, in the order named, then to join the Buffalo detachment and together clear the Niagara peninsula.

This was an excellent plan; it was aimed at proper and most important objectives in the right order; it was strictly practicable. Kingston was, next to Montreal, the point of primary importance. Its capture would have cut all lines of communication, both land and water, leading to the west and have insured the capture of all that territory. It would have wiped out the Ontario squadron and destroyed its base and dockyard. Thus Armstrong was absolutely correct in deciding that Kingston should be attacked first.

Unfortunately the leaders on the spot did not agree. They were influenced by greatly exaggerated reports of reenforcements arriving at Kingston. Dearborn went so far as to protest formally against his orders. Chauncey, we say it with regret, partly supported the army leader. He admitted that Kingston could be taken, but said that York's capture could be more easily accomplished. This was almost as wretched an argument as Hull had used in refusing to attack Fort Malden. As well might our commodore have said that he could defeat ten ships of the enemy, but that it would be easier to defeat one. The capture of Kingston would have been absolutely decisive, that of York only a partial success. In view of this opposition of the commanders in the field, the plan was changed. York was to be attacked first.

Once this decision was made Chauncey was all energy. On April 24, just as the ice broke up, he took the lake with a formidable flotilla: *Madison, Oneida, Fair American, Hamilton, Tompkins, Conquest, Asp, Pert, Julia, Growler, Ontario, Scourge, Lady of the Lake,* and the transport *Rover.* He had such an overwhelming superiority that he risked encumbering his ships with 1,700 troops. Dearborn was sick, so he entrusted the actual direction of the attack to General Pike. He was a splendid soldier, eager for this chance to gain distinction. "No man will load until ordered," his instructions ran, "except the light troops in front, until within a short distance of the enemy, and then charge bayonets; thus letting the enemy see that we can meet them with their own weapons."

West of York two batteries covered the harbor entrance. It was beyond these batteries and some three miles from the town that our troops landed. There was no resistance to the actual landing, but as Pike was forming up his men they received a sharp British counterattack, supported with field guns. The squadron now had its chance; its guns laid down a deadly barrage of grapeshot. This was more than any troops could be expected to stand—and the redcoats retired hastily. Our troops, delighted with this support from afloat, pressed on eagerly, drums and fifes playing the war song of those days, "Yankle Doodle." A stirring song it is too—even today—when the shrill high notes of the fifes mingle with the deep rumble of the drums. How those men must have marched! They had enjoyed a comfortable cruise, a good night's rest, a plentiful breakfast; had been rowed ashore by sailors and gained an easy victory. Now they were holding a dress parade, as it were, for their friends in the fleet. Yes, there was war with all its glamor —but Mars was ever a trickster: now he was preparing a rude surprise. Better march carefully, General Pike!

The schooners move in to within six hundred yards of the two batteries. Their long 32's raise havoc among the defenders, and they run off while still they can. They have one more trump to play, and it is a good one: yes, nothing less than a powder magazine. In this there lay five hundred barrels of powder and an immense quantity of shot and shell. Ignorant of the tremendous power lying dormant in this mass of explosive, the retiring Britishers touched it off. Seldom has there been such an explosion. Forty of their own men it killed. Of the on-coming Americans it killed or wounded 230. Among the mortally wounded was General Pike, a soldier we could ill afford to lose. Midshipman John Hatfield, in the landing party from the *Lady of the Lake,* was killed. Thus early had his naval career ended.

Under cover of this stratagem the British detachment made good their retreat; had time even to burn a fine 30-gun ship which was nearly ready for sea. However, we did take the *Duke of Gloucester,* together with a great quantity of valuable stores and equipment, the loss of which hampered British operations for months to come.

This expedition was notable for the perfect coöperation between Army and Navy. "I am under great obligations to Commodore Chauncey," Dearborn reported, "for his able and indefatigable exertions in every possible manner that could give facility and effect to the expedition." Sir Julian Corbett very aptly divided naval operations into two general types: those with the object of gaining the command of the sea by aggressive action against the hostile fleet; and those to exercise or take advantage of that command once it is gained. Chauncey was only partly successful in his campaigns against the British squadron to gain the command, but during the periods when he had the command— due to faster shipbuilding or partial victories in sea fights— he distinguished himself by getting for the army every advantage he could possibly derive from that command. In this respect his leadership was superb. No naval commander in history ever gave more loyal and effective support to his military confrères.

General Pike, mortally wounded, was carried to the shore and thence rowed out to the schooner *Pert*. Lossing gives us a picture of the last moments of this splendid soldier: "Just as the surgeons and attendants, with the wounded general, reached the little boat, the huzzas of the troops fell upon his benumbed ears. 'What does it mean?' he feebly asked. 'Victory,' said a sergeant in attendance, 'The British union jack is coming down from the block house, and the Stars and Stripes are going up.' The dying hero's face was illuminated with a smile of great joy. His spirit lingered several hours, and then departed. Just before his breath ceased the captured British flag was brought to him. He made sign for them to place it under his head, and thus he expired." Perhaps that flag is the royal standard now preserved at our Naval Academy, which is said to be the only British royal standard not now in the possession of its original owners.

On May Day our troops were reëmbarked. On the eighth they were landed at Fort Niagara. The squadron went on to Sackett's Harbor. With admirable foresight Chauncey sent Mr. Eckford and thirty carpenters to Black Rock to expedite the preparation of the ships there for sea. He was planning a skillful combination which ultimately was to result in our gaining Lake Erie. We must never forget that the commodore was primarily responsible for the upbuilding of our squadron on that lake and thus should share in the credit for its successes.

CHAPTER VI

SUCCESSES ON THE NIAGARA PENINSULA

MEANWHILE the British had been little satisfied with the accomplishments of their Lakes squadrons. Chauncey's attack upon Kingston in the fall had convinced them that to compete with our regular forces on the Lakes their squadrons also must be commanded and manned by personnel of the Royal Navy. In the early spring Captain Barclay, an officer of distinguished ability, had arrived at Kingston. He had assumed command of all the Lakes squadrons and commenced a construction program at Kingston and York which it was hoped would throw material superiority again into British hands. On May 15 Sir James Yeo, late of H.M.S. *Southampton,* arrived at Kingston with a large detachment of regular officers and seamen. He assumed general command over all forces on the Great Lakes and gave Barclay the direct command of the Erie squadron.

After a short refit Chauncey reappeared on May 25 off the mouth of the Niagara River. Two days later he covered in excellent style a landing of troops a mile west of Fort George. Perry had been called up from Erie and Chauncey had made him responsible for the actual landing of the expeditionary force, a service which he performed with marked distinction. The accurate fire of the little schooner *Hamilton,* close in to the shore, decided the fight along the beach. Once the landing was affected, our greatly superior numbers compelled the enemy to abandon the entire Niagara peninsula and retire with heavy losses to Burlington. Forts George and Erie fell into our hands. This was a splendid, almost decisive, success. Again coöperation of the two services had been perfect; a splendid spirit prevailed. General Dearborn reported: "Commodore Chauncey had made the most judicious arrangements for silencing the enemy's batteries near the point of landing. The army is under the greatest obligations to that able naval commander, for his indefatigable exertions."

In these days our military and naval services are giving most careful consideration to the great problems of coördinating naval and military forces in a combined campaign. These instances of highly successful coördination are well worthy of most careful study. In this respect Chauncey was well-nigh without an equal.

These successes on Ontario greatly influenced the march of events on Lake Erie. Our capture of York delayed Barclay's arrival at Amherstburg, near Fort Malden, until June 7. What is even more important, it delayed, and in many respects entirely prevented, the supply of proper equipment for his squadron. Governor General Prevost wrote the next month: "The ordnance, ammunition and other stores for the service on Lake Erie had been deposited at York for the purpose of being transported to Amherstburg, but unfortunately were either destroyed or fell into the enemy's hands when York was taken by them; and subsequent interruption to the communication, by the occupation of Fort George, has rendered it extremely difficult to afford the supplies Captain Barclay requires, which, however, are in readiness to forward whenever circumstances will permit it to be done with safety."

Now Chauncey had reasons of his own for desiring the expulsion of the British from the Niagara peninsula. As long as they held Fort Erie our ships in Black Rock could never reach the lake. You will recall, that counting upon the success of the combined attack, he had sent on some extra carpenters to get the ships ready. As soon as Fort George was taken, the commodore sent Perry down to Black Rock to make the final preparations. When Fort Erie fell that energetic officer commenced moving his ships at once. It was quite a job, for they had to be dragged up against the current by oxen as far as Buffalo. It was not until June 12 that Perry had the *Caledonia, Somers, Tigress, Ohio,* and *Trippe* ready to sail.

Perry now was face to face with a difficult problem, for Barclay had taken the lake and on the fifteenth was off Erie. Thus he had interposed between the two portions of Perry's squadron. He was greatly superior to each, and much faster. If he met either American detachment on the open lake we were doomed to certain loss of the Erie campaign. Perry was never good at waiting. He saw that, sooner or later, he must get the Buffalo detachment to Erie. Nothing could be gained by waiting, so he had better try now while his crews were in high spirits and eager for action. He put to sea with his five little craft, doubtless with many a fervent prayer. Perry was always a dashing fellow, a gambler, ready to risk all on a single throw of the dice, a characteristic essential to the highest type of leadership. Fortune usually favored him and she did now. A fog came on. Through it the five little ships sailed, slipped past their waiting enemy, and gained Erie on the eighteenth. This was one of the luckiest breaks ever had by our lucky country. In Erie Perry found that the schooners *Ariel* and *Scorpion* were completed and that the *Porcupine* and two large brigs had been launched. Brave Lawrence had just thrilled the country with a heroism which rose above defeat. Generous Perry, a man cast in the same heroic mold, named one of the brigs, destined to be his flagship, after his hero, "Captain Jim." Yes, soon there would be seen on her decks fighting worthy of her namesake.

CHAPTER VII

PREVOST BUNGLES HIS CHANCE

NOW, on the surface, things had been going beautifully, in accordance with plan—to use a World War
idiom. But unfortunately, as we have tried to point out,
the plan was vitally defective. We had been winning some
easy successes—well worth the winning too. But we had
neglected the decisive point, Kingston, the British naval base.
And we were now to pay for that neglect, pay dearly, and
only by the rarest of good luck miss complete, absolute,
decisive defeat. This is how it happened.

While Chauncey had been coöperating so finely with our
army, Sir James Yeo had been biding his time in Kingston.
He was hastening to completion the *Wolfe,* a fine ship-
rigged vessel of 23 guns. This event would send him far
to the front in the race of naval armaments on Lake Ontario. He and Sir George Prevost had been waiting pa-
tiently for this advantage so they could decide the war on
the northern frontier by a single blow—the capture of Sackett's Harbor. How delighted they must have been when intelligence arrived that Chauncey had left with his entire
squadron for Niagara. The American naval base was now
almost unprotected by reliable troops and our enemy had
an opportunity such as never again presented itself to
either side during the entire war.

On the day after Chauncey was so ably covering the landing of troops to take Fort George, a truly formidable expeditionary force suddenly arrived off Sackett's Harbor. Yeo
had six ships, mounting in all about ninety-two guns,
manned with regular crews and completely refitted for a

long campaign. On these vessels and in thirty large bateaux were 1,000 soldiers, practically all regulars. To make things certain Prevost had come in person to command the landing force.

On the twenty-ninth, after certain bombarding and cannonading, Prevost landed and formed up his regulars. Now in the garrison was the First Regiment of Light Dragoons, a regular organization, and considerable numbers of New York militia. In command of them was a certain Jacob Brown, called by courtesy a general; and, strange to say, he was! Brown formed up his men, gave them some sound instructions. But let him tell in his own words of the strange and disquieting incident that occurred: "My orders were that the troops should lie close and reserve their fire, until the enemy had approached so near that every shot might hit its object. It is impossible to execute such orders with raw troops, unaccustomed to subordination. My orders were in this case disobeyed; the whole line fired, and not without effect; but in the moment while I was contemplating this, to my utter astonishment, they . . . fled."

How was this for a way to defend key positions? Picture poor Brown as he found himself a general without an army. However, he did have the dragoons, and their resolute attitude calmed the fears of certain militiamen. Prevost, with the decision in his very hands, pursued his advantage in a very cautious and irresolute manner, for which he was long roasted by British military critics. He seemed to have the happy faculty of fumbling the ball just as our goal line was being passed. Like Chauncey, in this respect alone, he never quite had the nerve to give the coup de grace to a beaten army. Meanwhile Jacob Brown, after his *mauvais quart d'heure,* had been arranging a Marengo. Bonaparte had said, to the admiration of soldiers, only thir-

teen years before: "We have lost the battle, but there is
time to win another." Brown's mind, on this occasion, ran
along with the great conqueror's. He kept rallying his militia, formed them on his dragoons, and arranged a new
line of resistance. And, strangely enough it held. Prevost
was beaten back. Marengo had been repeated. There was
even a Dassaix, brave Colonel Bacchus of the dragoons, who
"fell nobly at the head of his regiment as victory was declaring for us." Yes, Brown had staved off defeat, nay
more than defeat—disaster. Prevost had lost his great
chance.

But, even though beaten back, the British attack had not
been without effect. Thinking that the British were victorious, the people at the naval base set fire to all the stores
and equipment, assembled there at such great expense. Before these fires could be extinguished over half a million
dollars of material had been destroyed. This greatly delayed
the commissioning of the fine corvette *General Pike,* then
almost ready for sea.

It was June 1 when Chauncey came back to his base and
learned the bad news. Without the *General Pike,* which he
had counted on to offset the *Wolfe,* he felt that the British
had the overwhelming superiority on the lake. He estimated
that their squadrons mounted 106 guns to his 62—a characteristic exaggeration of enemy strength. Arguing that it
would not be wise to risk complete defeat when a delay
of two months would insure his unquestioned superiority,
Chauncey withdrew from the lake and surrendered its temporary command to the enemy.

Yeo knew that his ascendancy would be short-lived: he
made haste to make the most of it. Taking on board a re-
enforcement of three hundred regular troops, he sailed with
his six ships for Burlington. Even before his arrival the

tide of Dearborn's invasion had begun to ebb. There had been a wild mixed-up fight at night in which two of our generals were captured. When Yeo's squadron came on the scene, Dearborn gave the order for a general retirement, fearing that the British would transport troops to storm Fort Niagara and thus cut his communications. While Chauncey had controlled the lake, most of our army's supplies had been carried in boats along the lake shore. Now this material could not be evacuated and fell into the hands of the enemy. Dearborn's whole campaign had been ruined by the loss of our control of Ontario. So clearly did sea power demonstrate its influence upon military operations that Dearborn received orders to remain on the defensive until the *Pike* was ready for sea and Chauncey could take the lake with superior strength.

On July 21 the *Pike* was ready for sea. Chauncey's new flagship was a splendid vessel, ship-rigged, with an exceptionally powerful battery of twenty-eight long 24's, of which fifteen could be brought to bear on either broadside. The same day our commodore took the lake. He sailed for Niagara to come again to Dearborn's assistance. A bombardment of Burlington proved ineffective, but in an attack on York a great quantity of stores were either captured or destroyed. This town seemed the weak link in Prevost's armor.

On August 7 the two squadrons came in contact off Niagara. While the opposing forces were approximately equal under average weather conditions, their vessels were so dissimilar that for nearly any given situation one squadron or the other would have a very marked advantage. The prize of a decisive success was so great that neither commander dared engage unless the conditions were in his favor. Add to this the fact that both the commodores were by nature cautious, and it will be seen why the Ontario campaign developed into endless long-range maneuverings rather than into downright fighting. Now for three days the squadrons played about without a shot being fired. On the fourth day, the tenth, there was a brief long-range cannonade, during which two of our schooners tacked toward the enemy without orders and were captured. Chauncey could have continued the action with the *Pike* alone, but felt that he must wait until he could receive the support of at least several other vessels. As these never reached a position of support, the action ended thus, with the honors of the day belonging to Yeo.

On September 7 Chauncey and Yeo again met and maneuvered without coming to grips. Two days later, however, there was a sharp fight off the mouth of the Genessee. Here Chauncey gained a decided moral ascendancy over his enemy and the temporary command of the lake. Yeo, with eleven casualties, decided that he had had enough and withdrew into Amherst Bay, where he submitted peacefully to a blockade. This campaign reminds us of Chinese warfare, or a duel with buttoned foils. It certainly is an extreme example of the idea that warfare is a battle between the wills of the two commanders.

CHAPTER VIII

PERRY'S SQUADRON REACHES THE LAKE

NOW let us return to Lake Erie, where operations of great importance were imminent and commanders of a different type held the stage: adventurous Perry and hard-fighting Barclay. General Proctor, after his retreat from Fort Meigs, meditated for a second time an attack upon Erie. Fortunately for us, the reënforcements he considered necessary could not be spared from the Niagara peninsula; there was now no Isaac Brock to use interior lines for daring combinations. The British general decided upon another attack upon Harrison—a more conservative operation. On July 13 he sailed for Sandusky; to cover his communications Barclay took the lake. Embarking one hundred soldiers at Long Point on the sixteenth he sailed for Erie. On the nineteenth he arrived off Perry's base and commenced a blockade.

By this time Perry's squadron, except for personnel, was ready for sea. The nine vessels which took part in the coming battle were.

Ships	Rig	Tonnage	Battery
Lawrence	Brig	480	2 long 12's; 18 short 32's.
Niagara	Brig	480	2 long 12's; 18 short 32's.
Caledonia	Schooner	180	2 long 24's; 1 short 32.
Ariel	Schooner	112	4 long 12's.
Scorpion	Schooner	86	1 long 32; 1 short 32.
Somers	Schooner	94	1 long 24; 1 short 32.
Porcupine	Schooner	83	1 long 32.
Tigress	Schooner	96	1 long 32.
Trippe	Sloop	60	1 long 24.

9 vessels   1671 tons   54 guns

In addition there was the *Ohio* schooner, with one long 24, which did not engage in the Battle of Lake Erie.

The commodore now had two problems: first, to obtain personnel to fill his crews; and second, to pass his ships over the five-foot bar at the harbor entrance in the face of the enemy. In May, Chauncey and Perry had estimated that it would require 740 officers and men to man the squadron. Early in July, Perry, impatient for the campaign to begin, said that he would take the lake with much less than that number. Chauncey thought this a most dangerous procedure. "I am at a loss to account for the change in Captain Perry's sentiments," he wrote to the Navy Department. "But if he can beat the enemy with half that number, no one will feel happier than myself." From this time on there was constant friction and misunderstanding between daring Perry and cautious Chauncey. Why Chauncey selected for his chief assistant an officer holding opinions so contrary to his own will always be a mystery.

By July 19, when Barclay showed himself off Erie, Perry still had only 170 men. Of these over fifty were sick. "Think of my situation," he wrote to Chauncey, "the enemy in sight, the vessels under my command more than sufficient and ready to make sail, and yet obliged to bite my fingers with vexation for want of men." Two days later, to relieve his feelings a bit, he took out three schooners and skirmished at long range. On the twenty-third he again wrote to his chief: "The vessels are ready to meet the enemy the moment they are officered and manned. Our sails are bent, provisions on board, and, in fact, everything is ready. Barclay has been bearding me for several days; I long to be at him." Here we have again the spirit of James Lawrence, who, in losing one fight, won many another for our Navy.

Later in the day Sailing Master Champlin arrived with a party of sixty-nine sailors from Lake Ontario. These men were of such poor quality that Perry felt he should protest. "The men that came by Mr. Champlin," he wrote on the twenty-sixth, "are a motley set, blacks, soldiers, and boys. I cannot think you saw them after they were selected." Apparently even in those times present-day methods of selecting men for transfer were already in vogue.

Perry's situation had now become very irritating, particularly to one of his high-strung, sensitive nature. We see from his letters that he needed no urging to take the lake and begin the campaign. Nevertheless, General Harrison, in fear of Proctor's new advance, was continually calling upon Perry for his assistance. The Secretary of the Navy, well knowing Perry's difficulties, was likewise insisting upon immediate action. On the other hand, Chauncey was continually urging delay and caution. His orders had just come in and certainly they struck a most discordant note. "The first object will be," they read, "to destroy or cripple the enemy's fleet; but in all attempts upon the fleet you ought to use great caution, for the loss of a single vessel may decide the fate of the campaign." Remember that Chauncey was Perry's immediate superior, to whom he was directly responsible for his conduct of operations.

Every principle of warfare demands that the junior shall obey the spirit as well as the letter of his superior's orders. But what if the junior knows that the orders are based upon an utterly false theory of war? "A battle," says Ian Hamilton, "is a swirl of 'ifs' and 'ands.' The commander who enters upon it possessed by some clear and just principle is like a sailing ship entering a typhoon on the right tack." Certainly it was far from a clear and just principle to tell a distant subordinate to destroy the enemy and not lose a

single ship. That was only to condemn him also to the same
system of Chinese warfare that Chauncey and Yeo were
playing on the Ontario chessboard. General Hamilton said
that *"wish to fight* and *will to win* are the surest victory get-
ters in the pack." So thought our commodore. He rightly
forgot any orders that Chauncey had ever sent him and
resolved to fight this campaign in his own way. As soon
as he had half a chance he was determined to take the lake
and fight, whenever and wherever his opportunity came!
And he did this with the full realization that the slightest
mishap, deserved or not, would be charged to recklessness
by his "play-it-safe" senior.

"The order that battle is to be sought *à tout prix* cannot
be issued," said Tirpitz, "but must be locked in the breast
of the person concerned." Perry was to seek a battle at
any cost even though his orders forbade it.

On the thirtieth there arrived sixty more sailors. A few
people from the surrounding country were induced to volunteer for four months. These fellows were evidently not
of a very high caliber, for it was of them that General
Harrison said that "numbers must give that confidence
which ought to be produced by conscious valour and intrepidity." But maybe the commodore can make something
better out of them. By this not over-satisfactory method of
recruiting, his total was brought to 320, including all the
sick. However, doubtless Barclay had to do some indis-
criminate recruiting also, and some of his fellows must have
been sick.

Perry decided now that he would go just as soon as his
opportunity showed. And to his delight, late on the thirty-
first, Barclay's sails faded below the horizon. The next day
was Sunday, August 1. The surface of the lake, as far
as he could see, was clear. He deliberated for a while,

like Caesar at the Rubicon. Then suddenly he issued the order to cross the bar. The die was cast!

This was a daring decision. Over the bar, at its deepest point, there were but five feet of water. Through this spot the schooners and sloop could be taken without difficulty. With the two brigs it was a different matter. It was necessary to remove their guns, ammunition, and stores, and even then it was very doubtful whether they could be pulled through. Had Barclay returned before the first brig had passed Perry could have opposed him with but schooners and sloops, plus some slight moral assistance from a battery of three long 12-pounders on the distant shore. The other brig would have been too far distant for her carronades to reach the enemy. However, it had to be done—as well then as later.

The guns and stores were removed from the *Lawrence* and she was towed toward the bar. Under the commodore's personal direction the men worked as never before; night and day they kept at it. Thus was much hard work saved afterward. For three days and nights the toil continued; anxious hours they must have been for our young commodore, for what could he have done had Barclay returned and staked everything on one resolute onslaught?

But luck is with us. At 8:00 A.M. the flagship comes through the mud and floats in the deep waters of the lake. But Perry does not stop to congratulate himself; he hurries with feverish energy the reloading of guns and stores. No sooner is this done than the British squadron reappears— just too late. Now, even without the *Niagara,* we are a match for them and they know it. Perry pushes out the *Ariel* and *Scorpion* to hold Barclay in play. That proves sufficient, for he is now in no mood for fighting. The *Niagara* comes through much easier. By nine in the evening

Perry is able to report that all the American squadron has reached the lake. The British withdraw. Perry can sleep easy now, if his fever will let him.

This feat of Perry of gaining the lake in the face of the enemy has always been accounted a most notable one, and very justly so. Even more than his battle does it illustrate his restless energy and bold decision.

Perry was anxious to finish the job, so he cruised for two days between Erie and Long Point to try to bring the enemy to battle. But Barclay, very properly, had retired to Malden to await the completion of his new ship, the *Detroit*. Our squadron then returned to Erie. There on August 9 Captain Jesse D. Elliott appeared with 100 men and officers; this brought the total, including sick, to 420. Chauncey deserves great credit for sending on these men, for he could have used them well in his own ships. Readers will remember that this was the period of his maneuvering off Niagara and the mouth of the Genessee and that Chauncey did not win his moral victory until August 10.

Elliott had been sent in order to command the *Niagara*. While doubtless an officer of high rank was required for this command, it was unwise to send a man so close to Perry on the Navy List and who had once been appointed to the chief command on Erie.

While Chauncey had been very decent in sending on the draft of men, in other respects he was hardly so helpful. For with Elliott came a letter of admonition. It concluded with an ominous paragraph, one which would have killed the spirit and *will to fight* of many a young fellow in Perry's shoes: "As you have assured the Secretary that you should conceive yourself equal or superior to the enemy, with a force in men so much less than I deemed necessary, there will be a great deal expected from you by your country, and

I trust they will not be disappointed in the high expectations formed of your gallantry and judgment. I will barely make the observation, which was impressed upon my mind by an old soldier; that is, 'Never despise your enemy.'" This is one of the most glaring instances of "passing the buck" which has come to our attention. It was all very well to say "Never despise your enemy." That was one of the maxims of fiery old Suvaroff, probably the most aggressive, daring, seemingly reckless, and highly successful general who ever led an army. But when Chauncey said it the meaning was far different than when Suvaroff did. For our commodore was just the fellow who would, to use an expression of General Hamilton, "see a Turk behind every bush, a battalion behind every hill, and a brigade behind every mountain." Chauncey's entire life was spent in avoiding the charge that he was despising his enemy, and he never got any further. By this letter Chauncey washed his hands of the whole Erie business—threw the entire responsibility upon Perry. If that reckless officer suffered any defeat, Chauncey was completely protected by the letter he had just written. Doubtless he kept a copy at hand to clear himself and tell the world, "I told you so."

Some time ago we gave our most favorable comment to an entirely different attitude on the part of Commodore Preble. He accepted the entire responsibility for the *Philadelphia* incident, and shared equally with Decatur in the credit for its success. Had Chauncey accepted full responsibility for Perry's conduct on Erie, he also would have received a large share of the credit. But as he repudiated in advance Perry's plan and methods and did much to break down his spirit at a highly critical time, he lost his chance to share in the glory of the most decisive naval victory of the war.

Perry was in anything but a happy mood when this letter heaped fuel on the fires of mental strain and actual fever. He had passed through days of terrible anxiety. He had been distressed by his conflicting instructions and Harrison's urgings. For months he had suffered terribly from fever which rarely left him. This last straw broke the camel's back. His temper flared up; he asked to be relieved. Yes, he wrote to the Secretary of the Navy: "The critical state of General Harrison was such that I took upon myself the responsibility of going out with a few young officers you had pleased to send me, with a few seamen I had, and as many volunteers as I could muster from the militia. I should not shrink from this responsibility; but, Sir, at that very moment I surely did not anticipate the receipt of a letter in every line of which is an insult." The Secretary used sound judgment. He made allowances for Perry's condition. He did not approve his request; told him to stick to his job. Thus he deserved a part of the credit for the coming successes.

Meanwhile Proctor had begun his attack upon Harrison. Already, on August 1, he had appeared before Sandusky. There we had a Fort Stephenson—also a certain Major George Croghan. There were only 160 soldiers, a solitary 6-pounder, and some weak palisades. Proctor had his redskins along. Our soldiers knew by this time what happened after a surrender or a Proctor victory. So they decided that, if they wanted to keep their scalps, there had better be no Proctor victory. In fact, they drove him back, killed or wounded 120 of his soldiers, and he had to retire to Malden. Yes, Proctor, you have won your successes, furnished plentifully your redskins with scalps, spread terror through our land. Now hard times are coming; soon you are going to make a famous ride rearwards; better get well

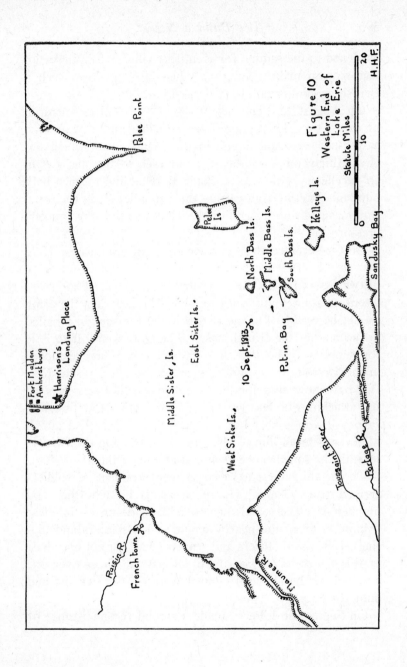

Fort Malden
Amherstburg
Harrison's
Landing Place

Pelee Point

Raisin R.
Frenchtown

Maumee R.

Middle Sister, Is.

West Sister Is.

East Sister Is.

10 Sept. 1813

Pelee Is.

North Bass Is.
Middle Bass Is.
South Bass Is.
Put-in-Bay

Kelleys Is.

Toussaint River

Portage R.

Sandusky Bay

0   10   20

Statute Miles

Figure 10
Western End of
Lake Erie

H.H.F.

hardened to the saddle, for Kentucky riflemen, flushed with
victory, can make good time when hunting down such a
British general as you have proved.

On August 12 Perry left Erie with his entire squadron
of ten ships. Three days later he came into Put in Bay,
a well-protected anchorage in the island group which lies
about thirty miles southeast of Malden. Here he was in
an excellent position to blockade Barclay and to keep both
him and Proctor from getting their supplies along the usual
water route from Long Point. That was the way to exert
pressure.

On the seventeenth Perry anchored off Sandusky. Here
two days later General Harrison, with his staff and a party
of twenty-six Indian chiefs, visited the flagship. Plans were
discussed for a joint attack on Fort Malden when the army
should be ready. On the twenty-third the squadron sailed
to reconnoiter the British base. The *Ohio* went off to Erie
for supplies. The British squadron was found anchored
in the Detroit River under cover of the guns of the fort.
We were now superior by two to one and Perry was all
for attacking the enemy as he found them. But first, unfavorable winds kept him off, and then a very bad attack
of fever induced him to abandon his plan. On the twenty-
seventh the squadron re-anchored at Put in Bay.

On the thirty-first a welcome reënforcement of soldiers
arrived from General Harrison. This brought the total
number of officers and men to 532, made up as follows:
volunteers from the nearby country, 45; soldiers and marines, 158; naval officers and seamen, 329, but not over half
of this figure were trained sailors. At all times over one
hundred of the above personnel were on the sick list and
unfit for duty.

On September 1 Perry made a second reconnaissance of

Malden, returning to his base on the sixth. These cruises gave his untrained crews much valuable experience and raised their morale.

If Perry was working under many disadvantages, Barclay also was not without his worries. Early in September his new ship, the *Detroit,* was completed. It had not been practicable to bring her armament to Malden, so Barclay had to mount on her deck the guns of the fort, a most miscellaneous collection. The rupture of their water communications had reduced the British forces in the Detroit area to a most serious situation—had virtually cut them off from the rest of Canada. The very Indians who had assisted Proctor so ably in his campaigns now became a liability rather than an asset, for they had to be fed. With the women and children, their numbers reached the total of 14,000. Flour for this many people could be transported only by water. Even cattle no longer were available in sufficient numbers to give them meat. Without food the Indians would certainly leave the British army, might even join Harrison. Proctor informed Barclay that he would have to evacuate the entire Detroit front if the command of the lake could not be regained.

Yes, it was certain that Barclay would have to fight Perry. The only question for him to answer was "When?" This was settled by Sir George Prevost. Himself cautious to the point of timidity where he had to run the risk, he had the habit of gallantly urging on his naval commanders in a spirit of nonchalant confidence. Yeo's successful skirmish with Chauncey had elated him and he wrote in light vein to Proctor: "Yeo's experience should convince Barclay that he has only to dare and he will be successful." On the seventh fifty regular seamen arrived from Montreal. Two days later Barclay took the lake to fight.

The British squadron was composed as follows:

Ships	Rig	Tonnage	Battery
Detroit	Ship	490	1 long 18; 2 short 24's; 6 long 12's. 8 long 9's; 1 short 24;
Queen	Ship	400	1 short 18.
Charlotte			1 long 12; 2 long 9's;
Lady	Schooner	230	14 short 24's.
Prevost			1 long 9; 2 long 6's;
Hunter	Brig	180	10 short 12's.
			4 long 6's; 2 long 4's; 2 long 12's; 2 short 12's.
Chippe-way	Schooner	70	1 long 9.
Little Belt	Sloop	90	1 long 12; 2 long 6's.

6 vessels	1460 tons	63 guns

The squadron was manned by about 440 officers and men, of whom 70 were regular seamen, 120 Canadians, and 250 soldiers. Doubtless Barclay, as well as Perry, had his proportion of sick.

There follows a concise comparison of the two squadrons:

Squadron	Ships	Personnel	Tonnage	Guns	Broadside
British	6	440	1460	63	459 pounds
United States	9	532*	1671	54	936 pounds

* Only 416 fit for duty on September 10.

While in displacement, personnel, and number of guns the squadrons were well matched, in weight of broadside we had a superiority of 2 to 1. To partly counterbalance this advantage in gunfire, the British guns were mounted in a smaller number of vessels, of more nearly the same type and speed, so that they could all be brought into action at the same time. A great part of our broadside came from very slow schooners, which Chauncey had conclusively demonstrated could not be maneuvered and brought into action with his larger square-rigged ships. Everything considered, Perry had a moderate, but not by any means overwhelming superiority, say about 10 to 7.

On the evening of the ninth our commodore called his captains on board the *Lawrence* to explain his plan of battle. It was an historic occasion, for all knew that decisive battle was imminent. What a thrill must have passed through the assembled captains when their young commodore, inspired by the impending opportunity to serve his country, gave his orders in language and manner which we may well call Nelsonic. If the enemy did not come out, he was to be attacked at anchor, or wherever found. There was to be no more delay. Then, with face flushed with fever, Perry told his captains that he wanted close action, where his short guns would have their full effect. The *Detroit* was to be the objective of the *Lawrence;* the *Niagara* was to attack the *Queen Charlotte;* the *Caledonia,* the *Hunter.* All were warned in the most emphatic language that they must keep closed up on the flagship. Perry knew there might be difficulty in getting his rear ships into the action, so he repeated to his captains part of Nelson's instructions before Trafalgar. "They were," he said later, "expressly instructed that 'if in the expected engagement they laid their vessels alongside those of the enemy, they would not be out of the way.'"

As the captains prepared to return to their ships Perry brought to them a blue flag, upon which in large, white, and somewhat irregular muslin letters were sewn those immortal words of dying Lawrence, DON'T GIVE UP THE SHIP! "When this flag shall be hoisted to the main royal masthead," the commodore said, "it shall be your signal for going into action." Ah, what a battle flag to fight under! Every vessel of our Navy today should carry an exact copy of this famous flag to be hoisted before going into action.

CHAPTER IX

THE BATTLE OF LAKE ERIE

NEXT morning—the famous tenth of September—sunrise disclosed on the northwestern horizon a cluster of six sails. The day long eagerly awaited by Perry had arrived. Instantly signals were flying to get under way and stand out of the harbor. At first the wind was unfavorable for this maneuver, blowing gently from the southwest. The commodore, still weak from the effects of his fever, redoubled his exertions to get the squadron formed for battle. While beating out of the harbor, Taylor, the sailing master, strove to gain every yard he could to windward to win the coveted weather gauge. This delayed the formation of the battle line; Perry, growing impatient, told him to run to the leeward of certain islands. "Then," Taylor answered, "you will have to engage the enemy to leeward." "I don't care," the commodore said, "to windward or to leeward, they shall fight today."

At ten the squadron cleared the islands; the wind shifted to the southeast, giving Perry the weather gauge. He used this favor of fortune to stand down upon the British fleet, determined to engage at the earliest possible instant.

Barclay too was in fighting mood. He had only a week's food left and for several days his men had gone without their usual ration of spirits. "They were reserved for the action," wrote one of the British officers, "and all consumed on that day." Barclay hove to his flagship and closed up his battle line on the port tack. The course was southwest. The ships had been freshly painted and battle flags flew from every masthead. It was a formidable show of naval power.

[401]

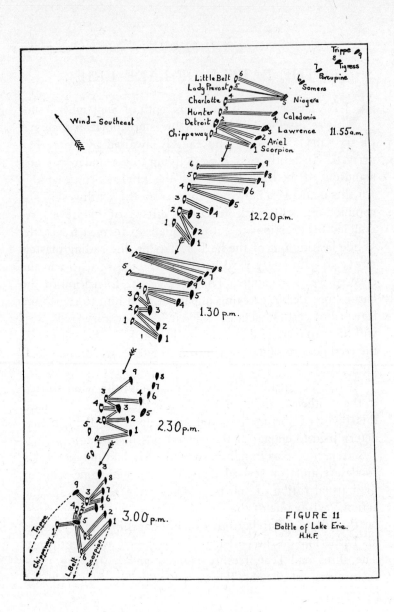

Wind — Southeast

Little Belt
Lady Prevost
Charlotte
Hunter
Detroit
Chippeway

Niagara
Caledonia
Lawrence
Ariel
Scorpion

11.55 a.m.

12.20 p.m.

1.30 p.m.

2.30 p.m.

3.00 p.m.

Trippe
Tigress
Porcupine
Somers

Trippe
Chippeway
L.Belt
Scorpion

FIGURE 11
Battle of Lake Erie.
H.H.F.

The British squadron was ranged in the following order: *Chippeway, Detroit, Hunter, Queen Charlotte, Lady Prevost,* and *Little Belt.* Barclay had the advantage of bringing his whole force into battle in a compact formation.

Perry also had formed his squadron in column, the customary battle formation. In the van he had placed the three brigs, *Niagara, Lawrence,* and *Caledonia,* followed by the schooners *Ariel, Scorpion, Somers, Porcupine, Tigress.* The little sloop *Trippe* brought up the rear. When his blue fighting flag was shown by the flagship lusty cheers resounded down the line of battle. At about three knots his ships edged in slowly toward the enemy. Food was served to the crews—men fight best on a full stomach! Whether stimulating drinks were issued, as on the British ships, is not stated, but it is probable that they were.

When the squadrons were apart three miles Perry first noticed the unusual dispositions of the British ships. To carry out his announced plan some changes would be necessary in his own line. In the van he placed the *Scorpion* and *Ariel* to beat down the weak *Chippeway.* Next he placed the *Lawrence* to fight the *Detroit,* the *Caledonia* to match the *Hunter,* and the *Niagara* to oppose the *Charlotte.* In the rear the four schooners and one sloop were to handle the *Prevost* and *Little Belt.* These dispositions would insure superiority at all points—if all ships could be brought into battle together. But that was a big "if."

The realignment completed, Perry turned his ships together to close the enemy. Over his port quarter a light breeze came. The weather was perfect; not a cloud was in the sky. In his eagerness to engage Perry carried rather too much sail on the brigs in the van. The schooners in the rear manned their great sweeps, but even with their aid could not keep closed up. This, however, was to be expected; it did not much concern the commodore. He was well used to slow schooners—let them come on as best they might. He had superiority of force and did not have to wait until conditions were all in his favor. He knew they never would be! He was resolved that, to use an expression of Paul Jones, "there would be disaster to someone" before the sun set upon that bright September day. And when our leaders enter battle in such a state of mind, it will usually be the enemy to whom the disaster occurs.

It was 11:45 A.M. when the first brown smoke puff appeared against the *Detroit's* side. She had fired her long 24 at extreme range, about a mile and a half. After five minutes of deliberate fire the first hit plowed its way through the flagship's bulwarks, scattering splinters over the deck. The commodore passed the word along the line to close up—each vessel to engage her designated opponent. By 11:55 the flagship had reached a position abreast the *Hunter;* now the long guns in the American van began to shoot. Stephen Champlin, commanding the *Scorpion,* fired the first round with his long 32. Lieutenant Packet in the *Ariel* commenced firing his four long 12's on the *Detroit.* At first the *Lawrence* could fire only one long 12, but the other was hauled over from the unengaged side. Thus in the van Perry had only six—later seven—guns against the ten long cannon of the *Chippeway* and *Detroit.* In the center the *Caledonia* with her two long 24's had rather the advantage over the *Hunter's* four long guns of smaller caliber, while the *Niagara,* with her two long 12's, was well matched with the one long 12 and one long 9 of the *Charlotte.* This assumes that Elliott brought over both his long guns to the engaged side, as Perry had done. In the rear the five small craft were entirely out of range, the last vessel being still two miles from the enemy. This possibly allowed the *Pre-*

Com.ᵣᵉ Oliver H. Perry

From an engraving by Henry Meyer, after the original painting by John W. Jarvis

COMMODORE OLIVER H. PERRY

From the original painting by Thomas Birch in the Pennsylvania Academy of Fine Arts. Photograph by W. Vivian Chappel

THE BATTLE OF LAKE ERIE

vost and *Little Belt* to do some shooting at the *Niagara* with four long guns. The advantage thus lay with the enemy in the first part of the fight.

The British vessels concentrated a great part of their fire on the *Lawrence;* she was suffering severely and unable to make effective reply. So at noon Perry brought her around parallel to the enemy and fired his carronades. It was no use; all their shot splashed short into the water. He headed in again for the enemy and passed the word by speaking trumpet to come to close action. The *Lawrence* now began to receive serious injuries aloft and man after man fell on her blood-stained decks. "It was twenty minutes," Roosevelt says, "before she succeeded in getting within carronade range, and during that time the action at the head of the line was between the long guns of the *Chippeway* and *Detroit,* throwing 123 pounds, and those of the *Scorpion, Ariel* and *Lawrence,* throwing 104 pounds."

It was about 12:20 P.M. before the *Lawrence* reached cannister range, or about 250 yards. Now for a second time she paralleled the enemy and opened on the *Detroit* with such of her guns as remained intact. The *Scorpion* and *Ariel* kept on the flagship's port bow at moderate range. An excessive powder charge blew the *Scorpion's* 24-pound carronade off its carriage and down a hatch; one of the *Ariel's* long 12-pounders burst. Being opposed only by the one gun of the *Chippeway,* these two vessels fired into the *Detroit's* bows with great effect.

The *Caledonia* engaged the *Hunter* at 1,000 yards. As two of her three guns were long 24's, it was correct for her to remain outside carronade range. The *Niagara* remained at a similar distance from the *Charlotte* and fired with her two long 12's, her powerful battery of eighteen 32-pounder carronades was entirely useless. The *Somers* came into the fight and fired on the *Charlotte* with her long 24. Thus the three vessels which now occupied the center of our line had a great advantage over the *Hunter* and *Charlotte,* throwing from their long guns ninety-six pounds of shot, to which the enemy could reply only with thirty-nine. As a consequence the *Charlotte* suffered very severely; her captain and first lieutenant were killed. Lieutenant Irvine saw that he could do nothing in his present position with his short guns, so now he made probably the finest tactical decision of the battle. Making sail, he surged past the *Hunter* and came into close action against the *Lawrence* with his short 24's.

Elliott possibly had some justification for keeping the *Niagara* at long range until Irvine made his brilliant maneuver—though we consider it very slight indeed. But now, after that vessel was firing at the *Lawrence* with her carronades, there can be no question but that Elliott likewise should have engaged at the closest range with every gun. However, he still continued at extreme range, where he was virtually out of the fight. The only possible excuse for his action was the impossibility of his making headway in the variable breezes, which might conceivably have been felt by the *Charlotte* and not the *Niagara.* The fact that the former's rigging had been injured while that of the latter was intact tends to decrease the possible validity of this excuse almost to zero.

The *Porcupine, Tigress,* and *Trippe* concentrated a long-range fire upon the *Prevost* and *Little Belt.* As our three vessels had between them two long 32's and one 24, the more numerous, but smaller, guns of the enemy were no match for them. The captain and first lieutenant of the *Prevost* were both severely wounded and after a determined resistance this vessel gradually drew out of the line. The *Little Belt* followed suit.

Irvine's able maneuver and Elliott's grave mistake soon produced a critical situation in the van; almost gave the enemy the victory; probably would have if a Perry had not stood upon the *Lawrence's* decks. Almost by a miracle his life was preserved amid the awful slaughter. Had the commodore fallen, who can say where the victory would have rested?

For the devoted flagship was rapidly being wrecked by the deadly carronade fire of the *Detroit* and *Charlotte.* "Every brace and bowline being shot away," Perry reported, "she became unmanageable, notwithstanding the great exertions of the sailing master. In this situation she sustained the action upwards of two hours within cannister distance, while every gun was rendered useless, and the greater part of her crew killed or wounded." In fact, out of a total of 103 fit for duty, 83 were killed or wounded. First Lieutenant John Yarnall had been wounded; Lieutenant of Marines John Brooks, and Midshipmen Henry Laub and Thomas Claxton killed. Perry himself, assisted by the purser and chaplain, fired the last gun at 2:30 P.M. The *Lawrence* was out of action.

Fortunately, the *Detroit* was in little better shape. According to Barclay, she "was a perfect wreck, principally from the raking fire of the gunboats." The commodore himself had received the eighth wound of his gallant career and had been carried below; his first lieutenant was mortally wounded.

The ships in the van had fought themselves to a finish. Such men as were still unwounded had exhausted themselves physically and mentally by three terrible hours of point-blank firing. Rigging had been wrecked, masts splintered, sail ripped and torn. The ships drifted aimlessly. Vessels in the rear, with rigging and spars still intact, came closer and closer into the action. In this way the *Niagara,* still uninjured, reached a position about five hundred yards outside the *Lawrence.* The crisis had arrived—the decision hung by a hair. Elliott had thus far been actuated by the greatest caution. He would not know from a distance how badly the British had suffered. If the *Lawrence* struck her colors was it not probable that he, as next senior in command, would give the signal for retirement? On the other hand, if by any means the *Niagara* could be brought into close range the victory still would be ours. How could Perry be certain of getting her into close action? Only by taking her there himself! "Finding that the *Lawrence* could no longer annoy the enemy," he reported, "I left her in charge of Lieutenant Yarnall, who, I was convinced, from the bravery already displayed by him, would do what would comport with the honor of the flag."

The commodore quickly shoved off in a small boat, pulled by four seamen. Over his arm was his blue fighting flag; he stood erect and in plain view of the two squadrons. It was a great moment of history—an inspiring episode.

> See! he quits the *Lawrence's* side,
> And trusts him to the foaming tide,
> While thundering navies round him ride,
> And flash their red artillery.—Old Song.

Fortune favors the brave—nearly always. Unscathed, the commodore reaches the *Niagara.* It is now nearly 2:40. Elliott, seeing doubtless that two captains are not needed for a single ship, volunteers to bring the schooners in the rear into closer action. He leaves in a small boat, possibly Perry's cutter, to carry out his mission. The commodore looks about a bit, weighs the situation for a few minutes, then decides to venture. "At 45 minutes past 2," he reports, "the signal was made for close action. The *Niagara* being very little injured, I determined to pass through the enemy's line."

Already the tide had begun to turn. Even though, at 2:40, the *Lawrence* had struck her colors, our captains were commencing to push the fight. Lieutenant Turner most gallantly sailed the *Caledonia* inside the *Lawrence* and brought her against the British flagship. Lieutenant Stevens brought the *Trippe,* originally at the end of the line, against the *Hunter*. He and Turner were exchanging signals proposing to board the *Detroit*. Here were captains after the commodore's heart.

Elliott also was doing good service. Boarding the *Somers,* he led the *Porcupine* and *Tigress* closer to the enemy and began to fire with grape and cannister. The British stuck to their guns manfully and the *Lady Prevost* and *Little Belt,* having been driven from their position in the rear of the line, reëntered the fight in the van.

The scene now was set for the coup de grace. Perry double-shotted his carronades, trimmed his sails to catch the freshening breeze, and headed for the center of the enemy's formation. The *Detroit* saw the danger, tried to wear to bring her starboard battery into play. This was a difficult maneuver with her wrecked rigging and she ran foul of the *Charlotte*. While in this helpless position both vessels received the raking fire of the *Niagara's* starboard battery at pistol shot; the shot which missed them crashed into the *Hunter,* which lay directly in the line of fire. At the same time the *Niagara's* port battery raked the *Prevost, Little Belt,* and possibly even the *Chippeway.* There are few cases in history where single broadsides have been so terribly effective. It was simply murder!

The slaughter was too great now even for Englishmen— with the traditions of centuries of naval supremacy behind them. At exactly three o'clock, just eight minutes after the *Niagara* broke the line, the *Detroit's* war flags fluttered down. "The ship lying completely unmanageable," wrote the senior officer on duty, "every brace cut away, the mizzen topmast and gaff down, all the other masts badly wounded not a stay left forward, hull battered very much, a number of guns disabled, and the enemy's squadron raking both ships ahead and astern, none of our own in a position to support us, I was under the painful necessity of answering the enemy to say we had struck, the *Queen Charlotte* having previously done so." The *Hunter* and *Prevost* also surrendered. The *Chippeway* and *Little Belt* tried to escape, but were run down and captured by the *Trippe* and *Scorpion,* respectively. Victory was complete. Sailing Master Champlin, of the *Scorpion,* fired the last, as he had the first, shot of the battle.

After such a long and closely contested fight the decision had come with startling suddenness. This, however, is a common occurrence in war and should be a reason for more and more perseverance, more and more resolution to fight to the finish. Many a great leader has fought for days and months—even years—without seeming to make progress, only suddenly to discover that his enemy has collapsed in a most unexpected manner. This psychological phenomenon is seen not only in war and battle but in the world of sport. Particularly in football is it noticeable. Tad Jones mentions it: "In nearly every well-balanced struggle—football or other—there comes a stage when victory and defeat hesitate a bit before ranging themselves with this side or that. Until this moment arrives one contestant may have built up an apparently winning margin and still know that success is not assured, while the other, though outplayed and left behind in the scoring, is not prepared to accept the loser's portion; but once it passes, the result no longer is in doubt and both parties to the fray are conscious of the fact."

Some time after Perry had left the *Lawrence* Yarnall had struck her colors, but in the heat of battle the enemy had no chance to take possession. Now that the battle had been decided the few unwounded men on the flagship made haste to rehoist her ensign. On the quarter-deck of this gallant ship Perry received the surrender of the British ships. Because of the determined resistance they had made, Perry permitted the captains to keep their swords—a courtesy accorded very frequently by our victorious commanders.

Unfortunately, the losses were very heavy on both sides. The British had forty-one killed and ninety-four wounded; we lost twenty-seven killed and ninety-six wounded. Perry made every effort to care for the poor wounded fellows, British as well as American. Here war ceases—a man is just a man. "Captain Perry has behaved in the most humane and attentive manner," Barclay wrote, "not only to myself and officers, but to all the wounded."

Immediately after the battle had been decided, Perry wrote in pencil on the back of an old letter his famous message to General Harrison: "We have met the enemy and they are ours: Two ships, two brigs, one schooner and one sloop. Yours with greatest respect and esteem, O. H. Perry."

His despatch to the Secretary of the Navy was worded in more formal style, but was received with equal delight. The victory was hailed with enthusiasm by the entire nation. States competed with the Federal Government in awarding swords and medals. Three months' pay was given each officer. Each seaman received $209 in prize money. It is difficult for us in these days to realize the place our Navy then had in the hearts of Americans.

This is one of the few battles of the War of 1812 which has aroused comment and criticism, doubtless caused by the unfortunate controversy between Perry and Elliott. Perry has been very freely criticized for having entered the battle in a careless and reckless fashion. We believe that this is due to an ignorance of the difficulty in bringing such an ill-assorted squadron into battle in proper order. The innumerable maneuverings on Lake Ontario—we can scarcely call them battles—demonstrate that it was an impossibility to bring slow-sailing schooners and sloops into the fight simultaneously with much faster square rigged ships and brigs. The reader will have a further proof of this before many pages. The situation which confronted Beatty at the commencement of the Battle of Jutland was closely analogous to that which Perry had to face on Lake Erie. Each engaged without waiting for his slower ships— in each case, we think correctly. Had they waited there never would have been a battle, or at least one which gave any promise of being decisive. We would hesitate long before criticizing a fighter like Perry for such a problematical error as this.

That the battle was ever in doubt was due to the failure of Captain Elliott of the *Niagara*. First, there can be no question but that he was guilty of disobedience of orders. To criticize him for this may seem inconsistent with our approval of Perry's failure to obey the spirit of his senior's instructions. There is, however, a decided difference. Perry received very general instructions from a senior at a great distance. Elliott received absolutely definite orders from a senior a few hundred yards away—and in battle. Furthermore, Perry's decision led him into battle with his entire squadron; Elliott's kept him out of battle when his comrades were being beaten. There is a grave difference here. Second, there are two charges in our present "Articles for the Government of the Navy" which could be laid against him:

"Art. 4 (17) Or does not, upon signal for battle, use his utmost exertions to join in battle;

"(20) Or does not afford all practical relief and assistance to vessels belonging to the United States or their allies when engaged in battle."

It is very possible that these provisions were written with Elliott's conduct in mind and with a view to prevent its recurrence.

Perry thought that there was glory enough for all and did not wish his glory dimmed by recriminations. So he referred to Elliott's part in the battle most generously: "At half past two, the wind springing up, Captain Elliott was enabled to bring his vessel, the *Niagara,* gallantly into close action." Elliott had such strong political backing that Congress was induced to award him a gold medal, with a fine Latin motto engraved thereon: "Who thinks nothing done while anything remains to be done." Think of it!

The effects of the battle were tremendous. When, a year later, the British delegates at Ghent demanded that an independent Indian nation be created within our present boundaries, our delegates, fortified by Perry's victory, could reply that it was "not necessary to refer such demands to the American Government for its instructions," and forthwith rejected the British proposals unconditionally.

After the action the squadron returned with its prizes to Put in Bay. The next day a heavy gale broke over the battered ships; the *Detroit* and *Charlotte* rolled out their masts. These two ships, with the *Lawrence,* were then used to house the wounded. The other vessels were prepared to transport Harrison's army to Canada. The latter had now been joined by Governor Shelby, familiarly known as "Old King's Mountain" from his part in that famous Revolutionary fight, and eleven regiments of Kentucky volunteers. On the twentieth commenced the transportation of the troops to Middle Sister Island. By the twenty-fifth 5,000 had assembled there in readiness for the enterprise. Colonel Johnson with a mounted regiment marched along the shore to Detroit. This time it would be different from Hull's campaign; now we had command of the lake. It was a wide road over which we could travel with ease and rapidity in any direction. The British could scarcely venture on its waters in a rowboat.

September 27 found the weather perfect. The army sailed at 9:00 A.M. in sixteen large vessels and one hundred small craft of various kinds. At four of the same day the landing was effected three miles east of Amherstburg. Soon afterward our vanguard was entering its streets to the rollicking tune of "Yankee Doodle." Fort Malden was found evacuated and from there Harrison marched to Sandwich, the squadron keeping pace with him along the Detroit River. On the twenty-ninth Sandwich and Detroit fell and on October 1 Johnson with his mounted riflemen joined.

Next day the united force set out in pursuit of Proctor along the shore of Lake St. Clair as far as the mouth of the Thames River. There the squadron was waiting with stores and ammunition. Up the river our troops marched; Perry kept pace for fifteen miles with the *Scorpion, Tigress,* and *Porcupine.* When shoaling water stopped them the commodore joined Harrison as a volunteer. He would be in at the kill.

Ten miles more up the river Harrison marched. On October 5 a brief, but sharp and decisive, action was fought.

33

U. S. Brig Niagara off the Western
Sister head of Lake Erie, Sept. 10th 1813
4. p. M.

Sir

It has pleased the almighty to give to the arms
of the United States a signal victory over their enemies
on this Lake. The British Squadron consisting of
two Ships. two Brigs. one Schooner & one Sloop
have this moment surrendered to the force under
my command, after a sharp conflict.

I have the honor to be
Sir Very Respectfully,
your Obdt. Servt.
O. H. Perry

The Honble William Jones
Secretary of the Navy

Facsimile of the original letter in the files of the Navy Department

PERRY'S DESPATCH

From an engraving after the painting by Alonzo Chappel

CHARGE OF THE KENTUCKY MOUNTED RIFLEMEN AT THE BATTLE OF THE THAMES

The Indian falling in the left foreground is Tecumseh.

Johnson's mounted Kentuckians charged through the dense forest upon the British regulars. Quite a cavalry charge this was! "One of the guns being deserted early in the action," reports Captain John Hall of the Canadian Regiment, "the troops near it gave way, and the consequence was a complete rout." Six hundred British prisoners were taken. Proctor made good his escape after a thrilling ride—already alluded to—galloping at top speed through the woods for sixty-five miles. That might be compared with Sheridan's famous ride to Winchester, with the exception that this was towards, while Proctor's was away from, battle!

Brave Tecumseh was killed; the Indians sued for peace. Only 250 British escaped, including General Proctor. "The general," adds Captain Hall, "is so fatigued by riding from the field of battle the other side of Moraviantown, through the wilderness, that he cannot write; and I am not much better." The famous Saratoga cannon, recaptured at Detroit, a second time fell into our hands. We almost feel a little sorry for poor Proctor.

During the action Perry acted as the general's aide and assisted him in forming the line of battle. "The appearance of the brave commodore," so Harrison reported, "cheered and animated every breast." Here was real example of coöperation between Army and Navy.

The campaign decided here, Harrison was ordered to the Niagara peninsula. On October 24 he sailed into Buffalo on seven of Perry's ships, only two weeks after his victory. Here it was found that Proctor's defeat had caused the British to withdraw from the entire peninsula and post themselves again at Burlington.

Perry soon received permission to turn over his command to Captain Elliott. His victory had given us Lake Erie for the rest of the war and the control of all its shores. The

power of the Indians was broken forever.   The possession
of all the immensely valuable territory south of the Great
Lakes was permanently assured to the United States.   Few
naval battles have given a more decisive impetus to the forward march of a nation to greatness.

CHAPTER X

CHAUNCEY MISSES HIS OPPORTUNITY

HAVING followed Perry and Harrison through the Erie campaign we must now return to a view of events upon Lake Ontario. You remember how at the beginning of the campaign General Armstrong, Secretary of War, had stated that Kingston should be the objective of our combined military and naval forces on Lake Ontario. Unfortunately the protests of Dearborn, partly supported by Chauncey, had induced him to abandon this entirely correct conception. As the campaign wore on and on without decisive results, Armstrong reverted to his original idea of an attack upon Kingston. Dearborn had proved his incapacity. Unfortunately, for political reasons, Armstrong felt compelled to give the command to General James Wilkinson, a man with a very shady reputation. He had been involved in the Burr episode in a most discreditable manner and Scott bitterly denounced him as an "unprincipled imbecile." Our old Chinese friend Sun Tzu said with justice that "the leader of armies is the arbiter of the people's fate, the man on whom it depends whether the nation shall be in peace or in peril." Yet our government selected such a man as Wilkinson to command our armies when both Brown and Scott were available, not to mention Jackson and Harrison.

Ou August 8 Armstrong described his idea to Wilkinson as follows: "Operations westward of Kingston, if successful, leave the strength of the enemy unbroken. It is the great depot of his resources. So long as he retains this, and keeps open his communications with the sea, he will not

[417]

want the means of multiplying his naval and other defenses, and of reënforcing or renewing the war in the West."

This was a remarkably lucid and correct estimate of the situation. After explaining that Kingston could be taken by a direct attack or indirectly by cutting the communications between it and Montreal, the Secretary concluded: "After this exposition, it is unnecessary to add, that, in conducting the present campaign, you will make Kingston your *primary object,* and that you will *choose* (as circumstances may warrant) between a *direct* and *indirect* attack upon that post."

Never did a general have more logical and correct orders than Wilkinson. The plan was perfect—what would the execution be? As there were only a few months before winter would set in, activity and speed were imperative. To insure these essentials, Armstrong took station at Sackett's Harbor so he could follow Wilkinson's operations and prod him on. Alas, he never dreamed what a task it would be—worse, we think, than that of the old woman in getting her pig over the stile in the familiar nursery rhyme.

To obtain the troops considered necessary, 3,000 were to be withdrawn from the Niagara peninsula and assembled at Sackett's Harbor. General Wade Hampton, who with 4,000 men was at Burlington, Vermont, was to demonstrate towards Montreal to attract the attention of the army toward that vital point.

On September 18, eight days after the Battle of Lake Erie, Chauncey sailed from Sackett's Harbor. On the twenty-fourth he arrived at Niagara and the next day commenced to embark troops.

Meanwhile, on the nineteenth Yeo had left Kingston with orders to escort supply ships to Burlington and then assist the army in an attack upon Fort George. On the twenty-

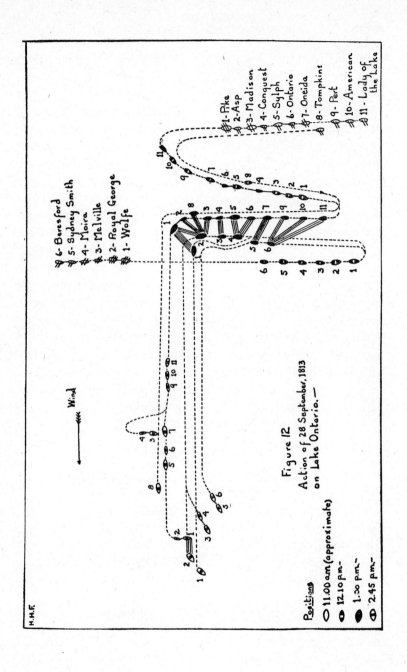

Wind

6 - Beresford
5 - Sydney Smith
4 - Moira
3 - Melville
2 - Royal George
1 - Wolfe

1 - Pike
2 - Asp
3 - Madison
4 - Conquest
5 - Sylph
6 - Ontario
7 - Oneida
8 - Tompkins
9 - Port
10 - American
11 - Lady of the Lake

Figure 12
Action of 28 September, 1813
on Lake Ontario. —

Positions
○ 11.00 a.m (approximate)
◑ 12.10 p.m.—
● 1.30 p.m.—
◐ 2.45 p.m.—

H.H.F.

fifth he discharged his stores at Burlington. Hearing that Chauncey was then at Niagara, Yeo gave up the projected attack and retired to York.

Now on the twenty-sixth Chauncey heard that Yeo was at York. Sending out the *Lady of the Lake* to reconnoiter, he soon verified this intelligence. He decided that it would be wise to beat Yeo before attempting to escort Wilkinson's army in small boats to Sackett's Harbor. On the twenty-seventh at 8:00 P.M., he sailed to seek out the enemy. His squadron scattered during the night. It took until eight in the morning to get it assembled. To increase its speed of advance the *Pike* took in tow the *Asp;* the *Sylph,* the *Ontario;* and the *Madison,* another schooner, probably the *Conquest.*

Soon afterward the British squadron was seen at anchor in York. With the schooners still in tow, Chauncey formed line of battle and stood down to engage. While our squadron was still three miles off the port, Yeo led out his squadron. He stood to the southward with a fresh breeze on his port beam. Chauncey had the weather position, so he ordered his ships to wear in succession and formed his line of battle on a course parallel to the enemy.

Here are the opposing squadrons:

UNITED STATES SQUADRON

Ship	Rig	Tonnage	Crew	Armament
Pike	Ship	875	300	28 long 24's.
Madison	Ship	593	200	24 short 32's.
Sylph	Schooner	300	70	4 long 32's; 12 long 6's.
Oneida	Brig	243	100	16 short 24's.
Conquest	Schooner	82	40	1 long 32; 1 long 24; 1 long 6.
Tompkins	Schooner	92	40	1 long 32; 1 long 12; 4 long 6's.

Ontario	Schooner	53	35	1 long 32; 1 long 12.
American	Schooner	53	35	1 long 24; 1 long 12.
Asp	Schooner	57	25	1 long 32; 2 long 6's.
Pert	Schooner	50	25	1 long 32; 2 long 6's.
Lady of the Lake	Schooner	89	15	1 long 9; 1 long 4.

11 vessels   2487   880   105 guns: 65 long; 40 short

BRITISH SQUADRON

Wolfe	Ship	637	220	1 long 24; 8 long 18's; 4 short 68's; 8 short 32's.
Royal George	Ship	510	200	1 long 24; 2 long 18's; 2 short 68's; 16 short 32's.
Melville	Brig	279	100	2 long 18's; 12 short 32's.
Moira	Brig	262	100	2 long 9's; 12 short 24's.
Sydney Smith	Schooner	216	80	2 long 12's; 10 short 32's.
Beresford	Schooner	187	70	1 long 24; 8 short 18's.

6 vessels   2091   770   91 guns: 19 long; 72 short

These two squadrons were similar in many respects to those on Lake Erie. We had a considerable advantage in tonnage, personnel, and number of guns; also the greater weight of broadside: 1387 to 1359. In the all-important matter of long guns we had an enormous superiority: 851 pounds to 201. Could we fight at long range, as Hillyar did off Valparaiso, this would give us a decisive advantage. However, it rested with the enemy to select the range, for he had his guns concentrated in a smaller number of ships, which in general were faster and better handled than ours. In particular, Chauncey was greatly hampered by the very dull sailing of the *Oneida* and the schooners. Already on many occasions he had found it impossible to bring his squadron into action together. If he wished to fight, he must bring his force into battle piecemeal; and Perry's experience showed that this had its disadvantages. Still, Chauncey had an advantage which Perry did not possess: the *Pike* was the largest by far of any ship in either squadron and she was armed with long 24-pounders. Even alone she could put up a good fight for a time against all Yeo's force. Unfortunately, her guns were poorly cast and had a habit of exploding at critical moments, which was disconcerting to their crews. In general, we may conclude that Chauncey's superiority on Ontario was about as great as Perry's on Erie. Let us see what use he made of it.

The two squadrons formed on parallel courses on the port tack and Chauncey led the American line in toward the enemy at a slight angle. Already his ships were greatly scattered—his line strung out for miles. The *Pike*, with the *Asp* still in tow, was a good distance in the van. Next was the schooner *Tompkins*, which had passed several of the larger vessels. Then came in order the *Madison*, towing the *Conquest*, the *Sylph*, towing the *Ontario*, and last, probably at great intervals, the *Pert*, *American*, and *Lady of the Lake*. Yeo led the British column in the *Wolfe*, followed by the *Royal George*, *Melville*, and *Moira*, all well closed up; last were the *Sydney Smith* and *Beresford*, some distance behind the other vessels.

At 12:10 P.M. the fleets were almost within gunshot. Yeo thought his schooners were in danger, so he signaled to tack in succession. Thus he would protect his rear and also threaten Chauncey's. "Perceiving his intention," the

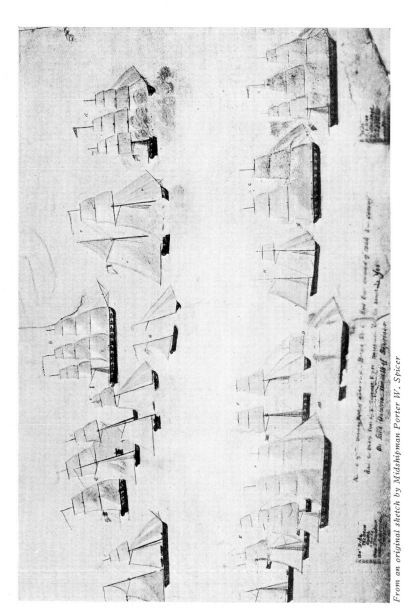

From an original sketch by Midshipman Porter W. Spicer

THE ACTION OF SEPTEMBER 28, 1813, ON LAKE ONTARIO

From an engraving by J. B. Forrest after the original painting by John W. Jarvis

Thomas Macdonough

latter reported, "I was determined to disappoint him; therefore as soon as the *Wolfe* (the leading ship) passed the center of his line and abeam of us, I bore up in succession (preserving our line) for the enemy's center; this maneuver not only covered our rear, but hove him into confusion." As the *Pike* commenced her turn the *Wolfe* and *Royal George* opened on her at 1,200 yards with their long guns. At last it seemed that we were to have a real fight.

Just as soon as the *Pike* finished her turn she let go with her 24-pounders. One of her bow guns burst, killed or wounded twenty-two men, blew up the forecastle, and put the bow pivot gun out of action. Such an accident at the first broadside is extremely disconcerting, to say the least. Sailors expect losses from the enemy guns, but hardly from their own. The bursting of one gun naturally creates a suspicion that others are liable to do the same. Undeterred by this initial disaster, Chauncey led his squadron into carronade range and the firing was as hot as anyone might wish. The commodore had not shown such combativeness since those old days when he commanded the *Constitution* in the Tripolitan bombardments.

At 12:25 the *Pike's* main topmast came down, but her gunners returned this loss with interest. Within five minutes they had shot down the *Wolfe's* main and mizzen topmasts and smashed her main yard. The British flagship fell out of the line and it looked as if the issue had been decided in fifteen minutes. But Captain Mulcaster saved the situation for Yeo by sending three well-aimed broadsides crashing into the *Pike*—the *Royal George* had reëstablished the fight.

Yeo cleared away his wreckage and brought the *Wolfe* back into the lead. The action again became furious. Most of the *Wolfe's* guns were silenced and her injuries aloft made it difficult for her to sail close-hauled. By 12:50 Yeo had had enough and he sheered off at right angles out of action. Mulcaster gallantly interposed the *Royal George* between him and the *Pike* and then followed his commodore to the westward; the other vessels did likewise. The battle had been won. It remained for Chauncey to make it decisive.

It certainly seemed that this time the commodore would make it so. He turned his flagship after the enemy and hoisted the signal to make all sail. "I continued the chase until nearly 3 o'clock," he said, "during which time I was enabled in this ship (with the *Asp* in tow) to keep within point-blank shot of the enemy, and sustained the whole of his fire during the chase." Yes, this must be right, for here the great defect of our squadron was again made evident— its very slow speed. The *Pike,* during the entire battle, received little effective support from the other ships. The *Tompkins* did well with her six long guns, one a 32-pounder, until injury to her foremast made her shorten sail. The *Asp* presumably was able to help some with her long 32. The *Madison* fired only a few broadsides; the schooner she was towing slowed her up; her guns were short-range carronades; so she soon dropped out of the fight. The *Sylph,* towing the *Ontario,* also fell astern. Her long 32's were mounted on pivots along the center line between the masts. This proved a most unsatisfactory method of mounting and kept her rate of fire very low. The *Oneida's* carronades fired only a few rounds. She was a dull sailer always and now her main topmast was wounded. The rear schooners certainly fired only a few shots, if any.

It seems probable that the *Madison* and *Sylph* would have done well to cast off the schooners which were reducing their speed. The order to make all sail might have been interpreted to that effect. Unfortunately, the *Pike* still kept her schooner in tow and this seemed to show that the commodore wished the other vessels to follow her motions. Chauncey seemed to be satisfied with the decision of his two captains, for he said that the commanding officer of the *Madison* "used every exertion to close with the enemy."

Thus during the two-hour chase Chauncey had to engage the enemy almost single-handed. He fired mostly on the *Royal George* and wounded her fore topmast. Captain Mulcaster continued to put up a splendid fight; in fact he was the hero of the day; his gunners sent several heavy shot into the *Pike* below her water line, so that all her pumps had to be used to keep the ship clear of water. The personnel losses, curiously enough, were surprisingly light. Except for the casualties caused by the bursting of the *Pike's* gun, we had only five wounded, all on the flagship. The British losses were six killed and thirteen wounded. "During our chase," Chauncey said, "one, if not two, of the enemy's small vessels, was completely in our power, if I could have been satisfied with so partial a victory." With our commodore in such a mood, it seemed certain that a few hours would give us the command of Ontario as completely as Perry had won that of Erie.

Both British and American armies viewed the fight which was to decide their fate. The suspense must have been agonizing for the British spectators at Burlington, for they knew the inferiority of their squadron. General de Rottenburg wrote: "My ulterior movements must now depend upon the issue of this action. I am prepared to meet disaster with fortitude and assure Your Excellency that any retrograde movement I may be compelled to make shall be done deliberately and without precipitation. The fate of the province must be decided in a few days."

General Wilkinson also was able to view the fight from

his headquarters at Fort George. "We could with the aid of our glasses," he wrote, "distinctly perceive that the British squadron was forced to leeward toward the head of the lake, and the action continued without intermission until we lost sight of the sternmost of our vessels about three o'clock. The issue must therefore have been decisive, because the breeze freshened without a change in its direction, and the narrowness of the lake made it impossible for the vanquished party to escape by any maneuver."

Poor Yeo must likewise have thoroughly realized what a pickle he was in. As well as Rottenburg, he knew what an effect his annihilation would have on the British cause. Better than Wilkinson he knew that he was beaten, badly beaten, and that he was caught in a veritable cul de sac. In no way, except by sailing overland, could he escape his eager pursuer. Imagine what must have been his surprise when at 2:45 he saw the *Pike* sheer away to the southward and haul to the wind on the port tack. Could it be that Chauncey was deliberately abandoning the pursuit? Yes, his eagerness had cooled. Apparently ashamed of the wild party he had just been enjoying, he again became conservative, cautious, careful Commodore Chauncey.

Yes, here was a Jutland—and another Jellicoe! Like that admiral, our commodore had a whole list of plausible excuses for not beating the enemy when he had him in the hollow of his hand. He said that the flagship was leaking badly; that the muzzles of four of his guns of the port battery had cracked; that this, with the actual bursting of one gun, "rendered their use extremely doubtful." How about his intact starboard battery which had not fired a shot? How about our other ships, on which not a single man had even been wounded? These vessels, without the *Pike,* could now have annihilated the British squadron.

But now there seems to have been "a gale of wind," though other accounts do not mention any such force this early in the day. With the two squadrons now only six miles from the head of the lake, this wind became in Chauncey's mind an element of grave danger: "I considered that if I chased the enemy to his anchorage at the end of the lake, I should be obliged to anchor also, and although we might succeed in driving him on shore, the probability was that we should go on shore also; he amongst his friends, we amongst our enemies."

Now please remember that we had a preponderance of long guns of over four to one. With that in view it certainly looks as though our squadron could have anchored outside the range of the enemy's carronades and pounded him to pieces with our long guns; this also would have allowed our ships to remain outside the range of any guns which might be mounted ashore. If this scheme were considered too dangerous by our commodore, he could have anchored his squadron out of range and waited until the weather improved, and then have continued the fight at any time and on his own terms.

But Chauncey's spree was over. The wild intoxication of battle had led him into terrible excesses, into fighting for hours at point-blank range. Think of it! But now at last the commodore had come to his senses; "had lost all memory of the joy of battle!" Chauncey never could learn to accept the "hazards of command." Few men have assumed greater responsibilities than Field Marshal von Hindenburg—few have made so many daring decisions and been so uniformly successful. Here is his carefully weighed opinion: "A commander who cannot or will not dare to stake his last resources for the sake of victory is committing a crime towards his own people. To act only on absolutely safe calculations, or win laurels which are not dependent on the courage to take responsibility, is to banish the very elements of greatness." How wonderfully true! If so when inferior in numbers, as he nearly always was, how much more applicable is this principle to cases such as we have under discussion—where we had a marked superiority and the enemy already had been beaten!

In justification for his decision, Chauncey alleged a reason almost as remarkable as that which Hull had advanced to excuse his Detroit fiasco. Listen to it: "I without hesitation relinquished the opportunity then presenting itself of acquiring individual reputation at the expense of my country." How, one might ask, could a commander in chief gain individual reputation in battle and harm his country? Perhaps we might find a case where a subordinate could do so, but how could a commander in chief? Can any reader think of a situation such as the commodore had in mind? It all sounds like what the fox said when his leap for the grapes fell short.

Personally, we confess to a devout wish that the commodore had given much more attention on that fateful day to enhancing his reputation. Had he been actuated by such a motive a victory would have been won which would have been most advantageous to his country. He himself would have entered the ranks of our great naval commanders between Perry and Macdonough. What a pity! What an example of the popular saying: "The man who stopped to congratulate himself on third base failed to make a home run."

In many ways Chauncey was a splendid officer. He had a fine peace-time reputation; was efficient, energetic, thorough, and patriotic to a high degree. But he could not fight. Long ago Brasidas, a Spartan, said: "Skill which cannot fight is useless!" It fell to Chauncey to illustrate this.

Since the commodore made a point of bringing up the issue of personal distinction, we must say a few words about it. To induce officers to put forth the extraordinary efforts so essential to success in war every incentive must be used. The desire for personal distinction has ever been, and is now, a most effective, and in our opinion an entirely proper, stimulus. As such it is an essential element in our naval power. It certainy had much to do with our success in the War of 1812; it is the basis of our present system of peace-time training. Our Navy will never reach its highest war-time efficiency unless its officers *in battle* strive for personal distinction.

After breaking off the action and abandoning the pursuit, Chauncey could, as we have pointed out, have anchored in the vicinity of the enemy, so as to be ready to renew the action when the weather moderated. Instead, he left Yeo completely and sailed for Niagara. For this he offered another strange reason. "I thought it important to communicate with General Wilkinson to ascertain when he meant to move with the army." Like the French admirals of the eighteenth century he thought entirely too much about ulterior objects and not nearly enough about the enemy's fleet.

On the first of October he arrived at Niagara and thus lost three whole days. He asked Wilkinson's advice as to the next step and, strange though it may seem, the general told the commodore just how to run his own show. Chauncey reported: "He thinks that the public service will be promoted by my watching Sir James at the head of the lake, and if possible preventing his return to Kingston, while he proceeded with the army for Sackett's Harbor. I shall, therefore, proceed immediately in quest of the enemy."

Yes, this is a strange chapter in our naval history. Wilkinson might have gone even a bit more into detail and shown the commodore that there was one well-recognized method of preventing Yeo from getting to Kingston—to annihilate his squadron. But perhaps this would have been a bit too blunt.

Despite all this criticism of our commander, the issue of the action still was favorable to our arms. Yeo was beaten and knew it, despite his bombastic reports of a victory. He knew that he could not afford to get into another fight. The British were astonished at Chauncey's failure to complete his success. General de Rottenburg wrote on the thirtieth: "After the action our fleet made for Burlington Heights to repair the damages, and a battery on shore had been erected for their protection. Major Moule reports this day that everything had been repaired. The enemy's squadron had the wind all yesterday and today, but never presumed to molest our fleet. What this can mean I am at a loss to account for, except that the wind blew very hard and they were afraid of coming on a lee shore."

Now it will be noted that all the British vessels were able to anchor in safety and that in two days they repaired all the damages received in the battle. Even to some degree their morale had been reëstablished and they were ready to make a further attempt to hold the lake, but not a very determined one!

CHAPTER XI

A BLOW IN THE AIR

DURING the forenoon of the second Wilkinson sailed for Sackett's Harbor; his 3,500 troops went in fifty bateaux and a number of small sailing craft. As soon as the last boat had cleared the river before the southwesterly breeze, Chauncey sailed to seek out the enemy.

Early the same morning Yeo was informed of Wilkinson's sailing; he took the lake to try to intercept him. At 10:00 A.M. the two squadrons came into contact. The breeze was light and Yeo was able to avoid contact all that day and the next. He retired into the cul de sac at Burlington. Chauncey failed to follow him. On the fourth the weather was hazy and the commodore sent out the *Lady of the Lake* to reconnoiter. He was losing chance after chance. What prevented him from going with his whole squadron along with the schooner?

Now Yeo's entire squadron was at anchor off Burlington. The schooner, slipping into reconnoiter, saw two gunboats, which must have been apart from the rest of the squadron, and ran back in the evening with this entirely misleading report. Chauncey came to the false conclusion that Yeo had passed him to the eastward and might be threatening Wilkinson. So he got up anchor and made all sail in that direction. Just as the *Lady of the Lake* was making her unfortunate reconnaissance the expeditionary force arrived at Sackett's Harbor.

Our squadron made splendid speed down the lake before the northwesterly gale and at 3:00 P.M. of the fifth made out a detachment of seven small vessels near the False Ducks. They proved to be gunboats carrying two companies of the De Watteville Regiment from York to Kingston. Only one sloop with thirty soldiers on board got away. One was beached and burned by the enemy. Five were taken; soldiers and sailors to the number of 270 were made prisoners. On the sixth Chauncey brought his prizes into Sackett's Harbor. Yeo had followed him down the lake; on the same afternoon he came into Kingston.

Deserters from our army had kept General de Rottenburg well informed of Wilkinson's projected movements, and the general had seen our expedition start off down the lake. Suspecting a blow at vital Kingston, De Rottenburg sent off on October 2 the 49th and 104th Regiments and the Voltigeurs. In numerous bateaux they skirted the northern shore of the lake, ready to land in case of attack by our squadron. On the ninth this convoy arrived at Kingston. Here for once Chauncey had neglected to make the most out of his temporary command of the lake. Said the Kingston *Gazette:* "These three gallant regiments, together with our brave Militia who are pouring in from all quarters and have already assembled in considerable numbers, will be a sufficient reënforcement and with our present respectable garrison will be able to repel any force the enemy may be able to bring against us."

Yes, perhaps so, if led by a Wilkinson! But, had our forces been led by Jacob Brown or Winfield Scott, perhaps your garrison of 2,200 of all arms might not have been quite so sufficient as General de Rottenburg would have wished. Had it been possible for Tennessee Jackson to have devoted a month to the Kingston problem, he might have coined at an earlier date that famous epigram, "To the victors belong the spoils."

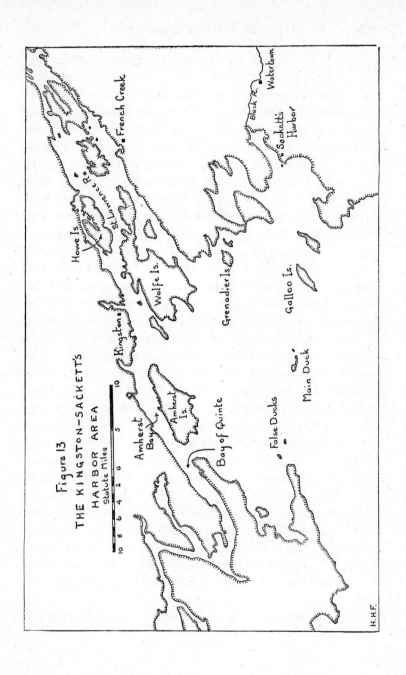

Figure 13
THE KINGSTON-SACKETT'S
HARBOR AREA
Statute Miles

But why indulge in such phantom wishes? Let us come back to facts and Wilkinson. No sooner had that general arrived at Sackett's Harbor on the fourth than he protested in person to the Secretary of War that a direct attack upon Kingston was impracticable. Armstrong insisted that the direct attack must be made, provided that: first, Yeo be kept out of Kingston; second, its garrison be not largely reënforced; third, the weather be favorable. Now all three contingencies had come to pass, Armstrong felt constrained to yield to his general in the field. An indirect attack was now in order. Perhaps it might accomplish something.

Yes, surely something must be done with the formidable army which our War Department had collected for the fall campaign. By October 7 there were 6,000 troops at Sackett's Harbor. Colonel Scott was preparing to join with the 800 regulars remaining at Niagara. Harrison was coming on with 1,300 of his best troops. Already General Wade Hampton had crossed Lake Champlain to Plattsburg; had marched northward along its western shore and thence westward to the Chateauguay River. There since September 24 he has been causing great concern to the enemy. Governor Prevost had written home: "The position of Major General Hampton at the Four Corners on the Chateauguay River is highly judicious, as at the same time he threatens Montreal and obliges me to concentrate a considerable body of troops to protect it, and has it in his power to molest the communication with the Upper Province and impede the stores required there for the navy and army."

So much can a position do—so far can we make geography fight our campaigns. But to do more a general is needed, and one not "under the influence of a too free use of spirituous liquors." Also soldiers—not those of whom it was said that "a spirit of subordination was foreign to their views." Reassure yourself, Prevost! Wade Hampton has it in his power to do much—but will do nothing! Nothing on his own initiative—nothing even when ordered!

As our forces lay inactive in Sackett's Harbor, delusions of grandeur began to form in military minds. We cannot attack Kingston close at hand—let us attack Montreal at a great distance. Distant fields look greenest! Yes, let's attack Montreal. How will that be for an indirect attack on Kingston? The idea is a good one, if practicable. Wilkinson will drift down the St. Lawrence in boats, draw in Hampton, seize that great key point of the entire frontier. But, alas, the generals are not nearly as good as their plans, and the weather undeniably is even worse.

Had he been well, Wilkinson would scarcely have been equal to his task, and now he was sick. General Delay seized the command. Not until October 17, well along toward winter, did Wilkinson commence moving his army to Grenadier Island, covered by Chauncey from a position of readiness near Main Duck Island. The weather was terrible: rain almost incessant; cold boring from within; gales roughening the waters, blowing the tops off the waves. Not until the twenty-eighth was the movement of the main body completed.

By this time the decision to attack Montreal has been definitely announced. The transportation of the army to the mainland at French Creek begins; is completed, except for the rear guard, November 2. This is the day that Captain Mulcaster ventures out with the *Melville, Moira,* and two schooners and attacks our people at French Creek. There is a full hour of sharp cannonading; at dusk the British vessels, hit a number of times, withdraw; our casualties are but ten. Late in the day Chauncey's squadron enters the river. The next morning he anchors at the eastern end of Wolfe Island three miles above our camp. Here he will keep Mulcaster from further attempts.

On November 5 Wilkinson started down the river with some 7,000 troops. Chauncey, much concerned lest Yeo should attack Sackett's Harbor in his absence, loyally remained at the head of the river to cover Wilkinson's rear. In the evening of the sixth the army halted seven miles short of Ogdensburg and the general expressed a despatch to Wade Hampton. In it he stated definitely that he would attack Montreal. Wade Hampton was to join him and bring on several months' provisions from Lake Champlain. He was careful to state that even without these provisions, his army could carry through the campaign. "I have submitted the state of our provisions to my general officers," he told Hampton, "who unanimously agree that it should not prevent the progress of the expedition!" At last it seemed that we might get some action!

But no. Wade Hampton decided otherwise. On the eighth he received the letter at Four Corners, and lost no time in replying that, due to lack of provisions, he must decline to coöperate with Wilkinson; on the contrary it was imperative that he must retire to Lake Champlain. On the twelfth, at Cornwall, Wilkinson received Hampton's reply. Alone he felt unable to carry through his plan. The campaign was over. Crossing to the American shore, he went into a second Valley Forge at a little village, French Mills.

Chauncey remained at the head of the St. Lawrence until November 10. Then, having seen Wilkinson well on his way, he went to Sackett's Harbor. Here he received a request to bring Harrison's detachment on from Niagara. On the fifteenth our squadron was there and immediately embarked the troops. On the twenty-first it stood into Sackett's Harbor, after having fought through a heavy gale.

"The troops and seamen suffered extremely," the commodore tells us, "as they were wet from the commencement of the gale until their arrival here. The water was so deep on the berth deck that they were obliged to scuttle it to let the water off yet the men arrived in better health than could have been expected." The squadron went into winter quarters; it well deserved its rest.

Our concentration to the eastward had reduced the troops at Fort George to a paltry hundred men. On December 10 this most important key point was evacuated. On the nineteenth the enemy crossed the river and stormed Fort Niagara. On the thirtieth they burned Buffalo and destroyed at Black Rock the *Ariel, Trippe,* and *Little Belt.* Thus, our immense concentration had been misdirected. While we were still unbalanced through this blow in the air our opponent had countered sharply where our defense had weakened.

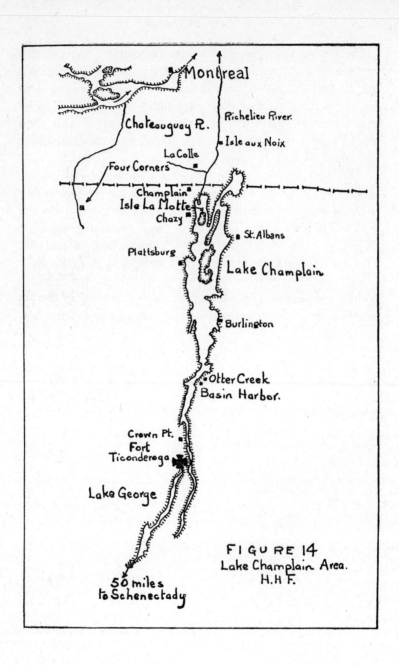

Montreal

Chateauguay R.

Richelieu River.

Isle aux Noix

La Colle

Four Corners

Champlain

Isle La Motte

Chazy

St. Albans

Plattsburg

Lake Champlain

Burlington

Otter Creek
Basin Harbor.

Crown Pt.
Fort
Ticonderoga

Lake George

FIGURE 14
Lake Champlain Area.
H.H.F.

50 miles
to Schenectady

CHAPTER XII

THE CAMPAIGN ON LAKE CHAMPLAIN

HAVING thus brought to a conclusion the campaign of 1813 on the Great Lakes, let us trace for a few moments the minor happenings on Lake Champlain. When war was declared Lieutenant Sidney Smith was in command of two small gunboats, based on Basin Harbor, Vermont. Two sloops and four bateaux were pressed into service and armed with one long 18-pounder each. The British had three small gunboats on the Richelieu River. We exercised the command of the lake.

In the fall of 1812 the Department sent up Lieutenant Thomas Macdonough to take over the command of the American flotilla. He set to work with energy and in the next spring commissioned two large sloops, the *Growler* and *Eagle*. On June 2 he sent these two craft into the Richelieu under Smith. That officer ran down the river with a following wind in pursuit of British rowing galleys until the fortifications on Isle aux Noix stopped him. It had been better for Smith if his own discretion had stopped him before running that far into a blind alley. For, when he tried to withdraw, he found that he could not. Current and wind swept him back; the galleys fired on him with cannon; soldiers along the river banks swept his decks with musketry; he was in a veritable death trap. Four long hours he fought. Then the *Eagle* sank and the *Growler* grounded. Their crews surrendered. Doubtless Smith, when he knew surrender was inevitable, did what he could to injure his ships beyond repair. But in this he had little success, for both were salvaged by the British and commissioned with the names *Chubb* and *Finch*.

[439]

Now the control of the lake passed into the enemy's hands and in July they sent an expedition against Plattsburg. In two sloops, three galleys, and forty-five long boats, 1,400 men cruised up the lake. The undefended village they pillaged with sufficient thoroughness and sailed home with their booty.

Undeterred by those reverses, Macdonough was building up a new squadron. By August 6 he had organized a flotilla of three sloops and six galleys and promptly regained the command of the lake. On September 19 he carried Hampton's army down the western lake shore and protected their line of communications while they remained posted at Chateauguay.

Before coming to a description of the 1814 campaign let us glance over the situation in Europe. Only thus will we have a proper background for our studies. During the fall of 1813 the great Napoleon had been beaten back to the frontiers of France. Confident that he could soon remedy the situation to which his unfortunate Russian adventure had reduced him, he had entered the campaign of 1813 with a new army and radiant hopes. Now the terrible retreat from Leipzig had shattered his new organizations as surely as the Russian campaign had the Grand Armèe. Marshal Soult, fighting every step, had been forced back by Wellington into southern France. Italy, the first of Bonaparte's conquests, had been lost forever to the French eagles. Thus every indication pointed to the complete overthrow of Napoleon early in 1814. How were we to withstand the assaults of that victorious army and navy which had at last worn down the greatest of conquerors? What chance would Wilkinsons and Hamptons have—what chance for even a Macdonough?

In February, 1814, Wilkinson found that French Mills

was a poor place in which to winter an army. The hardships of the troops brought back memories of Valley Forge. So General Brown, known to us as victor in the fight at Sackett's Harbor, marched off with 2,000 troops to that place. Wilkinson went across to Plattsburg with the remaining 3,000. General Izard, who had relieved Wade Hampton, was wintering across the lake at Burlington.

Brown went on to Niagara and there, ably supported by Winfield Scott, he waged a hard-fought, equally balanced campaign which did credit to both armies. The result was a perfect deadlock.

Yeo and Chauncey expanded their fleets to remarkable size. One of the British vessels at the close of the year mounted 102 guns. This campaign also continued equally balanced and indecisive. The two commanders alternated in exercising the control of the lake, depending upon which had launched the last ship. Here was a real race of naval armaments. Shipbuilding rather than fighting determined which fleet had the temporary control. The hazard of a pitched battle was so great that neither commander would fight while he was inferior—and why should he when in a few weeks his carpenters would give him another ship and the material preponderance? As the United States was on the defensive in 1814 this state of affairs worked to our advantage. Now Chauncey's Fabian strategy was quite effective. The fact that he prevented Yeo from gaining definite command of the lake influenced Wellington to refuse the command of the British armies in Canada, as he believed that nothing decisive could be accomplished on land until the command of the Lakes had been assured. Thus clearly did even a general see from over the ocean the decisive influence of naval power on the frontier lakes.

During 1814 there was little activity in the Erie region.

We held the undisputed command of the lake, but an attempt to recapture Fort Mackinac failed through overconfidence and carelessness.

In 1814 Lake Champlain became the decisive theater of war on the norther frontier and we must examine in detail the important operations which developed in this sector. Honorable peace or long continued warfare depended upon young Thomas Macdonough—his resolution, strategy, and tactics!

During March Wilkinson proceeded north and attacked a British force stationed along the La Colle River, which ran eastward into the Richelieu just north of the border. A poorly conducted skirmish lost him his command and Izard came over to Plattsburg to relieve him. Macdonough continued to build up his flotilla at Otter Creek, Vermont. Captain Pring, Royal Navy, took charge of the British naval forces fitting out in the Richelieu.

The British were ready first. Pring had learned that we had launched the fine 26-gun ship *Saratoga* on April 11 and he was anxious to try his hand with Macdonough before this powerful reënforcement could join him. On May 10 he entered the lake and anchored behind Providence Island with the brig *Linnet*, five sloops, and thirteen galleys. As soon as Macdonough heard of this movement he called upon the army for assistance; a battery of seven 12-pounders was constructed at the entrance to the creek and manned by light artillery and bluejackets. On the fourteenth Pring attacked with eight galleys and a bomb vessel, but accomplished nothing. On May 29 Macdonough took the lake with overwhelming force and based his squadron on Plattsburg.

Meanwhile, momentous events had been occurring in Europe. During the winter months negotiations between regularly appointed peace commissioners had been taking place in Ghent. Each side presented two demands. We asked for the repeal of the Orders in Council and the end of impressment. They demanded that an independent Indian state be established within our frontiers and that we acknowledge British military and naval dominance on the Great Lakes. Thrown in for good measure there was to be rectification of the Maine frontier.

Among the many unpleasant episodes of this war the strong and courageous attitude of our commissioners at Ghent stands out in bold contrast to our weak and vacillating negotiations with the Tripolitan pirates. "It is not necessary," our envoys replied to these arrogant insults, "to refer such demands to the American Government for instructions. They will only be a fit subject of deliberation when it becomes necessary to decide upon the expediency of an absolute surrender of national independence."

Not gaining their ends by diplomacy, the British decided to win them by force. On April 11 Napoleon abdicated and they commenced moving large detachments of Wellington's army to America. Four strong brigades were to go to the Canadian frontier; another to attack Washington; while several more were to make an attack in force upon New Orleans to get a strangle hold upon the Mississippi River. Few people realize today that the British were determined in 1814 to strike us with their full strength and forever cripple our national power by limiting us to the Atlantic coast line. If they could win the state of Maine, gain the control of Lake Champlain and the Great Lakes, exercise a protectorate over an Indian state in the northwest, hold the line of the Mississippi, seize Mobile Bay from Jackson's militia, and buy Florida from their ally, they would be indemnified for long years of conflict and revenge themselves upon the rebels of 1776. Nor would they ever have been confronted by those American demands for naval parity which have so disturbed Britannia's rule of the wave in recent years.

The British attitude in 1814 is well summed up by a letter which Commissioner Gallatin wrote home in June: "You may rest assured of the general hostile spirit of this nation, and its wish to inflict serious injury on the United States; that no assistance can be expected from Europe; and that no better terms will be obtained than the *status ante bellum."* Not very pleasant reading for President Madison, as his feeble hands endeavored to steady the heavy, jerky tiller of the leaking ship of state while it wallowed in the trough of the mountainous seas. But perhaps there are some rather obscure members of the crew who can lend a hand, spread a sail, get steerageway, steady our ship on its course again. Yes, perhaps so: for up on the northeast border is a young naval lieutenant; down in the far southwest is a militia general. Perhaps something can still be done!

As soon as the British military preparations were under way their diplomats showed a desire to prolong the peace negotiations until after the various campaigns to humble the Yankees had been completed. One of them wrote home to the foreign minister: "If our campaign in Canada should be as successful as our military preparations would lead us to expect, if our commander does his duty, I am persuaded we shall have acquired by our arms every point on the Canadian frontier which we ought to insist on keeping." Yes, it certainly looked as if this were to be an historical example of the perfect coördination of policy with strategy. But, fortunately for us, there was an "if." Wonder if Governor Prevost will do his duty—as counted upon by British statesmen?

CHAPTER XIII

PREVOST'S OFFENSIVE

ON JULY 12 the first brigade of reënforcements arrived at Montreal. With it came orders for Prevost to accomplish "the entire destruction of Sackett's Harbor and of the naval establishments on Lake Erie and Lake Champlain." By August 14 the other brigades had arrived. Prevost had now 30,000 bayonets, a tremendous force! All save 2,500 were regulars, veterans of many a hard-fought campaign. How will ill-drilled Yankees stand against these famous red-coats?

One brigade was stationed at Kingston. Prevost concentrated 14,000 troops between the Richelieu and St. Lawrence Rivers for an invasion of New York. "Vermont has shown disinclination to the war," he wrote on August 5, "and, as it is sending in specie and provisions, I will confine offensive operations to the west side of Lake Champlain." There, Vermonters, is a rare compliment to add to your history books.

Now Prevost, in his operations on the Great Lakes, had been made aware of the necessity of having naval command of lakes, as well as seas. So he ordered the building of a great frigate at Isle aux Noix. She was to carry thirty-seven large guns and be named the *Confiance*. On August 25 she slipped down the launching ways into the Richelieu. Her construction was assisted by Americans—no, that is not a typographical error. Macdonough reported the seizure of six spars, evidently intended for use as the lower and top masts of the *Confiance*, while they were being towed toward the Richelieu. "The turpitude of many of our

[445]

citizens in this part of the country," he wrote, "furnishes the enemy with every information he wants."

Meanwhile our people had also been getting some information of the enemy and General Izard had been making such preparations as he could to meet the impending invasion, in the face of active treason on the part of the governor of Vermont, who ordered all soldiers from that state to return home. Fortunately these soldiers replied to their governor, "Your proclamation has produced no effect." By August 1 Izard had assembled a force of 4,500 men at Champlain, five miles below the border. As an imitation of Wellington's Torres Vedras lines, he was hastily constructing field works about Plattsburg.

At this crucial moment Izard received from the Secretary of War the most astonishing orders a general ever received —to proceed with his whole force to Niagara! "I will make the movement you direct, if possible," he replied, "but I shall do it with the apprehension of risking the force under my command, and with the certainty that everything in this vicinity but the lately erected works at Plattsburg and Cumberland Head will, in less than three days after my departure, be in the possession of the enemy." Nevertheless, on August 29 he started off by way of Schenectady and the Mohawk Valley. He had obeyed his orders literally.

General Macomb, with 3,500 militia of the rawest variety, was left to hold the bag. Over eight hundred of his soldiers were sick. In his entire force was but one organized battalion. Macomb saw that his only chance was behind fortifications. So he assembled his miscellaneous companies and detachments at Plattsburg and turned them to with pick and shovel on the line of trenches across the neck of the peninsula south of the Saranac River. "To create an emulation and zeal among the officers and men in completing the works," he said, "I divided them into detachments, and placed them near the several forts; declaring in orders, that each detachment was the garrison of its own work and bound to defend it to the last extremity." This was an excellent way in which to get some fighting out of militia— about the only one in fact.

Macdonough, at anchor in Plattsburg Bay, had:

Ship	Rig	Tonnage	Crew	Armament
Saratoga	Ship	734	240	8 long 24's; 6 short 42's; 12 short 32's.
Eagle	Brig	500	150	8 long 18's; 12 s. 32's.
Ticonderoga	Schooner	350	112	8 long 12's; 4 long 18's; 5 short 32's.
Preble	Sloop	80	30	7 long 9's.
6 Galleys		420	246	6 long 24's; 6 s. 18's.
4 Galleys		160	104	4 long 12's.
14 vessels		2244	882	Broadside: long 480 lbs; short, 714 lbs.

On September 2 Captain Downie, Royal Navy, assumed command of the frigate *Confiance* and the British squadron:

Ship	Rig	Tonnage	Crew	Armament
Confiance	Ship	1200	325	31 long 24's; 6 s. 32's.
Linnet	Brig	350	125	16 long 12's.
Chubb	Sloop	112	50	1 long 6; 10 short 18's.
Finch	Sloop	110	50	4 long 6's; 7 short 18's.
5 Galleys		350	205	3 long 24's; 2 long 18's. 4 short 32's; 1 s. 18.
7 Galleys		280	182	3 long 18's; 4 s. 32's.
16 vessels		2402	937	Broadside: long, 660 lbs; short, 532 lbs.

All these figures have been taken from Roosevelt, who has made a most careful analysis of this campaign.

On September 3 Prevost camped at Champlain, 14,000 strong. Next day he marched to Chazy. On the fifth he bivouacked five miles south of that place. Downie was working night and day to get the *Confiance* ready. Pring with the rest of the squadron boldly took the lake, occupied Isle La Motte, and guarded the communications of the army. Had he not exposed himself to a counterstroke?

Macdonough's reputation has been made so secure by his decisive victory that historians have not thought it worth while to examine his measures during the week preceding it. The commodore evidently had decided to keep in his carefully prepared defensive position in Plattsburg Bay, and to let nothing lure him out. The policy of a passive defensive is never without grave disadvantages. It gives the initiative to the enemy—and now Macdonough had it for the taking. The time was ripe for a naval offensive, not a defensive. Our naval squadron was relatively much stronger and more efficient than our militia army and should have been our "first line of defense" on this occasion.

It is admittedly dangerous for a writer, whose knowledge of a situation existing a century before must necessarily be incomplete, to suggest that a leader should have taken measures other than those he did, particularly as those brought decisive success. Still we must suggest that Macdonough had now a perfect opportunity to take the offensive. He was overwhelmingly superior to Pring and we see no reason in the world why he should not have destroyed him or at least have driven him into the Richelieu. This would have brought Prevost to an abrupt stop, his water communications cut. As it was late in the season, it might have brought the campaign to an end.

Furthermore, it is by no means certain that Macdonough could not have anchored his squadron off the entrance to the Richelieu in such a manner as to have prevented Downie from ever coming out, even with the *Confiance*. The British must have towed the ships in single column out of the river against the current, and this in the face of a raking fire which they could have returned only with their bow chasers. We are free to admit that there was risk in such aggressive action, but was it as great as staying in Plattsburg Bay with our rear protected by some raw, untrained militia against the assault of the finest soldiers of the world in overwhelming strength?

We have but one object in this discussion. Nothing succeeds like success—and success places the seal of approval upon the methods used to win it. The Austrian admiral at Lissa said to "ram everything gray" and so well did his plan succeed that the ramming idea would not down for fifty years. Also, as Thucydides said, "many schemes which are ill-advised have succeeded through the still greater folly which possessed the enemy." This we think was the case on Lake Champlain. We would not like to see the stamp of approval placed upon Macdonough's strategy, to serve as a precedent for future commanders. Fortunately for us the British strategy was more faulty than ours, and in tactics Macdonough was superb. But of that readers will soon be able to judge for themselves.

On the sixth the British marched the remaining eight miles to Plattsburg. Their advance was disputed sharply by small detachments of regulars under Appling, Wool, and Sproul, assisted at times by the gunfire of Macdonough's galleys. Macomb reported: "The militia could not be prevailed on to stand, notwithstanding the exertions of their general and staff officers; although the fields were di-

vided by strong stone walls, and they were told that the
enemy could not possibly cut them off. The state dragoons
of New York wear red coats and their being on the heights
to watch the enemy, gave constant alarm to the militia, who
mistook them for the enemy, and feared his getting in their
rear."

The splendid British veterans, although they lost two
hundred men in the fighting, treated their foes with superb
contempt. "So undaunted was the enemy," Macomb said,
"that he never deployed in his whole march, always pressing
on in column." The Americans withdrew over the Saranac
River, destroyed the bridge, and occupied the intrenchments.
They checked weak attempts of the enemy to feel out our
strength.

Meanwhile Captain Downie had been hastily organizing a
crew for the *Confiance*. He had received some drafts of
sailors from the naval vessels at Montreal and some soldiers
from the Thirty-ninth Regiment. On the seventh the ship
was towed up the river against wind and tide. On the
evening of the eighth she arrived at Chazy. Here Downie
assumed command of the entire squadron. Pring kept the
Linnet.

The figures tabulated above as to the relative strengths
of the opposing squadrons favor the British. But these
theoretical advantages were counterbalanced, at least to
some extent, by certain practical disadvantages. The *Confiance* had been very hastily organized. Her crew were
poorly trained and knew neither each other nor their officers.
Downie had little knowledge of the capabilities of his squadron, which he saw only three days before the decisive battle
was fought. Prevost could have greatly increased the fighting strength of the British squadron by allowing it more
time to be shaken down and welded together; but on the

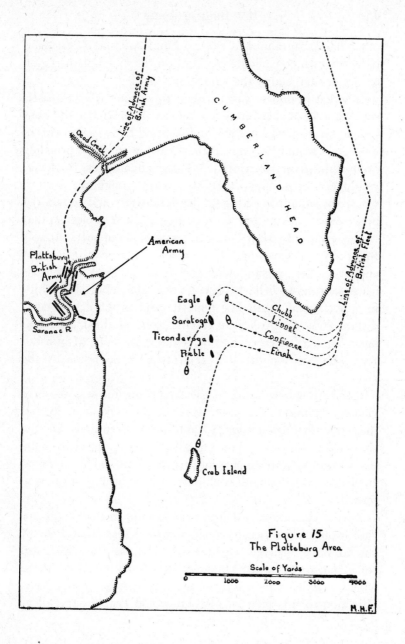

Figure 15
The Plattsburg Area

Scale of Yards

0   1000   2000   3000   4000

M.H.F.

other hand, autumn was near at hand and speed was vital if he were to consolidate his hold on the Champlain region before winter ended the campaign.

In a battle under way between squadrons whose vessels could not be maneuvered together with precision the concentration of power in the *Confiance* and their superiority in long guns would have given the British a marked, probably even a decisive, superiority. These advantages, however, would not be so important in a battle fought at anchor, where the squadron acting on the defensive could be moored in a compact formation with springs on their cables, so that its vessels would afford each other mutual support. It was for these reasons that Macdonough elected to fight at anchor. This decision, after the *Confiance* joined the British squadron, we believe a correct one. He moored his ships in a north and south line opposite and about 2,500 yards distant from the American fortifications south of the Saranac. He had taken care to place his vessels out of gunshot from the position the British army took up north of the river.

On the northern flank of the American line was the brig *Eagle,* 20 guns; in the center were the ship *Saratoga,* 26, and the schooner *Ticonderoga,* 17; on the southern flank was the sloop *Preble,* 7 guns. The ten galleys were in the rear of the line in readiness to support any critical point. Thus arrayed for battle, Macdonough could expect to fight almost on even terms.

As the chances of a battle between the squadrons at anchor would be so nearly equal, it would seem that Prevost should have ordered Downie to blockade the American squadron, while he used his enormous superiority ashore to storm or at least reduce by siege the American works. His objection to this plan was that it would enable our galleys to support Macomb's troops. But even with this possible handicap it is scarcely conceivable that his 14,000 veterans, eager to fight and end the campaign, could have been repulsed by a force, including sick, of 4,700 troops, of whom only 1,500 were regulars. The conditions were hardly the same as those at New Orleans, where the militia had been seasoned by long fighting against the Indians and had an incomparable leader. Once Macomb's lines were stormed, gunfire from the shore must have driven Macdonough into Downie's arms. Finally, even though Prevost might be checked, he still had the naval attack as a last resort. This should have been made before a southerly wind.

The governor, however, decided that there should be a simultaneous naval and military attack. As he had been ready several days before Downie reached the lake, his impatience increased daily. As the culmination of a series of letters urging haste, he wrote on the ninth: "In consequence of your communication of yesterday I have postponed action until your squadron is prepared to coöperate. I need not dwell with you on the evils resulting to both services from delay."

Downie replied that he would sail at midnight, but a strong southerly wind prevented him from so doing. Prevost did not like this at all. He wrote: "In consequence of your letter, the troops have been held in readiness, since six o'clock this morning, to storm the enemy's works at nearly the same moment as the naval action begins in the bay. I ascribe the disappointment I have experienced to the unfortunate change of wind, and shall rejoice to learn that my reasonable expectations have been frustrated by no other cause."

Downie was infuriated by the implied reprimand. "This letter does not deserve an answer," he said to Pring, "but I will convince him that the naval force will not be backward in their share of the attack." And so brave Downie did, at the cost of his life and of the campaign.

Pring remonstrated with his commodore against the plan for a combined attack. Downie replied that he counted much upon the fortifications being stormed during the naval action and the American vessels being forced to move, "whereby we shall obtain decided advantage over them during the confusion." If the commodore really relied upon the successful execution of such an extremely difficult form of the concentric attack he was counting upon a degree of perfection which has seldom, if ever, been obtained in war. To bring two columns upon the battlefield from opposite directions is difficult enough. To concentrate from opposite directions a naval and a military force in such a way as to have the interacting effect Downie hoped for is beyond the realm of possibility.

CHAPTER XIV

MACDONOUGH DESTROYS THE BRITISH SQUADRON

EARLY on the eleventh the wind became fair from the north-northeast. Before daylight Downie weighed anchor. While he fired signal guns as a notification of his movements, there is no mention of Prevost having heard or understood this signal. At 7:30 A.M., the squadron hove to off Cumberland Head. The commodore pulled out in a small boat to reconnoiter the American squadron. He devised a concentration on our van, somewhat on the order of Nelson's famous dispositions for the Battle of the Nile. Here was the plan:

Confiance to sail close-hauled to a position to windward of the *Eagle;* then to wear and sail before the wind, wrecking the *Eagle* with her starboard broadside; finally to moor head and stern across the *Saratoga's* bow.

Linnet and *Chubb* then to concentrate on the *Eagle,* already damaged by the flagship.

Finch and ten gunboats to hold in play the *Ticonderoga* and *Preble.*

Now there was one great difference between the dispositions on Lake Champlain and those at the Nile. There Nelson had made his attack with a strong following wind. Here Downie would have to beat up against light, puffy, shifting breezes coming over the high wooded ground on Cumberland Head. This was to have an important effect upon the execution of the British plan of operations. Could he have waited for a southerly breeze, a concentration on Macdonough's southern flank would have been more effective.

[455]

During the reconnaissance Downie had seen no activity on shore. Now as he rounded Cumberland Head with his ships in line of battle there still was no sign of the army's expected assault. However, having gone thus far, he felt it necessary to carry on. The moral effect would have been bad to have canceled the attack now. The signals had been called, the ball snapped, the players were in motion; now only the referee's whistle could end the play!

Once the *Confiance* got in the lee of Cumberland Head the wind became so light and baffling that it soon became apparent that she could not get far enough to windward to carry out the plan. She could head no higher than the *Saratoga;* Downie laid her so. He would engage as best he might; would make a gallant fight of it. He would show Prevost that the navy would do its part!

"As the British squadron stood bravely in," Roosevelt writes, "young Macdonough, who feared his foes not at all, but his God a great deal, knelt for a moment, with his officers on the quarter-deck; and then ensued a few minutes of perfect quiet, the men waiting with grim expectancy for the opening of the fight." At 8:30 A.M. the long guns of the American squadron broke the silence. On the flagship Macdonough aimed and fired the first shot; it struck the *Confiance* in the bow, killing several men. That vessel, coming on at a sharp angle, had to stand a heavy fire for several minutes without firing a single shot in return. Only the British galleys, with their bow guns, could return our fire.

Finally Downie brought the *Confiance* to anchor, backed his sails to tauten the cable and bring his guns to bear, and then fired a tremendous broadside. He was only four hundred yards on the *Saratoga's* beam and his guns had been double-shotted; the heavy 24-pound balls pierced the Ameri-

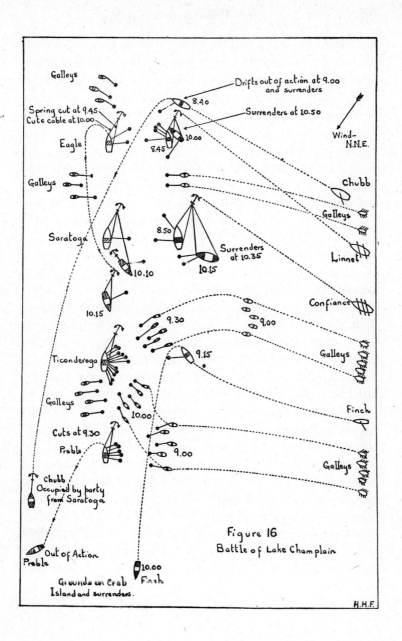

Figure 16
Battle of Lake Champlain

can flagship through and through, smashed guns from their mountings, covered her decks with clouds of jagged splinters, killed or wounded forty men.   Well for us that we had a Macdonough for captain here and that for two years he had been training officers and men for just such bloody business as this!

The *Linnet* came to anchor about three hundred yards from the *Eagle* and slightly forward of her beam; the *Chubb* headed up for a position off her bow.   Two British galleys and six Americans fought at this end of the line.   On the southern flank the *Finch* and ten galleys attacked the *Ticonderoga, Preble,* and four American galleys.

Commencing on the northern flank, let us view the action in detail.   The sloop *Chubb* was first to come into action against the *Eagle,* Master Commandant Robert Henley. She received such a heavy pounding that before it was possible to anchor, her bowsprit and main boom had been shot away.   She drifted helpless through our line and surrendered to a boat sent out from the *Saratoga.*

The *Linnet* proved a tougher customer and she received assistance from an unexpected source.   Several of the bow guns of the *Confiance* could not be made to bear on the American flagship, so they opened on the *Eagle* at moderate range.   Their great 24-pound balls crashed into her and one cut the spring on her cable which kept her broadside on the *Linnet*.   This casualty threw the *Eagle* into the wind and exposed her to the raking fire of the hostile brig, upon which none of her guns could be brought to bear.   "The *Eagle*," Macdonough reported, "not being able to bring her guns to bear, cut her cable and anchored in a more eligible position between my ship and the *Ticonderoga*."   Thus tactfully did the commodore refer to an incident which nearly lost him the battle.

From an engraving by B. Tanner after the original painting by H. Reinagle

BATTLE OF LAKE CHAMPLAIN

Compare with the next illustration viewed from the northeast. The large vessels from right to left are: *Linnet,* *Saratoga, Eagle, Confiance* (in foreground), *Ticonderoga* and *Preble.*

From an old engraving

BATTLE OF PLATTSBURG

As viewed from the British army position north of the Saranac River.

The two flagships had proved themselves well matched. "The *Saratoga* suffered much," Macdonough reported, "from the heavy fire of the *Confiance*. I could perceive at the same time, however, that our fire was very destructive to her." Within fifteen minutes Commodore Downie was killed and Lieutenant Robertson assumed command. Thus the fight went well until the *Eagle* was forced from her position at the head of the line. That permitted the *Linnet,* after driving off some galleys, to spring her broadside upon the *Saratoga*. She commenced a well directed raking fire into the bows of that ship. First Lieutenant Peter Gamble was killed and the commodore was twice knocked unconscious. Third Lieutenant Silas Duncan was badly wounded. The situation became very critical. Henley relieved it somewhat by anchoring the *Eagle* by the stern, to use her undamaged port broadside against the *Confiance.*,

On the southern flank the action had been hardly and evenly fought. The *Preble* made a wretched showing against the British galleys. They forced her out of the line after she had received only two casualties. After this weak effort she took no further part in the battle. On the other hand, the *Ticonderoga* drove the *Finch* out of action with heavy losses; she grounded on Crab Island and surrendered to the soldiers in hospital there. The British galleys now concentrated upon the *Ticonderoga* and attacked her in the most determined manner. Their repeated attempts to board were beaten back by cannister and musketry. Lieutenant Cassin, in command, stood upon the taffrail and calmly directed the defense amid showers of cannister, grape, and musketry. It was in this fine ship that Midshipman Hiram Paulding, then only seventeen, received his baptism of fire; passing from gun to gun, he fired pistols into their touchholes to ignite their powder charges.

Meanwhile the *Saratoga* and *Confiance* were fighting themselves out. One after another our guns were dismounted; in several cases overcharges had recoiled the carronades from their stands. Twice the enemy's hot shot had set the ship on fire. Fifty-five shot pierced her hull. Fortunately, after the first broadside the fire of the enemy had been rather too high and most of his shot had passed just over the bulwarks—a sign of poor gunnery training. The situation on the *Confiance* was almost as bad: nearly all her engaged battery was out of action; killed and wounded covered the decks; her masts were bundles of splinters; and her rigging shot away. The poor state of training of her crew reduced the effectiveness of her remaining guns; after the action one was found to contain two round shot in a canvas bag rammed home and wadded without a powder charge; another had two cartridges and no shot; while a third had a wad below the cartridge, so that the latter could not be ignited through the touchhole.

At length the *Saratoga* had not a single gun intact in her engaged broadside, and the *Confiance* only four! Macdonough had foreseen just such a situation—and was prepared. "Our guns on the starboard side being nearly all dismounted," he said, "a stern anchor was let go, the bower cut and the ship winded with a fresh broadside to the enemy's ship." Here was a "masterpiece of maneuver"!

Could the *Confiance* duplicate the *Saratoga's* maneuver? "All great events," Napoleon said, "hang by a single hair." And here was an illustration of his saying—if a broken old fellow at Elba still was interested in the philosophy of war! The British flagship had both her port bower anchors and her stern anchor shot away. All Robertson could do to swing the ship was to run a line from her starboard quarter to her riding cable and heave in on this line while slacking off on the cable itself. This was a long process and by the time the *Confiance* was half way around the *Saratoga* had completed her maneuver and was raking her from bow to stern with her port guns. Already she had been hulled by 105 round shot; over half her crew had been killed or wounded; many of the remainder were frantically working her pumps to keep down the water in the holds. "The ship's company declared," so Robertson reported, "that they would stand no longer to their quarters, nor could the officers with their utmost exertions rally them." The great frigate was beaten. At 10:35 her colors were lowered. The battle was won. The campaign, as we shall later see, was thereby decided.

Macdonough next turned his broadside on the *Linnet* and in fifteen minutes forced Pring to surrender. The water had risen a foot above his lower deck and his wrecked spars and rigging prevented any attempt at escape. The British galleys also surrendered. Macdonough reported: "Our galleys were about obeying with alacrity, the signal to follow them, when all the ships were reported to be in a sinking state; it then became necessary to annul the signal to the galleys, and order their men to man the pumps. I could only look at the enemy's galleys going off in a shattered condition, for there was not a mast in either squadron that could stand to make sail on; the lower rigging being shot away, hung down as though it had been just placed over the mastheads."

As soon as the decision was won the commodore wrote a brief despatch to the Secretary of the Navy: "The Almighty has been pleased to grant us a signal victory on Lake Champlain in the capture of one frigate, one brig, and two sloops of war of the enemy."

The commodore received the British officers on his quarter-deck. Treating them with elaborate courtesy, he insisted that they should retain their side arms. "I have much satisfaction," Captain Pring reported, "in making you acquainted with the humane treatment the wounded have received from Commodore Macdonough; they were immediately removed to his own hospital on Crab Island and furnished with every requisite. His generous and polite attention to myself, the officers, and men, will ever be gratefully remembered." Rarely have we won a victory where our prisoners have not testified to the generous treatment they have received. We confess to a lively pride in such a naval tradition.

Macdonough gave our losses as fifty-two killed and fifty-eight wounded. Roosevelt believes that the latter figure included only men hurt badly enough to be sent to the hospital; he places our total loss at about two hundred. He estimates the British casualties at over three hundred, stating that 180 killed or wounded were taken out of the *Confiance* alone. These figures offer mute testimony to the desperate character of the fighting.

CHAPTER XV
PREVOST RETREATS

R EADERS will remember how Prevost had arrayed his
troops for the assault on the tenth at 6:00 A.M. On the
eleventh, however, he made no preparations until Downie
was sighted at 7:00 A.M., coming down the far side of
Cumberland Head. He then ordered that an assault should
be made by about one and a half of his four brigades. He
seems to have made his arrangements in a most leisurely
manner, for it was not until 8:30, when the naval action
commenced, that his artillery preparation began. Under its
cover three assaulting columns advanced to ford the river.
At two places the attacks seem to have been intended only as
diversions, for they were made in a half-hearted manner.

The third column, however, crossed the river in great
strength and reduced the defenders to an extremely perilous
situation. But just when it seemed that he was doomed to
annihilation, Macomb received assistance in an unexpected
manner. Let Prevost tell his own story:

"Scarcely had his majesty's troops forced a passage across
the Saranac and ascended the height on which stand the
enemy's works, when I had the mortification to hear the
shout of victory from the enemy's works, in consequence of
the British flag being lowered on board the *Confiance* and
Linnet, and to see our gunboats seeking their safety in
flight. This unlooked-for event deprived me of the coöperation of the fleet, without which the further prosecution
of the service was become impracticable. I did not hesitate to
arrest the course of the troops advancing to the attack, because the most complete success would have been unavailing,

[463]

and the possession of the enemy's works offered no advantage to compensate for the loss we must have sustained in acquiring possession of them."

This is a remarkable statement—sounds like Hull and Chauncey rolled into one. Truly, some queer ideas of warfare were then prevalent on the northern frontier. Prevost's argument was a most technical one; he neglected the moral factor. He could afford a considerable loss to defeat and capture Macomb's army, which undoubtedly lay within his power. His losses in no case would have exceeded the eight hundred men who deserted from his army in the subsequent retreat. If Macomb's defeat after Macdonough's victory would have had little permanent strategical effect, it would at least counteract the enormous moral effect of Macdonough's victory.

A British writer, quoted by James, ably sets forth this viewpoint:

"Did not the loss of our fleet require a military set-off? And did not that loss absolutely impose it upon Sir George, as an imperious duty, to furnish that set-off, by capturing the enemy's army, to prevent the effect which a retreat, under such circumstances, must produce, ornamented, as he well knew it would be, by American gasconade? The mischievous effect of the Plattsburg business has been, and will be, incalculable, both in America and in Europe; for that will be heard in many countries and places, where it will not be known, that the commander alone was to blame, and the army under him indignant on the occasion. Were the events of Sir George's command, and especially the expeditions to Sackett's Harbor and Plattsburg, to become examples for the British army to follow; from possessing the hearts of lions, they would soon be reduced to the timidity of lambs; and the future inquiries of military men would be, not who

had ably done his duty, but who had avoided a battle, or
who had continued to escape unhurt."

Unfortunately, the name of this writer is not recorded; we
heartily approve his opinions, which are applicable not only
to the Plattsburg business but to the more recent events of
the World War. Propaganda evidently was as much a
weapon then as today, and it seems that American "gasconade" was something to be feared even by those masters of
propaganda, the British.

On the evening of the battle Prevost commenced his retreat. He moved in such unseemly haste that he was eight
miles away before we discovered that he had left Plattsburg.
He had to destroy great quantities of stores; more were left
intact, together with many sick and wounded. Eight hundred men deserted from his army during this short campaign, mostly during the retreat. Instead of making a renewed attack in another direction, possibly towards Sackett's
Harbor, Prevost decided that he had had enough. His army
went into winter quarters south of Montreal.

Macdonough and Macomb received every honor a grateful country could give. After a small British force had captured Washington with ease—old Joshua Barney and his
seamen alone adding any luster to American arms—the news
of a decisive victory over so powerful an enemy expedition
was welcome to both government and people. It was doubly
welcome to our peace commissioners at Ghent. On September 27 they had been depressed by the evil news of our capital's capture, which had much weakened their position. On
October 21 they were correspondingly overjoyed at the great
news from Lake Champlain. Gone now were the British
arguments for a rectification of the Maine frontier; even
Wellington advised that their demands were untenable. He
refused the command of the armies in Canada, saying that

soldiers could accomplish nothing until sailors had gained the command of the Lakes.

Conditions in Europe, even after Napoleon's overthrow, were far from settled. The allies already had begun their haggling over the spoils. There was a strong party in Russia which favored America and this gave the British considerable concern. The European nations, well remembering England's high-handed procedure on the seas, were now throwing their moral assistance to us. Powerful movements looking toward the restoration of Napoleon to the throne of France were known to be gathering momentum.

Conditions were far from good in England. The financial situation was very bad. Merchants and shipowners had looked upon Napoleon's downfall as the end of their troubles. Now they found that their losses from Yankee privateers far exceeded those caused by the French and their allies. They filled the press with their remonstrances. The people were war-weary—they had fought for twenty years. Why go on when there was nothing really to fight about? When it seemed impossible to gain any decisive successes? Prevost with his great expedition had brought only discredit to the British arms. The attack upon New Orleans was meeting with delay upon delay. Surely it now was time to bring the war to a close.

On the day before Christmas the treaty was signed by the commissioners at Ghent. As Gallatin had predicted, it provided for the *status ante bellum*. It was, in fact, a moral victory for the United States. Already the obnoxious Orders in Council had been repealed. While impressment of our seamen was not mentioned in the treaty, its practice was discontinued forever.

CHAPTER XVI

JACKSON SAVES NEW ORLEANS

B UT though the war had ended, the greatest danger with which our country has ever been threatened was impending. England had long seen the decisive importance of gaining possession of the mouths of the Mississippi River and in June had commenced moving an expedition of overwhelming strength to take New Orleans. James Durand, then serving on H.M.S. *Pactulus,* had seen the troops leaving the Bordeaux River. "They said that, since they had whipped Napoleon, they would have no trouble in subduing the United States. If they had known that General Andrew Jackson was awaiting them, they would have laughed another way." No, Durand, old fellow, we doubt that Old Hickory at that time would have given them cause for concern. We would ourselves have felt concern had we seen those 12,000 veterans preparing to brush aside our hastily gathered militia, supported by Patterson's tiny flotilla of gunboats, which, as we have seen, had been found unsuited even for enforcing the embargo.

Once in possession of New Orleans, there is every probability that the British government would have insisted upon its retention—treaty or no treaty. The hold thus obtained on the Mississippi River would have checked for many a year our westward march. Very probably it would have added to the British Empire the vast territories west of the river.

But, fortunately for us, an incomparable soldier stood between the enemy and their goal. By his superhuman efforts, Andrew Jackson composed internal dissensions, built defenses, recruited, assembled, equipped, and trained soldiers, and imparted to them his own marvelous energy and courage, his stalwart patriotism, and unalterable resolution. Master Commandant Daniel Patterson most sturdily supported him with his flotilla: the 16-gun armed merchantman *Louisiana,* the 14-gun schooner *Carolina,* five gunboats, and two sloops. All but the two former were captured in Lake Borgne by a boat assault of one thousand men. Lieutenant Thomas ap Catesby Jones, who commanded them, made a brave defense—in which at least ninety-four of the enemy were killed or wounded and several of their boats sunk. This action, incidentally, was a perfect demonstration of the uselessness of gunboats. Jefferson had admitted that they were valueless on the high seas; now it was shown that they could not perform the one service for which they were specially designed.

Patterson used the *Carolina* to assist Jackson in a night attack which resulted in severe losses to the enemy. But next morning the strong current prevented the schooner from escaping the British batteries ashore so Patterson set her on fire and abandoned ship. The *Louisiana,* Master Commandant John D. Henley, delayed the enemy's advance and then took station off the flank of Jackson's cotton-bale breastwork. On January 8, 1815, ten thousand British soldiers, mostly veterans of the Peninsula campaigns, advanced to the assault. Led in person by heroic Pakenham, they fought with utmost gallantry and determination—lived fully up to their reputation. But it was of no use. Old Cotton-bale Jackson had no time to think up a good epigram; but what he said was probably much to the same effect as "They shall not pass!" Nor did they—which is more important. Their general killed, their line of battle enfiladed by the *Louisiana's* long 24's their ranks literally mowed down by the musketry of Lafitte's pirates and miscellaneous militia —which here stood to their posts as never before, or since— the invaders were glad to leave those inhospitable Louisiana shores. Again was the famous axiom of Hermocrates demonstrated: "Rarely have great expeditions, when sent far from home, met with success." Thus did Andrew Jackson keep the West safe for the United States.

The war taught many lessons. Of these the greatest and most instructive were those learned by the politicians of the Jeffersonian, or pacifist, school. One of the leaders of that school was Secretary of the Treasury Gallatin. He expressed his opinions in no uncertain manner:

"The war has been productive of evil and of good, but I think the good predominates. Independent of the loss of lives, and of the property of individuals, the war has laid the foundation of permanent taxes and military establishments, which the Republicans had deemed unfavorable to the happiness and free institutions of the country. But under our former system we were becoming too selfish, too much attached exclusively to the acquisition of wealth, and, above all, too much confined in our political feelings to local and state objects. The war has renewed and reinstated the national feelings and character which the Revolution had given, and which were daily lessening. The people have now more general objects of attachment, with which their pride and political opinions are connected. They are more Americans; they feel and act more as a nation; and I hope that the permanency of the Union is thereby better secured."

Now began that national development which future historians may account the most remarkable movement in world history. Our naval victories in the War of 1812 to a very great degree commenced that movement.

WE DELIVER THE TRIBUTE FROM THE MOUTHS OF OUR CANNON

O UR story does not end with President Madison's proclamation of peace with Great Britain on February 18,
1815. Just as a few months later the episode of Waterloo
was to form a tragic epilogue to the great Napoleonic drama,
so in the story of our early Navy a brief postscript is
necessary to bring it to a fitting conclusion.

Readers will discover other reasons for telling the dramatic story of the famous Mediterranean campaign of 1815.
They will see Stephen Decatur, much buffeted about by fate
of late, receive again the smiles of fortune. They will read
of how good old Bainbridge came back into the ring again
for a final round against his old enemies. They will remember the uncertain, fumbling manner in which our squadrons
went about their business in those first Mediterranean campaigns, and in what a week-kneed compromise they came to
an end. Now they will see a startling change of method:
downright fighting and straightforward diplomacy combined in just the proper proportions. In the old days there
had been much boasting of "delivering tribute from the
mouths of our cannon," only to present sixty thousand good
American dollars to the Bashaw after trying to lick him for
three long years. Now at last those old boastings were to
be made good—and in a manner we much enjoy. Let's see
how!

After peace had been negotiated with Tripoli in 1805,
Consul General Tobias Lear had been left at Algiers to
keep the American Republic in the good graces of the deys.

But as the latter were subject to change without notice by assassination or other forms of violent death, Lear's life had been anything but a merry whirl of pleasure. Except for an occasional cruise, our men-of-war had disappeared from the Mediterranean, a fact much regretted by the consul general. However, for several years the annual tribute had sufficed to satisfy the desires of the Algerians.

But once the war with Great Britain commenced on June 18, 1812, the situation rapidly became more and more involved for Tobias Lear. The British influence in Algiers naturally was very considerable and they used it all to embroil the Dey with the United States and thus give Algiers the status of an allied, or, if you prefer, an associated, power. They said that "the American flag would be swept from the seas, the contemptible Navy of the United States annihilated and its maritime arsenals reduced to a heap of ruins." The British agent further promised that the United States should never be allowed to have a vessel larger than a frigate. Sounds rather like a Treaty of Versailles to us—with the United States in the position of Germany. But to the Dey it seemed really quite plausible. So he decided upon war.

It was a simple matter to find a pretext. The first was some laughable hocus-pocus about the difference in measuring time by sun and moon—not very intelligible to us. But, at any rate, the Dey figured that we had underpaid him some $27,000 in the seventeen years we had been paying him tribute. Tobias Lear was in a most untenable position and to keep the peace he agreed to the Dey's demands. Diplomats are good at staving off the evil day. When Lear's report reached Washington, it must have made the comptroller of the Treasury, or whoever then battled with such problems, scratch his head in wonder. But he did not have to ponder long over such a problem of accounting, for the Dey soon found another *casus belli* which would work just as well. It seems that the annual tribute of naval stores did not suit his exacting taste.

So the Dey fired out poor old Tobias Lear—really we feel quite sorry for him—in most unceremonious fashion, specifying that "he would not have a consul in his regency who did not cause everything to be brought exactly as ordered." And why should he have one, when the British government most kindly sent down two large ships with equipment enough in their holds to fit out the entire Algerian squadron?

We think this a rather expensive bargain for the British for the Dey's corsairs caught only one American ship, the little brig *Edwin* with a crew of ten men. As she was bound from Malta for Gibraltar the British could just as well have taken her themselves and saved the extra expense. But for Algiers the alliance proved not only expensive, but positively disastrous. Ill blows the wind that profits nobody; the only nation which profited from the alliance was the one against which it was directed—the United States.

Tunis and Tripoli followed the lead of their big brother, Algiers. It seems that an American privateer, the *Abellino*, began operating with success in the Mediterranean and sent two prizes into each of these ports. Their rulers had no hesitation in turning the prizes over to the Royal Navy, an unneutral act which one fine day they would much repent.

During the war with Great Britain there had been no opportunity for us to devote to chastising these Mediterranean pirates for their insolence. However, once peace was proclaimed, this became a live subject. Our leaders had learned some lessons of statesmanship and they had a strong, fully armed and manned naval force just waiting for somewhere to go. The speed and firmness with which we acted was a striking contrast with the watchful waiting of previous years. In the short space of one week the President transmitted to Congress an estimate of the situation made by Mr. Secretary Monroe—who soon would be thinking of certain doctrines which are still talked about. He added a recommendation that war should be declared against Algiers and even asked that Congress make "such provisions as may be requisite for a vigorous prosecution of it to a successful conclusion." Congress took his advice and declared war.

By this time many of the ships of the war-construction program were nearing completion. Our naval strength had become far more formidable than ever before. Two powerful squadrons were ordered to prepare for sea in all haste. Stephen Decatur was to command the first. To select him for a command of such importance so soon after the *President* disaster was a striking proof of the confidence which the government had in his abilities. At New York he hoisted his commodore's pennant on the fine new frigate *Guerrière*, 44 guns. Round him gathered his old war comrades, officers who had served with him in the *United States* and *President*.

To join his broad pennant in New York came the *Macedonian*, 38, *Constellation*, 36, *Epervier*, 18, *Ontario*, 18, and five small brigs and schooners for inshore work. On May 20 the squadron made sail for the Mediterranean, while Bainbridge continued preparing and assembling the second squadron to reënforce it, should this prove necessary. In the *Guerrière* sailed Consul General William Shaler. He, Decatur, and Bainbridge were designated commissioners with full powers to negotiate peace with the piratical powers.

On June 15 Decatur arrived at Tangier. There he heard
that the Algerian admiral had sailed only a few days before
for Carthagena, in his flagship, the 40-gun frigate *Mashouda*. The admiral, called Rais Hammida, was noted for
his fine seamanship and desperate bravery. From a seaman
he had risen to chief command and during recent years had
won a series of brilliant successes. Five years before,
off Gibraltar, with three frigates he had offered battle to a
Portuguese ship of the line and three frigates, only to have
it declined. His fleet consisted of five frigates, six sloops-
of-war and one schooner. It mounted 360 guns, against
Decatur's 210. Our guns were much heavier than those
on the Algerian ships and it is probable that our total weight
of broadside would have exceeded theirs, had it been worth
while for anyone to have recorded such data. On the other
hand, the Algerian crews were larger than ours. They were
very well trained and experienced in warfare, after their
own fashion. Naturally they could not be compared to
those unequalled sailors who manned the American squadron.

The Algerians knew nothing of our declaration of war
and still less of the impending arrival of such a powerful
American squadron. Consequently their own fleet was
widely scattered. Our commodore, knowing the advantage
he had in this respect, wished to surprise the Algerians and
open the campaign with a striking, perhaps decisive, success. So he sailed quickly on the track of the unsuspecting
Mashouda. As he passed Gibraltar more definite information arrived: Hammida was waiting off Cape de Gatte for
tribute of half a million dollars owed him by His Most
Catholic Majesty of Spain.

Dawn of June 17—the day before Waterloo—found the
American squadron some twenty miles south of the cape.

It was scattered on an irregular scouting line, the *Constellation* being farthest to the southward and somewhat in advance of the flagship. When it became fully daylight the *Constellation* hoisted the signal: "Enemy in sight." The squadron soon made her out to be a large frigate lying to under topsails. Knowing that Hammida would never suspect that an American squadron would be in the Mediterranean, Decatur continued his approach under easy sail without disclosing his nationality. The Algerians would then certainly think that the approaching ships were British; in fact, two of them, until very recently, had been.

When distant about a mile the *Constellation* carelessly broke one of her battle ensigns. Now the secret was out. In a minute the agile Moors were seen crowding into the rigging and setting their sails. The *Mashouda* gathered headway and started to run back to her lair. But the hunters were too many—she would never reach it. First the swift-sailing *Constellation* headed her off, opening up at long range. One of her shot wounded Hammida, but he bravely kept the deck. There was evidently no escape to the southward so he tacked toward Carthagena.

But this time the *Guerrière* intercepts the foe. Decatur drives down his great flagship, determined to give the Moors a practical demonstration of how the Yankees fire broadsides. On bowls the towering frigate. The Algerians open with muskets from their tops and shoot down four men on the *Guerrière's* decks. Decatur is not ready yet, holds his fire until he is yardarm to yardarm and every gun can bear. Along the covered gun deck every 24-pounder is double-shotted; above are the 42-pounder carronades, even more terrible at that short distance. Like a rolling thunderclap the broadside roars and deadly shot pierce and smash the *Mashouda's* stout timbers—kill and wound her sailors.

Coolly, the Yankee gunners reload, fire a second time. Brave Hammida is killed—never will he deliver to his ruler that Spanish tribute. His men leave their guns, run below. Only the musketeers in the tops keep on fighting. The *Mashouda* is beaten!

Thinking that the enemy will now surrender, Decatur hauls ahead and ceases his fire. He has not escaped unscathed. Three of his people have been killed and eleven wounded. The bursting of one of his own 24-pounders has killed three more and wounded seventeen. We had not learned after many such disasters how to cast our guns.

The Algerian makes another try to get away. This time John Downes is in his path. The last time we have seen this young fellow was on a tragic day off Valparaiso, when he rowed out through the *Phoebe's* cannonade to see if there was anything he could do to help the *Essex* in her death throes. Now he commands the *Epervier* and sails her into close action against his much larger, but badly crippled, opponent. In twenty-five minutes he fires off nine resounding broadsides; then his enemy surrenders. Her loss is not very heavy: only 30 killed and wounded out of a crew of 436. Had Hammida lived doubtless she would have put up a stouter fight.

We claim no special credit for the tactical features of this fight, except for John Downes's bold handling of the *Epervier*. But from a strategic viewpoint the surprise and capture of the enemy's flagship within a week of his arrival in Europe was a success of which Decatur might well be proud. The *Philadelphia* incident had now been reversed. This time we had the frigate and the prisoners, trump cards in the diplomatic game soon to begin.

The *Mashouda* was sent into Carthagena under escort of the *Macedonian,* while the rest of the squadron continued

From an engraving by Henry Meyer after the original painting by John W. Jarvis

STEPHEN DECATUR

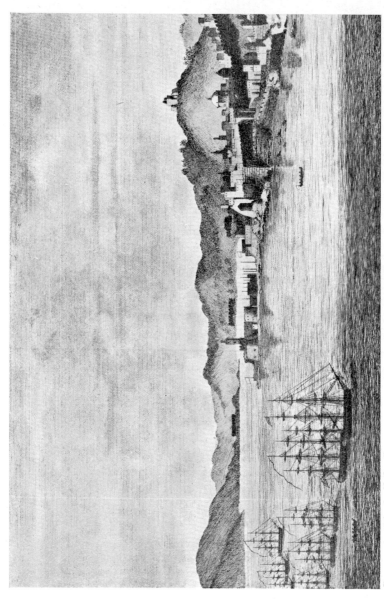

From an engraving by N. Jocelin

THE UNITED STATES SQUADRON BEFORE ALGIERS, JUNE 30, 1815

their combing of the Spanish coast. On the nineteenth the hunting again was good. The strong 22-gun brig *Estido* was chased ashore near Cape Palos. Twenty-three of her crew were killed and eighty-three made prisoner. The rest escaped to the shore in their boats, where it is presumed that their reception was not over cordial. The prize was floated and sent into Carthagena.

By this time the alarm probably had been given to the other Algerian men-of-war. But by sailing at once to Algiers Decatur hoped that he could prevent them from getting home. On the twenty-ninth of June the squadron anchored off the port, a tremendous fortress mounting over five hundred guns. The captain of the port paid the usual visit of courtesy to the visiting flagship and was dumbfounded to hear that Decatur had taken two ships and held five hundred prisoners as hostages. He was asked to give the Dey a letter from the President which stated in blunt language the terms which alone would be acceptable to the United States. Decatur further informed him that the treaty would be negotiated on board the *Guerrière* or not at all.

Next day the Algerian reported on board again, this time with full powers to negotiate. Decatur and Shaler, fortified by recent successes, gave him our ultimatum. The following were its principal points: all tribute to cease; no more American ships to be captured; no more Americans to be enslaved; all American vessels to be treated hospitably in Algerian ports; in case of war between the United States and another nation, Algiers to maintain a strict neutrality; all Americans now in slavery to be surrendered immediately and repaid for the loss of their personal effects; the owners of the *Edwin* to receive ten thousand American dollars in cash. After agreeing to these provisions the envoy asked for a truce of three hours in which he might obtain the signature of the Dey. "Not one minute," Decatur answered. "If your squadron appears before the treaty is actually signed by the Dey, and sent off with the American prisoners, *ours will capture it!*" Thus at last we did begin to speak the only language which the African pirates could understand—*terror*. Would that William Eton had been there to hear it!

An hour after the envoy left the *Guerrière* an Algerian man-of-war was sighted approaching the port. Signal to chase her was hoisted. The *Guerrière* had cleared for action and was just making sail, when the Dey's boat was seen pulling out in haste. In her bow flew the white flag—the signal that the treaty had been accepted and signed. The prisoners came on board, overcome with joy and gratitude at their unexpected relief. Yes, the Navy was now paying some really worth-while dividends, and Stephen Decatur again was sitting on the top of the world. It was only fifteen days since he had arrived in Tangier; in that short time he had forced the Dey to practically an unconditional surrender.

There is a story of how the Algerian ruler gave the British consul a piece of his mind. "You told us," he is reported to have said, "that the Americas would be swept from the seas in six months by your navy, and now they make war upon us with some of your own vessels." History does not record what reply the consul made.

The two prizes had been considerably shot up and would have required extensive repairs before they could be sent across the Atlantic. So as a *beau geste* Decatur returned them to the Dey. He had only recently come into power and was suffering for the sins of his predecessor in office. This would save his face with his subjects and make him better disposed toward us. We thought it politic to ease his position a bit.

Thus was Decatur's main task completed. He sent home the *Epervier* with a draft of the treaty. Unfortunately she was lost at sea with every soul on board. Her captain, Lieutenant John T. Shubrick, thus ended a most gallant and active career.

It took some time to carry into effect the terms of the Algerian treaty and to return the prizes and prisoners. This accomplished, and the *Macedonian* having rejoined, Decatur sailed eastward to finish his job. We have seen that during the recent war an American privateer had sent two prizes into Tunis and a like number into Tripoli. The Bey of Tunis had allowed the British brig *Lyra* to recapture the prizes in his harbor. And the Bashaw of Tripoli had permitted a like violation of neutrality by the brig *Paulina*. In each case the piratical ruler doubtless had received his commission from the British consul. Now they were to pay in full.

On July 27 the squadron anchored off Tunis. The commodore gave that Most Illustrious and Most Magnificent Prince, the Bey of Tunis—for so diplomatic courtesy required that he be addressed—just twelve hours in which to hand over $46,000 in payment for the two prizes. The consul presented the demand. "Why," asked the Bey, "do they send wild young men to treat for peace with the old powers?" But within the time limit the brother of the prime minister came out with the cash. The stock of Tunisian Piracies Preferred would not this year pay its usual dividend.

Decatur visited pleasantly for a few days with the Bey. Then he again sailed to the east, toward the scene of his famous exploits of past years. On August 5 he dropped anchor off the well-known citadel of Tripoli. For a time the Bashaw made a bluff at resistance—marshaled his troops, manned his batteries. But when he saw that bombardment was imminent he sent out $25,000 and saluted the American flag with thirty-one guns. Ten Christian slaves also were surrendered. In recognition of the kindness of Mr. Nissen, the Danish consul, to Bainbridge and his men, the commodore specified that two Danes be released.

Thus after many years, did we deliver our tribute from the mouths of our cannon!

Sending the rest of the squadron back to Gibraltar, Decatur proceeded in the *Guerrière* to Sicily, where the captives were landed. He next went to Carthagena. While proceeding down the Spanish coast toward Gibraltar the *Guerrière* fell in with a powerful Algerian squadron, four frigates and three sloops. As they came down in a menacing manner, Decatur cleared for action; told his crew that, if the enemy fired first "we'll take the whole of them." The squadron in line of battle passed close aboard. The customary hail was made from the Algerian flagship: "Where are you bound?" Decatur took the speaking trumpet and shouted back: "Where it pleases me!"

In August William Bainbridge with his reënforcing squadron had arrived at Gibraltar. It included our first ship of the line, *Independence,* 74, the frigates *United States,* 44, and *Congress,* 36, and eight smaller vessels. He paraded this formidable force before Algiers, Tunis, and Tripoli in a way which must have given the old fellow much satisfaction.

On October 6 the combined squadrons assembled at Gibraltar. It was the most powerful concentration of naval power thus far made by the United States. Under Bainbridge's flag were one ship of the line, five frigates, two sloops, and ten smaller vessels—eighteen sail in all. The familiar names of many of these vessels, *Guerrière, Mace-*

donian, and *Boxer,* not to mention the *Epervier* which had just left, and the *Java* which soon would arrive, did not, it is said, conduce much to the friendliness with which our people were greeted by the officers of the garrison and of His Majesty's ships in port. In fact, dueling became, we are told, quite a favorite outdoor sport.

Bainbridge and Decatur went home with a part of the fleet. Commodore John Shaw stayed in the Mediterranean to sit on the lid. The Algerian pot soon began again to boil, the fire under it having been lighted in a most peculiar manner. After Decatur had released the American captives for nothing and had been paid for their effects and their ship, Lord Exmouth appeared with six of the line and other vessels. He had come, it seems, to ransom off some thousands of Neopolitan and Sardinian captives. This he did for some $400,000. British historian James claims that this was a real bargain sale; possibly it was from their viewpoint.

But it had other results. It made the Dey very sad that he had yielded so quickly to Decatur. However, Decatur now had sailed away. Doubtless it would be possible to bluff the other naval commanders. He soon found that John Shaw was not a good man to bluff; nor was that young fellow who had just come out in the *Java,* Captain O. H. Perry!

Shaw soon heard what was in the wind, so gathered in his ships. On April 8 he appeared off Algiers with three frigates and two sloops and commenced making some dispositions of a rather menacing nature. In fact, he was making his arrangements to commence a cannonade of the Algerian men-of-war in port. He seems to have thought better of this, and substituted a much more inoffensive scheme—to carry the Dey's batteries by assault. A night attack was to be made in boats by twelve hundred men, led by Captains Charles Gordon and O. H. Perry. Scaling ladders were constructed to storm the batteries, and cutlasses and boarding pikes brightened up on the grindstone. Unfortunately a French captain tipped off the Dey as to what was to happen and he hastened to ratify the treaty with due ceremony. We can never think of this episode without sincere regret. The contemplated attack would have given the marines something to sing about!

And so ended the Mediterranean campaigns. Until the World War, practically never again did we have to fight, or even to threaten to fight, in those blue waters. The events of 1815 made a lasting impression.

Although those cruel deys, beys, and bashaws caused us a lot of trouble for almost two score of years, we owe them a vote of thanks. For by their efforts, and theirs alone, was created the United States Navy. And they, later assisted by their British allies, established it in the hearts of Americans, proving beyond the slightest doubt that a navy was vitally essential to our national security and public welfare.

This ends our story. Its telling, we fear, has not been worthy of those gallant officers and hardy men whose exploits rang around the world. But we hope that it has brought you something of the action and atmosphere of that golden age. "Treasure it in your minds," wrote Conan Doyle, "and pass it on to your children, for the memory of a great age is the most perfect treasure that a nation can possess. As the tree is nurtured by its own cast leaves, so it is these dead men and vanished days which can bring out another blossoming of heroes, of rulers, and of sages." Amen!

Times change. Events march swiftly. Forward we must look. But perhaps a glance back over our shoulder into the past may light our path and steady our footsteps!

LIST OF OFFICERS AND MEN MENTIONED HEREIN
FOR WHOM DESTROYERS ARE NAMED

(See Index for page)

Number	Name of Ship	Name and Rank of Officer or Man	Ships on which serving
DD22	*Paulding*	Rear Admiral Hiram Paulding	*Ticonderoga*
DD27	*Sterett*	Lieutenant Andrew Sterett	*Enterprise*
DD28	*McCall*	Lieutenant Edward R. McCall	*Enterprise*
DD29	*Burrows*	Lieutenant William Burrows	*Enterprise*
DD30	*Warrington*	Commodore Lewis Warrington	*Peacock*
DD31	*Mayrant*	Captain John Mayrant	*Bon Homme Richard*
DD33	*Trippe*	Lieutenant John Trippe	*Gunboat No. 6*
DD36	*Patterson*	Commodore Daniel Todd Patterson	*Carolina*
DD37	*Fanning*	Lieutenant Daniel Fanning	*Bon Homme Richard*
DD38	*Jarvis*	Midshipman James C. Jarvis	*Constellation*
DD39	*Henley*	Captain Robert Henley	*Eagle*
DD43	*Cassin*	Captain Stephen Cassin	*Ticonderoga*
DD45	*Downes*	Captain John Downes	*Essex*
DD46	*Duncan*	Commander Silas Duncan	*Saratoga*
DD47	*Aylwin*	Lieutenant John Cushing Aylwin	*Constitution*
DD52	*Nicholson*	Captain Samuel Nicholson	*Dolphin*
DD58	*Conynham*	Captain Gustavus Conyngham	*Surprise*
DD59	*Porter*	Commodore David Porter	*Essex*

DD60	*Wadsworth*	Commodore Alexander Scammel Wadsworth	*Adams*
DD66	*Allen*	Master Commandant William Henry Allen	*Argus*
DD68	*Shaw*	Captain John Shaw	*Enterprise*
DD69	*Caldwell*	Lieutenant James R. Caldwell	*Gunboat No. 9*
DD74	*Manley*	Captain John Manley	*Lee*
DD75	*Wickes*	Captain Lambert Wickes	*Reprisal*
DD77	*Woolsey*	Captain Melancthon Taylor Woolsey	*Oneida*
DD86	*Stevens*	Captain Thomas Holdup Stevens	*Trippe*
DD97	*Murray*	Captain Alexander Murray	*Constellation*
DD98	*Israel*	Midshipman Joseph Israel	*Intrepid*
DD104	*Champlin*	Captain Stephen Champlin	*Scorpion*
DM10	*Ludlow*	Lieutenant Augustus C. Ludlow	*Chesapeake*
DD113	*Rathburne*	Captain John P. Rathburne	*Providence*
DD116	*Dent*	Captain John H. Dent	*Nautilus*
DD117	*Dorsey*	Midshipman John Dorsey	*Gunboat No. 9*
DD123	*Gamble*	Lieutenant Peter Gamble	*Saratoga*
DD128	*Babbitt*	Lieutenant Fitz Henry Babbitt	*President*
DD130	*Jacob Jones*	Captain Jacob Jones	*Wasp*
DD140	*Claxton*	Midshipman Thomas Claxton	*Lawrence*
DD141	*Hamilton*	Lieutenant Archibald Hamilton	*United States*
DD143	*Yarnall*	Captain John Joliffe Yarnall	*Lawrence*
DD149	*Barney*	Commodore Joshua Barney	*Rossie*
DD150	*Blakeley*	Captain Johnstone Blakeley	*Wasp*
DD165	*Meredith*	Sergeant Jonathan Meredith, U.S.M.C.	*Gunboat No. 6*
DD166	*Bush*	First Lieutenant William S. Bush, U.S.M.C.	*Constitution*

DD167	*Cowell*	Master John G. Cowell	*Essex*
DD177	*O'Bannon*	First Lieutenant Presley N. O'Bannon, U.S.M.C.	*Argus*
		Ordinary Seaman Daniel Hogan	*Constitution*
DD183	*Haraden*	Captain Jonathan Haraden	*General Pickering*
DD224	*Stewart*	Rear Admiral Charles Stewart	*Constitution*
DD229	*Truxtun*	Commodore Thomas Truxtun	*Constellation*
DD230	*Paul Jones*	Commodore Paul Jones	*Bon Homme Richard*
DD232	*Brooks*	First Lieutenant John Brooks, Jr., U.S.M.C.	*Lawrence*
DD236	*Humphreys*	Naval Constructor Joshua Humphreys	——
DD245	*Reuben James*	Boatswain's Mate Reuben James	*Constellation*
DD246	*Bainbridge*	Commodore William Bainbridge	*Constitution*
DD250	*Lawrence*	Captain James Lawrence	*Chesapeake*
DD254	*Rodgers*	Commodore John Rodgers	*President*
DD258	*Aulick*	Commodore John H. Aulick	*Enterprise*
DD259	*Turner*	Captain Daniel Turner	*Caledonia*
DD261	*Delphy*	Midshipman Richard Delphy	*Argus*
DD263	*Laub*	Midshipman Henry Laub	*Lawrence*
DD265	*Edwards*	Midshipman William W. Edwards	*Argus*
DD267	*Ballard*	Lieutenant Edward J. Ballard	*Chesapeake*
DD271	*Morris*	Commodore Charles Morris	*Adams*
DD275	*Sinclair*	Captain Arthur Sinclair	*Argus*
DD290	*Dale*	Commodore Richard Dale	*Bon Homme Richard*
DD292	*Reid*	Captain Samuel Chester Reid	*General Armstrong*
DD296	*Chauncey*	Commodore Isaac Chauncey	*General Pike*

DD300	*Farragut*	Admiral David Glasgow	*Essex*
	Somers	Farragut	
DD301	*Hull*	Lieutenant Richard	*Intrepid*
		Somers	
DD330	*Macdonough*	Commodore Isaac Hull	*Constitution*
DD331		Commodore Thomas	*Saratoga*
		Macdonough	
DD340	*Perry*	Commodore Oliver Haz-	*Lawrence*
		ard Perry	
DD341	*Decatur*	Commodore Stephen	*United States*
		Decatur	
DD345	*Preble*	Commodore Edward	*Constitution*
		Preble	

BIBLIOGRAPHY

The publications below listed were principally consulted and followed in the preparation of this book. The author makes grateful acknowledgment to the writers named.

Life and Letters of John Paul Jones by Mrs. Reginald De Koven.

Commodore John Paul Jones by A. S. Mackenzie.

Paul Jones by Seitz (a compilation of contemporary British newspaper accounts).

Life and Character of Paul Jones by J. H. Sherburne.

Cruikshank's Documentary History (a complete compilation of letters relating to the Lakes Campaigns, 1812-14).

Our Navy and the Barbary Corsairs by Gardner W. Allen.

Official Letters of Military and Naval Officers (1812-1815) by John Brannon.

History of the Navy by J. Fenimore Cooper.

History of the Navy by Edgar S. Maclay.

The American Navy by Rear Admiral F. E. Chadwick.

Sea Power in its Relations to the War of 1812 by A. T. Mahan.

A Naval History of the American Revolution by Gardner W. Allen.

Pictorial Field Book of the War of 1812 by B. J. Lossing.

The American Revolution by John Fiske.

The American Merchant Marine by W. L. Marvin.

Naval History of Great Britain by William James.

Naval Occurrences With the Americas by William James.

American State Papers.

The Naval War of 1812 by Theodore Roosevelt.

Memoir of Commodore David Porter by Admiral David D. Porter.

James Durand—An Able Seaman of 1812, with notes by George S. Brooks.

James Lawrence by Rear Admiral Albert Gleaves.

Commodore John Rodgers by C. O. Paullin.

Ships' Data—U. S. Naval Vessels by the Navy Department.

Official Reports of Paul Jones.

A Gunner on Old Ironsides by Moses Smith (the *Golden Book,* October, 1927).

Many points were elucidated or verified by an examination of the archives of the Navy Department.

INDEX

A

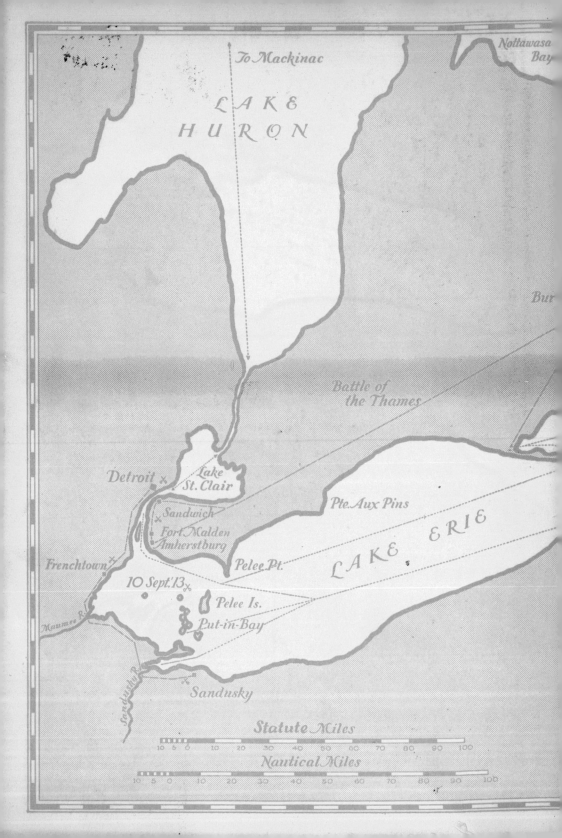

LAKE HURON

To Mackinac

Nottawasa Bay

Bur

Battle of the Thames

Detroit

Lake St. Clair

Sandwich

Fort Malden

Amherstburg

Frenchtown

10 Sept.'13

Maumee R.

Pte. Aux Pins

Pelee Pt.

LAKE ERIE

Pelee Is.

Put-in-Bay

Sandusky R.

Sandusky

Statute Miles

10 5 0   10   20   30   40   50   60   70   80   90   100

Nautical Miles

10 5 0   10   20   30   40   50   60   70   80   90   100